Master Painter: Warner E. Sallman

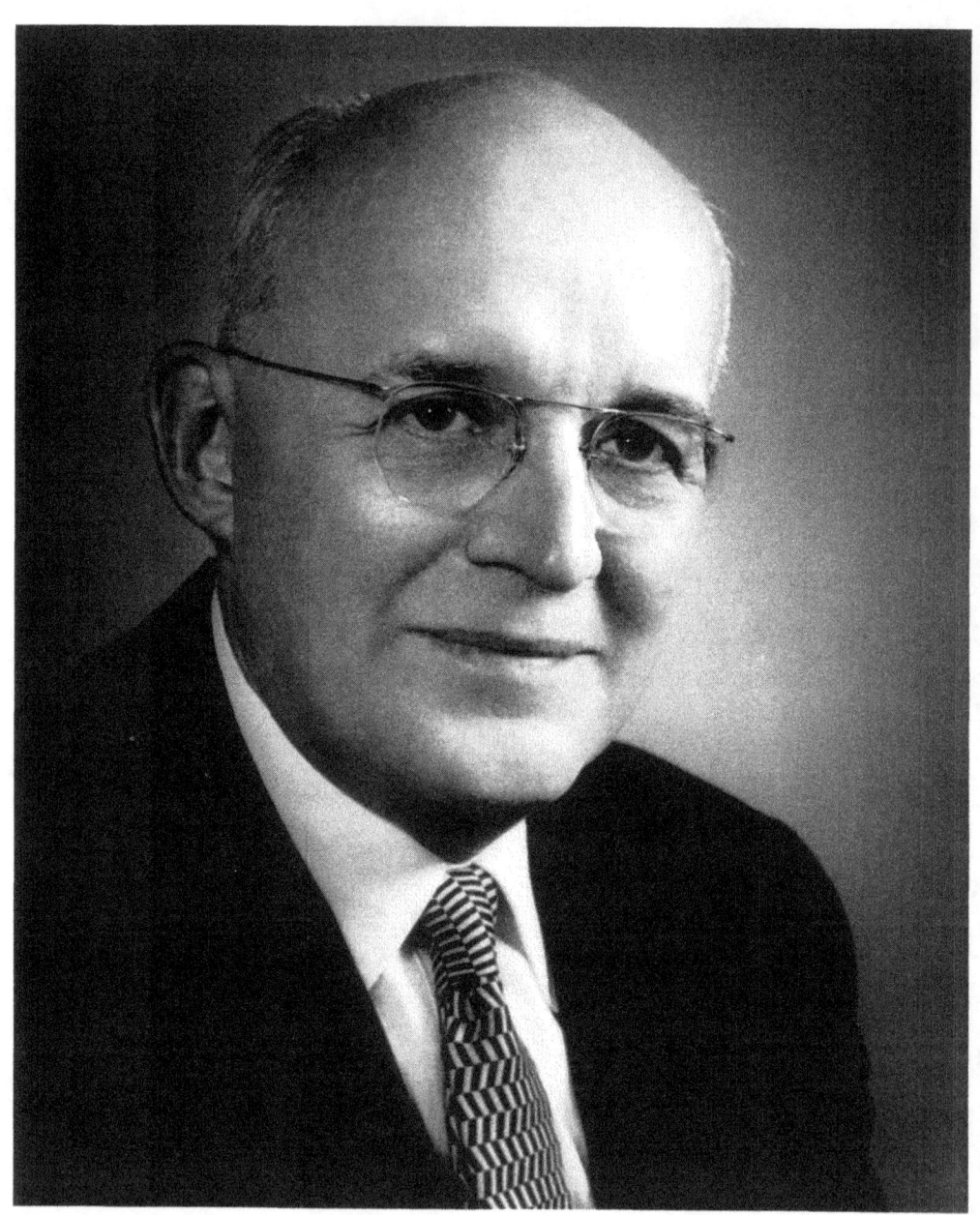

Warner Sallman

Master Painter: Warner E. Sallman

by Jack R. Lundbom

WIPF & STOCK · Eugene, Oregon

Wipf and Stock Publishers
199 W 8th Ave, Suite 3
Eugene, OR 97401

Master Painter
Warner E. Sallman
By Lundbom, Jack R.
Copyright©1999 by Lundbom, Jack R.
ISBN 13: 978-1-4982-341-6
Publication date 3/16/2015

To
Dorothy O. Lundbom
my mother
and
my aunt
Virginia M. Ohlson

Table of Contents

Preface

This book should have been written long ago. When I was at Yale, in the mid-1980s, I was shocked to discover in three tiers of books on artists and sculptors in the Reference Room of Sterling Library no mention of Warner Sallman. I looked in the *Art Index*, from its first volume in 1929 on through 1981, and not a single entry for Warner Sallman or a single mention of the Sallman *Head of Christ* under the listing "Jesus Christ." The same was true when looking at *Repertoire International de la Litterature de l' Art (RILA)* and *Bibliographie d'Histoire de l'Art (BHA)*, standard reference works in the art field–nothing. An American artist active in religious circles for over forty years, with one painting of religious art known around the world and others known all across the United States and Canada, and not a single biographical sketch or as much as a paragraph about the famous Christ head. Only later did I come upon two brief biographical sketches, one in *The Swedish Element in America*,[1] and another in a 1945 volume of *Who's Who in Chicago and Illinois*.[2]

I was actually not the first to be surprised. Back in 1942, the director of the Art Institute in Chicago received a letter from a woman in the New York Public Library requesting a biographical sketch of the Chicago artist, Warner E. Sallman, "who in 1924 painted a picture of Christ entitled 'The Son of Man.' The letter continued, "The New York Public Library art department has no data on this artist, and he is not listed in the latest Who's Who in American Art."[3]

Sallman's lack of notoriety in professional art circles can be explained by the fact that he made no attempt to put himself forward as a Chicago–or even a Swedish-American–artist. He had no exhibitions of his works, and his public life consisted largely of appearing before church and community groups to do chalk drawings, usually of his Christ head. Sallman was a member of the Swedish Mission Covenant, now the Evangelical Covenant Church, a small American denomination not widely known. Outside the Covenant his connections were mainly but not exclusively with Methodists, Lutherans, the Salvation Army, and the Church of God of Indiana. Public exposure was then limited within the larger American Church.

Perhaps of equal importance was his own attitude regarding personal fame. Sallman intended the Christ he painted to be foreground. He himself was background. The time has come, nevertheless, for a broader public to know the man

1. Vol 3 (Chicago: Swedish-American Biographical Society, 1931).
2. (Chicago: A. N. Marquis).
3. Letter sent by a Miss Irma Hilgedick dated April 16, 1942.

who stands behind the paintings and other artwork bearing the Sallman signature. The Warner Sallman story is a fascinating story of a gifted man, with humble beginnings, who overcame disappointment, ill health, and personal limitations in order that he might live out a vision, i.e., that his artwork be not simply for the enjoyment of humankind, which for many would have been a laudable enough goal, but preeminently for the glory of God and the practical end that people might be instructed in the ways of God and his son, Jesus Christ.

The idea of writing a book on Warner Sallman was conceived a number of years ago by Sylvia Peterson, Director of Children's Work for the Covenant Church (1947-1956), and a close friend of Sallman's. She is responsible for much of what has been written thus far about Sallman's "ministry of Christian art." Sylvia was unable to follow through on her idea, but she fervently hoped that someone else who knew Warner Sallman would.

I accepted the task early in 1984, following a visit to the Jim Sallman home in Rockford, Illinois, at which time the idea of my writing a book was discussed. Family permission came soon afterwards to go ahead with the research and writing. Jim and Gene Sallman have been a great support throughout the work. Indeed, without their help the book could scarcely have been written. I also received invaluable help and unqualified support from Richard and Marion Sallman, and from Everett Sallman. A visit with Richard and Marion in Texas in February 1988 was of benefit, as I was granted access to resources in their possession. Linda and I also joined Richard and Marion for a festive celebration on Åland (Finland) in June 1991, when the Sällman homestead was opened and a 750th anniversary of the parish church of Föglö rounded out a memorable weekend of activities. That was a very special time, thanks to the gracious hospitality of Sällman relatives, Gunhild Sällman Karlström and Karin Sällman Ilemyr, who, together with their families acted as our hosts. Hjordis Sundblom, a family friend of the Sällmans, initiated the plans for a Sällman reunion and was a large part of its planning.

My good friend Sylvia Peterson gave her unqualified support to the present undertaking, sharing generously with me published and unpublished materials, typed and handwritten notes, and enriching me with countless hours of happy conversation about Warner. I owe her a great debt. I regret she could not live to see the fruit of our joint labor.

Many individuals–too many, unfortunately, to mention–assisted in the research that went into the writing of this book. Some showed me Sallman artwork in churches, schools, hospitals, and other institutions, providing in addition invaluable interpretive background. I should like, however, to single out a few people for special thanks: Sigurd Westburg and Timothy Johnson, archivists at Covenant Archives; Walter Osborn, archivist at Crowell Library, Moody Bible Institute; Kevin Leonard, archivist at the United Library of

Garrett-Evangelical Theological Seminary; Mary McIsaac, archivist at the School of the Art Institute in Chicago; Joy Rich, of the Archives and Research Center of the Salvation Army, formerly in New York City; and especially Paul A. Marshall, archivist at the Albert G. Pepper Library of the Salvation Army School for Officers' Training in Chicago. All were generous with their time and gracious in sharing records at their disposal. Other personnel in the following libraries provided me with kind access to research material in their possession: the Sterling Library of Yale University, the Jesuit-Krauss-McCormick Library at the Lutheran School of Theology at Chicago, the Mellander Library of North Park Theological Seminary, the Ryerson Library of the Art Institute at Chicago, the Chicago Public Library, and the library of the Chicago Historical Society.

Professor David Morgan of Valparaiso University, and Dr. Jason Knapp, director of the Jessie C. Wilson Galleries at Anderson University in Anderson, Indiana, were most cooperative in coordinating their research on Sallman, underwritten by a grant from the Lilly Foundation, with my own. Discussions with them and their colleagues were very fruitful. Help of a different sort, but no less important, was given early on in the project by Charles Bates, who invited me to spend a day at the Kriebel and Bates office in Indianapolis. Others too have given much-appreciated support and encouragement at various stages along the way, among whom I gladly mention Craig Anderson, LeRoy Carlson, Ralph P. Hanson, Helen Fredrickson, Dr. Paul L. Holmer, and the late Dr. Karl A. Olsson. My mother, Dorothy Lundbom, and my aunt, Dr. Virginia M. Ohlson, supported the project from its visionary stage on through to completion, and near the end, particularly, help came from both in tangible and intangible ways. To them I warmly dedicate this book. My wife Linda, who, in addition to being the ideal companion she is, served in the present endeavor as my resident artist and art critic—as good of one as I could wish for.

Thanks also goes to my sister Virginia, and her husband, the late Reverend Quentin Larson, who made available to Linda and myself, at a crucial juncture, their cottage on Sunset Lake near Iron River, Michigan in the winter of 1992. There, surrounded by deep snow in the quiet woods of Michigan's Upper Peninsula, I wrote uninterrupted for two weeks. Later in the spring, the Reverend Craig Anderson and his wife Dotty kindly made their summer home on Big Bay de Noc in the Upper Peninsula available to us for the same purpose. My thanks to them as well. Final preparation of the manuscript was done while I was serving as interim pastor of the Evangelical Covenant Church of Menominee, Michigan. My thanks to this congregation for granting me the necessary time to finish the work.

Scripture passages are taken from the King James Version (KJV) and Revised Standard Version (RSV) of the Bible. Hymn titles, also authors and translators of hymns, derive from Evangelical Covenant Church hymnals

(Chicago: Covenant Book Concern / Covenant Press / Covenant Publications), and are cited: *CovH* 1931; *CovH* 1950; *CovH* 1973; and *CovH* 1996.

Permission has been kindly granted by the Swedish-American Historical Society to use excerpts from my article, "Warner Sallman and His 'Head of Christ,' published in *The Swedish American Historical Quarterly* 47 (1996), 69-83.

Permission to reproduce Sallman artworks have been kindly granted by Covenant Publications, Chicago: "Son of Man" (1924) charcoal; by Covenant Archives, Chicago, for the originals: Thorn-crowned Christ (1926); "Portrait of the Rev. C. A. Björk" (1935); and "Thine Is the Power" (1951); for the following pictures in the booklet, "Short History of the Swedish Evangelical Lutheran Mission Congregation (of Lake View), 1886-1911": the church exterior and interior, also Pastor August Pohl; for the following publications in *Förbundets Veckotidning*: "Frid på Jorden" in *FV* 263 (Dec 24, 1918), 1; Resurrected Christ Rising from the Crucified Christ in *FV* 359 (Mar 30, 1920), 1; "Tell Me the Old, Old Story" in *FV* 397 (Dec 21, 1920), 1; "Self-Denial, Self-Indulgence" in *FV* 410 (Mar 22, 1921), 1;"Memories of Julotta" in *FV* 449 (Dec 20, 1921), 1; and "A Thank Offering?" in *FV* 500 (Nov 27, 1923), 1; for the following publications in *The Covenant Companion*: "Son of Man" in *CC* Old Series 3:2 (Feb 1924), 1; Family Altar of the American Home in *CC* Old Series 3:11 (Nov 1924), 1; and the Edgewater Covenant Church "Head of Christ" in *CC* 56:8 (April 21, 1967), 9; for the publication in *Our Young Covenanters*: Gypsie Girl in *OYC* 2:33 (Aug 14, 1932), 1; for the publications in *Our Covenant Little Folks*: Portrait of Olga Lindborg in *OCLF* 15:38 (Sept 23, 1945), 1; and The Children's Friend in *OCLF* 16:32 (Aug 11, 1946), 1.

By the Chicago Historical Society: for picture of a life class at The Art Institute; by The Salvation Army National Headquarters, Alexandria, VA: for the following publications in *The War Cry*: Apostate Religionists in *WC* Central 939 (Dec 24, 1938), 23; Woman at the Well in *WC* Central 1004 (Mar 23, 1940), 10-12; "The Flight into Egypt" in *WC* Central 1089 (Nov 8, 1941), back cover; The Christmas Story in *WC* Central 1147 (Dec 19, 1942), front cover; The Wise Men in *WC* Central 1147 (Dec 19, 1942), 18; "A Home Away from Home" in *WC* Central 1200 (Dec 25, 1943), back cover; the Salvation Army Frieze at Chicago's Century of Progress (1933-34) in *WC* Central (Aug 5, 1933), 8-9; and the "Chalice of Antioch" in *WC* Central (Aug 4, 1934), 16; and by the Mt. Greenwood Corps of the Salvation Army, Chicago: for the original, "The Ascension" (1941).

By the Wilson Galleries, Anderson University, Anderson, IN: for the following originals: "Head of Christ" (1940) oil; "(Christ in) Gethsemane" (1941) oil; "Crown of Thorns" (1941) watercolor; "Christ at Dawn" (1945) oil; "Christ Our Pilot" (1950) oil; "Behold the Lord" (1952) watercolor; The Annunciation"

(1953) watercolor; Mary and Baby in Manger (1954) watercolor; "Power and Glory" (1957) oil; "It is Finished" (1958) watercolor, chalk and pen; "The Holy Communion" (1958) watercolor, chalk and pen; The Road to Emmaus" (1961) oil; "The Story of Gethsemane" (1964) oil; and "Portrait of Jesus" (1966) oil.

By the Evangelical Covenant Church, Braham, MN: for a reproduction of "The Ascension" (1934), an oil, as it appeared in the old church; by the First Covenant Church, Iron Mountain, MI: for a reproduction of "The Ascension" (1939), an oil, as it appeared in old church; by the First Covenant Church, Red Wing, MN: for the original, "Christ in Gethsemane" (1940), an oil; and a reproduction of the same artwork as it appeared in the old church; by the Bethlehem Covenant Church, Stephenson, MI: for the original, "The Good Shepherd" (1943), an oil; by the First Covenant Church, Fort Dodge, IA: for the original, "Christ Knocking at the Door" (1947), an oil; by the Evangelical Covenant Church, Norway, MI: for the original, "Christ Knocking at Heart's Door" (1953), an oil; and by the United Evangelical Covenant Church, Gladstone, MI: for the original, "His Presence" (1960), an oil.

By the Bethany Methodist Home, Chicago: for the original, "Mary and Martha with Jesus" (1954), an oil; by the United Hospital Center, Clarksburg, WV: for the original, "The Master Healer" (1960), an oil; by the Iowa Methodist Medical Center, Des Moines, IA: for the original, "The Great Physician" (1958), an oil; by Everett Sallman: for the original, "Abraham Lincoln and His Son" (1963), a watercolor; the picture of Warner Sallman (12 years), with LeRoy and Violet at left (1904); the picture of Warner Sallman Age 15 (1907); and the reproduction of Sallman before his "Head of Christ" at Covenant Village, Northbrook (1967) oil; by James Sallman: for the picture of Warner Sallman at 60; the family picture of Warner, LeRoy, and Violet Sallman, with parents Christine and Elias Sallman; the wedding picture of Warner and Ruth Sallman; the picture of Warner Sallman in his attic studio; the family picture of Warner and Ruth Sallman, with Everett, Richard and Jim as young boys; the picture of Warner Sallman completing a "Head of Christ" chalk at North Park College; the picture of Warner Sallman receiving an honorary Doctorate of Humanities degree from West Virginia Wesleyan College in 1962; the picture of Warner and Ruth Sallman, with Everett, Richard and Jim behind them, on the occasion of the Sallman's 50th Anniversary, May 31, 1966; by Marion Sallman: for the original, "Christ at Prayer" (1957), in charcoal; by Patsy Needham: for the unfinished original of Men on Road to Emmaus (n.d.) an oil; and by Norman Andrews: for the original of "Rev. C. J. Andrews" (1959), a charcoal.

Jack R. Lundbom
Clare Hall, Cambridge, August, 1998

Abbreviations

CA	*The Christian Advocate*
CC	*The Covenant Companion*
CF	*The Children's Friend*
CHo	*Children's Hour*
CovH	*Covenant Hymnal*
CW	*The Covenant Weekly*
CYT	*Covenant Youth Today*
EH	*The Epworth Herald*
FV	*Förbundets Veckotidning*
K&B	Kriebel and Bates Inc.
KJV	The King James Version of the Bible
LHJ	*The Ladies Home Journal*
MFU	*Missions-Förbundets Ungdomstidning*
MM	*Moody Monthly*
MV	*Missions-Vännen*
OC	*Our Covenant*
OCLF	*Our Covenant Little Folks*
OCY	*Our Covenant Youth*
OJ	*Our Juniors*
OYC	*Our Young Covenanters*
RSV	The Revised Standard Version of the Bible
WC	*The War Cry*

Prologue

The Sallman *Head of Christ* is one of the most familiar pictures of Jesus of all time. Across America one sees this work in homes, churches, chapels, hospitals, and other places public and private. The *Head of Christ* appears in framed prints and on wallet-size cards, on bookmarks, calendars, funeral cards, Bibles, buttons, stickers, and stationery. It is even found on lamps, clocks and china. One sees the picture around the world–in homes and churches mainly, but also in the marketplace with other religious artifacts. Over 500 million prints of the *Head of Christ* have been sold, and an equal number of the other combined Sallman works. That adds up to a billion pictures, a truly astonishing total.

In February 1999 it is seventy-five years since Sallman did his first charcoal of the famous picture. Since 1941, when the first prints of the *Head of Christ* in oil were made available to the public, the picture has come to have an enormous impact on Christians across North America–Protestants mainly, but also Roman Catholic and Eastern Orthodox Christians. With some justification this picture–and others by Sallman–are called the "icons of American Protestantism."[1]

Most people have come to know the Sallman artwork through reproductions. They have not gone to museums to see originals, as most famous artworks find their audience. Indeed, many do not even know that oil originals of the well-known pictures exist. In part this public ignorance is because, until 1986, the *Head of Christ* and other oils were kept in a small office in Indianapolis, Indiana, or crated and stored in a back room warehouse.

Nevertheless, stories are legion about how the Sallman *Head of Christ* has impacted people's lives. At one of Sallman's personal appearances in San Diego, the chalk he had just finished drawing was offered to the person making the largest contribution to missions. A woman offered $500.00. When she came forward to receive the picture, with tears in her eyes she told those assembled, "I want this drawing because, when Sallman drew it, Christ became real to me for the first time in my life, and I have accepted him as my Savior."[2]

Sallman's charcoal version of the famous picture was displayed on Chicago public transportation beginning in the 1930s, and the story is told of a desperate alcoholic, having deserted his wife and family and living currently in poverty, saw the picture on a streetcar and was captured by it. He himself had been an artist. Getting off the streetcar, he passed a mission where he saw a chalk of the same Sallman picture. He went into the mission, and inquired of the superintendent where he might locate the artist. He was directed to the Edgewater Mission Covenant Church on Chicago's north side, where he went to meet Sallman. Moved by Sallman's friendliness, the man returned to the mission and made a commitment to Christ. Later he was reunited with his wife and family.[3] Many, many incidents of a similar nature have taken place over the years. Not all individuals were artists nor did they all personally meet Sallman, but because of his picture their broken lives were put back together, and they were brought to a living faith.

The impact of Sallman's *Head of Christ* has been worldwide. Dr. Charles Goff, well-known churchman and pastor for many years of the Chicago Temple, related to Sallman personally an incident that took place on his round-the-world tour in 1953:[4]

> He said he was leaving a church in Manilla, in the Philippines, after preaching the Sunday morning sermon. In the company of a number of prominent people in the city…on their way to dinner, a Chinese man[5] broke through the circle of friends and exclaimed, "You saved my life! You saved my life!"
>
> "I saved your life?" Goff replied. "You must be mistaken in your identity."
>
> "No, no, you have something to do with Sallman's painting of Jesus."
>
> Goff said, "Yes, he is a good friend of mine."
>
> "Well, during the Japanese War I was captured by an enemy raiding party and dragged into the interior jungle…I pleaded with them not to kill me, saying, 'I am a Christian, I am a Christian.' It was all to no avail. Then they found in my wallet a small print of the Sallman *Head of Christ* which they passed around from one to another.…When it came back to the leader of the group, and some remarks were made which I did not understand, my wallet and the picture was handed back and I was told I could leave. I was unharmed."

More recently, the Sallman picture was seen by Doris Johnson in Shanghai in 1992. Doris was returning to the land of her birth. Her parents had been China missionaries until 1927, when the Communist uprising forced them to leave. The pastor of the 5000-member Shanghai Protestant Church told Doris before she left for home, "Tell any Christians that you encounter in the United States that this picture means so much to the Chinese, and we have no idea how many Chinese Christians are in glory today, influenced in part by that picture."[6]

In the United States things have taken a somewhat different turn. A few years ago a Sallman *Head of Christ* in the hallway of a public high school in Bloomingdale, Michigan became the center of a controversy over the display of religious pictures in public places.[7] A court order, issued in February 1993, required that the picture be taken down. This was later modified to a ruling requiring only that the picture be covered. The argument prevailed that this was not an ordinary picture, but rather one conveying an essential Christian witness.

In these pages will be told the largely unknown story of the artist who painted the well-known *Head of Christ*, along with other religious pictures such as, *Crown of Thorns* (1941), *Christ in Gethsemane* (1941), *Christ at Heart's Door* (1942), *The Lord Is My Shepherd* (1942), *His Presence* (1946), *Christ Our Pilot* (1950), *The Road to Emmaus* (1961), and *Portrait of Jesus* (1966). Lesser-known works, many of which are preserved only in archives and are therefore inaccessible to the general public, will also be surveyed. In all, over 500 paintings and drawings will be placed in their historical, social and religious context. But the primary story being told is that of Warner E. Sallman, master painter.

[1] David Morgan, *Icons of American Protestantism: The Art of Warner Sallman, 1892-1968* (Valparaiso, IN: Valparaiso University, 1994); see also. Morgan, "Imaging Protestant Piety: The Icons of Warner Sallman," *Religion and American Culture* 3 (1993), 29-47.

[2] Dorothy C. Haskin, *Christians You Would Like to Know* (Grand Rapids: Zondervan Publishing House, 1954) 71.

[3] Ibid., 71-72.

[4] In a letter to Sylvia Peterson dated 27 March 1955. Sallman had heard the story from Goff a week earlier. Goff later repeated the story in his introduction of Sallman to the Union League Club on 4 November 1957.

[5] In some published versions of this story, e.g., William F. McDermott, "Christ...According to Sallman," *Christian Herald* 79/1 (January, 1956): 19, the man is identified as a Filipino. But in Sallman's own account of the conversation he had with Goff about the incident, the man is said to be Chinese.

[6] Lou Ann van Fossen, "Return to China: Touching the Past Gives Hope for the Future," *inSpirit* 16/1 (1993): 21.

[7] David Crumm, "Debating Jesus' Place: Student Sues to Remove Portrait from Hall," *Detroit Free Press*, 11 January, 1993, 1A, 8A.

I

Talking Small Living Big

> Too many Christians talk big and live small. What we really need are
> Christians who talk small and live big.
>> (Professor Paul Holmer, Yale University)

He liked to say of himself that he was just an ordinary man. Those who
knew Warner Sallman would agree with this self-appraisal, but they would
be quick to add that there was also something about this man that was quite
extraordinary. One could see the blend in his quiet, unassuming manner, and in
his humility about accomplishments, which, by the mid-1940s were already
numerous. At the close of World War Two the Sallman *Head of Christ* was
known worldwide, and well on its way to becoming the most widely-distrib-
uted work of religious art in human history.

My earliest remembrances of Sallman were on the streets of North Park. He
was my neighbor, living just a block and a half north of where I lived on
Spaulding Avenue. As a young boy I remember his friendly hellos when we happened to pass. Occasionally he would stop to chat, which was a normal
occurrence in our community, but not always a normal occurrence when an
older man passed a young boy. Our families were friends. My grandfather,[1] like
Sallman, was a painter, only his work consisted of interior decorating and sign
painting. We never talked about painting, or about art for that matter, just the
more ordinary things going on. If our conversation had any focus it was probably on what I happened to be doing. Warner Sallman was an "other-centered"
person. Our encounters always left me with a good feeling. I was glad I knew
this man, and that he knew me.

My most memorable visit, and one of the last, came just after I had decided
to enter the Christian ministry and begin North Park Seminary. We chanced to
meet again on the street, and I told him about this surprising turn of events in
my life. He was visibly pleased, and said I must come by when it was convenient as he wanted to give me some prints.

A few days later I called and arranged a visit. When I came to his house, a
robust man of seventy greeted me at the door. Sallman was well-built, athletic,
about six feet tall and weighing 190 pounds. He was quietly enthusiastic about
my coming, making me feel—as was his custom toward all callers at his home
over the years—that he was more pleased at my coming than I. This time I
paused to look with more attentiveness than usual at the original *Head of Christ*,

hanging in the hallway. We talked about his midnight vision, which I had heard recounted before. Now, however, I listened more carefully as he told me that the sketch done at night was but a 3-inch-high prototype in pencil, and that he did the charcoal the following day. He said he did the pencil immediately for fear of losing the picture if he waited until morning.

Once we were in the living room he was talking and moving about quickly, showing me recent paintings and telling me what he was currently working on. Then he went to his studio, returning a few minutes later with a generous number of prints. All the well-known pictures were present—*Christ in Gethsemane, Christ at Heart's Door, The Lord Is My Shepherd, Christ Our Pilot,* and the *Head of Christ*—those I had admired many years ago, when, as a young boy I used to ride my bike up to Covenant Bookstore on Francisco Avenue and look at them there. He also brought his *Abraham Lincoln,* the recently-completed *Road to Emmaus,* and a modern Christ atop the world, which he called *Power and Glory.* I had not seen these before. The latter two he was particularly anxious to show me. The *Road to Emmaus,* he explained, was done after more careful research into the terrain and flora of Palestine. Gone were the tall mountains of *The Lord Is My Shepherd,* replaced with rolling hills typical of the area north and west of Jerusalem. *Power and Glory,* with its refracted light, was an attempt to depart from the realism characterizing his earlier paintings. Warner went back to get a few more prints.

I was taken back by his generosity. I told him that since he had given me a number of duplicates I would now have to give some away to my friends. He thought this a good idea. Perhaps he was hoping I would do that. Before I left, he took the time to sign them all. I noticed his large hands. He also told me how to mount the prints on masonite, without the use of glass.

Sallman's quiet manner did not come across as weakness. He was a strong and vigorous man. His handshake was firm. His speech was animated and direct. He could even be bold, particularly when it came to giving testimony to his faith. He was very much a man of action, a man with a purpose, a man whose life you had the feeling was going somewhere.

Those who remember him from Edgewater Covenant, which was his home church, know how eager he was to greet strangers Sunday morning, Sunday evening, and any other time, making sure they felt welcome. Many newcomers Ruth and he invited home for dinner. Over the years Sallman taught a young people's Sunday School class at Edgewater, which endeared him to an entire generation younger than he. His longtime friend from Edgewater, Edgar Swanson Jr., said of Sallman at the time of his death,

> For nearly the entire history of this church, he was a vital part of the fellowship. Even if he had never lifted a palette or brushed a single stroke, his presence in our fellowship would have been long remembered...

Strangers could always say, "I met Warner Sallman at Edgewater." The very old and the very young were special marks of his attention and love. His feelings of concern for the lost and the straying were constantly expressed.

Sallman's 1926 Sunday School class consisted of young women. One Sunday he was having particular difficulty in getting a point across. Frustrated, he pulled from his pocket a piece of letter paper, and quickly sketched, in pencil, a picture of Christ with a crown of thorns (*Thorn-crowned Christ* 1926). "This," he said, "is what I mean." Seated directly in front of him was Beatrice Ringquist, into whose lap the paper fell. The sketch survives, and is the closest thing we have to the pencil *Head of Christ* done just two years earlier, which is not extant.

Shortly after the Reverend Ralph Hanson came to Chicago to be Secretary of Foreign Missions for the Covenant Church, in about 1944, his eldest son took sick and was diagnosed as having a terminal disease. Sallman lived only a short distance from the Missionary Home into which the Hansons had moved, and upon hearing the news, he immediately went over to express his concern. With him he brought along a print of his recently-completed *Christ at Heart's Door*, and gave it to the Hansons. The visit and the gift were much appreciated. Sallman also suggested a doctor who might be able to help. The treatments begun soon afterward led to the son's eventual healing.

Olga Lindborg was Sallman's senior, but a great admirer of his, also a good friend. For many years she was Director of Children's Work for the Covenant Church. Olga was an extremely talented woman, knowledgeable about history, archaeology, and art–particularly religious art, which she strongly advocated using for the illustration of Bible stories.[2] In the summer of 1945 she lay sick in Swedish Covenant Hospital and had not much longer to live. Sallman made frequent trips to visit her. One day he came, and before going into the hospital room he stopped to inquire about her condition from one of the nurses. The nurse told him that Olga was not eating. Sallman proceeded to the room, and upon entering said, "Olga, they tell me you're not eating. Can't you think of anything you would like?" "Well," she said, "there's that hot cereal Ruth makes, which would taste good. I sometimes wish I could have some of that."[3] Sallman immediately left the room, went the short distance to his home and prepared some of his wife's cereal to bring to the hospital. Before leaving home, he took from the cupboard a setting of their best china. Back at the hospital, in the most elegant manner possible, Sallman fed Olga the hot cereal she said she could eat.[4]

Sallman's attention to strangers was not limited to the confines of the Edgewater Church. The story is told of one errand of mercy Sallman went on following a chance meeting with Elvira Hedstrand. Elvira's husband, the

Reverend G. F. Hedstrand, edited the *Covenant Companion* that published Sallman's original Christ head. On this particular day when Sallman met Hedstrand, she had a sad look on her face. Sallman asked what was wrong. She told him her next door neighbor was sick, and feeling very much alone. Sallman inquired as to precisely where she lived, and within a short time was at the neighbor's home with a basket of fruit. He also carried a picture of his *Head of Christ* that he left with the woman. He told her simply that it was "a picture of his friend." The woman was Jewish. The next day the woman told Mrs. Hedstrand that the nicest man had been to her home and left a basket of fruit, also a picture. She said she asked him who he was and where he lived, but all he said was that he was "just a neighbor from up the street who was concerned about her and wanted to offer some help."[5]

The Mission Covenant Church has its roots in Lutheran Pietism where mission has always meant not simply verbal witness, but deeds of kindness and mercy. Sallman often spoke about his faith—in church, on the street, in his home, on the telephone, and while at work. He was a frequent visitor and occasional speaker at Chicago's downtown rescue missions. But speaking did not come easily to him, and so more often his witness was expressed in deeds, rather than words.

Sallman's modesty and self-effacement enhanced his stature among those who knew him, but these same characteristics led to obscurity on the larger scene. Though his paintings became widely known, Sallman himself did not. To an earlier generation within the Covenant Church, the Methodist Church, the Salvation Army, and Chicago-area congregations of many denominations, he was well known, largely because of personal appearances to do his chalk talks. Today he is less well known in these constituencies, including his own Covenant Church. On the larger American scene, as well as internationally, he is an obscure figure or otherwise unknown.

Any embarrassment this lack of notoriety causes friends and admirers today would not be felt by Sallman himself if he were alive. Sallman wanted his art, since it consisted largely of depicting the person of Christ, to gain the attention rather than he himself. The scripture he most frequently cited to describe his work and what he the artist was really about was 2 Corinthians 4:5-6:

> For what we preach is not ourselves, but Jesus Christ as Lord, with our-selves as your servants for Jesus' sake. For it is the God who said, "Let light shine out of darkness," who has shone in our hearts to give the light of the knowledge of the glory of God in the face of Christ.

Sallman also often cited Philippians 2:8-11, which again describes the Christ Sallman was painting and a mode of living that he, the artist, sought to emulate:

And being found in human form he humbled himself and became obe-
dient unto death, even death on a cross. Therefore God has highly
exalted him and bestowed on him the name which is above every name,
that at the name of Jesus every knee should bow, in heaven and on
earth and under the earth, and every tongue confess that Jesus Christ is
Lord, to the glory of God the Father.

Sallman then was not a seeker after personal fame; whatever fame he achieved
came in spite of efforts on his part to see that he himself remained in the background.

Sallman's self-confidence—also his love of gadgetry—can be seen in a story
told by Nils W. Lund, Dean of North Park Theological Seminary, about how
Sallman persuaded him one day to make a radio. Lund gave this account:

A number of years ago I came to see Warner on business—some church
activity—and I noticed a radio on his mantel. I commented on it—it was
such an unusual piece and had such sweet music. "You can make them
yourself," he said. "But," I replied, "I don't know anything about
radio." "Get a blueprint and a soldering iron," he said. He directed me
what to buy. I bought the radio parts and then spent about three days
in assembling it. Materials—batteries, a loud speaker, and a
transformer—amounted to $100.00. Transformers were very expensive
in those days—$11.00 a piece. My wife said, "That thing will never
play."

Soon after Warner said he would be coming over. He came about
10 o'clock. Some gadgets were missing so he went and got them. At
10:30 we were going strong. We tinkered until about 2 o'clock in the
morning when the music finally came....I have always liked Warner's
tremendous enthusiasm. I call him my chief consulting engineer on the
radio.[6]

Warner Sallman was first and foremost a Christian, a Pietist Christian upon
whom the impression was made that Christ must remake you into his own
image, and any glory you receive belongs ultimately to God, and must be given
back to God. The following is his own personal testimony:

I believe everyone who has committed himself to Christ our Lord
desires to serve him with whatever gifts or talents he may possess. On
this premise, with Jesus Christ as my guide, it has been my goal to yield
whatever abilities God has given me to his honor and glory. It seemed
that my talent for painting and illustrating developed in me from early
youth, and by divine direction I was led step by step toward a ministry

of Christian art. I give God glory for whatever has been accomplished by my efforts to bring joy and happiness to people throughout the world.

Paul Fryhling, pastor for many years of the First Covenant Church in Minneapolis, called Sallman the layman who inspired him most. Fryhling said,

No one in my acquaintance has so truly sought only the glory of Christ in a real sense. He has put into practice the theme of John the Baptist: "He [Christ] must increase and I must decrease"...Sallman doesn't seem to be a great man, but his quiet influence is really tremendous. He is selfless, humble, and a devout servant of Christ.[7]

A close neighbor and friend, the Reverend Carl Philip Anderson, who for many years was editor of the *Covenant Companion*, said about Warner Sallman:

It was my privilege to become acquainted with Warner Sallman early in life and to observe him as a neighbor and friend for more than a quarter of a century. Like the Lord whom he followed in his daily walk he was a man of strength, compassion, and humility. One of my strongest impressions of him is of a man who delighted in helping others, gave generously of himself and his talents in living out his life as a follower of Christ, and was a model of humility, shunning ostentation and totally without pride.[8]

Professor Emeritus Paul Holmer of Yale once said, "There are many Christians who talk big and live small. What we really need are Christians who talk small and live big."[9] Sallman was a Christian who talked small and lived very big. The same can be said of Ruth, his faithful companion of fifty-two years who was a remarkable woman in her own right. She even more than he talked small and lived big during what had to be the most critical juncture in all their married life, a time when hopes and dreams were put to the test, and commitments for a future life together could only be made with great courage. Sallman considered the crisis pivotal, and in retrospect attached not a little significance to it in the working out of his ministry of Christian art.

In the early summer of 1917, Warner and Ruth had been married a year ago May and were now expecting their first child. Warner was working as a commercial artist in downtown Chicago, employed by Meyer Both Studios where he was designing men's fashions. Although a war was being waged on the other side of the Atlantic, the Sallmans' world seemed bright. At twenty-five Warner was prospering financially. Then serious illness struck. Sallman recalled the feeling: "It seemed like a cloudless sky, but storm clouds already were forming below the horizon."[10] Some years before he had developed a tumor on the right side of his neck, down near the shoulder. A surgeon from Augustana Hospital removed it, and it seemed to have healed. But now a major complication erupted in the same area, and the pain was acute. Sallman went to several doctors who prescribed a variety of treatments, but the problem only got worse.

Finally he consulted a specialist, Dr. Cardinal Quinn, who conducted extensive tests. The report came back that Sallman was seriously ill. Sallman asked to know the whole truth, and was told that he had tuberculosis of the lymph glands. Quinn recommended surgery that would consist of injecting a new serum into the spinal column. This procedure had met with favorable results in certain patients. Moreover, it was about all the hope the doctor could give. Without surgery, said Quinn as he took hold of Sallman's arm, "I cannot give you much hope beyond three months."[11]

The doctor's words jolted him. He left the office so dazed that he nearly stepped in front of a passing car. He made his way to the streetcar for the trip home. He also began to do some thinking. "What shall I do?" he asked himself. "Shall I tell Ruth the whole truth, or conceal what the doctor has said until after the baby is born?" Ruth was due in September, a mere two months off. Warner was afraid the news would so upset her that complications might develop. He prayed. Then suddenly the conviction swept over him that his wife was a brave woman, possessing deep faith, and that she would be able to take the news. He resolved to tell her everything.

When he arrived home he told Ruth the news, not minimizing the words "three months to live." She received the words calmly, saying she had known the seriousness of his condition all along. A feeling came over Warner that Ruth was indeed a rock, and that through her the Lord would guide the two of them aright. Ruth's next words were most extraordinary. Warner recalled them as follows:

> "Let God's peace come into your heart, Warner," she told me, putting her arms around my neck and looking squarely into my face, her eyes aglow with love. "We'll pray and whatever is God's will for us, we gladly will do it. In three months we can do a lot for Him; and if it be His will to spare our life together for a longer period, we will thank Him for it and go ahead serving Him."[12]

They prayed together. Warner could not remember the precise words, only that they did not ask God for a longer life span. Their prayer was for God's blessing and guidance, echoing the words Jesus prayed in Gethsemane: "Thy will be done."

The next morning on his way to work Sallman was walking down the "el"[13] steps at Twenty-second Street when he noticed a big poster he had not seen before. Apparently it had been put up during the night. It read, "Foods that build or destroy," and advertised a series of articles in the *Daily News* about proper diet. This, he thought, was his answer from God, and he hurried to buy a newspaper.

Sallman had not wanted surgery, in part because the young couple didn't have the money. Also, Sallman had always been somewhat his own doctor, having thought at one time that he would enter the practice of medicine. Ruth for her part did not put much stock in diets. Besides, she was in the habit of cooking rich foods and baking buttery pastries, for which Swedes are justly famous. Now her husband would have none of them. Much discussion and prayer followed. Warner resolved nevertheless to follow the diet strictly and he did. He also went to a health clinic to build up his body strength. There he found out that he had extremely low blood pressure. The doctors at this clinic were divided about the swelling–about the size of a plum–on his neck. One claimed it was cancer; the other said tuberculosis. Subsequent treatments, however, brought the swelling to a head and finally it broke open.

Gradually the pain grew less, and there were signs the disease had ameliorated. After many months the healing was complete. Sallman thought his attitude had something to do with it, also the wondrous healing power of nature. But in everything–including the sign catching his attention that morning when he was on his way to work–Sallman discerned the guiding hand of God. He believed God was the Great Healer. For him God had performed another of his miracles. "It was progressive, not spontaneous," he said, yet a miracle all the same.[14]

The implications this experience had for living out of his life also dawned upon Sallman in progressive fashion. He now began to feel that he was living on borrowed time, and his immediate regret was that he had not done more in the way of service for his Lord. If he should die, what sort of testimony would survive? Thoughts of death became very real for Sallman. He decided that, should he die, a Bible was to be placed in his hands when they buried him so people would know that little else really counted in his life.

Greater things, however, were just around the corner. Sallman now became possessed with a great sense of urgency for the task that had begun to unfold before him, which was of devoting himself and his life to a ministry of Christian art. He began to drive himself, at times too hard. Now completely recovered, Sallman believed that all the talent God had given the artist must be dedicated to God's service. With a renewed spirit, then, he was on his way rejoicing.

[1] Otto F. Ohlson, who built a two-flat in North Park in 1925, three years after Sallman built. In this building, 5254 North Spaulding, our family lived.

[2] Olga E. Lindborg, "Choosing Pictures That Illustrate Bible Stories I-II,"

The Teacher's Companion 2/4 (September 1923): 5-6; 2/5 (October 1923): 6-7. This publication by the Mission Covenant Church appeared only in 1922-1923, after which it was succeeded by *The Covenant Companion*.

3 Reported by Sylvia Peterson to the author during a visit to her home in February 1986.

4 Olga Lindborg died on 11 August 1945 at Swedish Covenant Hospital; see *Our Covenant Youth* 26/36 (9 September 1945): 3.

5 Reported by Sylvia Peterson Knudson in "Over the Coffee Cup," *The Covenant Companion* 63/2 (15 January 1974): 15.

6 Dictated by Nils W. Lund to Sylvia Peterson, Sylvia Peterson's unpublished notes, n.d.

7 From "Sallman's Reward Was Portraying Glory of Christ" by the Reverend Fryhling in the *Minneapolis Star*, 16 April 1960 as told to Willmar Thorkelson.

8 Carl Philip Anderson, "Recollections and Reflections on the Life of Warner Sallman," n.d.

9 Paul Holmer, conversation with author, 7 June 1983.

10 Warner Sallman, "The Story Behind this Painting, " *Guideposts* 16/2 (February 1962): 8.

11 Ibid., 8-9.

12 Ibid., 9.

13 The "el" (short for "elevated") is Chicago's above-ground rapid transit system.

14 Sylvia E. Peterson, "The Ministry of Christian Art," *The Lutheran Companion* 55/14 (2 April 1947): 11.

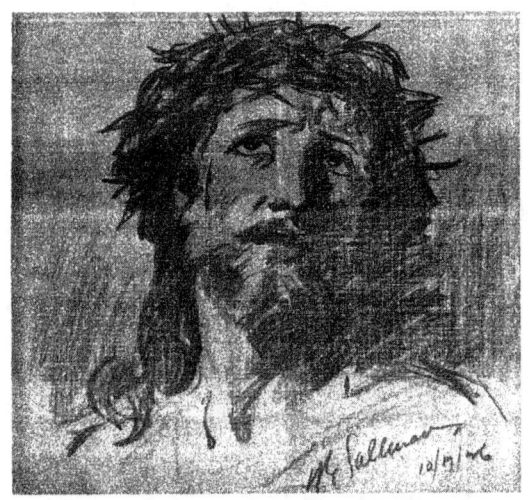

Thorn-crowned Christ (1926) pencil.

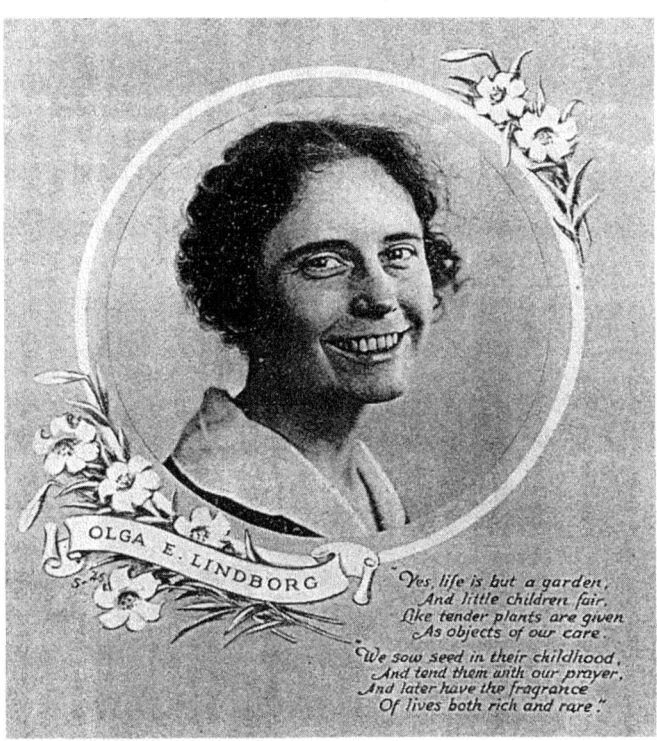

OLGA E. LINDBORG

"Yes, life is but a garden,
And little children fair,
Like tender plants are given
As objects of our care.

We sow seed in their childhood,
And tend them with our prayer,
And later have the fragrance
Of lives both rich and rare."

Olga Lindborg, Director of Children's Work for the
Mission Covenant Church

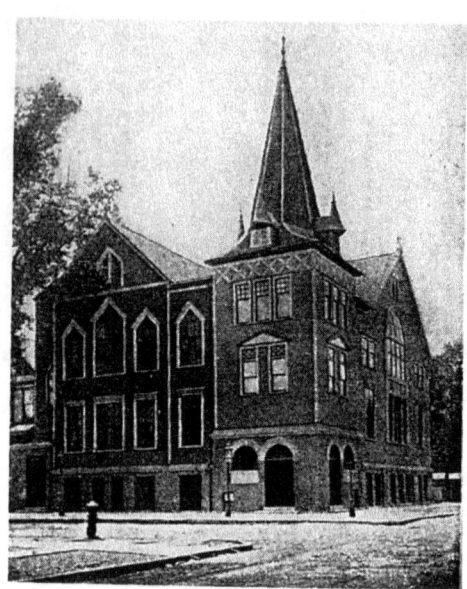

Lake View Mission Covenant
Church, School Street and Kenmore
Ave., Chicago

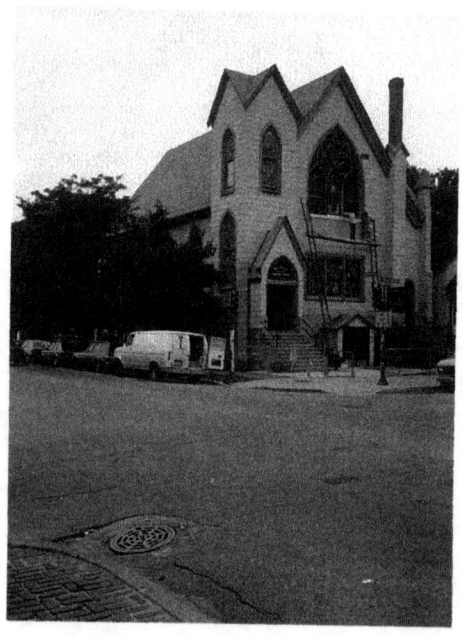

Centennial Methodist Church,
Wellington and Sheffield, Chicago

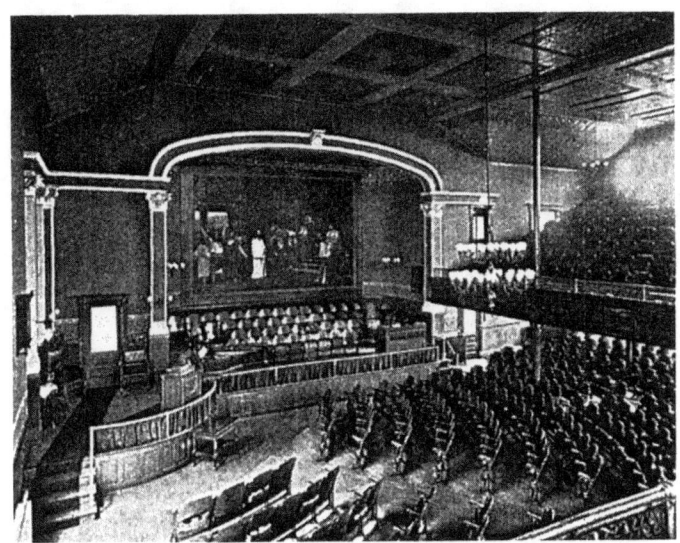

Interior of Lake View Mission Church, with Munkacsy's *Christ Before Pilate*, above the choir loft.

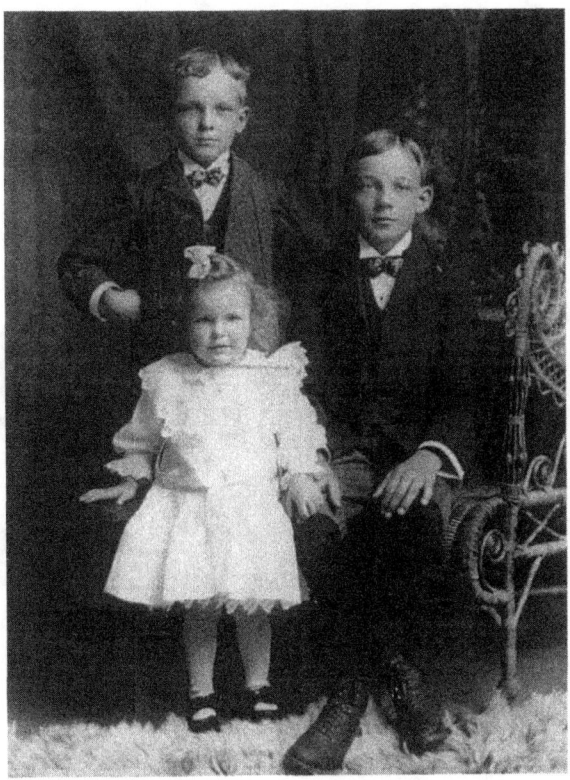

Warner (12 years), with LeRoy and Violet at left (1904)

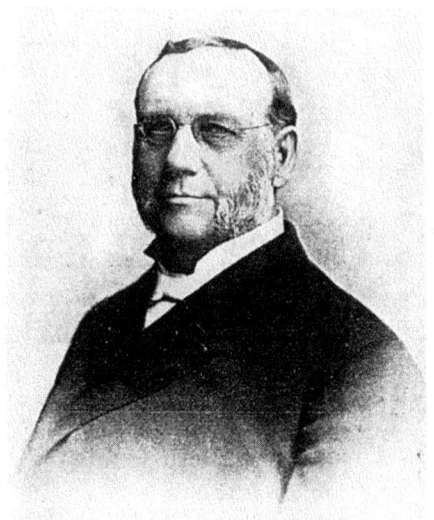

Pastor August Pohl of the Lake View
Mission Covenant Church

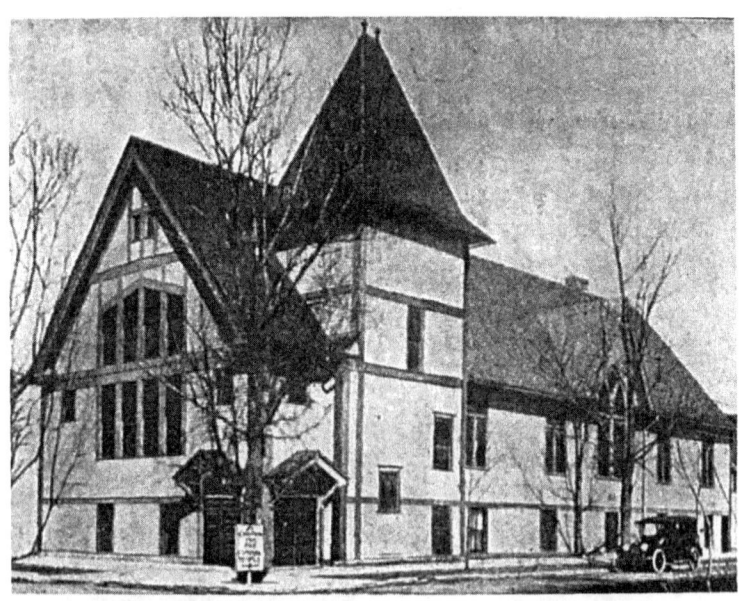

Waveland Avenue Congregational Church, Waveland and
Janssen, Chicago

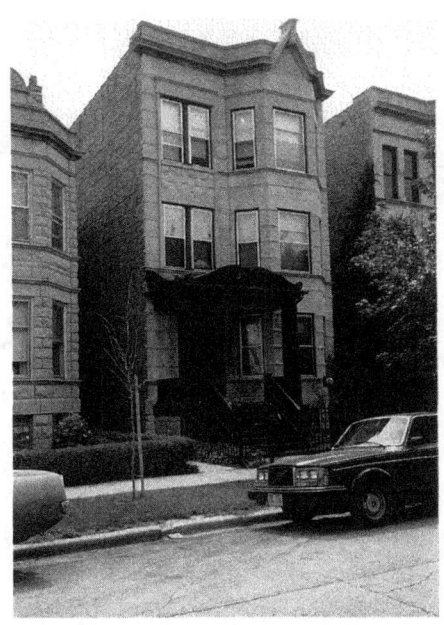

Sallman residence on 3631 N.
Maple Square Avenue

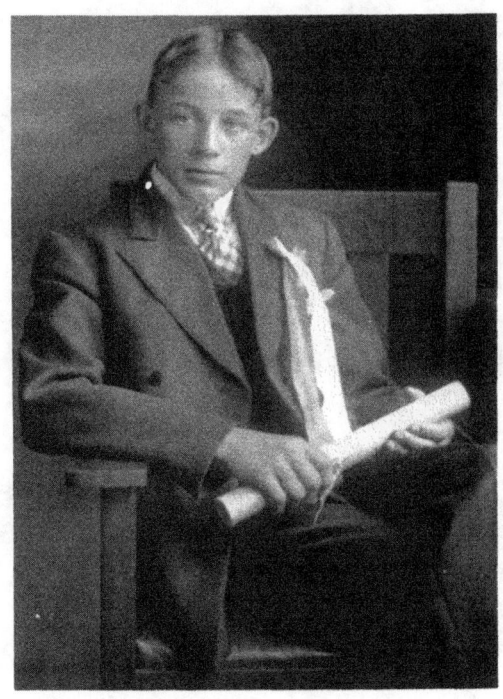

Warner Sallman, age 15 (1907)

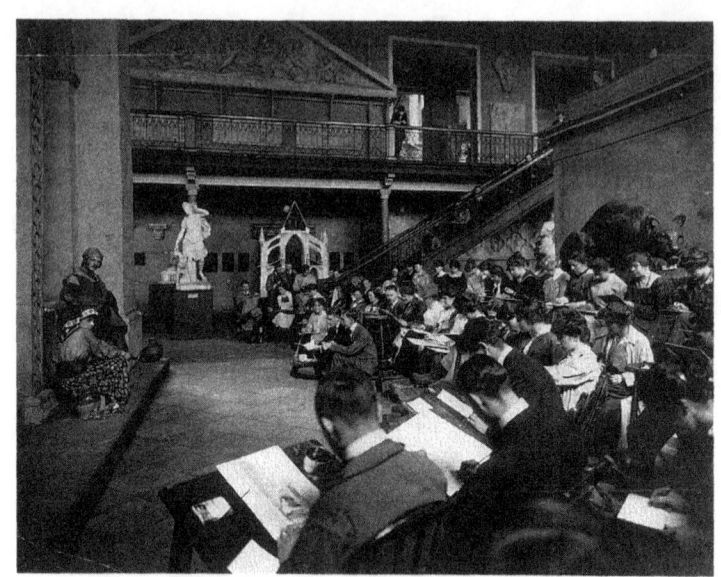

Life class at the Chicago Art Institute, before 1918

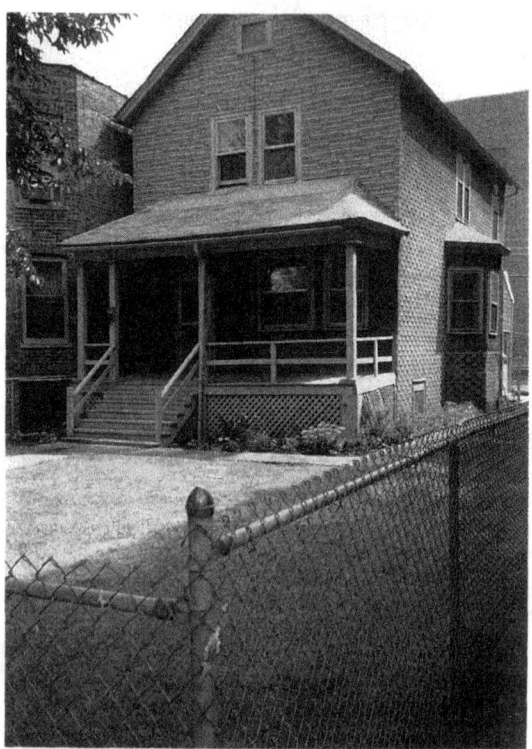

Sallman residence on 5111 N. Ashland Avenue

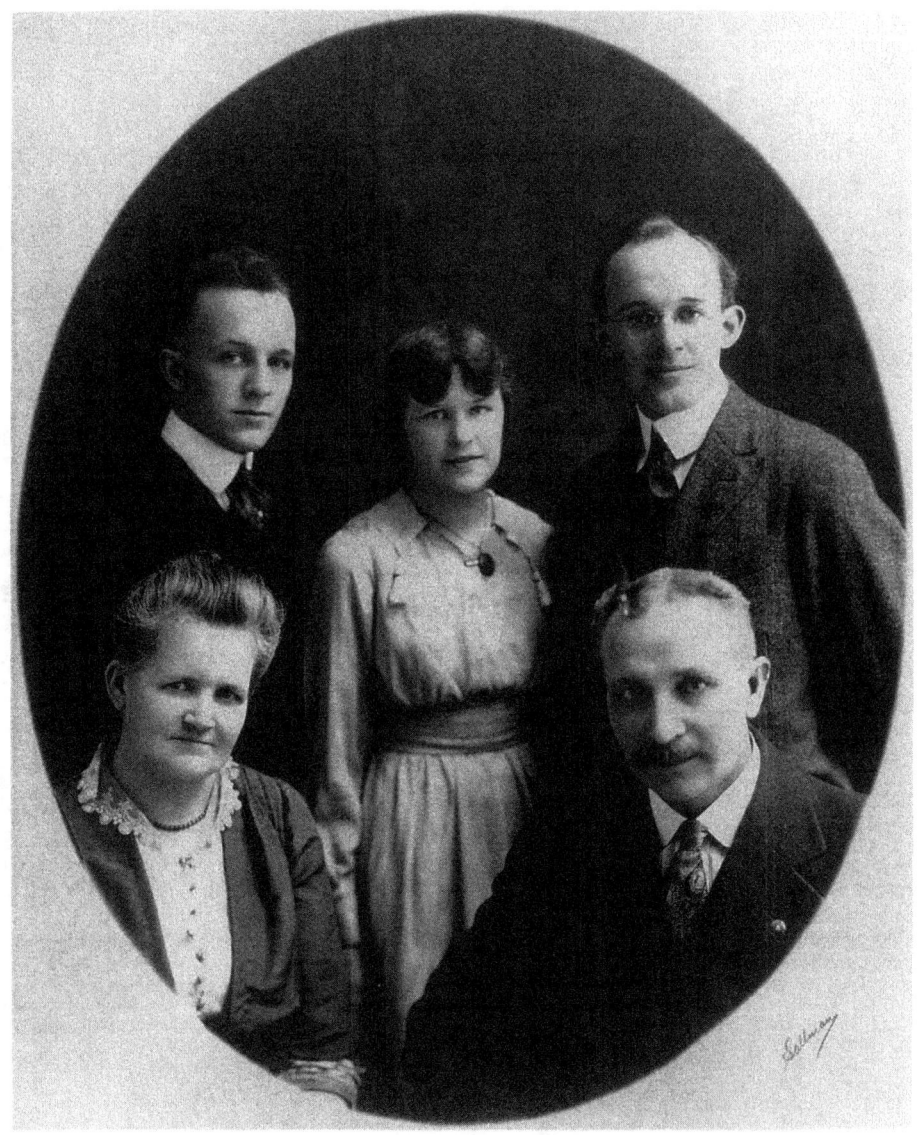

Family of Warner Sallman; back row: LeRoy, Violet and Warner; front row: Christine and Elias Sallman

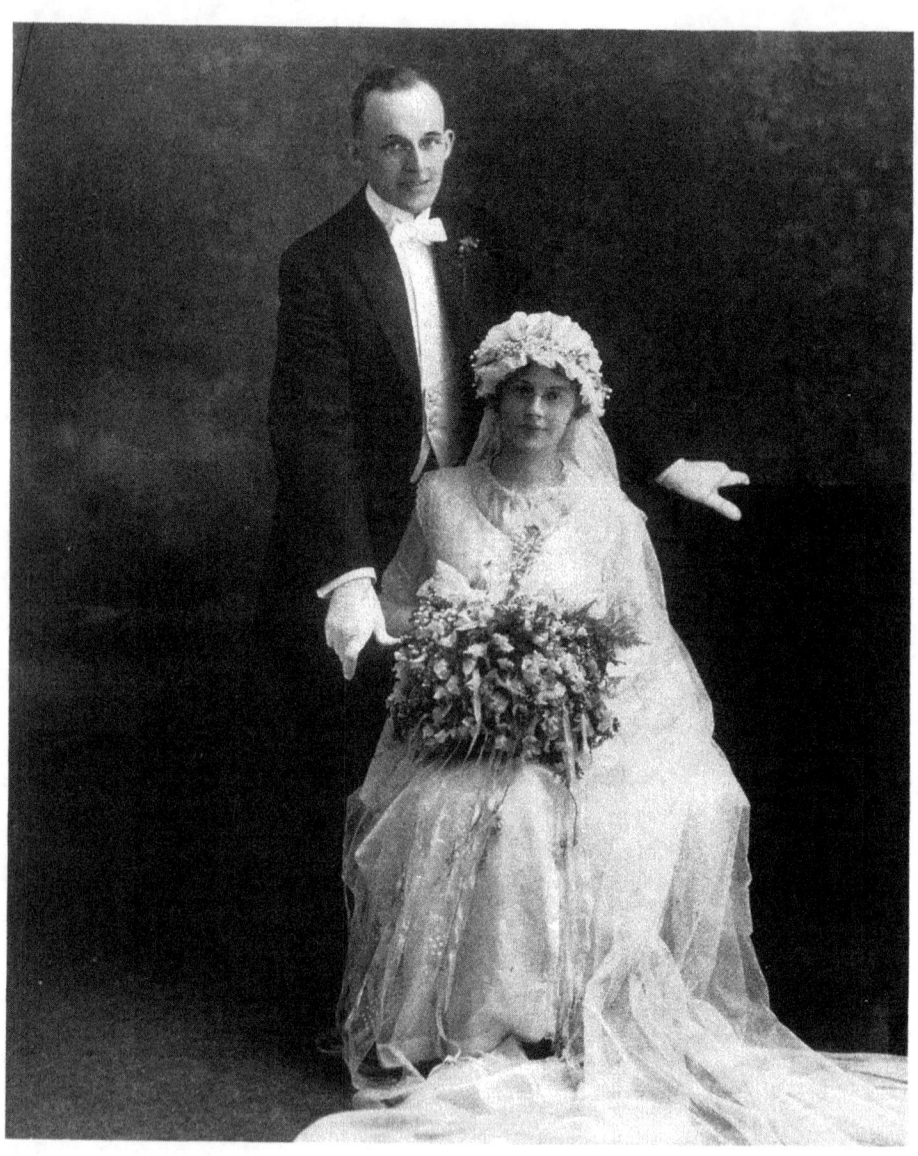

Warner and Ruth Sallman's wedding picture

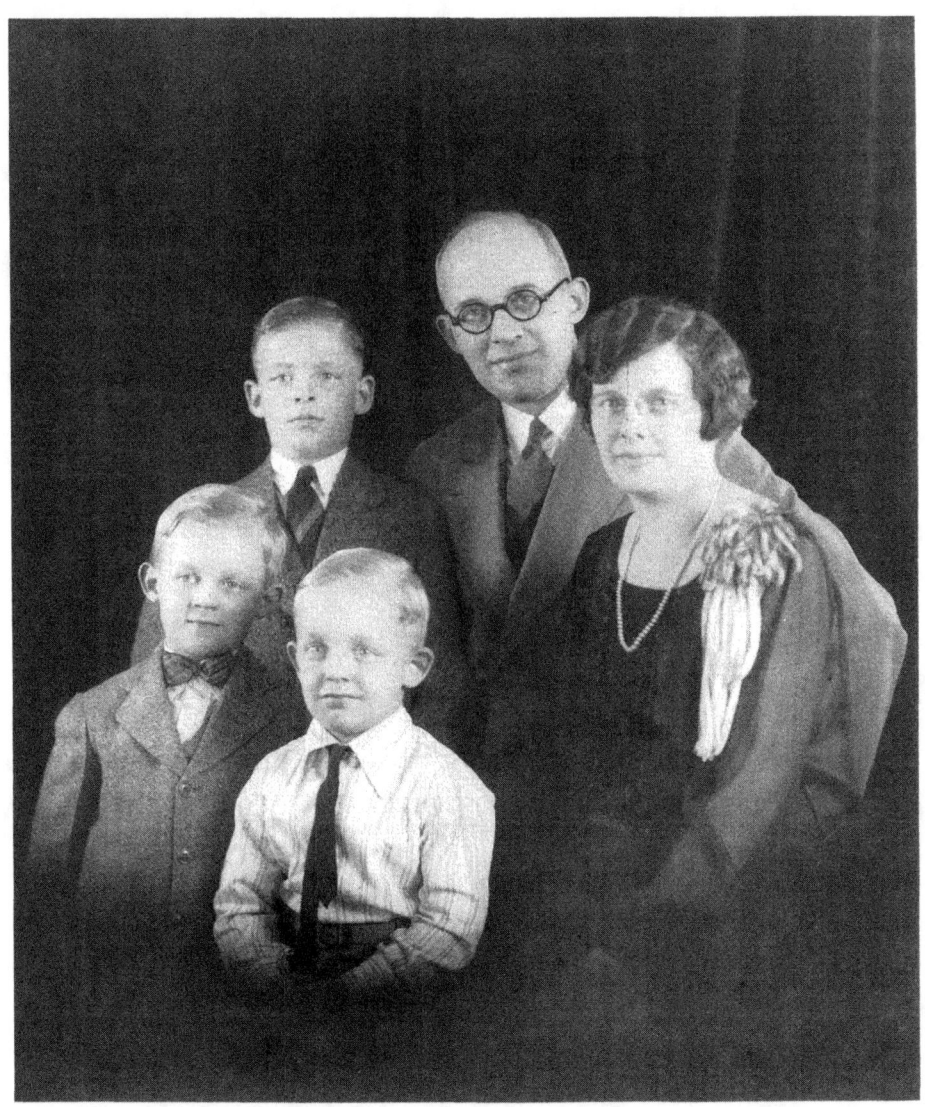

Warner and Ruth Sallman with Everett, Richard and Jim as young boys

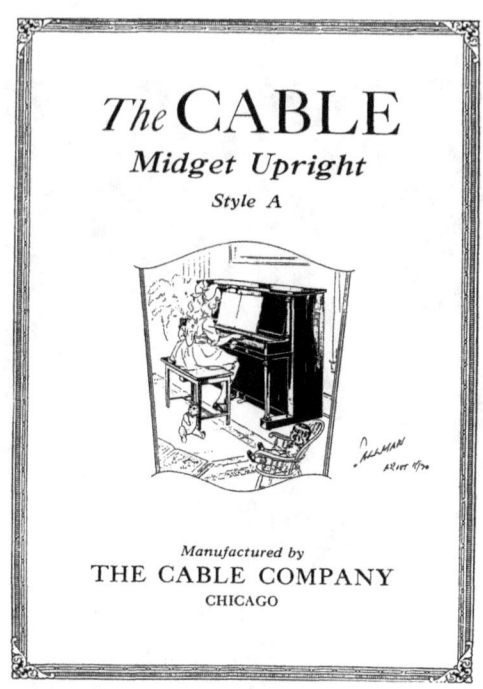

Cable Midget Upright (1920) pen.
Printed advertisement

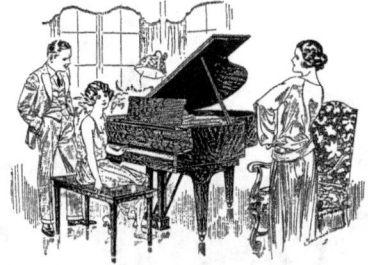

Pianos in Walnut (1920) pen.
Printed advertisement

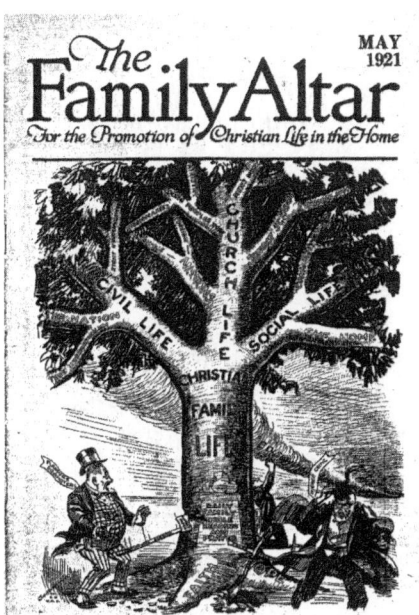

Christian Family Life (1921) pen.
Printed in *The Family Altar*

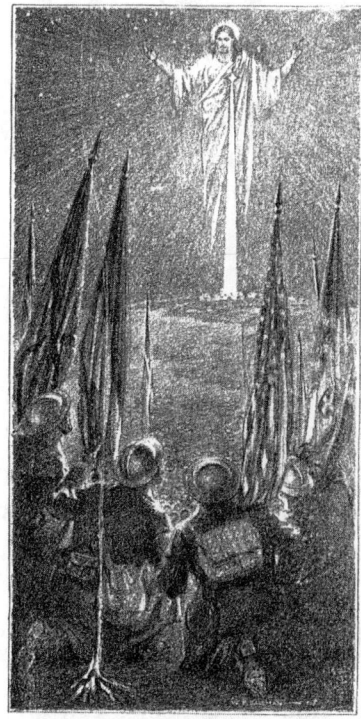

Frid på Jorden [*Peace on the
Earth*] (1918) pen. Printed in
Förbundets Veckotidning.

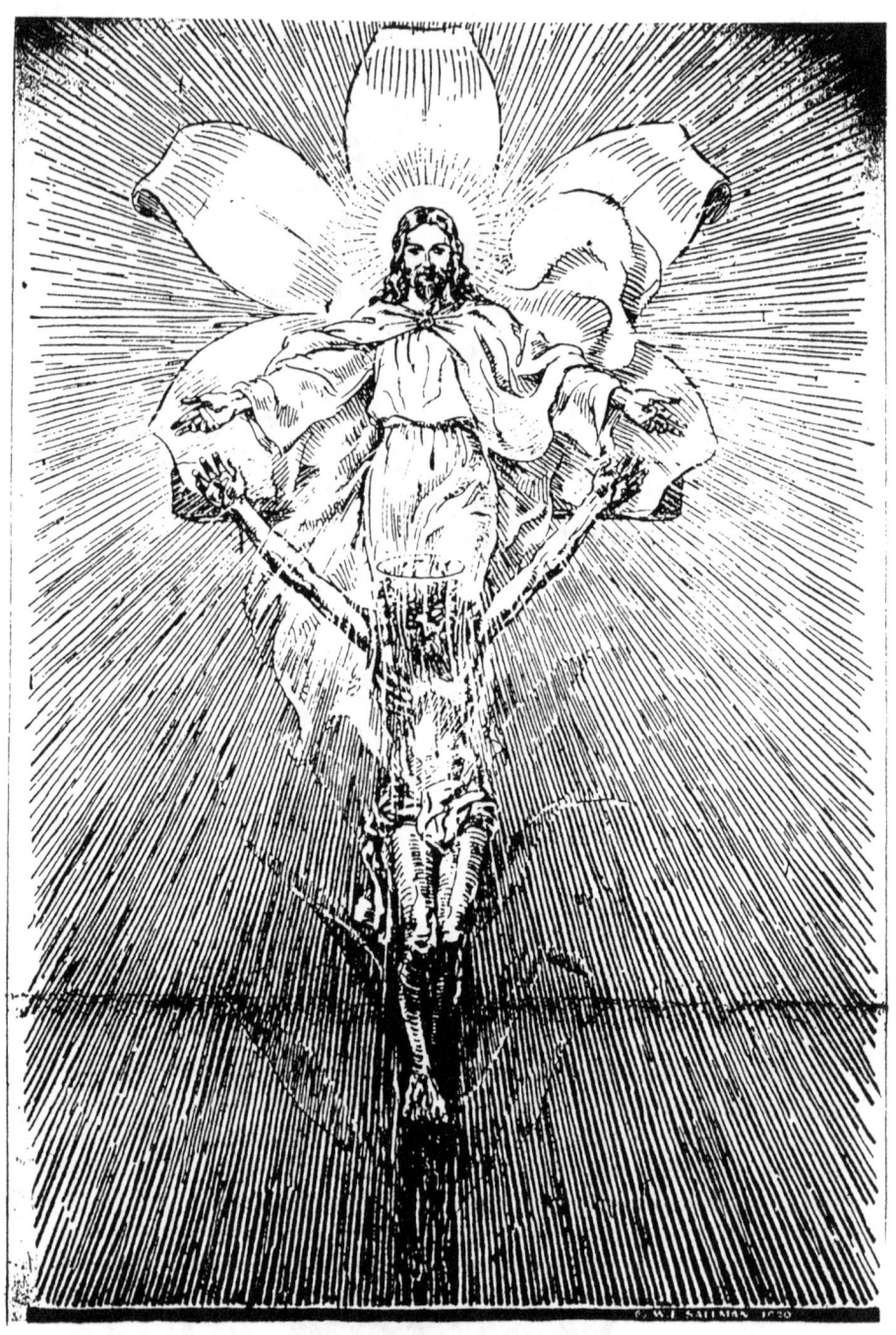

Resurrected Christ Rising from the Crucified Christ (1920) pen. Printed in *Förbundets Veckotidning*.

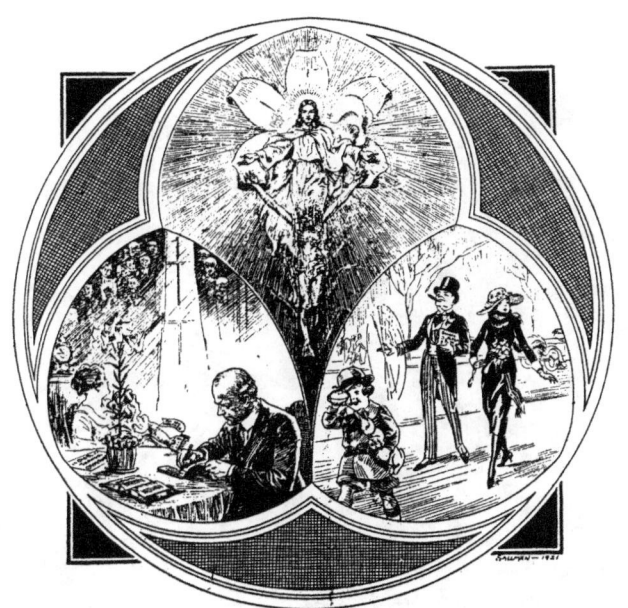

Self-Denial, Self-Indulgence (1921) pen. Printed in *Förbundets Veckotidning.*

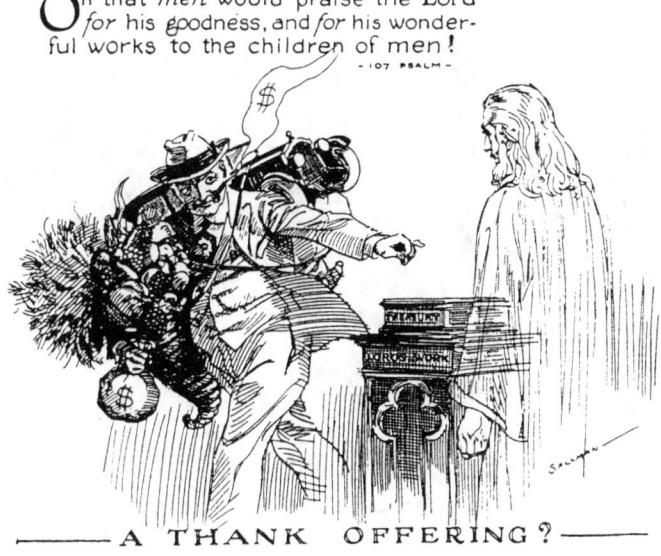

A Thank Offering? [1923] pen. Printed in *Förbundets Veckotidning.*

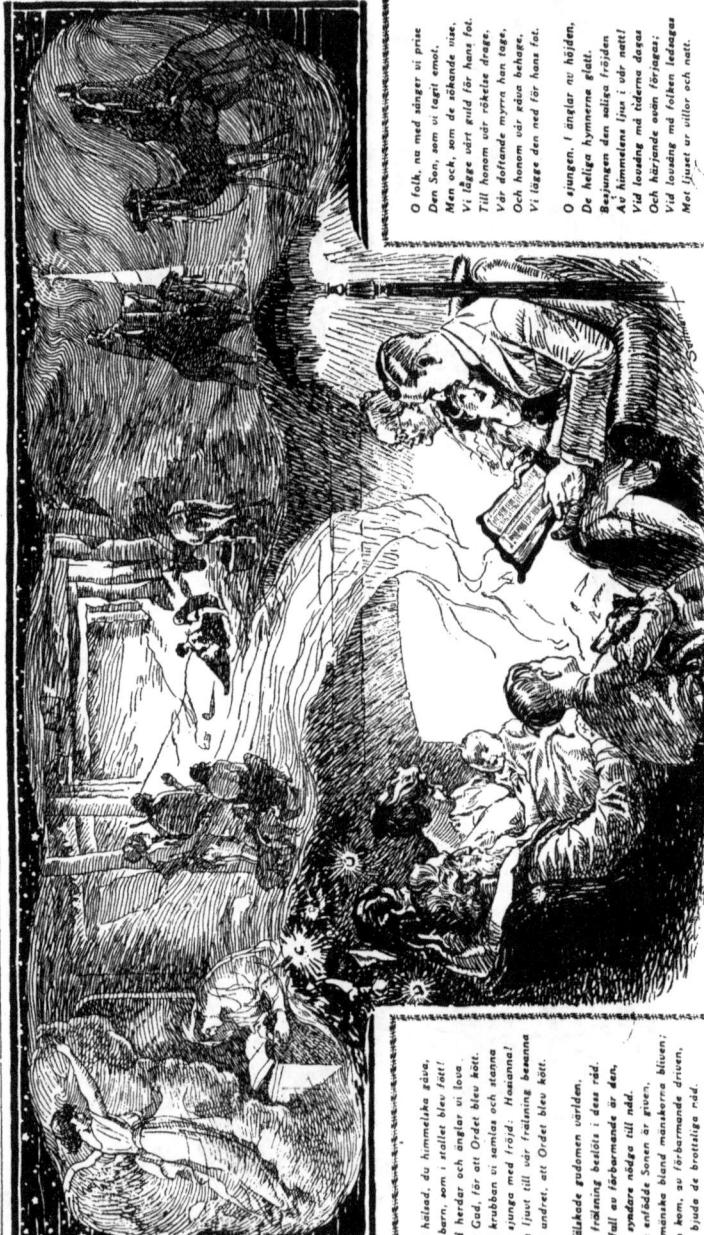

Var hälsad, du himmelska gåva,
Du barn, som i stallet blev fött!
Med herdar och änglar vi lova
Vår Gud, för att Ordet blev kött.
Vid krubban vi samlas och stanna
Att sjunga med fröjd: Hosianna!
Och ljus till vår frälsning besanna
Det undret, att Ordet blev kött.

Så älskade gudomen världen,
Att frälsning beredts i dess råd.
Så full av förbarmande är den,
Att syndare nådiga till nåd.
Den enfödde Sonen är given,
Er människa bland människorna bliven;
Han kom, av förbarmande driven,
Att bjuda de brottsliga nåd.

O folk, nu med sånger vi prise
Den Son, som vi tagit emot.
Men ock, som de sökande vise,
Vi lägge vårt guld för hans fot.
Till honom vår rökelse dråge,
Vår doftande myrra han tage,
Och honom vår ädira behage,
Vi lägge den ned för hans fot.

O sjungen, I änglar av höjden,
De heliga hymnerna glatt.
Besjungen den saliga fröjden
Av himmelens ljus i vår natt!
Vid lovsång må tiderna draga
Och härjande ovän förjagas;
Vid lovsång må folken ledsagas
Mot ljuset ur villor och natt.

Tell Me the Old, Old Story (1919) pen. Printed in *Förbundets Veckotidning.*

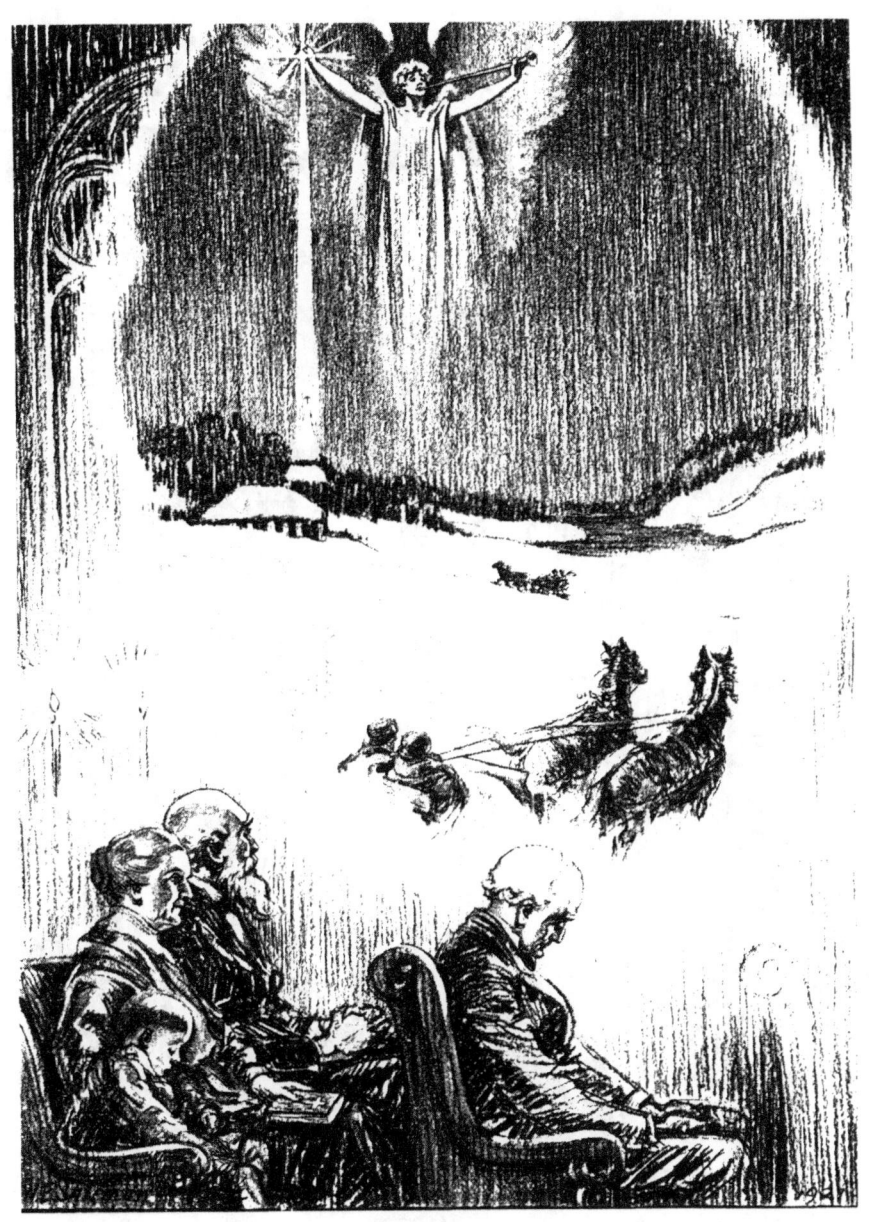

Memories of Julotta (1921) charcoal. Printed in *Förbundets Veckotidning.*

The COVENANT COMPANION

| VOLUME III | NOVEMBER, 1924 | NUMBER 11 |

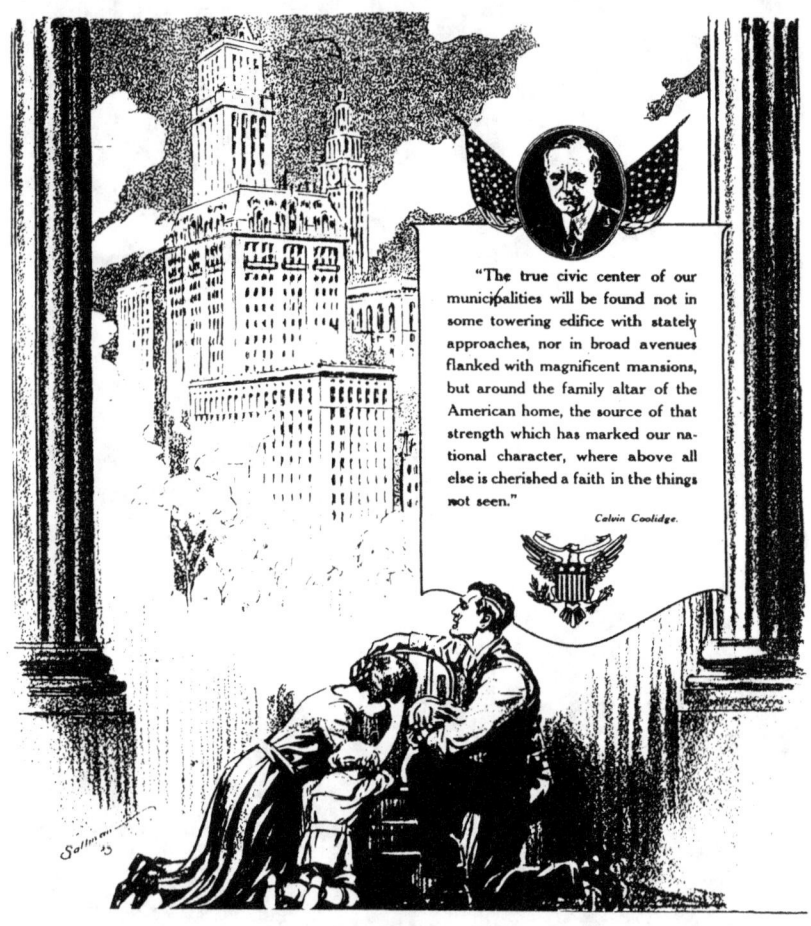

"The true civic center of our municipalities will be found not in some towering edifice with stately approaches, nor in broad avenues flanked with magnificent mansions, but around the family altar of the American home, the source of that strength which has marked our national character, where above all else is cherished a faith in the things not seen."

Calvin Coolidge.

Family Altar of the American Home (1923) medium unknown. Printed in *The Covenant Companion.*

Our Covenant
Little Folks

VOL. XVI   AUGUST 11, 1946   NO. 32

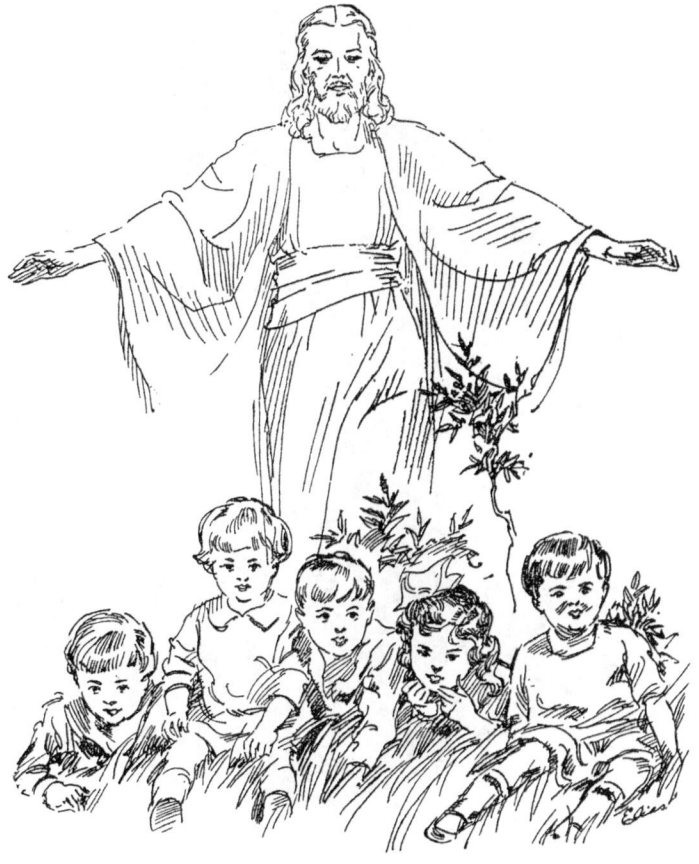

The Children's Friend [1946]

The Children's Friend [1946] pen. Printed in *Our Covenant Little Folks.*

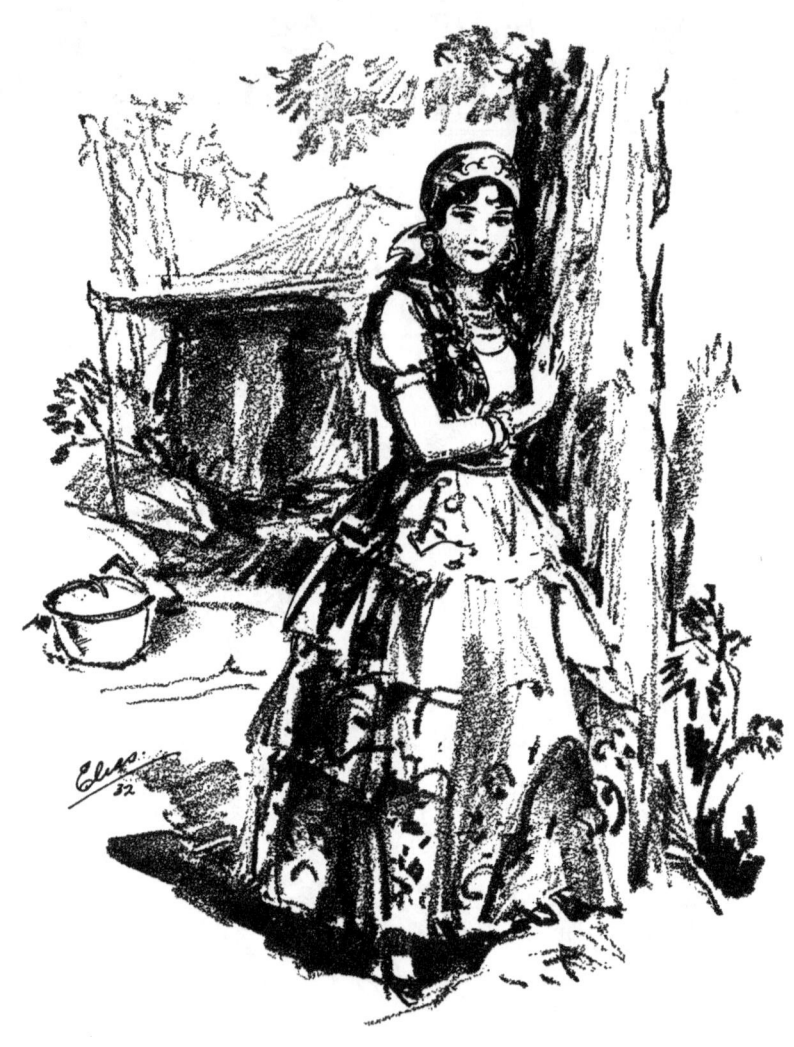

Gypsy Girl (1932) charcoal. Printed in *Our Young Covenanters.*

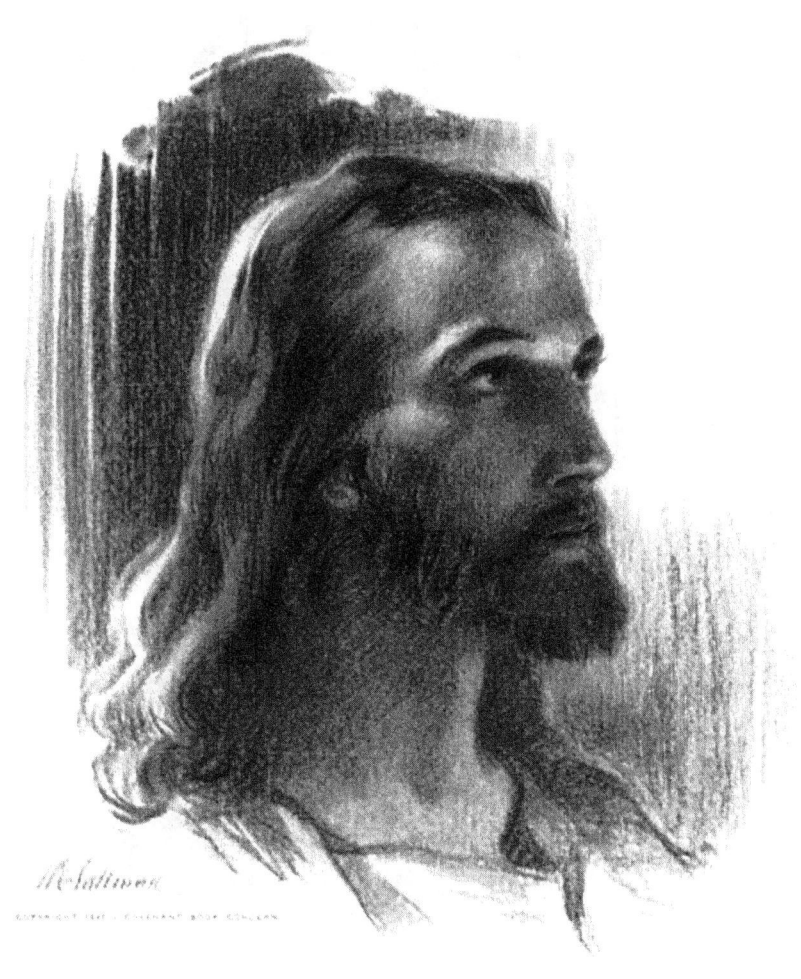

Son of Man (1924) charcoal. Printed in *The Covenant Companion.*

The COVENANT COMPANION

February, 1924

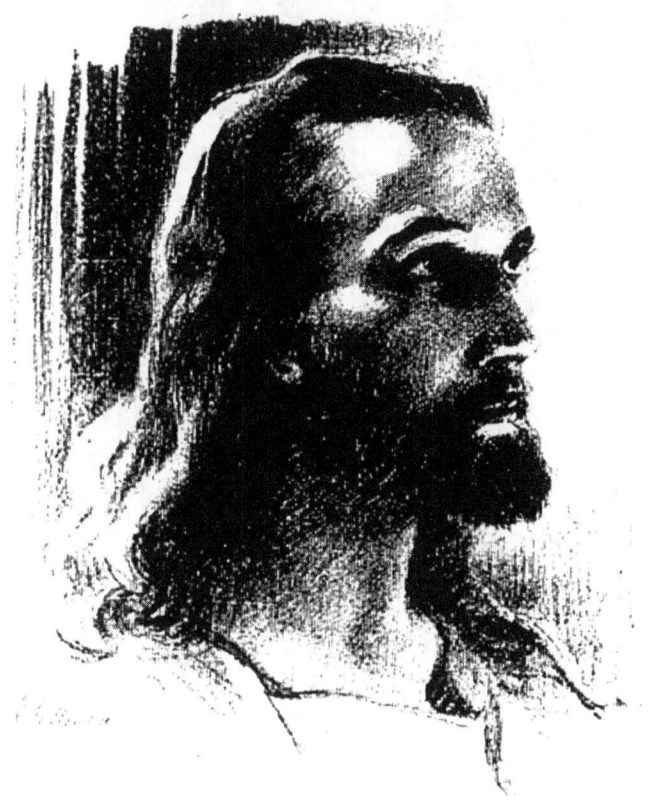

CHRISTIAN LIFE NUMBER

Son of Man as it appeared on the front cover of the 1924 *Covenant Companion*.

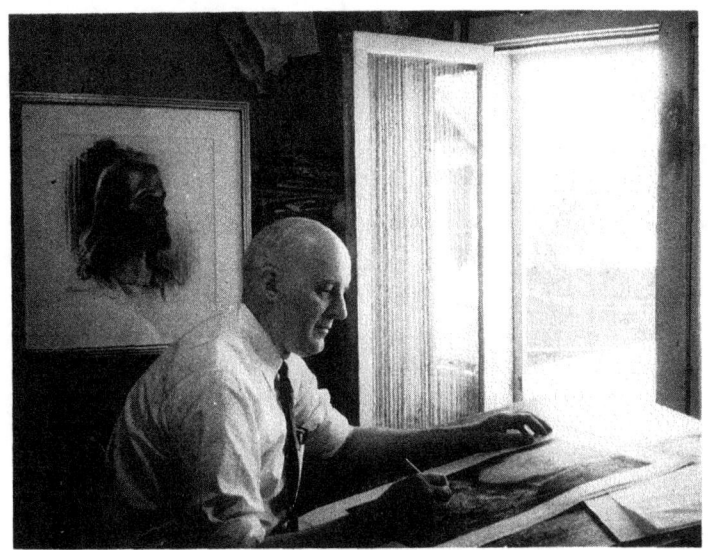

Warner Sallman in his attic studio.

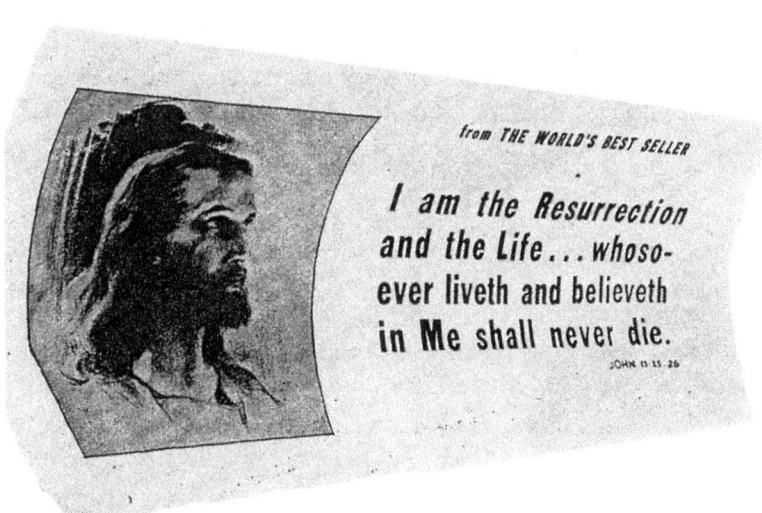

Best Seller advertising on Chicago transportation.

II
"Before You were Born I Consecrated You"

Now the word of the Lord came to me saying, "Before I formed you in the womb I knew you, and before you were born I consecrated you." (Jer 1:4-5)

Experiences and formative influences set the course a life takes. Warner Sallman's life contained a number of both, besides the illness that focused his resolve to embark on a ministry of Christian art. Some were small, some large. Some came before his illness, some after. Perhaps because a number of these experiences took place during his early years, Sallman came to believe that God had been directing his life all along.

Sallman's ancestors were Swedish, on his father's side people now called Finland Swedes. His paternal grandfather, Petter Anselm Sällman, was a Baltic sea pilot who worked out of the harbor town of Mariehamn in the Åland Islands linking Sweden to Finland. Åland, which earlier belonged to Sweden, was called by Napoleon when harboring designs on Finland, "the keys to the trunk." Since the Napoleonic Wars, Finland has owned Åland, but the islands are inhabited almost entirely by Swedes, who populate also the southwestern corner of the Finnish mainland. The Sällman family has lived for three centuries or more on the island of Föglö.

The present Sällman homestead dates from 1867, located in the small village of Bråttö on the southern tip of Föglö. It is still in the family, owned by grandchildren—two sisters and a brother—of Warner's uncle, Anders Gustav Sällman. The house is well-preserved, sitting at the end of a winding road some distance in from the island's main road.

Inside the house ceilings are a low seven feet above floor level. The kitchen is large, as is one of two downstairs bedrooms. A Swedish tile stove stands in the corner of the large bedroom. Upstairs are two bedrooms, and an attic to one side. The house is comfortable, even though without electricity or running water. A well is just outside the front door. Around the main house are other buildings from what was once a small working farm. The homestead is surrounded on three sides by water. On a clear day one can look out to other islands not far distant. The Sällmans now come out to Åland only during the summer, living the rest of the year in Sweden.

Warner's father, Elias Sällman, was born on the homestead, the youngest of six children. Elias had three brothers, Carl Petter, Anders Gustav, and Johannes

Anselm, and two sisters, Ida Maria and Anna Sophia. Johannes (later John), Ida and Elias emigrated to America, leaving Anders to take over the farm. Anders was also a pilot like his father, guiding ships through the islands. The firstborn, Carl Petter, died at five years. Anna Sophia, who was handicapped and confined to a wheelchair, died at fourteen years.

Elias as a young boy often accompanied his father on sea voyages. These gave him a deep affection for the sea, which stayed with him the rest of his life. But Elias had no affection for the life of a seaman, so before he was twenty the decision was made to emigrate to America. Brother Johannes had emigrated six years earlier, and his sister Ida four years earlier. Elias left Åland on 6 May 1886 for Chicago.

Elias Sallman settled in the Swedish immigrant community on Chicago's near north side. Two years after arrival, he was living on Oak Street near Sedgwick[1] and employed downtown as a clerk. Brother John lived with him and worked at the same location, which was 200 Adams Street. Elias later took up work as a carpenter and cabinet maker, being employed at the First National Bank in downtown Chicago, where he worked for many years.

Warner's mother, Christina Larson, came from Värmland, the province in Sweden known for clear lakes ringed with birch trees, and for its artists and poets. She emigrated from the town of Kristinehamn in late 1886 or early 1887, just after her eighteenth birthday. Christine–her name after arriving in America–came to Chicago where an older sister who emigrated ahead of her was living. This sister owned a laundry on the corner of Sedgwick and Hobbie, and Christine began working there soon after she arrived.

Elias was one of the young men who patronized the sister's laundry, and a friendship soon developed between him and Christine. This eventually led to their marriage in June 1891. The new couple made their home further north in Lake View, in a two-storey frame house on Oakdale Avenue, near Racine.[2] In this house, on 30 April 1892, Warner Elias Sallman was born.

At the turn of the century the Lake View community, which centers around Clark and Belmont, was on Chicago's growing edge, and had been so for nearly two decades. Already in the 1880s Swedes were beginning to relocate there from the near north side. A decade later schools were built, and both the Swedish Lutherans and the Swedish Mission Covenant people possessed large new churches. Warner's Uncle John moved to Lake View in 1889.

When Warner was two years old, the family moved to West Noble (later Barry) Avenue, near Racine. Then sometime within the next two years, they moved again, this time into a stylish hewn-stone three-flat a short distance away on Clifton Avenue,[3] where they lived until 1902. Two- and three-storey brick buildings with gray-white facial stone, nicely hewn, distinguish the Lake View and Edgewater neighborhoods, also other Chicago neighborhoods on both north and south sides that were built up about the turn of the century.

Warner attended the Robert Morris School through the fourth grade. A brand new school when he attended, it is now gone. School lay just a few blocks east of where the Sallmans lived.

Sallman had four siblings: LeRoy and Violet who grew to adulthood, Paul who died at 16 months, and Dewey who died at two and a half years. LeRoy, or Roy, became an artist at Vogue-Wright Studios in Chicago. Violet married Haddon Sundblom, the artist who created the famous Santa Claus for Coca-Cola.[4] The Sundblom family was also from Åland.

Dewey's death made a deep impression on Warner, who was eight years old at the time. One noon he came home from school and found Dewey seriously ill in his mother's arms. He had the croup. The doctor had been called, but had not yet come. Warner was asked to run to the nearby drugstore for medicine. He did so, and recalled the wait there as being an eternity. Once the medicine was in hand, he ran the entire way home, only to find out upon arrival that his brother had died. He said later, "I went into the living room, crawled under the davenport and cried. Not until evening could I be persuaded to come out."[5]

Warner had just learned a song at school, with lyrics from a poem by Eugene Field:

Wynken, Blynken and Nod one night
Sailed off in a wooden shoe
Sailed on a river of crystal delight
Into a sea of dew.

"Wynken, Blynken and Nod" now became associated with his brother's death, and it remained so ever after. In fact, a connection was made in Warner's mind between this song and anything tragic. After Dewey's death, Warner dreamed of being a doctor so he could make people well.

A short time earlier another tragedy had occurred, this time for a family named Ekdahl who lived in the same building as the Sallmans. Gustav Ekdahl worked as a window washer at Marshall Fields downtown. One morning on his way to work he developed a severe headache. He went to his coat pocket for headache pills, but discovered they had been left at home. Although quite a few blocks from home, he nevertheless decided to return. This event also made a deep impression on young Warner, who remembered Mrs. Ekdahl's superstitious remark upon the sight of her husband. "Now," she said, "what is going to happen? He came home!"[6] Late that afternoon, she received word that her husband had fallen out of a window and been crushed to death.

Tragedies have a heightened effect when striking close to home. In the case of Mr. Ekdahl, the Sallmans lost a good neighbor and friend. It was in the Ekdahl home where Warner discovered Gustave Doré's, *The Bible, Illustrated,* which made such an impression on his young mind. The library in the Sallman home consisted simply of a Bible, a hymnbook, and a few other old books from Sweden. But the Ekdahls had a fine library, and thanks to their generosity, young Warner was given access to it. Warner, no more than four years old at the time, remembered lying stretched out on the floor, looking with fascination by the hour at Doré's pictures. He said,

> I believe this has been the strongest and greatest individual influence in my life, not only when it came to drawing and painting, but also in that it brought about an early conviction regarding the reality of God.[7]

Sallman said his teachers at school were surprised to hear him speak highly of Doré's art. They were opposed, it seems, to showing tragic scenes to children. But Warner held to his favorable opinion of Doré when talking to the teachers.

Outranking all other influences in Sallman's early life was the nurture he received in the Christian faith. Warner's parents both possessed a deep, personal religious faith. His father, after arriving in America, came under the influence of the gifted Covenant preacher, the Reverend Carl A. Björk, as well as the more widely-known evangelist, Dwight L. Moody. Moody's large tabernacle was but a short distance from the Swedish community on Oak Street. Warner's mother found her spiritual home among the Mission Friends (later the Mission Covenant Church). When Elias and Christine moved to Lake View, they became part of the Lake View Mission Covenant Church. In 1892, the year Warner was born, that congregation built a new church on the corner of School Street and Kenmore Avenue[8] that had a seating capacity of 600.

From his earliest years Warner attended the Lake View Mission Covenant Sunday School. One of his teachers, Hanna Martenson, he remembered with particular fondness. Another teacher for whom Warner had special affection was August Clauson. When he was twelve, Warner did an oil painting that he presented to Clauson as a gift. The painting depicted a scene from the American West—a horse and a man drinking out of the same pool of water. The painting is extant.[9]

On Sunday afternoons friends took Warner to another neighboring Sunday school, which Warner remembered as being held a Methodist church on Wellington Avenue. Classes here were conducted in English, the language Warner now used in school. Sunday School at Lake View Mission Covenant was still held in Swedish.[10] The Methodist church was likely Centennial Methodist, located at Wellington and Sheffield, an easy walk from the Sallman home, and the only known Methodist church in the area. Centennial Methodist was a German-speaking congregation. The Lake View Mission Covenant records report that in 1884 the church was renting facilities from a nearby German congregation so it could hold Sunday afternoon meetings and organize a Sunday School. Possibly, Lake View Mission Covenant was conducting afternoon

Sunday School classes in Centennial Methodist Church, which would be the classes Warner remembered attending. Centennial Methodist was one of the earliest churches in Lake View. The frame building still stands, although it has not been a Methodist church for many years.[11]

In both of these church buildings Warner discovered artwork that impressed itself upon his young mind. At Lake View Mission Covenant a large sanctuary painting caught his attention, a reproduction of *Christ Before Pilate* by the Hungarian master Mihaly von Munkacsy (1844-1900).[12] At Centennial Methodist, Warner noticed the beautiful stained glass windows. He recalled sitting one day in a distant pew, "The church was dark, but light streamed through the bits of glass that brought the agony and loneliness of Gethsemane to my childish mind."[13] Here also beautiful floral picture cards were distributed, which Warner was delighted to take home. "I'd like to be able to paint like that," he remembered saying to himself.

In 1902 the Sallmans moved further north into an elegant stone-front three-flat on Maple Square Avenue, now just west of Wrigley Field.[14] Their apartment was on the third floor. The family lived here for seven or eight years, after which they moved into a frame house on Ashland Avenue, the final family residence.

The Sallman home was a happy home. Both parents loved music, and the children did as well. For a time Roy took lessons on the violin. Many an evening was spent having family musicals. While both parents could play the guitar, his father also played a Kimball reed organ. Warner recalled many musical evenings with his father at the organ and his mother playing the guitar.

Both parents also gave Warner early encouragement to draw and paint. Beginning when Warner was about four, his mother helped him sketch simple figures, the sort he later did in illustration work. His father's skills were in painting–both in watercolor and oil–and from an early age Warner was busy trying to emulate him. A beautiful oil Elias did of the landscape around his Åland home survives.[15] In 1905 Elias began evening classes at the Chicago Art Institute, where his skills were developed further.

Elias liked to go out into the country to paint landscapes, and now and then for companionship he would take Warner along. Frequent trips were also made early on Sunday mornings to Lake Michigan, where, after nostalgic thoughts about home were overcome, Elias would do a watercolor. Elias is said to have been so homesick for the sea and its ships that sometimes he would just sit by the lake, think about his childhood days, and cry. Warner was delighted when his father returned home with the watercolors, and more pleased yet when he said that the next time he went down to the lake Warner–and perhaps a friend or two–could go along.

At home Elias had a small studio for drawing and painting where Warner, along with his brother, sister, and friends from the neighborhood, received their first art lessons. Warner remembered spending much time in his father's studio. When he was about ten he attempted his first oil, which was of a bob-o-link clinging to the side of a reed. This work was followed by a home scene that he displayed atop the sewing machine in the kitchen hoping it would elicit some comment from his mother or father. This picture Warner took to school to show his teacher, who was impressed enough that she took it around to show the other teachers. It was then put up for display.

This early acceptance of Sallman's artwork took place at the James G. Blaine School at Grace and Southport, where Warner graduated from the eighth grade. While at the Blaine school Warner recalled making classroom charts, mottoes and posters—in pen and ink and in color. Friends said that some day he would surely become an artist. At Blaine Warner impressed his teachers with more than just his artwork. A 1903 letter from one teacher to his mother survives, which comments favorably on Warner's demeanor at age eleven:

> In my many years of experience in the schools I have but few boys that have given me the pleasure and the comfort that Warner has. Although he is not among the very quickest, he is always so careful, attentive, and above all, so thoughtful and considerate, that he will make friends wherever he goes. A mother may well be proud of such a boy, and I hope he may be the comfort to you that he was to me during this year.[16]

Warner was confirmed at Lake View Mission Covenant in a class of nearly sixty. He was, by his own admission, a lively boy. The confirmation class met on Saturday, and one session in particular Warner remembered vividly. The pastor, August Pohl, was late in coming, and with class assembled and waiting Warner seized the opportunity to stage a performance. He recalled,

> I got up behind the small pulpit where the preacher usually stood and began to carry on a class session as the pastor did—except that it was filled with humor. I had gotten the class into peals of laughter.[17]

The pastor slipped in quietly. How long he had been there Warner did not know, but upon seeing him Warner hurried to his seat. Much to his surprise, Pohl summoned him not to scold, but rather to give a word of affirmation. Placing his hand on Warner's head, he said, "I watched what you were doing, and somehow I can't help but hope it is prophetic. I would like to see you become a preacher some day."[18] The pastor's words made an impact. Now instead of wishing to be a doctor, Warner's thoughts turned toward the ministry. He would be a preacher.

After confirmation Warner with a number of his friends began attending the Waveland Avenue Congregational Church at Waveland and Janssen, just a block south of the Blaine School.[19] The family residence on Maple Square was now further distant from Lake View Covenant. The Waveland Avenue Church gave Warner exposure to a church more indigenous to American culture, and this broadened him in important ways. He joined a Bible class, a baseball team, and the Keystone Club, which was a literary group. In front of this Keystone Club, Warner gave his first chalk talk. He also lettered signs for Prohibition parades, and did a portrait of Abraham Lincoln, which he presented to the parish. In addition, he became a member of Christian Endeavor, and joined the choir.

In 1908, when Warner was sixteen, he had a pivotal religious experience at the Waveland Avenue Church.[20] At a meeting conducted by a visiting evangelist, said to be a Pastor Munro, an invitation was given, at which point young Warner knelt in his pew and quietly told God he believed Jesus Christ to be his Savior. A public testimony was later made. What did it all mean? Warner summed it up in these words:

> My burden of sin and guilt was removed, and I shall never forget the thrilling joy of that moment of experiencing God's redeeming grace. Since that time my life has been based on that experience, and has been directed toward serving God in every way.[21]

This testimony echoes that of countless others touched by pietistic and revivalistic movements of the nineteenth and early twentieth centuries. There was a personal awakening to Christian faith, a release from sin and guilt, and a fresh experience of God's grace, leaving one filled with unspeakable joy. Warner's testimony possessed all these elements and the remainder of his life showed an unmistakable indebtedness to this experience.

Sallman's artwork was also indebted to this life-changing experience. One cannot fully appreciate the Sallman depictions of Christ—which, to a large extent, show Christ resurrected, victorious and powerful—without knowing something of pietistic and revivalistic Christianity. The victorious life is rooted in a victorious Christ. Depicting a victorious Christ represented a new turn in religious art, born on American soil and produced by an indigenous American artist.

[1] The address was 119 Oak before 1909, and after that year 408 Oak. The Chicago City Council passed an ordinance on 22 June 1908, amended and put into effect in 1909, which changed city street numbers in the interest of greater

standardization. The location in question was Oak near Sedgwick (Sedgwick is 400 West).

2 Specifically 1130 Oakdale Avenue, after the renumbering of 1909 mentioned in the previous note.

3 The address was 741 North Clifton, just south of Belmont Avenue. The street number after 1909 (see note 1) was 3118 North Clifton. This building, and the ones on Oakdale and Barry, were still standing in 1990.

4 Sundblom redesigned Santa in red and white for Coca-Cola's 1931 winter advertising campaign.

5 Sylvia Peterson's unpublished notes.

6 Sylvia Peterson's unpublished notes.

7 Sylvia E. Peterson, "The Ministry of Christian Art," *Lutheran Companion* 55/14 (2 April 1974): 10.

8 Kenmore Avenue was originally Baxter, and for a time also went by the name of Osgood.

9 It is in the possession of Clauson's daughter, who lives in North Park.

10 Maintaining the Swedish language was important to the people of Lake View Covenant. In the history of their church it is recorded that classes in the Swedish language were held in the basement of the church beginning in 1893, coinciding with the arrival of Reverend Constantin Olson as pastor, to make sure that the children of the immigrants learned the mother tongue. These classes continued until 1908.

11 For many years this building has been home to a Japanese Christian Church. Before them a Jewish congregation worshipped there, who replaced some of the stained glass windows in the sanctuary with a Star of David.

12 A picture of this painting at the front of the Lake View sanctuary appears in *Missions-Förbundets Ungdomstidning* 1/14 (18 June 1912): 9; also in a booklet entitled *Kort Historik öfver Svenska Evangeliska Lutherska Missionsförsamlingen i Lake View, Chicago 1886-1911*: 30 (available in Covenant Archives, North Park University). A reproduction, with an accompanying article on Munkacsy, appears in the *Ladies Home Journal* 27/16 (1 December 1910): 11; as well as in *Our Covenant Youth* 24/14 (4 April 1943): 1; *Our Young Covenanters* 14/14 (2 April 1944): 1; and Cynthia Pearl Maus, *Christ and the Fine Arts*, revised and enlarged ed. (New York: Harper & Bros., 1959): 359. The original is in the John Wanamaker Collection, Philadelphia, Pennsylvania.

13 T. Otto Nall, "He Preaches as He Paints," Our Covenant Youth 24/49 (5 December 1943): 3.

14 1098 Maple Square Avenue; after renumbering 3631 Maple Square. Today the address is 3631 N. Magnolia.

15 It resides in the Everett Sallman private collection.

16 Letter from Ida Schifflin to Ruth Sallman, 25 June 1903.

17 Reported to Sylvia Peterson, Sylvia Peterson's unpublished notes.

18 Ibid.

19 The church building dates from 1899 and was still standing in 1990, although it was substantially rebuilt after a fire in 1952. In 1984 it was occupied by a Romanian Pentecostal (Philadelphia) congregation.

20 Sallman remembered this experience occurring just prior to a Chapman-Alexander Evangelistic Campaign, said to have been held in Chicago in 1908 (Warner Sallman, "Put Your Hands to Work, Your Heart to God," *The Covenant Companion* 49/3 [15 January 1960]: 3). But according to the book, *Charles M. Alexander: A Romance of Song and Soul-Winning*, published by Alexander's wife and J. Kennedy Maclean (London: Marshall Brothers, 1920) 172-173, the Chapman-Alexander Campaign came to Chicago in October-November of 1910.

21 Warner Sallman, "My Greatest Spiritual Experience," *Chicago Daily News*, 10 March 1953, 30. See also Sallman, "Put Your Hands to Work, Your Heart to God," *The Covenant Companion* 49/3 (15 January 1960) 3.

III

The Lost Trunk

Depressed because his trunk had been lost, and in a quandary because of the letter received from his father, Sallman decided to return home.

(New York, September 1912)

Graduation from eighth grade marked the end of Sallman's formal schooling. Warner considered going to Lake View High School, and even went there to register, but because of doubts about making the grade, and a desire to work, he chose not to enroll.

Sallman's father may or may not have known about his son's thoughts of becoming first a doctor, then a preacher. His desire, in any case, was that Warner take up music. Fatherly advice therefore seems to have prevailed as Sallman went about looking for his first job. That summer, an opening was advertised at the J. C. Deagan Musical Bell Factory on Clark Street, not far from the Sallman home. The company made bells and other musical instruments, also musical novelties. Sallman answered the ad, and was hired. They placed him in the department where caps for chimes were made. After a while he was moved to other departments, ending up finally in the finishing department, where his job was staining xylophone cases. The stain had to be applied by hand, and before long Sallman's hands were so colored that the stain would not come off. He requested a change, but Deagan said if Warner wanted to progress he would have to remain for the time being with staining. Not wanting to do that, Sallman was let go. Progress would have to come some other way.

Sallman then apprenticed at an art studio, where, for seven months he labored without pay. This work, however, he enjoyed, enough so that it made him begin to think seriously about doing art for a living. Friends had been encouraging him in this direction for some time.

For Warner, 1907 and 1908 were pivotal years. During this time Sallman made key decisions about where his priorities lay, and what steps needed to be taken in preparation for his life's work. We have already spoken about his experience in 1908 at the evangelistic meeting. The previous November he enrolled in the evening school of the Chicago Art Institute, where his father was taking classes.

During the next five or six years Sallman's life had a certain tentativeness about it, which is to say there was more seeking than finding. Sallman attended school on and off. He also changed jobs a number of times. Nevertheless,

Sallman received valuable training both at school and in the professional studios where he worked. Personal contacts made during this time also proved their value later on. By 1913 Sallman's work at the Art Institute would gain public recognition, and he would be well established in a job.

Critics have sometimes imagined that Sallman was without formal training, that he lacked experience drawing from nude and costumed models, and that approval was never given him by some recognized master. However, he actually experiences all of these, but by the time his religious art work commenced, all were well into the past.

Sallman began in the Art Institute's evening school, attending classes three evenings a week. His first enrollment was in an "antique" class that began November, 1907.[1] In antique classes drawings were made from plaster casts. The Art Institute had a fine collection of casts made from classical sculptures in the museums of Europe. These pieces were brought to Chicago for the Columbian Exposition in 1893. Afterwards, they were presented to the Art Institute, which was just opening its new building on Michigan Boulevard.

In the fall of 1908 and later in 1910, Sallman signed up for a "life" class in the school of drawing and painting. Life classes used live models, both nude and costumed. Today these classes are called "figure drawing and painting." Some of Sallman's pencil sketches of nudes done in a life class have survived (*Nudes* [1913]).

During the day Sallman worked downtown. At first just getting a job proved to be difficult. Sallman recalled how one day in 1909, when he was seventeen, he went about the Loop armed with names of artists gleaned from the telephone book and samples of his work. However, as he approached the entrances to the various studios he was too hesitant to go in. One day, however, Sallman was able to muster enough courage to walk into the studio of Crane and Borresen. Borresen turned out to be a very cordial man, and after looking at Sallman's samples he said he would gladly teach him, but at present could not afford to pay him salary. Sallman agreed nevertheless to his proposal. After three months he was given $1.00 a week, enough to pay his carfare. After three months, Sallman took on added duties, but with no increase in pay. So shortly thereafter, he decided to leave Crane and Borreson.

Sallman then took a job as office-boy with the Newman-Monroe Company, a design and illustration firm in the First National Bank Building. His salary here began at $1.00 a week, and was raised to $3.00 a week after three months. Though this job lasted only six months, the time here proved valuable because Sallman was able to meet a number of professional illustrators through Mrs. Newman who was herself an artist.

In 1910 Sallman took a job with Meyer-Both Studios, at the time the largest illustrator of fashion in the United States, employing no less than eighty-five illustrators.[2] Sallman began as a model for Semour Frank, a prominent fashion illustrator, at a salary of $5.00 a week. He learned a great deal from Frank, and after serving an apprenticeship was given the opportunity to illustrate on his own, primarily focusing on men's fashions. His tenure at Meyer-Both lasted eight years.

Also in 1910, Sallman began attending the Edgewater Mission Covenant Church where his friend, Fred Pamp, was student pastor. He recalled that the first person to greet him there was Enoch Anderson, his future father-in-law. This congregation had organized a year earlier, in 1909, as a result of outgrowth from the First Mission Covenant Church and Lake View Mission Covenant. The Sallmans had now moved north, and were living on Ashland Avenue. Sallman immediately became active in the Edgewater Church, becoming a member in 1911. He helped organize a young men's group and joined the choir, where he met Ruth Anderson, his future wife.

In 1912 restlessness once again descended upon the young artist and he decided to go to New York City, where he would stay for one year. So in early September Sallman quit his job at Meyer-Both and made preparations to leave for New York, packing his art supplies, some samples and a typewriter in a large trunk. The trunk was heavy, so heavy in fact that when they came to pick it up one of the men was overheard exclaiming, "What in the world has he got in there—lead?"

On the train ride to New York Sallman developed a severe headache. By the time he arrived at the Twenty-third Street Young Men's Christian Association (YMCA), where arrangements had been made to stay, his condition had worsened.

Upon arrival, a concerned YMCA desk clerk remarked, "Don't you feel well?" Sallman said he certainly did not. The clerk suggested Sallman get some black coffee, but finding out that the grill was closed, he kindly fixed him a cup. Sallman's condition, however, did not yield to so easy a remedy. Sallman remained ill in his room for the next three days, during which time the clerk checked in on him periodically and brought him food from the grill.

To make matters worse, Sallman's trunk had not arrived. After he felt better he walked to the station to make an inquiry. Those at the station knew nothing of the trunk's whereabouts. He returned on subsequent days, but the reply was the same. In the interval Sallman visited museums and became generally acquainted with the city. He also called on some art studios, but there was nothing to show prospective employers because his samples were in the trunk. A number of individuals expressed interest in hiring him, but little more—except at Talman Studios.

At Talman they were convinced of his ability, and knowing of his prior employment in Chicago they offered him a job, although like the other studios they wanted to see some of his work. The position offered was in England where Sallman would be a company representative. The one condition was that he agree to stay two years. Sallman grew excited. This offer appeared to be just the experience he was looking for, and he hastened to write letters home. He wrote his parents, also to Ruth, with whom he had been corresponding the whole time he was gone, telling them about the fine offer he had received.

Soon after Warner received the only letter his father ever sent him. Elias did not want him to go to London, and the point was conveyed in the clearest of terms. About the same time Sallman received another letter—this one special delivery from Meyer at Meyer-Both. Some work had just come in that he very much wanted Sallman to do, and would he consider coming back? If so, Meyer promised him a $50.00 bonus and a raise in salary from $65.00 to $75.00 a week.

Depressed because his trunk was lost, and in a quandary because of the letter received from his father, Sallman decided to return home. He wrote Meyer saying he would accept his offer. But before leaving New York City he decided to make one last trip to the station to inquire about his trunk. This time Sallman was urgent, telling the railway agent that something had to be done because he was leaving the city. Permission was granted for him to accompany one of the men into the shed where trunks were stored. They walked past rows and rows of trunks. Finally, in one corner, at the bottom of a pile, Sallman spied his trunk. When they opened it, they discovered that some of the drawings and the typewriter had been damaged because of the enormous weight pressing on it. Nevertheless, what had been lost was found, and Sallman sent the trunk back to Chicago. Asked later whether he thought the find was "coincidental," he replied, "No, providential!"[3]

The return to Chicago definitely seemed providential, for elements of Sallman's life began to fall into place. Sallman was warmly welcomed by his former employer, and classes at the Art Institute were resumed on 30 September. He had been gone about three weeks.

At the Art Institute Sallman took evening classes throughout the fall, and during most of next year. A life class with Antonin Sterba went from 30 September 1912 to 25 July 1913, and an illustration class with Walter Clute went from 4 August until 5 September 1913. In January 1913 Sallman increased his class load, and had his status upgraded to life student in the day school. From January to April of that year he was enrolled in a life class taught by Professor Sterba in the Day School. The following September he began sixteen lessons in painting from Wellington Reynolds, another day school faculty.

Among the distinguished faculty at the Art Institute from whom Sallman received instruction was one who took particular notice of his work, Walter Marshall Clute, who taught in the evening school. Clute himself had attended the Art Students' League of New York, after which he became a pupil of Benjamin Constant and Jean-Paul Laurens in Paris. Both were affiliated with the Académie Julian, one of the well-known art studios of the late nineteenth century.[4] Laurens was a noted painter, specializing in historical murals. Professors Sterba and Reynolds of the Art Institute faculty had also studied under Constant and Laurens.

Sallman had the singular good fortune of finding favor with an artist of national reputation such as Clute. Clute even nominated Sallman as one of a select number of students at the 1913 graduation ceremony to receive a citation for work in illustration.[5] Sallman was proud of this honor, although he did not attend the 20 June graduation to receive it. Incredulous as it may seem, he said his boss would not let him off work. Another honor Sallman received about the same time was having an oil of his selected for inclusion in the Art Institute's *Circular for Instruction* in 1913-1914 (*Mother Knitting* [1913]).[6] A home scene of a woman—his mother, in all likelihood—sitting in a chair knitting, this painting was seen by one of his friends to be a portent of better things to come. A letter to Sallman dated 30 June 1913 reads,

> With page 42 of the Art Institute catalogue before me I feel as though I had to let you know the hopes which your pleasing picture has raised. Criticisms from "lay-parties" are not, as a rule, very welcome to artists, but one has to be verily blind if he fails to notice the atmosphere of the picture, the light that falls from the lamp on the white tablecloth striking the birdcage in passing, the baby's outstretched arms, the many thoughts both serious and pleasant that mingle and play on the grandmother's features, as she knits, and she is a careful knitter, who realizes the value of time; other duties won't let her remain in that chair very long...
>
> We all here congratulate you and now, here is a wish for the $425. scholarship next year. May it be yours...[7]

The scholarship money probably did not come. Sallman took an illustration class from 4 August to 5 September, but no classes were taken during the following year.[8]

While Sallman was working at Meyer-Both and attending the Art Institute, a friendship developed with an older artist named U. S. Abell. One day as the two were working on fashion designs, others in the studio were trying to persuade Sallman to join a party the sort of which he had no interest in joining. Abell spoke up in support of Sallman's demur, and a friendship ensued.

Artists in most every age have developed reputations for being loose and unprincipled. Sallman therefore had to defend himself from time to time for keeping their company. To one person who doubted whether anybody in the profession could possibly have character, Sallman replied, "The notion that all artists are rogues and libertines is false. We had an organization of Christian artists in Chicago and the membership numbered almost a hundred."[9]

Sallman particularly enjoyed the walks he and Abell took down Michigan Boulevard on their way to the Art Institute. Their conversation frequently turned to the Scripture. Sallman expressed the desire to one day become a painter of religious pictures. Abell, who did religious cartooning, suggested that Sallman take a Bible class at Moody Bible Institute. So Sallman joined a Bible study class that met Saturday evenings.

One Saturday, Dean E. O. Sellers of Moody called Sallman into his office. He had heard that Sallman was an artist, and said he wanted to share with him the hope that some day an artist would portray Christ as forceful and masculine, rather than weak and effeminate, as was most often the case. This meeting probably took place in January, 1914,[10] shortly after Sallman enrolled in the Bible class. Sellers went on to say that according to his reading of the Bible, Jesus was very masculine:

> He walked the great distance from Jerusalem to Capernaum—a distance as great as from Milwaukee to Chicago. He slept out under the stars. He was sun-tanned and strong. He drove money-changers out of the temple.[11]

These words stayed with Sallman, and after his Christ head in oil was painted, many remarked that the look on the face was indeed forceful, masculine, sun-tanned and strong.

On 31 May 1916, Warner Sallman married Ruth Edith Anderson. The Reverend C. J. Andrews performed the ceremony in the Edgewater Covenant Church. Ruth, as we mentioned, had caught Warner's attention in the Edgewater church choir. She also played the organ. Among these and other fine qualities, Warner found in her a stability that he said exceeded his own. He called her "his brake." She was his inspiration and most trusted critic—in short, a perfect all-around companion.

After marriage Warner and Ruth lived with her parents on Ashland Avenue. Then in 1922 they built a brick bungalow in North Park,[12] a community west of Edgewater currently being developed by a land association aimed at selling lots to people wanting to be located near the Covenant school, North Park College. Here Warner and Ruth lived the remainder of their married life, and here they raised their three sons, Everett, Richard, and James.

During the years 1917-1924 Sallman was busy establishing a family and working as an artist downtown—mostly in commercial studios, but some of the time in studios of his own. In 1917-1918 he was also attending to his health, which returned only gradually.

Sallman left Meyer-Both in 1918, a year after Everett was born. He then worked briefly for Toby Rubovits, who was a fashion designer and engraver. After this, two years were spent as chief illustrator for Sidney B. Egan, a national advertiser copy writing for the Kling-Gibson Advertising Agency. Then in 1923, probably early in the year, Sallman opened up his own studio on Jackson, but later moved to another studio in the old Tribune Building at LaSalle and Lake. His final employment, before becoming freelance in 1932, was as illustrator for Olsen-Schmid Studios, where he worked from 1924-1932. During the 1920s Sallman did advertisements for Cable pianos (*Cable Midget Upright*, 1920; *Pianos in Walnut*, 1920), toothbrushes, trucks, men's fashions, and a host of other items.

In 1918, having pretty well recovered from his serious illness of a year ago, Sallman began doing artwork for *Förbundets Veckotidning* (*FV*), the Swedish-language Covenant Weekly published in Chicago by the Mission Covenant Church. This publication began Sallman's "ministry of Christian art." Likewise, Sallman began as principal illustrator for an array of Mission Covenant publications. He continued in this capacity on a regular basis through 1932-1933, and on a less regular basis until about 1946. Some work during 1928-1934—and possibly after—was done under the name "Elias."

Just prior to drawing his famous Head of Christ, Sallman made some acquaintances, which, in retrospect seemed to him to take on particular importance. At the Central YMCA, just a short walk from his studio in the Tribune Building, Sallman came to know John Meredith, General Secretary for the Family Altar League, who invited him subsequently to do a cover for the *Family Altar*. His contribution was a cartoon on *Christian Family Life* (1921).

About the same time Sallman became acquainted with Dr. E. L. Eaton who held the chair of astronomy at the University of Wisconsin. One day as Eaton was defending theistic evolution at a street meeting, countering the claims of Darwin, Huxley and others, Sallman stopped to listen.[13] Sallman also got to know George L. Robinson, an Old Testament scholar widely traveled in the Near East who in 1913-1914 served as director of the American School of Oriental Research in Jerusalem. Sallman listened with interest as Robinson reported on his archaeological work in Palestine, and how the finds increased his faith.[14] Eaton and Robinson were both integrating Christian faith with newly-expanding disciplines of human learning. Sallman faced the challenge of integrating Christian faith with his practice of art, but he needed more biblical training to do so.

Sallman, in fact, was already taking steps in both directions, attending now a noontime Bible class at the Central YMCA. Leading the class was a young Methodist seminarian from Garrett Biblical Institute, Charles Ray Goff. Goff went on to become minister of Chicago Temple, and an internationally-known churchman. He was very personable, possessed with a deep voice and given to firm conviction. But what really impressed Sallman as he sat and listened, was the straightforward way in which Goff presented the gospel. Sallman said his portrayal of Jesus was so vivid that he could feel the Savior's presence in the classroom. He now began to see a Jesus who lived on the level of ordinary people. Sallman remembered particularly a series of talks by Goff entitled, "The Essential Equipment for Work." Later Sallman generously credited Goff for inspiring him to draw his *Head of Christ*. But there was another inspiration behind the famous sketch of 1924, about which we will say more in a moment.

[1] I stated earlier ("Warner E. Sallman: A Centenary Tribute to a Covenant Artist," *The Covenant Companion* 81/7 [July 1992]: 9) that Sallman enrolled at the Art Institute when he was sixteen. In November 1907, however, he was fifteen. The problem stemmed from the fact that in the Art Institute's *Circular for Instruction* he was not listed as a student in 1907-1908, yet registration records tell us he took an antique class beginning 4 November 1907. He therefore began at the Art Institute when he was fifteen.

[2] Meyer-Both was located south of the loop at 2314 South Indiana Avenue, near Cermak.

[3] Sylvia Peterson, *Warner Sallman and his Ministry of Christian Art*, Pamphlet, January 1984, 3

[4] Nikolaus Pevsner, *Academies of Art, Past and Present* (Cambridge: Cambridge University Press, 1940) 226. See also William Rothenstein, *Men and Memories* (New York: Coward-McCann Inc., 1931) chapter 4: "Paris and 'Julian's," 36-50.

[5] The Art Institute's official graduation records for 1913 incorrectly list Sallman's name as "Walter Salman." The last name is a simple spelling error. The wrong first name may stem from confusion with the prior listing of Sallman's nominating faculty member (Clute), whose first name was Walter. The same mistake is repeated on Sallman's day school registration card for 1912-1913, where, in another hand, his name is written as "Walter E. Sallman." All other surviving Art Institute records have both names correct. My thanks to archivist Mary McIsaac at the School of the Art Institute for allowing me to check registration and graduation records of the School.

[6] *Circular for Instruction*, (1913-14), 42.

[7] G. E. Kattenbach to Warner Sallman, 30 June 1913.

[8] According to the biographical entry in *Who's Who in Chicago and Illinois*, Sallman continued at the Art Institute until 1918. But registration and tuition

cards from the Art Institute show only two classes in the Evening School after 1913, one taken from 13 October 1919 to 18 January 1920, and a final class in life and portrait painting with George Oberteuffer in the fall of 1927.

9 T. Otto Nall, "He Preaches as He Paints," *Our Covenant Youth* 24/49 (5 December 1943): 3.

10 There is a slight chronological problem here. According to the biographical entry in *Who's Who in Chicago and Illinois*, Sallman began classes at Moody Bible Institute in 1912, and continued until 1917. But in the *Moody Student* (21 September 1951): 3, it refers to Sallman as "an Evening school student of 1910," at which time the interview with Sellers is said to have taken place. Extant records at Moody indicate only that Sallman took an evening course from January to March 1914.

11 Sylvia Peterson's unpublished notes.

12 5412 North Spaulding Avenue.

13 See E. L. Eaton, *Our Spiritual Life: An Examination of the True Basis of Our Spiritual Life—Regeneration—In the Light Both of Science and Revelation* (Milwaukee: Advocate Publishing Co., 1911).

14 See George Livingstone Robinson, *The Bearing of Archaeology on the Old Testament* (L. P. Stone Lectures, Princeton Theological Seminary; New York: American Tract Society, 1941).

IV

Covenant Illustrator

Between the two world wars Warner Sallman acted as the Covenant Church's primary illustrator.

Once he had recovered from his serious illness Warner Sallman began doing illustration work for the Mission Covenant Church, which continued on a regular basis for fourteen years, then less regularly for another twelve–until about 1944, at which time his commitment was largely to Kriebel and Bates. Sallman's first contributions–in pen sketch, charcoal and watercolor–were to *Förbundets Veckotidning* (*FV*), the Swedish-language *Covenant Weekly*. Many of these artworks reappear in subsequent issues, also in English-language papers published by the Covenant, such as *The Covenant Companion* (*CC*), *The Covenant Weekly* (*CW*), *Our Young Covenanters* (*OYC*), *Our Covenant Youth* (*OCY*), *Our Juniors* (*OJ*), *Our Covenant Little Folks* (*OCLF*), *The Children's Friend* (*CF*), and *Children's Hour* (*CHo*). The Covenant and the General Conference (Swedish) Baptists jointly issued the latter publication. Sallman also produced original sketches for these other papers, which, except for the *Covenant Weekly*, were written for children and young people. He illustrated other Mission Covenant publications as well, including books.[1] Between the two world wars Warner Sallman acted as the Covenant Church's primary illustrator.

Sallman's first two drawings appear in the 24 December 1918 Christmas issue of *Förbundets Veckotidning*. The one, *Frid på jorden*, or *Peace on the Earth* (1918), depicts Jesus with outstretched arms positioned behind a star sending down its beam over Bethlehem. In the foreground, behind flags, are American soldiers of World War I. This artwork also appears on the Christmas 1918 issue of *Edgewater Missionsblad*. The other, *Mänskorna ett gott behag*, or *Goodwill to the People* (1918), portrays a man walking through snow carrying a Christmas tree. A dog follows behind. In the background lies a Swedish-looking church and a snow-covered house. Both titles appearing as captions come from Luke 2:14, and were known additionally to Sallman's audience from the popular Swedish-American Christmas song, "Lyssna."[2]

Sallman did a pen sketch, *Hope for the New Year* [1918], for the year-end issue of 31 December. Here Humanity and War are personified as a huddled woman and a soldier, respectively. Old man 1918 attempts to restrain War, who carries a chewed-up sickle. Incoming 1919 is flooded in background light. A soldier behind Humanity looks toward that light.

Sallman's contributions to the 23 December 1919 Christmas issue continue along a seasonal theme. For the front page he did *Winter in Sweden* (1919), a sketch of a snow-covered house behind a picket fence. Birds eat here from a shock of corn on the light post in front of the house; birds also eat from off the path. An apparently popular picture, it appears a number of times in Covenant papers. *Angels Blowing Trumpets* (1919), two sketches of winged angels blowing their trumpets right and left, illustrates the front page of this Christmas issue. Churches lie in the background. The captions, "Ära vare Gud" ("Glory be to God") and "Frid på jorden" ("Peace on the earth"), come again from Luke 2:14 and the Christmas song, "Lyssna." The fourth page of the same issue carries another winter sketch, *Christmas Tree with Snow-covered House* [1919].

During the 1920s, Sallman continued contributing to the Swedish-language *Förbundets Veckotidning*. The switch to reading English—among adults—did not take place until the 1930s. Sallman sketched primarily for Easter, Thanksgiving and Christmas issues, when editors wanted seasonal artwork in their pages. One very successful Easter sketch, *Resurrected Christ Rising from the Crucified Christ* (© W. E. Sallman 1920), was published initially in *FV* for 30 March 1920. Here the resurrected Christ, framed in an Easter lily, rises not out of a tomb, but out of the Christ who was crucified. Written below is "Den sanna Påskliljan" ("The true Easter lily"). The face, although a frontal view, has similarities to Sallman's later *Son of Man* (1924). This sketch appears in the *FV* Easter issue for 1924, as well as in other Covenant papers—by itself, and in the collage *Self-Denial, Self-Indulgence* (1921). It was also later modified for a bulletin cover (*Thine Is the Victory!* 1952).

Easter drawings went beyond simple depictions of the biblical story, just as Christmas and New Years drawings included the realities of a world war. *Self-Denial, Self-Indulgence* printed in *FV* for 22 March 1921, consists of a collage of three sketches, including the prior year's *Resurrected Christ Rising from the Crucified Christ*. The two additional sketches show contrasting responses made to the Easter message. In the one, a husband and wife sit at a table preparing to give their Easter offering, which, in the Covenant Church went each year to missions. The husband writes a check as the wife holds a bank for the world's children, who are sketched in the background. In the other, a crying child walks ahead of fashion-clad parents "going their worldly way." The title above the picture of Christ reads, "Supreme Sacrifice", and the title below the pictures of the Easter people reads, "Self-Denial—Self Indulgence."

For the Easter issue of 11 April 1922, Sallman produced *Mother Reading the Easter Story* (1922), a pen sketch of an aged mother sitting at a table with her finger pointing to the Easter story in John 11:25-26. Sallman did numerous pictures of people sitting before open Bibles. The model for this woman was likely his mother. Sallman's contribution to the 1923 Easter issue of *FV*, *Christ Holding an Easter Lily* (1923), depicts a young-looking Christ that looks nothing like the Christ of *Son of Man*, which Sallman will draw a year later. For the *FV* Easter issue of 7 April 1925, Sallman sketched *Jesus Leaving Gethsemane* (1925) in which Roman soldiers and Jewish leaders lead Jesus, bound at the hands, from the Garden of Gethsemane.

For the 1920 Thanksgiving issue of *FV* Sallman submitted *Tacksägelse*, or *Thanksgiving* (1920). Here again a man sits alone at a table with hands folded on an open Bible. Below the scene appear three verses from the Swedish hymn, "Tack, O Gud" ("Thanks to God").[3] The Sallman cartoon for the 1923 Thanksgiving issue of *FV*, *A Thank Offering?* [1923], conveys a message concerning the ingratitude of the wealthy. Here a man loaded down with a horn of plenty, an automobile, and a sack of money, walks away from a church pulpit on which is written, "Treasury, Lord's Work." A dollar sign appears in the smoke of the man's cigar. Behind the pulpit, hidden but nevertheless present, is Jesus looking on. The look of this profile strongly resembles that in *Son of Man*, which Sallman will draw two months later.

For the Christmas issue of 21 December 1920 Sallman submitted *Tell Me the Old, Old Story* (1919), a sketch of a family sitting before the hearth. The father reads from the Bible. Smoke from the fire contains three additional sketches of the Christmas story: the angel appearing to Mary; shepherds arriving at the stable; and wise men following the star to Bethlehem. The following year Sallman did *Memories of Julotta* (1921) for the *FV* Christmas issue, which was 20 December 1921. In this sketch four parishioners—one a child—sit in a candle-lit church. Outside others arrive in horse-drawn sleighs. Julotta is the Swedish pre-dawn Christmas service.

Christmas contributions to *FV* for 1922-1925 were primarily winter scenes of snow-covered churches, houses, or pine trees. In some, angels announce the Christmas message by blowing trumpets, playing harps, or emitting stars. One sketch features Christmas bells. Artwork in non-holiday issues of *FV* during 1920-1925 consists of a couple sketches supporting mission work in Alaska. In the 22 February 1921 issue, *Here Am I, Lord, Send Me* (1920) depicts a man with a suitcase looking at a sign calling for "5 Mission-Spirited Men" to take charge of five government schools in Alaska. Below is printed, "Here am I, Lord; send me" (Isaiah 6:8). The 15 March 1921 issue contains *Eskimo Child* [1921], a sketch of a young Eskimo dressed in a parka.

During 1926-1928 nothing original by Sallman appears in the pages of *FV*, only reprints of his earlier sketches. In 1926 Sallman completed his first large painting of the Ascension for the Mission Covenant Church in South Bend, Indiana, and in 1927 he began doing chalk drawings of the *Head of Christ* out in the churches. In 1928 original sketches by Sallman do appear, however, in the

English-language *Covenant Companion,* and in a political magazine called *Lightnin'.*

In 1929 Sallman continued contributing to *FV,* but this was his last year for the Swedish-language paper. He did not contribute to the 1929 Christmas issue, and in 1930-1933 only reprints appear. The shift was being made to English in the Covenant, and Sallman's contributions therefore went to the denomination's English-language papers, primarily those for children and youth.

A total of eight artworks were done for *FV* in 1929—three appearing in March issues. For 12 March Sallman did *Young Man Kneeling on Jesus* [1929], an adaptation of a well-known nineteenth century European painting of a young man kneeling on the lap of Jesus with hands folded. Its theme was "Come to me all who labor and are heavy laden, and I will give you rest" (Matt 11:28). The well-known work had been published earlier in *Missions-Förbundets Ungdomstidning* (*MFU*), another Covenant paper for youth, where it appears under the caption, "Den bäste vännen" ("The best friend").[4] In the 19 March issue appears *The Lamp of My Life* (1929), a sketch of a man sitting before an open Bible looking up at a picture of the Crucified. Later, the 16 September 1933 *War Cry* Central would reprint this sketch. For the 26 March 1929 issue of *FV,* the Easter edition, Sallman contributed *Christ Rending the Veil* (1929). Here a resurrected Christ ascends in a flood of light. To the right one thief hangs from the cross, within the light. The other thief is not seen. Below the scene is a man's face and a serpent. The rent veil of the temple frames the entire image. A later watercolor, *It Is Finished* (1958 © K&B 1958), develops this sketch further.

For the 2 April 1929 issue of *FV* Sallman drew *Waldenström on the Radio* (1929), a cartoon of Covenant leader Dr. P. P. Waldenstrom, with a copy of *Förbundets Veckotidning* in hand, speaking into a radio microphone the exhortation of Paul about love being without hypocrisy (Romans 12:9-11). In the 9 April issue, the sketch *Look and Live* (1929), takes aim at materialistic philosophy seen as being destructive to the Christian faith. Compare *Christian Family Life* (1921).

The issues of 4 June and 18 June carry two advertisements by Sallman for radio station KFLV in Rockford, Illinois. A man and woman sit in chairs and listen to "Tryggare kan ingen vara" ("Children of the Heavenly Father")[5] in the pen sketch *Turn the Radio On* (1929). The man holds an open Bible. *Radio Audiences* [1929] was a pen sketch reflecting KFLV's four listening audiences: two women in the hospital; a mother at home with children; a man playing pool; and three men out of doors.

Sallman's final sketch for *FV,* which appeared in the Thanksgiving issue of 26 November 1929, was *Pilgrims on Their Way to Church* (1929). Depicted here was an early New England family of father, mother, daughter and son leaving home on their way to church.

Two editors primarily were responsible for enlisting Sallman's services on behalf of Covenant publications: G. F. Hedstrand and Olga Lindborg. Long-time writer and editor of Covenant papers, the Reverend Hedstrand is best remembered as the editor of the *Covenant Weekly*. Lindborg served as director of Children's Work for the Covenant, as well as editor of its children and youth papers. With her considerable knowledge of art, particularly religious art, she strongly advocated its use in the illustration of Bible stories.

Once Sallman began contributing to the English-language papers of the denomination his focus was largely upon youth. He produced very little artwork for the *Covenant Weekly*, the Swedish edition of which was successor to *Förbundets Veckotidning*, and the English edition of which was successor to the *Covenant Companion* Old Series. Most of what appears in the pages of *CW* consisted of reprints. For the June 1935 issue of *CW*, however, Sallman did sketch *Four Covenant Presidents* (1935), a piece in connection with the Covenant Golden Jubilee celebrated that year.

Contributions to the *Covenant Companion* Old Series extended from 1924-1933. Some of the smaller pieces were unsigned. He began with his most famous sketch, the charcoal Christ head entitled *Son of Man* (1924). It appears on the cover of the February 1924 issue. The *Companion* reprinted it again in 1930 and 1932, as did the *War Cry* in 1933.

Artwork for the *Covenant Companion, Our Covenant Youth, Our Young Covenanters, Our Juniors, Our Covenant Little Folks,* and other youth papers appears primarily—though not exclusively—in holiday issues. Sallman contributed *Palm Sunday* (1934) for *OYC* in 1936, which was a charcoal of Jesus, hand upraised, riding a donkey. Other hands to the side hold palm branches and throw flowers. The picture appeared in an *OJ* of the same date.

The Easter issues of both *CC* and *OCLF* contain Sallman sketches. Sallman's *Up from the Grave* (1924) decorates the cover of the 1924 Easter *CC*. In this sketch an ascending Christ rises from the tomb over Roman soldiers lying stricken in the foreground. A winged angel at left points to a tomb flooded in bright light. For the 1942 Easter issue of *OCLF* Sallman submitted a pen sketch done earlier, *Behold I Am Alive* (1930), which showed Christ rising out of a dark tomb. Easter lilies appear in the foreground. A simulated etching of Christ and upper Easter surroundings—including three crosses on a distant hill—give a look of brightness. A boy and girl look at a large Easter lily growing among tulips in Sallman's *Tis Easter, Tis Easter* [1946], printed in the 1946 Easter issue of *OCLF*. Below the scene is printed, "'Tis Easter, 'tis Easter!' the flowers say."

Sallman's *Harvest Time* (1924), probably a watercolor, anticipates Thanksgiving for the front cover of the October 1924 *CC*. Farmers mound more hay on an already-full horse-drawn wagon. For the actual Thanksgiving issue in November, *Family Altar of the American Home* (1923) focuses on the family and prayer. A family of four pray around a chair. Large neo-classical pillars stand to the sides and skyscrapers stand in the distant background. A quote from Calvin Coolidge on the right states that "the true civic center of our municipalities will be found... around the family altar of the American home."

For Mother's Day 1950, Sallman submitted a charcoal, *Mother Holding Baby* (1950), for the *Children's Hour*. Were it not for the American-looking mother, this sketch could be Mary holding the baby Jesus. Sallman produced no Christmas sketches for the youth papers, only a winter scene, *Snow-Covered Tree and Bush* (1923), in brown and white, which appeared on the January New Year's issue of *CC* for 1925.

In non-holiday issues Sallman's artwork centers around three themes: prayer, teaching and evangelism. The 1924 Thanksgiving drawings, *Family Altar of the American Home* (1923) and *Prayer of an Aged Minister* (1928) both emphasize prayer. In the latter pen sketch for the 21 January 1933 issue of *CC*, an aged minister kneels before a chair and prays. Over the fireplace appears a vision of his younger self preaching. The minister's prayer is that he not be forsaken when he is old. This sketch was reprinted a number of times—as a unity, or one part only of the minister praying or his younger self preaching.

Since Sallman taught Sunday School over the years, it is no surprise to see in his artwork an emphasis on the teaching ministry of the church. For the front cover of the September 1924 issue of *CC* he produced *Saved for Service* (1924), a sketch of men and women sitting at classroom desks. The teacher up front looks along with the class at the board, where the theme of the work is written:

SAVED for SERVICE
STUDY to shew thyself approved unto GOD, a workman that needeth not to be ashamed, rightly dividing the word of truth. II Tim 2:15

The Christian life for Sallman meant more than accepting God's gift of salvation. It involved service to others, and a beginning of Christian learning.

Christian learning comes to the fore again in *The Benediction of Christian Education* [1929], a front cover sketch for the 17 April 1929 issue of *CC*. Here a bearded old man teaches a group of young people. The outline form of a hidden yet present Christ, with arms outstretched, stands behind the man. The man holds a Bible on his lap, and with the left hand directs the attention of the class to the Christ figure.

The July 1949 issue of the *Children's Friend*, a paper issued by the Covenant East Coast Conference, published *Girls Bible Class* (1943), a charcoal and pen sketch. Here a woman teaches a girls' Bible class out of doors, presumably at the conference summer camp in Cromwell, Connecticut. The girls sit on a hilltop with Bibles and notepads in their laps. The teacher points towards a clouded sky. In the clouds is a cross, and in front of the cross a line of flags.

Evangelism is the theme of *The Compassionate Christ* (1944), a pen and charcoal collage that appeared first on the front cover of the *Christian Advocate* for 15 February 1945. It was reprinted in *OYC* for November 11, 1945. It was reprinted in *OYC* for 11 November 1945. A thorn-crowned Christ here looks down upon a globe swirling in space. Below a hand set over against clouds carries the Christian flag. Accompanying the picture is a verse from Frank Mason North's hymn, "O Master of the Waking World."[6]

For the 11 August 1946 issue of *OCLF* Sallman sketched *The Children's Friend* [1946]. The work bears the signature "Elias," and may therefore be earlier. This same year Sallman also completed his oil, *Jesus, the Children's Friend* (1946 © K&B 1947). The present sketch is another Jesus in outline, hidden yet present, standing behind five small children who are sitting and lying on the ground. Jesus' outstretched arms with palms face down signifies Jesus' care over his small friends.

Numerous sketches for the various youth papers illustrate stories. Subjects from both the Bible and modern life sought to capture youthful imaginations: a) children of the world; b) the Old West; c) gypsies; d) birthday parties; and e) animals—sheep and dogs.

An illustration in *CW* for 13 February 1940, *He Loved the Sheep* [1940], addresses children's love of animals and seeks to illuminate the hidden years of Jesus' boyhood. Here the boy Jesus is pictured with sheep and a sheep dog. He holds a sheep.

Sallman sketches in *OYC* during 1931-1937 primarily illustrate stories. Most appear in *OJ* for the same date. Published in *OYC* for 15 February 1931, the pen sketch, *Riding the Pony Express* (1930) plays on the themes of adventure, life in the Wild West, and the conflict between Indians and white settlers. In this sketch Indians chase a settler riding the post route. Arrows whiz by his head. The accompanying article is entitled "When Dave Rode the Pony Express." Ethnic differences are brought out in *Chinese Boy Working on Model Airplane* (1930), a story illustration for "Friendship on a Non-stop Flight" in *OYC* for 19 April 1931.

Both *Japanese Woman Carrying Baby* (1929), published in *OYC* for 12 June 1932, and *Gypsy Girl* (1932), published in *OYC* for 14 August 1932, display a fascination with ethnic differences. In the former a Japanese mother carries a baby on her back. Its first printing illustrates a story entitled, "Little Folks in China." But later reprints of the sketch in *OYC* and *OJ* for 25 March 1934 and 4 August 1935 accompany stories about the Japanese. *Gypsy Girl* accompanies a story by Helen A. Larson entitled, "Betty and the Gypsies." In this charcoal, a gypsy girl with a headband and full skirt stands by a tree. A tent is in the background.

The *OYC* issue of 9 July 1933, uses a Sallman charcoal *A Birthday Party* (1932) to illustrate a story of the same title. In the charcoal, four children—three girls and a boy—sit together with a dog. The boy holds a softball; one girl holds a book in her lap; another is wearing roller skates; and a third girl listens to the others talk. *Woman with a Dog* [1937], published in *OYC* for 19 September 1937, also focuses on animals. A woman, stands in front of a farm house, telling her dog to put down the stick in its mouth. Underneath it is written, "Whenever we chide her for wrongdoing, she picks up a stick."

Of a more serious nature, *Talking about Sunday School* (1935), a charcoal published in *OCY* for 17 November 1935, focuses on Covenant young people teen-aged and older. Here a teenage brother and sister talk about Sunday School. The conversation centers around William Tyndale's translation of the Bible, and a Home Missions offering that will be taken next Sunday. An accompanying article by Olga Lindborg is entitled, "Good Stewards."

Sallman's *Son of Man* sketch for the 1924 *Companion* was done to inspire young people to live the Christian life. Subsequent artwork in the various Covenant papers had the same goal. Illustrations for Easter served as a reminder of the central event in Christian faith: the Resurrection. Other drawings promote family life, underscore the importance of prayer, encourage Christian learning—particularly Bible study—and mandate evangelism for the church and the individual believer. Thanksgiving pictures attempt to teach gratitude and inspire tangible giving to the Lord's work. Some sketches, of course, appeal simply to a sense of adventure, the youthful imagination, and the ordinary fun children and young people typically experience.

When looked at as a whole the Sallman illustrations for Covenant papers show a remarkable balance between men and women, boys and girls, young and old, Americans and non-Americans, clergy and laity, prominent leaders and every day folk. It is not surprising then that people of every description—in the Covenant and without—came to appreciate this artwork and the artist himself.

[1] Olga E. Lindborg, "Elias," *Our Covenant* 4 (1930): 14.

[2] John Holstedt, "Lyssna, lyssna, hör du ängla sängen," 1898.

[3] August Ludvig Storm, "Thanks to God for My Redeemer," 1891, trans. Carl E. Backstrom, *Covenant Hymnal* 1996, #657.

[4] *Missions-Förbundets Ungdomstidning* 3/9 (5 May 1914): 1.

[5] Lina Sandell, "Tryggare kan ingen vara" ("Children of the Heavenly Father"), trans. Ernst W. Olson *Covenant Hymnal* 1996, #87.

[6] *Covenant Hymnal* 1973, #547.

V

'The Thrilling Vision'

Suddenly about two o'clock I came out of my fitful attempts at sleep with a clear, beautiful image of the *Head of Christ* startlingly vivid in my mind. I hastened to my attic studio to record it. I made a thumbnail sketch, working as fast as I could in order that the details of the dream might be captured before fading out of my mind. Next morning I made a charcoal drawing from it. (Warner Sallman, A Night in January, 1924)

During the early 1920s Sallman had wanted to do an artistic representation of Jesus. Three sketches, in fact, had already been published in *Förbundets Veckotidning* prior to January 1924, two of them bearing striking similarities to *Son of Man*. The earliest known published Sallman face of Christ is in *Resurrected Christ Rising from the Crucified Christ*, dated 1920, and printed in the March 1920 *FV*.[1] It is a frontal view with hair and facial similarities to *Son of Man*. *Christ Holding an Easter Lily* in the 1923 Easter issue of *FV*[2] has a different face, although someone knowing that Sallman sketched it might perhaps see similarities to *Son of Man*. An earlier frontal sketch of the face of Christ from 1914 is also extant, but it looks more like a Hofmann rendering.

The most interesting Christ sketch prior to January 1924 was in *A Thank Offering?* (1923), a front page cartoon published in *FV* just two months before *Son of Man*.[3] The head is seen only from the back and one side, nevertheless the hair and profile of the nose and eye bear unmistakable similarities to *Son of Man*.

The story of how *Son of Man* came about begins in 1923 when the Reverend G. F. Hedstrand, editor of a new Mission Covenant youth publication, entitled the *Covenant Companion*,[4] invited Sallman to be the publication's art editor. Sallman actually volunteered his services, without pay, for the magazine's first year. The first issue was December 1923, and for the cover Sallman secured a painting from his brother-in-law, Haddon Sundblom, the artist who a few years later created the classic Santa Claus for Coca-Cola.[5] For the cover of January 1924 Sallman got a contribution from his friend Walter Ohlson. Hedstrand had a "Christian Life" issue planned for February 1924, and Sallman decided to do this cover himself. His task was in some fashion to "challenge young people to a staunch and faithful Christian life."[6] He said,

I thought to do the face of Christ. My first attempts were all wrong. Finally there were only twenty-four hours until delivery date. I tried again and again the preceding evening, but the impressions that came to my mind were futile. I felt disturbed and frustrated. I went to bed at midnight, restless in spirit, but did ask God once more to give me the vision I needed. Suddenly about two o'clock I came out of my fitful attempts at sleep with a clear, beautiful image of the *Head of Christ* startlingly vivid in my mind. I hastened to my attic studio to record it. I made a thumb-nail sketch, working as fast as I could in order that the details of the dream might be captured before fading out of my mind. Next morning I made a charcoal drawing from it.[7]

The thumbnail sketch was about 3 inches square, in pencil. The charcoal done the next morning was 22 inches by 22 inches, and this drawing was the one Sallman delivered to the engraver shortly before the 4:30 P.M. deadline. He remembered being satisfied that what he reproduced was almost precisely what he had seen in his dream.[8] The name *Son of Man*, given later, was suggested by a friend.

This "thrilling vision," as he called it,[9] was never understood to be an isolated experience or one without a human dimension. In another recollection Sallman remarked:

Of course, many experiences went into the preparation of the picture. I know that, and I am not foolish enough to think that it came in a moment of time as simply as this account may seem to suggest...The nine years I spent in evening classes at the Chicago Art Institute went into that picture...My experience drawing fashions on a kind of assembly line that included dozens of other artists, which put my religious convictions to a severe test, went into that picture. My sickness when I was given but three months to live, and then recovered by an act of faith, went into that picture. And there were the experiences that came to me through a number of men.[10]

Sallman goes on to mention friends he acquired before making the drawing—E. O. Sellers, E. L. Eaton, George Robinson, John Meredith, Charles Goff, and U. S. Abell of whom we spoke earlier. "All these people, and many others too numerous to mention, deserve part of the credit for any recognition that may have come to me for the *Head of Christ*."[11]

Sallman also had to answer the charge that his drawing of the Christ head was influenced by a painting of Léon Augustin L'hermitte, *Friend of the Humble* (1892), which was housed in the Boston Museum of Fine Arts. As a boy he saw this painting on journal cover, cut it out, framed it, and gave it as a gift to his mother.[12] About this he said: "I don't wonder that people say the L'hermitte painting influenced my drawing. Isn't everything we create a composite of what we have subconsciously stored through the years?"[13]

Sallman's Easter cover for the 1924 *Companion*[14] was a fully-resurrected Christ ascending from the tomb on Easter morning. The face here is not the face of *Son of Man*. Sallman did the September and December *Companion* covers as well, and in the December issue Hedstrand thanked him for his artwork of the past year. Sallman continued doing artwork for the *Companion*, and in 1930 and 1932 the magazine reprinted his Christ head.[15]

The response to the picture, which at first came primarily from Covenant people who had seen it on the cover of the *Companion*, was positive. Some did ask, however, why there was no eye contact, why the face looked away, and not straight at the viewer. Sallman answered that the face looked up and away because Jesus was "set to go to Jerusalem" (Luke 9:51).[16] When pressed for a further interpretation, Sallman said he hoped all of the following qualities were present in the picture: kingly bearing, masculine strength, courage and equanimity, high intellectual faculties and powers, divine love and kindness, tenderness, compassion, sympathetic understanding with humility, and resolute serenity. In this picture Jesus was one on the march to the cross,the savior of the world, as well as the personal savior of all who put their trust in him.[17] A rather comprehensive answer.

Sallman also thought Jesus to be of beautiful countenance, citing Song of Songs 5:15: "His appearance is like Lebanon, choice as the cedars." But at the same time he believed that the Lord's face was brutally marred in accordance with the description of the Suffering Servant in Isaiah 53:2-5: "He was despised and rejected of men…He was wounded for our transgressions, he was bruised for our iniquities; upon him was the chastisement that made us whole, and with his stripes we are healed."[18]

About seven thousand copies of the February 1924 *Companion* were printed, six thousand of which went out to subscribers. Requests came in for extra copies, until finally the supply was exhausted. People continued to want copies, but Sallman and the publisher agreed that there was no need for a second run. Sallman said he pretty much forgot about the matter as he busied himself with new work.

Then about a year later Frederick Emrich, Home Missions Secretary for the New England Congregationalists, asked his friend the Reverend Fred Pamp, who was then pastor of the Covenant Congregational Church of Boston, where he might get a print of the Sallman Christ head suitable for framing, and said he would pay any price. Pamp contacted Sallman, and Sallman is said to have supplied him with a copy. The question now had to be raised again whether more copies ought to be made.

Sallman was reluctant to make more prints, but finally he went ahead and had cuts done by a local engraver, who struck one thousand copies on special chemio stock. These were highlighted, half tone, life-size copies in black and white. All was done at Sallman's own expense. On high quality paper, these prints were now suitable for framing, and Covenant Book Concern offered them for sale. Sallman kept the original, and hung it in his upstairs studio. Only later was it placed where most people remember it—in the hallway inside the front door.

Within eight to ten years all the prints were gone. Many were given away.[19] Some went with new subscriptions to the Salvation Army's *War Cry*,[20] and some with new subscriptions to the *Covenant Weekly*.[21] Later, after a new run, Covenant Book Concern sold prints also in "sepia" (brown), which was the color of the original on the cover of the *Companion*.[22] Most of these prints—both black and white and sepia—went to Covenanters. One will see them yet today in Covenant homes and Covenant churches.

All this took place without the drawing ever having been copyrighted. Sallman did not want it copyrighted. When he sent the drawing to the engraving company that ran off the first one thousand prints, the engraver asked him who held the copyright. Sallman said no one. The engraver said, "I'll tell you what's going to happen. Some of my friends, who are not Covenanters, are going to take this picture, copyright it, and make a lot of money." Sallman said he didn't care. The picture was given to him, and he wanted it to "be as free as the air."[23] It was finally decided that since the *Covenant Companion* was registered at the post office, the post office would get prior rights were any such claimed. Only in 1941, when the Christ head in oil was copyrighted by Kriebel and Bates, did Sallman finally copyright his earlier charcoal. He then sold to Covenant Book Concern the exclusive rights to reproduce the 1924 Christ head in black and white and in sepia.[24]

Not until a decade later did the Christ head begin to gain broader recognition. When the 1933-1934 Chicago Worlds Fair, called A Century of Progress, was held, the fair displayed the picture in the Hall of Religion, where Sallman had other artwork in exhibits of the Salvation Army and American Bible Society. In 1933 the Salvation Army Central Headquarters in Chicago also asked for and received permission to reprint *Son of Man* in the *War Cry*,[25] which introduced the picture to a new audience of several thousand.[26]

Then in 1934 the Messenger Corporation of Auburn, Indiana asked Sallman to do a pastel of his Christ head for a 1935 Roman Catholic Scripture Text Calendar it was preparing, suggesting he add a halo. Sallman complied, which sent the picture into thousands of Roman Catholic homes.[27] For a 1938 calendar Sallman did *The Blessed Mother* (1936), a rendition of Mary, and for a 1939 calendar a third pastel, *Woman, Why Weepeth Thou?* (1936), which was of Mary Magdalene with Jesus on Easter morning.

In 1935 Sallman did what is believed to be his first Christ head in oil. It was a large painting, measuring 66 inches square and done with a silver background. A large border on all sides made the entire work 8 foot square. The painting was displayed at the Mission Covenant Golden Jubilee, held that June in a tent on the campus of North Park College.[28] The next week it appeared in the same tent at evangelistic meetings conducted by Charles F. Weigle, a personal friend of Sallman's. Later the painting was presented to Weigle as a gift. The North Park Covenant Church raised the money, said to be about $150 or $200, by selling neckties.

That same year the 1924 Christ head was given an additional boost by John Timothy Stone, pastor emeritus of Chicago's Fourth Presbyterian Church and president of McCormick Theological Seminary. Stone wrote a friend saying that Sallman's picture of Christ was nearest to his own conception of how the Savior might have looked. Sometime earlier[29] a student had brought a Sallman Christ head into Stone's class that the student had found in a Chicago bookstore.[30] Sylvia Peterson gives the following account of this incident:

> …Dr. John Timothy Stone, then president of McCormick Theological Seminary, suggested to his senior class that they make a search for a picture which to them was the most accurate representation of the Christ. After a period of three months they brought in their selection found in art shops and galleries. Included in the group were many of the old masterpieces. But on the first vote the picture receiving first place was not one of these, but one by an unknown artist. It was Warner Sallman's charcoal drawing of the *Head of Christ*.[31]

More copies of the 1924 Christ head were made at Stone's urging, which helped increase the picture's popularity. The supply of one thousand original prints had finally run out, so Covenant Book Concern paid for a new run, which was done in both black and white and sepia. In 1937 the 1924 Christ head was also reprinted in the Christmas issue of the *War Cry* for the Central and Southern Territories, the largest press run yet.[32] Here it appears in burnt orange. In 1937 Sallman painted another oil of the Christ head, this one for the Scandinavian Lutheran Mission Church in Nelson, British Columbia. It was done on masonite, set over against a background of blue sky with pink clouds.

In March 1938 the 1924 charcoal began appearing in Chicago streetcars and buses as the result of an advertising venture called Best Seller Publicity, organized by Josephine Peterson. After riding one day to the Loop from her home in Jackson Park, where she sat looking at ads for chewing gum, whiskey, Sloan's Liniment, hair wash, Sal Hepatica, candidates for aldermen, and home-loan plans, Peterson decided that advertising signs in Chicago streetcars and buses might better contain edifying verses from the Bible, which, after all, was the world's "best seller." Artwork was needed, and so Peterson enlisted the services of Sallman and other Chicago artists to help prepare 11 by 28 inch advertising cards. These other artists included Walter Ohlson, Vaughn Shoemaker of the *Daily News*, and Coleman Anderson of the *Chicago Tribune*. Some of these cards displayed the 1924 Christ head. Other Sallman drawings were used as well. One, entitled *Christ Looking at the City*, was used on public transportation as late as 1957. The campaign spread to 120 other cities, where the Sallman artwork was used not only on public transportation, but also on large billboards.[33]

At the close of the 1930s the 1924 Christ head had become quite popular. Covenant Book Concern had now sold over a million prints,[34] and people were asking for it in color. A pastel had been done, and the picture was being drawn before live audiences in colored chalk.[35] Sallman had also experimented in oil. By 1940 then, Sallman was quietly at work attempting another painting of his 1924 Christ head in oil.

[1] *Förbundets Veckotidning* 359 (30 March 1920): 1; reprinted in *Förbundets Veckotidning* 520 (15 April 1924): 1; *Covenant Companion* Old Series Sunday School Teacher's Edition 7/4 (April 1928): front cover; and numerous times afterwards.

[2] *Förbundets Veckotidning* 465 (27 March 1923): 1.

[3] *Förbundets Veckotidning* 500 (27 November 1923): 1.

[4] The new magazine was actually launched in June 1922 as the *Teacher's Companion*. The change in name to the *Covenant Companion* came with the December 1923 issue.

[5] The Sundblom Santa in red and white was done for Coca-Cola in 1931.

[6] Warner Sallman, "Head of Christ," *The Upper Room* 23/4 (September-October 1957): 3.

[7] Warner Sallman, "The Story Behind This Painting," *Guideposts* 16/12 (February 1962): 10.

[8] T. Otto Nall, "He Preaches as He Paints," *Our Covenant Youth* 24/49 (5 December 1943): 3.

[9] Warner Sallman, "My Greatest Spiritual Experience," *Chicago Daily News* (10 March 1953): 30.

[10] Nall, "He Preaches as He Paints," 3.

[11] Ibid.

[12] Margaret Anderson, "His Subject Shaped His Life," *War Cry* Central 2136 (9 December 1961): 8. Anderson lists the painting as *Friend of the Lowly*, which appears to be simply another English title for the painting (see *The Friend of the Lowly* in Ripley Hitchcock [ed.], *The Art of the World 2*). L'hermitte's other famous work in the New York Metropolitan Museum of Art is entitled, *(Jesus)*

Among the Lowly (1905). This painting also goes by the name *Among the Poor in Heart* (see M. Hamel, *The Salons of 1905*, plate facing page 14). There is, however, a mistake in Anderson's mention of the cover of a *Ladies Home Journal*, since no L'hermitte painting appears on any *Ladies Home Journal* cover. See further the discussion in chapter XII. Some years later the Methodist Book Concern was selling prints of *Friend of the Humble*; see the ad together with a picture in the *Epworth Herald* 40/9 (2 March 1929): 24. The picture appears again in the *Epworth Herald* 41/15 (12 April 1930): 13; 42/14 (4 April 1931): 6; also in *Our Covenant Youth* 17/16 (19 April 1936): 3. The painting, *(Jesus) Among the Lowly*, is printed in the *Epworth Herald* 40/47 (23 November 1929): front cover; 41/16 (19 April 1930): 14; and 42/9 (28 February 1931): 19.

13 M. Anderson, "His Subject Shaped His Life," 8.

14 *Covenant Companion*, 3/4 (April 1924).

15 *Covenant Companion*, 9/5 (3 March 1930) and 11/24 (11 June 1932).

16 Sallman, "Head of Christ," 3.

17 Ibid.; Sallman, "Two Artists Depict Christ: Warner Sallman and Birger Sponberg..." *The Covenant Companion* 49/16 (15 April 1960): 8.

18 Sallman, "Two Artists Depict Christ," 8.

19 Olga E. Lindborg, "Another Picture of Jesus," *Our Covenant* 17 (1942): 70-71.

20 See e.g., *The War Cry* Central 661 (26 August 1933): 11.

21 The offer of a free print of the 1924 *Head of Christ* for new subscriptions to the *Covenant Weekly* was made on page 8 of the 7 July 1936 issue. The offer was still alive in 1938.

22 A sepia Christ head appears on the cover of the *Covenant Companion* 63/1 (1 January 1974).

23 Nall, "He Preaches as He Paints," 4.

24 *The Covenant Weekly* 38/4 (28 January 1949): 6.

25 *The War Cry* Central 661 (26 August 1933): front cover.

26 Exact circulation figures for the *War Cry* Central issue, the only territory in which the Sallman sketch appeared, are unavailable. Central Territory *War Cry* sales for the Christmas issue of 1937 were 515,933 (letter from Joy Rich at the Salvation Army Archives and Research Center, NYC, dated 30 December 1987), but the Christmas issue sold many more copies than the August issue.

27 Lindborg, "Another Picture of Jesus," 71.

28 *The Covenant Weekly* 24/26 (25 June 1935): 1; *Missions-Vännen* 61/26 (25 June 1935): 4.

29 Sylvia Peterson said the year was "about 1933;" see Peterson, "The Ministry of Christian Art," *The Lutheran Companion* 55/14 (2 April 1947): 10-12; idem, "The Brush that Ministers," *Our Covenant* 23 (1948): 82.

30 Said to be a Baptist bookstore on Belmont Avenue.

[31] Peterson, "The Ministry of Christian Art," 11.

[32] *The War Cry* 887 (25 December 1937): 12. Sales for the Central Territory were 515,933. No figures are available for the Southern Territory (letter from Joy Rich in the Salvation Army Archives and Research Center, NYC, cited in note 26).

[33] *Our Covenant Youth* 27/42 (20 October 1946): 4-6. See also Tennessee Bergsten, "After 55 Years—Still a Silent Witness," *Power for Living* 50/4 (6 September 1992): 2-3, 6-7.

[34] Jane Gardner, "Mental Image Is Model for Christ Sketch," *Chicago Tribune*, (6 June 1954), Neighborhood sec., part 3, 1.

[35] Glenn D. Everett, "Story of a Great Picture," *The Link* (April 1958): 15. This article, printed for Protestant Armed Forces personnel, is an imaginative account but unfortunately flawed by a number of inaccuracies. Everett may, nevertheless, be correct in reporting a request by students for a colored chalk in 1939. A 1939 color chalk of the Christ head survives from the Edgewater Covenant Church.

VI

The Salvation Army Connection

One Salvationist remarked after seeing the completed interior of
Cherokee Hall, that Sallman had created "the most colorful and elaborate stage we have ever seen in a Scout camp."

In the early twentieth century, close ties existed between Swedish Americans of
the Mission Covenant Church and the Salvation Army.[1] By 1887
Scandinavian Salvationists had organized their own department with divisional
headquarters in New York, Chicago and San Francisco. Mission Covenanters
and Salvationists were therefore friends and often relatives of one another.
Gunnar Erickson, a Salvation Army officer in the 1930s and 1940s, came originally out of the Mission Covenant Church in Evanston and counted among
his personal friends Covenant presidents T. W. Anderson and Clarence Nelson,
also Warner Sallman. It was Erickson who engaged Sallman to do the painting
for the Salvation Army Hall on 59th Street.[2]

A very special relationship also developed between Warner Sallman and
Salvation Army officer R. Lewis Keeler, though exactly how the friendship
began is not known. Keeler was nine years younger than Sallman, but like
Sallman, was an artist who had studied at the Chicago Art Institute. The two
could have met there, or perhaps in the Chicago group of Christian artists
about which we spoke earlier.[3] In any case, when Sallman later expressed gratitude to the Salvation Army for helping him decide to leave the commercial art
field to do full-time religious artwork, he singled out Lewis Keeler as one who
gave him much-needed encouragement.[4] It was Keeler who requested Sallman's
1924 *Head of Christ* for the cover of the 26 August 1933 *War Cry* Central.
Keeler himself had done a face of Christ for the 7 January issue of that year.

About the time Keeler published Sallman's Christ head he succeeded in per-
suading his friend to do additional artwork for the Army. These were
Depression years, a time when artists did not exactly find their telephones ring-
ing off the hook.[5] Sallman was asked to do a major work for the Army's exhibit
at the Century of Progress in 1933-1934, the interior artwork for newly-built
Cherokee Hall at Camp Shagbark in Camp Lake, Wisconsin, and to make peri-
odic contributions to the *War Cry*—mainly its Christmas and Easter special
issues.

Sallman's contribution to the Army's Fair exhibit, which was set up in the
south wing of the Hall of Religion,[6] consisted of a frieze of thirty drawings in

sepia crayon, 28 inches by 32 inches in size, which portrayed international aspects of the Salvation Army's work. It encircled the exhibition room ten feet or so above floor level. The drawings were done in three colors. Included were portrayals of William Booth's conversion in 1844, William and Catherine Booth carrying the gospel to people in the slums of East London, three men sitting at a table officially naming the Salvation Army in 1877, and Salvationists of Norway, Sweden, Finland, New Zealand, Korea, Australia, Zululand, Alaska, and elsewhere, set over against backgrounds representative of their countries.[7] It was a significant work.

Sallman did a similar frieze at the Fair for the American Bible Society. This exhibit consisted of six paintings—whether in watercolor or oil is not known—depicting significant people and occasions in the history of the Bible among English-speaking people: the singing Saxon cowherd Caedmon; the venerable scholar Bede; Translator John Wyclif; Translator William Tyndale; The Court of King James; and Mary Jones, the legendary Welsh girl remembered for so ardently seeking a copy of the Bible.[8]

In 1934 Sallman spent six weeks painting murals and stage scenery in Cherokee Hall at Salvation Army's Camp Shagbark. The camp was newly-built, made possible the year before by the generosity of Will Rogers, who turned over $50,000 from a series of radio talks to the Salvation Army with the one stipulation that the money be used in some way to benefit the unemployed.[9] The Central Territory of the Salvation Army decided to use their portion of the Rogers donation to expand existing facilities at Camp Lake, Wisconsin.

At the dining room end of Cherokee Hall Sallman painted a frieze similar to those done at the Century of Progress, only here the scenes depicted Indians. At the other end of the hall was a rustic auditorium. Here Sallman painted the stage scenery, including life-size wooden cut-outs of Indians, complete with braces to make them free-standing.[10] The latter served as backdrops and to provide concealment for stage productions.[11] One Salvationist remarked after seeing the completed interior of Cherokee Hall, that Sallman had created "the most colorful and elaborate stage we have ever seen in a Scout camp."[12] Sallman was presumably paid—like other Works Project Administration (WPA) workers—from the Rogers' donation. Cherokee Hall was ready when the first camp opened in July 1934.[13]

Sallman's *War Cry* contributions began, as we mentioned, with the reprinting of *Son of Man* on the cover of the 26 August 1933 Central issue. Keeler printed it again—in burnt orange—in the Christmas issue of 1937, also in subsequent issues. For the 16 September 1933 *War Cry* Central Sallman contributed *The Lamp of My Life* (1929), a sketch done originally for *Förbundets Veckotidning*. Then for the front cover of the 1933 Christmas issue, Sallman submitted a watercolor of wide-eyed children framed by a Christmas tree and

Christmas toys, *Christmas Light in Children's Eyes*. Though the piece is undated, its signature suggests that the work could be from as early as 1910.

In 1935 appeared artwork that was done specifically for the *War Cry*. *Sunday School Kickoff* (1934), in *WC* Central for 5 January 1935, and *On to 50,000 Campaign* (1935), in *WC* Central for 27 July 1935, were cartoons promoting increased Salvation Army Sunday School membership. These were followed by *World for God Campaign* [1935], a pen sketch done for the *WC* Central issue of 25 September 1935. This supported an Salvation Army evangelism effort that had as its goal the "winning of one million souls." Evangeline Booth, with Bible in hand, is seen here preaching to a vast multitude.

Thus began a series of artworks in charcoal, pen sketch, and watercolor describing the Salvation Army's work of evangelism and social ministry. *Miracle and Menial Tasks* (1938) were five charcoals done for the *WC* Central Easter issue of 16 April 1938. They accompanied an article by P. LeRoy DeBevoise on the mission of the Salvation Army in the light of Jesus' ministry and redemptive sacrifice. Three sketches portray mission in terms of extended hands.

Achieving with Christ (1941) portrayed the work of the Salvation Army in nine pen sketches done for *WC* Central 3 January 1942. These sketches, surrounding a nearly-full Christ figure in watercolor, show a band playing, a choir singing, scouts carrying food to the needy, a woman teaching Sunday School, a man praying with two other men, a nurse reading to a sick woman in bed, a man giving a homeless man a bed, a nurse tending babies in a hospital nursery, and a man visiting another man in prison.

Some artwork stays with strictly biblical themes, although even here themes were chosen with the larger purpose of supporting evangelistic outreach. For the front cover of *WC* Central, 8 November 1941, Sallman did a charcoal, *Christ on the Clouds* (1941 © Warner Sallman 1941), where Christ is framed by the rent veil of the temple. The portrayal, however, is neither resurrection nor ascension, but the Second Coming. Below one sees explosions taking place on earth. An accompanying poem speaks of Christ's return. *Thorn-crowned Christ on the World* (1942), in three-color crayon and possibly watercolor, is a thorn-crowned face of Christ in front of a clouded world and appears in *WC* Central for 24 October 1942. This piece was done in support of Christian evangelism. Except for the wide-open eyes, this Christ head compares with the one on *The Veil of Veronica* (circa 1615), by Domenico Fetti, which is in the National Gallery of Art in Washington, DC. A year earlier Sallman did *Crown of Thorns* (1941 © Warner E. Sallman 1943; © K&B 1956), a watercolor in which the head tilts slightly and glances downward. This artwork was published in *WC* Central for 17 April 1943—its first known printing.

Once *Christ in Gethsemane* (1941 © K&B 1942) had been completed for Kriebel and Bates, Sallman did a charcoal of the face in this picture for *WC*

Central, 25 October 1941, appearing under the title, *Our Redeemer* (1941). The *War Cry* has since printed other K&B pictures: *His Presence* (1946 © K&B 1947), on the front cover of *WC* Easter for 6 April 1985; *Christ Our Pilot* (1950 © K&B 1950), on the front cover of *WC* for 7 November 1987; and the *Head of Christ* (1940 © K&B 1941), on the front cover of *WC* for 13 May 1989.[14]

One significant change here from Sallman's earlier stint as Covenant illustrator is that oils are now being submitted and published in color. Of fifteen major artworks done for the *War Cry* between 1941 and 1944, thirteen were oils or probable oils. One was a pastel, and the medium of the other is unknown. Included here is a head of Christ, portrayals of the Easter and Christmas stories, and pictures juxtaposing the Easter and Christmas stories to realities of World War II and the Salvation Army's concern for men and women in the Armed Services.

Sallman oils begin appearing in the 20 December 1941 Christmas *War Cry*. A *Bethlehem Shepherd* (1941) illustrated a Christmas story, and three others artworks were scenes from the biblical Christmas story. On the front cover appears *The Prince of Peace* (1941 © Salvation Army 1941), a close-up of the baby Jesus sleeping in the Bethlehem stable. *The Boy Jesus* (1941 © The Salvation Army 1941), which Sallman did at Camp Shagbark, appeared inside. In this work, the young Jesus stands next to Joseph, his father. Joseph sits on a carpenter bench instructing his son.

On the back cover was *The Flight into Egypt* (1941 © The Salvation Army 1941), a painting of Mary and Joseph with the baby Jesus traveling at night to Egypt (Matt 2:14). Mary, with Jesus in her arms, rides a donkey; Joseph walks alongside. Earlier Keeler had printed Hans Lietzmann's *The Flight to Egypt* on the back cover of *WC* Central for 29 June 1935. Inside the front cover of the present issue he included another Flight to Egypt painting from the House of Art in New York.

Head of Christ (1942 © Warner E. Sallman 1942) is a probable oil Sallman is said to have done for the Salvation Army when Kriebel and Bates refused the *War Cry* permission to print the 1940 oil. It was published on the front cover of the *War Cry* Easter issue, 4 April 1942. On the back cover was *Consider the Lilies* (1942 © The Salvation Army 1942),which took its theme from Matthew 6:28. Jesus here is walking with three disciples pointing to lilies, daffodils and other flowers growing along the side of the path.

The Christmas issue for 19 December 1942 contained three Sallman oils. On the front cover was *The Christmas Story* (1942 © The Salvation Army 1942), a collage consisting of a serviceman reading his New Testament against the background of an American flag. To the left and slightly above is a Bethlehem scene—Mary, Joseph and the baby—lighted by a heavenly beam that is shining down on an open New Testament.

Inside was *The Wise Men* (1942 © The Salvation Army 1942), which showed two wise men standing and a third on one knee greeting the heavenly star. They and their camels are at a stopping place for the night. An article accompanying a black and white reprint of this picture in *WC* Central for 18 November 1944 stated that six thousand prints had been sent to the Salvation Army East African Territory, where they now appeared in "many an African hut." On page 31 of the same issue was Sallman's *Faithful unto Death* (1942 © The Salvation Army 1942), a picture in an unknown medium of a soldier on the ground close to death. His eyes are open and a smile is on his face as he looks up to the Christ who is beckoning him.

On the front cover of *WC* Central Easter for 24 April 1943 was *The Christ Triumphant* (1943 © The Salvation Army 1943), a rising Christ about to pass over stricken Roman soldiers who lie face-up in the foreground. A winged angel stands next to an empty background tomb. Inside the issue was *Christ Carrying the Cross* (1942 © The Salvation Army 1943), a pastel of Jesus carrying his cross up a modern Golgatha. An analogy is intended here to the soldier laboring in wartime under a loaded pack. Rockets and canon fire light up the background. On the back cover appears *The Unseen Easter Guest* (1943 © The Salvation Army 1943). Here a hidden yet present Christ, with hands behind his back, stands behind an Army chaplain who is reading from his pocket Testament to soldiers on a South Pacific beach.

For the front cover of the 25 December 1943 Christmas issue Sallman did *Thoughts at Christmastime* (1943 © The Salvation Army 1943). In this picture a helmeted soldier, carrying his rifle, looks up to a star-studded sky where he sees, at the upper right, his wife tenderly holding their young daughter. On the back cover appears *A Home Away from Home* (1943 © The Salvation Army 1943), a picture of two servicemen at a Salvation Army post drinking coffee and listening to carolers. On the background wall is a picture of wise men on camels going toward the light of Bethlehem.

Sallman's last paintings for *War Cry* special issues were two oils done for the Christmas issue of 23 December 1944. On the front cover appears *Lest We Forget* (1944 © Warner Sallman 1944), which was a young boy and girl standing before a Christmas candle. Above the candle light hangs a World War II window star signifying that a family has lost a son in the war. On the back cover is *Madonna and Child / Babe of Bethlehem* (1944 © Warner Sallman 1944; © The Salvation Army 1944), another painting of Mary and the Christ child.

Sallman also did story illustrations for *War Cry* Christmas and Easter issues—in watercolor, charcoal, crayon and pen. Between 1935 and 1943 over thirty artworks illustrated some fifteen Christmas and Easter stories, with titles such as, *Roman Soldiers and Barabbas* (Easter 1936); *Horse Riders at Bethlehem* (Christmas 1936); *The Centurion of Faith* (Easter 1938); *Woman at the Village*

Well (Easter 1940); *Servant of the Bethlehem Inn* (Christmas 1942); *Pilate and Claudia* (Easter 1943), and so on.

Sallman's artwork for the *War Cry* covered a period of slightly more than ten years—from 1933 until the end of 1944. By 1944 his commitment was largely to Kriebel and Bates. Christmas and Easter issues were published in Chicago for all four territories, which meant Sallman artwork was now finding its way into the homes of millions. The usual run for the Christmas issue was 4.5 million, and the Easter issue 3 million.

Sallman's other work for the Salvation Army consisted of oil paintings for Salvation Army chapels and meeting halls. Three are known to have been done—two quite large—and all are extant. The first was an *Ascension* painted in 1941 for Scandinavian Corps #16 on 59th Street in Chicago. Earlier Ascension paintings had been done for the Mission Covenant Church in South Bend, Indiana (1926), the Mission Covenant Church in Braham, Minnesota (1934), and the Swedish Mission Church in Iron Mountain, Michigan (1939). All portray the scene described in Acts 1:11. The Scandinavian Corps painting, unusually rich in color, is an estimated 9 to 10 feet in width, and 6 to 7 feet in height. Its shape simulates three-paneled European altar paintings. The tops here are rounded, with the center panel higher than those on either side. The South Bend, Braham, and Iron Mountain paintings, in their original settings in the old churches, were styled similarly.

The present painting was done at the time the 59th Street auditorium was being remodeled. An older artwork had been painted over, much to the dismay of the artist who did it, and a sum of money had been donated and an additional amount raised for a new painting. Gunnar Erickson contacted his friend Warner Sallman to see whether he would do the work. Sallman came out, evaluated the setting, and suggested a painting of the Ascension. The auditorium was not large, seating with a balcony only four hundred people. The painting was done for a reported sum of $400.00.[15] Sallman did it at home, then brought it down to the 59th Street location himself where he stayed just long enough to supervise the mounting and do final touch-ups.

The painting was moved to Mt. Greenwood in 1971. Because the new facility was not ready when the 59th Street facility was vacated in 1965, the painting had to be stored a few years in a basement. At Mt. Greenwood it was remounted and hung at the front of the chapel. In spite of the dismounting, remounting, storage and transit the painting is in remarkably good condition.

Watching Jesus ascend into the clouds are the eleven disciples, positioned differently than in the South Bend and Braham paintings, but similarly to the Iron Mountain painting. The disciple third from the left with no staff in hand has both hands extended upward. The center disciple has the left hand, not the right, raised. The disciple third from the right holds a staff in the left hand.

What Sallman seems to have done, both here and in the Iron Mountain painting, is to have taken two disciples from the South Bend painting—the one third from the left, and the one third from the right—and interchanged them. The Christ figure in the present painting is exceptionally well done. The face is like the face on the 1924 and 1940 *Head of Christ*.

The Good Shepherd (1943) was done two years later for the Evanston Scandinavian Corps. This large oil, about 9 foot square, hangs in an upstairs auditorium. It is basically the same painting as *The Lord Is My Shepherd* done the previous year for K&B (1942), and similar to *The Good Shepherd* done in 1943 for the Bethlehem Covenant Church in Stephenson, Michigan. Because the present painting is square, part of the top and bottom of the K&B version is missing. The painting is also not as bright and vivid as the well-known version—the colors are light blue and the background mountains less distinct. Nevertheless, changes from the famous work are slight, e.g., one sheep is without horns, the rock in front of the bush at the upper left is positioned differently, and there is no dark passageway in the background mountain. The face of Jesus is also slightly different from the face on the well-known picture— a bit more elongated. Still, the black sheep is there, the lamb is carried in Jesus' arms, and Jesus holds his same staff.

This painting was also done at the time of a remodeling. The individuals responsible for contacting Sallman were Ethel Barber and her husband, an Evanston judge, who was chairman of the Corps' Advisory Board. A service of dedication was held after the painting was hung, but Sallman took sick, and was unable to attend.

In 1964 Sallman did a *Head of Christ* for the chapel of the Rehabilitation Center for Homeless Men (now the Salvation Army Adult Rehabilitation Center) in Minneapolis. It measures 3 feet by 4 feet and has a white background. The face looks almost exactly like the face on the 1940 oil, but the shadowing and shirt outline are like the color pastel done for the Messenger Corporation. Sallman noted at the lower left © Messenger Corp. 1935.

John and Margaret Troutt secured the painting for the Minneapolis facility, which was newly-built in 1964. They visited Sallman in Chicago and asked simply for a *Head of Christ* in chalk. When they came to pick up the finished work, they discovered to their surprise a Christ head in oil awaiting them. Sallman said, "When you told me where the picture would hang, I wanted the men to have my best."[16] The Troutts brought the painting to Minneapolis and presented it to the center, where it was placed on a side wall in the 250-seat chapel. In 1992 the painting was relocated to the Central Territorial Headquarters in Des Plaines, Illinois. At the lower right, together with Sallman's signature and the date, are three Scripture verses: Heb 12:2; Phil 2:8-11; and II Cor 4:6.

[1] Edward O. Nelson, "Recollections of the Salvation Army's Scandinavian Corps," *Swedish Pioneer Historical Quarterly* (October 1978): 257-276; idem, *Hallelujah! Recollections of Salvation Army Scandinavian Work in the U.S.A.* (Chicago: The Salvation Army, 1987).

[2] Gunnar Erickson, phone conversation with the author.

[3] Suggestion made by Paul Marshall to me in a letter dated 17 November 1987.

[4] *The War Cry* Central 1902 (15 June 1957): 19.

[5] Paul Marshall letter cited in note 3.

[6] Merle J. Hamilton, "Religion at the Fair," *War Cry* Central 650 (10 June 1933): 9; see also "Religion, History, and Progress Featured at Fair," *War Cry* Central 710 (4 August 1934): 16.

[7] See pictures of the exhibit and of some of the Sallman artworks (in black and white) in the *War Cry* Central issues of 29 July 1933, back cover; and 5 August 1933, 8-9.

[8] These drawings are mentioned in an American Bible Society publication, *The Exhibit of the American Bible Society at the Century of Progress Exposition Chicago, 1933* (New York: The American Bible Society, n.d.), although Warner Sallman is not named as the artist. See also "The Bible at the Century of Progress Exposition" in *Bible Society Record* 78 (September 1933): 88-89.

[9] *The War Cry* Central 665 (23 September 1933): 5, 10; also 666 (30 September 1933): 4; and 759 (13 July 1935):front cover.

[10] See them over against the stage scenery in the *War Cry* Central 713 (25 August 1934): 9.

[11] Paul Marshall, "Warner Sallman Receives 'Well Done,'" *The War Cry* 68/26 (29 June 1968): 15; supplemented by a letter from Marshall to me dated 17 November 1987.

[12] *The War Cry* Central 709 (28 July 1934): 11.

[13] Ibid.

[14] On page 6 of this issue, besides the incorrect year given for the K&B copyright of the *Head of Christ* appearing on the cover (It should be 1941, not 1940), the note says mistakenly that the picture on page 3 is the same as the 1940 oil on the cover. It is not. The picture on page 3 is a probable oil which Sallman gave to the Salvation Army for publication on the front cover of *WC* Central Easter 1110 (4 April 1942). On page 4 the same picture in the older issue is reproduced. See *Head of Christ* (1942 © Warner E. Sallman 1942) in Appendix II.

[15] Gunnar Erickson, phone conversation with the author

[16] Margaret Troutt, "Gospel Artist," *War Cry* 101/5 (31 January 1981): 5.

VII
The Head of Christ and Other Paintings in Oil

The now-famous *Head of Christ* was painted in 1940 at home. It was another experiment…When the oil was finished it simply rested quietly in the living room, for a while on the piano.

The 1930s were lean years for artists. Many were on WPA, and those who owned homes struggled to meet mortgage payments. Sallman had neighbors and friends in North Park who lost their homes in the Depression, and others who nearly did. In 1932 he began freelancing, and was fortunate the next two years to receive the large commissions for the Century of Progress and Camp Shagbark. In 1934 Sallman painted an Ascension for the Mission Covenant Church in Braham, Minnesota, and in 1935 some work came his way in connection with the Covenant Golden Jubilee. For this latter celebration he did his first *Head of Christ* in oil.

Other work had to be taken wherever he could get it. Sallman was asked to do a few portraits of Covenant leaders, also the wife of one. Six are known to have been painted and are extant. In 1934 Sallman painted a portrait of T. W. Anderson, commemorating Anderson's arrival in Chicago to assume the presidency of the Mission Covenant Church. Another portrait was done the same year of Signe Lund, wife of Nils W. Lund, who was Dean of North Park Seminary. In 1935 portraits were painted of former Covenant president, the Reverend C. A. Björk, and North Park science professor, C. J. Wilson. In 1939 Sallman did two more portraits of Covenant pastors, F. M. Johnson and Otto Högfeldt.

In 1938 the invitation came to do some five hundred illustrations for the *Thorndike Century Senior Dictionary*, being prepared by E. L. Thorndike of the University of Chicago. It was a welcome assignment, but now he needed help.

About this time a young artist named Elmer Carlson arrived in Chicago from Iron Mountain, Michigan. Carlson was a sign painter, aspiring to work one day in an art studio. Iron Mountain held little promise for a young man with such a dream, in fact, it barely had work enough for painters willing to paint anything. In Chicago Carlson found the market for his skills scarcely better. Then a friend happened to introduce Carlson to Warner Sallman. Sallman asked to see some of his pen and ink drawings. After studying them carefully, Sallman asked Carlson if he would be willing to help with some dictionary illustrations—about 500 of them? Indeed he would!

Carlson remembers working with Sallman in his attic studio in the summer of 1938:

> I shall never forget the heat of that first summer. A couple of fans stirred the air around a bit, but no air-conditioning cooled our sweaty bodies. Sometimes the heat became so unbearable we both stripped down to our undershirts and shorts. We were glad that clients were not in the habit of dropping in to check on our work. But we needn't have worried. Warner's wife, Ruth, would have called up a warning before they mounted the stairs.
>
> Every day started with a short prayer that God would guide our hands as we worked. There were so many pen-and-ink drawings to be made, and so little time in which to complete them. We made layouts first, followed by the finished art, which was to be reduced three times in reproduction. Warner always commended me for my work, but there were times I believed I could have done better. I felt so relaxed working beside him. He never intimidated me in any way. I tried my best to please him.
>
> Part of my work consisted of trips downtown to Chicago's main library where I spent many hours researching data on machinery, animals, and buildings—all the things we were expected to illustrate. I drew dozens of maps—areas all over the world—giving dates of their boundaries following the various wars. I learned more geography than I had ever learned in school.

After the dictionary work was completed, and with a letter of recommendation from Sallman in his portfolio, Carlson had no difficulty getting work. In 1954 he went out on his own, establishing the Carlson Studios of Creative Arts in downtown Chicago. Carlson's son, Bob, also received instruction from Sallman.

Sallman had no protégé per se, nevertheless a few young artists like Elmer and Bob Carlson received instruction from him, and assisted him in work he was doing. Some did clouds and sky on large church paintings. Stan Ekman, who went on to become a fine artist, found in Sallman a warm friend and helpful instructor, as did Howard Ellis, a student from Garrett Seminary who frequented Sallman's downtown studio for instruction and encouragement. Ellis went on to do some original art, a few pieces of which are on permanent exhibit at the Upper Room Chapel and Museum in Nashville, Tennessee.

In early 1940, with the dictionary work complete, Sallman returned to painting oils. Before year-end three large paintings of Hofmann's *Christ in Gethsemane* would be completed for Mission Covenant churches in Lund, Wisconsin, South Chicago, Illinois, and Red Wing, Minnesota. Early in the year Sallman would paint another oil, one that would eclipse every other done by Sallman before or after.

The now-famous *Head of Christ* was painted in 1940 at home. It was another experiment. Sallman had done at least two other oils of his popular picture—the more recent on masonite. He was worried at the time about the white lead he was using, fearing it would yellow with age. Then after a bit of research he discovered that the old masters used white canvas in order for the light to penetrate the color. This precluded the need for white lead. So Sallman did the present oil on canvas, without the use of white lead.

Impetus for doing this painting may also have come from a request, in February of that year, that Sallman do a *Son of Man* in oil for the North Park Seminary Class of 1940. They wanted it for a class gift that they could present to the school. Sallman earlier had done an oil of science professor C. J. Wilson (*Portrait of C. J. Wilson* 1935), which was presented as a gift to North Park from the college class of 1935. Kenneth Strom, a member of the seminary class of 1940, had collected $35.00 from twelve class members and visited Sallman at home in February. He left the money with Sallman, with Sallman promising he would come up with something.[1]

When the oil *Head of Christ* was finished it simply rested quietly in the living room, for a while on the piano. Later it hung over the mantle. Jim Sallman remembers a family conversation that transpired one Sunday when they were sitting around the dinner table. Warner said, "Maybe I should give it to North Park," pointing to *Head of Christ* over the mantle. The reaction was spontaneous. "No," said Jim, "we want to keep that here at home." Ruth suggested Warner give the painting to the Art Institute, an idea she followed up on by writing to the Art Institute asking for an application blank. Warner was surprised. He had no idea they were that fond of the painting. At the time, nothing was decided.

Sometime later Fred Bates came to the house to visit. He and Anthony Kriebel were associated with Gospel Trumpet Company (later Warner Press)[2] in Anderson, Indiana. Gospel Trumpet was the publishing house of the Church of God of Indiana. Sallman had come to know both men through Covenant Bookstore, after they began promoting his 1924 Christ head in charcoal. Bates' errand on this particular day was to discuss Sunday School art, possibly to request a small size of the charcoal Christ head for use in making plaques.[3] When he stepped into the living room, however, he saw the Christ head in oil hanging over the mantle, and the conversation turned to it immediately. Both he and Kriebel had been encouraging Sallman to do the 1924 sketch in oil. In their opinion the charcoal appealed mainly to "arty-types;" what the masses wanted were religious pictures in color.

"What do you intend to do with it?" asked Bates. Warner said he didn't know. No plans had been made. Bates expressed interest in securing the painting for reproduction, arguing that it deserved to be marketed for the whole world to behold. They discussed things a bit more. Finally an arrangement was made whereby Bates would return a week later with Kriebel, who was Gospel Trumpet's business manager, and at that time a decision would be reached. Sallman promised no deal would be made before the two of them came.

A week later Bates and Kriebel called at Sallman's home, and a decision was reached to turn the painting over to them. Sallman called his friend Al Nordberg, who was manager of Chicago Offset Printing Company, and arranged for a meeting. The three men, Kriebel, Bates, and Sallman, then drove to see Nordberg. The painting went with them. Together with other executives of Chicago Offset, the four discussed printing the picture by lithograph. They also made a few suggestions for improvement. It was then decided that after Sallman completed his touch-up work Chicago Offset would proceed at once to make plates and print a run of pictures ranging in sizes from 2½ inches by 3½ inches to 16 inches by 20 inches.

The following day Sallman met again with Kriebel and Bates to work out details of a contract. The two men would form a business partnership that would own the painting and hold its copyright. Kriebel and Bates would also retain control over the distribution of prints. It was decided that Gospel Trumpet would sell and promote the Sallman picture in the "Protestant Field." By "Protestant Field" was meant Protestant Church publishing houses and Protestant dealers of Christian literature, such as Bible and religious bookstores. Kriebel and Bates would themselves sell and promote the picture in the larger market, which included Catholic stores and dealers, also secular gift shops and distributors of books and pictures. Sallman, for his part, would receive payment for the painting plus royalties after each run of pictures. The contract also covered future paintings that Sallman promised to do for Kriebel and Bates.

By late November the touch-ups were completed and the first color prints of *Head of Christ* were ready to roll off the Chicago Offset press. A number of preliminary runs had to be made, and in early December Sallman was still making minor changes on the portrait, to remove, in his words, its "hardness and harshness...[yet] without sacrificing [its] strength and masculinity."[4] Kriebel sent Sallman a check for $100.00.

In the same letter Sallman said copyright matters had been attended to, presumably referring to the oil. But there was also a copyright Sallman himself had on an earlier crayon portrait that had to be clarified. Sallman presumably worked this out separately with Kriebel and Bates and the W. M. Welch Company, who owned the plates. The 1924 charcoal still lacked a copyright. This too needed clarification—both legal and otherwise.

By mid-January 1941 Sallman realized there were problems as a result of the contract made with Kriebel and Bates. The issue centered around rights to the 1924 *Head of Christ* in charcoal, and the person at the center of the controversy was Robert Norstrum, manager of Covenant Book Concern. Norstrum felt Covenant Book Concern possessed rights in handling the 1924 Christ head, and that these rights had been infringed upon once Kriebel and Bates secured their rights to market the Christ head in oil.

Sallman went to see Norstrum in his office on 14 January. He explained in detail everything that had transpired since the middle of November. Norstrum was bitter, threatening to blacken the names of Kriebel and Bates at a religious book store convention scheduled to be held next month in downtown Chicago. According to Sallman, "[Norstrum] was going to stand up on the floor of that meeting and tell them of how he had been robbed by these designing men."[5]

Bates called Norstrum later in the week, inviting him to the Morrison Hotel to see their display and talk the situation over. Norstrum refused and repeated his threat to "smear Mr. Kriebel and Mr. Bates" at the association meeting.[6]

Sallman, in view of the crisis now developing, sent a formal letter later that week to Warner Press in care of Kriebel and Bates:

> Because of possible difficulties and misunderstandings arising from your new reproduction of my painting of the Christ head, I wish to make a statement herewith, that,—in no way have you been guilty of making any secret or unethical efforts to procure the exclusive reproduction rights of my work. The original drawing always has been and is now my property. The Covenant Book Concern [has] purchased previous prints from me for resale purposes, acting as distributors...[7]

Sallman makes no mention of it, but the problem with Norstrum must certainly have stemmed from the fact that no copyright had been taken out on the 1924 picture. Sallman had not wanted it. It was, he said, "to be as free as the air." Norstrum, on his part, seems to have assumed rights by Covenant Book Concern over the charcoal, or perhaps was just afraid that now with Kriebel and Bates getting rights to the oil—which was the same basic picture as the charcoal—Covenant Book Concern would lose the privileged position it had in distributing the charcoal. Though Nostrum's position on the issue remains unclear, a year later, when the matter was discussed before the Covenant Board of Publication, Norstrum said he expected Nordberg to have asked his consent before giving Kriebel and Bates permission to publish the oil, and by not doing so had "sold the Covenant down the river."[8]

Sallman talked again the next week to Norstrum on the telephone, and followed up the conversation with a letter the same day to Covenant President T. W. Anderson. The letter brought Anderson up to date on what had been happening, and reiterated the complete confidence Sallman had in the business practices of Kriebel and Bates. Both, he said, were "honorable Christian gentlemen."[9] Sallman did admit, however, that there were numerous angles to the matter that needed to be explained. One, no doubt, was the lack of a copyright on the 1924 picture.[10] Sallman also told Anderson that he would either meet personally with the Board of Publication or else provide them with a written statement reciting all the facts.

The following week, on the afternoon of 27 January, Sallman, Nordberg, and Norstrum met in Nordberg's office for two hours. Sallman called it "quite a session," but said a proposal for reconciliation and peace was made. This was conveyed to Kriebel by telephone.[11] Norstrum promised to cooperate with Kriebel and Bates and try to erase the negative consequences that had occurred thus far. He also agreed to talk with Kriebel and Bates when it was convenient. Some concessions seem to have been made, although we do not know what they were. Correspondence regarding the Norstrum affair breaks off at this point, and does not pick up again until December.

In the meantime Sallman was experiencing financial difficulties. It seems he was not able to collect sums for work already completed, and he was even talking about a "possible change in occupation." Reluctantly he informed Kriebel and Bates of his tight financial situation, but in the same letter thanked them for a check they had just sent him for $100.00.[12]

When the correspondence on the Norstrum affair picks up again in December 1941,[13] Sallman is still discussing the "Norstrum complications" with Nordberg. This time the issue is comments Norstrum had already made to religious publishers and booksellers. A gentleman of Scripture Press had heard about the "injustice" done to the Covenant, and to Sallman personally, and said he resented such "smart business practices."[14] Sallman went to see Mr. Victor Cory of Scripture Press personally and in relating the entire story, smoothed the complications between Scripture Press and Kriebel and Bates.

On 16 December Nordberg called a meeting of the Covenant Board of Publication for 11 o'clock in the morning. Nordberg was chairman of the board. Sallman and Norstrum were both present. Nordberg opened with a summary of attacks that had been made on Kriebel and Bates, after which Sallman was given an opportunity to tell his story. Then Norstrum was given the chance to speak. His story was the same as a year ago, although it was now revealed that he had expected Nordberg to consult him before giving Kriebel and Bates permission to publish the Christ head in oil and that in not doing so he had "sold the Covenant down the river." Some emotional discussion followed. Nordberg asked for a vote of confidence, and said that if vindicated he would resign from the board because he no longer had confidence in Norstrum's management of Covenant Book Concern. The board responded by giving Nordberg a unanimous vote of confidence, but they would not hear of his resignation. The matter, for all intensive purposes, was now closed.

A year then after the controversy began it was settled. The Covenant Board of Publication had vindicated Kriebel and Bates, and affirmed that the Covenant had not been wronged. So far as copyrights were concerned, by the end of 1941 *Son of Man* was under copyright, and Covenant Book Concern became its eventual owner. Copyright for the *Head of Christ* in oil remained with Kriebel and Bates.

Prints of the oil *Head of Christ* went out early in 1941. Chicago Offset shipped them to Gospel Trumpet in Indiana for distribution. The first run of one hundred thousand copies sold out in two months. Several more runs were made. By the end of 1941 the distribution total was well in excess of a million. The following year the company received orders for an additional three million prints, many of which went overseas with men and women in the military. By 1985 the painting had sold over 500 million copies. Combined sales of the other thirty-five Sallman paintings were said then to be another 500 million, adding up to one billion reproductions total.[15]

Sallman received $500.00 for the oil Christ head from Kriebel and Bates. Later they gave him $500.00 more, evidently feeling that the price they paid was too low. Sallman, of course, also received royalties on the prints. But in spite of phenomenal sales he never became rich. For each of the subsequent paintings the contract stipulated that Sallman would be paid $100.00 plus royalties. After the pictures became more accepted, and Sallman became more widely known, an adjustment was made in July 1943, increasing the amount Sallman received per painting. In October 1944 Kriebel and Bates paid Sallman an additional $2000.00 for all the paintings done thus far, which established the price at about $1000.00 per painting. This amount remained constant for most of the Sallman oils thereafter, including those done for churches and other institutions. For some very large paintings Sallman received as much as $1500.00. Though not rich, Sallman had enough to live on, an accomplishment for an artist in any age. And he was grateful. Kriebel and Bates, for their part, established a viable business, but profits were never such that either partner became wealthy.

The Sallman originals went to Kriebel and Bates where a few were hung on office walls, but the majority were kept in storage and never put on exhibition. Only recently has a public exhibition of the best-known paintings—and others not so well known—become possible with the acquisition, in 1987, of the entire Kriebel and Bates collection by Anderson University and Warner Press in Anderson, Indiana. The 140 or more original pieces now form a Sallman Collection in the Jessie C. Wilson Galleries of Anderson University.

The North Park Seminary Class of 1940 received another Christ head to present to the school. For them Sallman did an oil over a black and white print.

This painting, which is basically the same as the copyrighted version, except for a white background, was completed in August 1940. After its presentation to North Park it was hung in the school chapel in Old Main. Today the painting resides in Covenant Archives at North Park.

Beginning in early 1944 Kriebel and Bates opened a Chicago office from which it carried on business operations and coordinated work with Sallman and Chicago Offset. Before having their own office there, Kriebel and Bates had set up Sallman in an office in downtown Chicago. The hope was that Sallman would be productive there, but just the opposite occurred. People began stopping by to visit, or to see what Sallman was currently working on, and finally it became apparent to Kriebel and Bates—and also to Sallman—that some change had to be made. Too much time was being consumed in public relations, and not enough time doing the paintings both artist and sponsoring company wanted completed. Sallman therefore closed his downtown office and moved home. There his wife Ruth could monitor phone calls and knocks at the door, which came steadily. Kriebel and Bates remained in their downtown office until December 1945, at which time they moved both operations and paintings to Indianapolis, Indiana.

Sallman's first oil for Kriebel and Bates after the *Head of Christ* was a rendition of *(Christ in) Gethsemane* (1941 © K&B 1942), this one his own. Like most artists, Sallman developed themes from others preceding him, and here inspiration came from the *Christ in Gethsemane* painting of Johann Heinrich Hofmann (1890). When we say this rendition was his own, we mean to distinguish it from five known replications of the Hofmann classic that Sallman did for Covenant churches in 1940 and 1941. In Hofmann's *Christ in Gethsemane*, which was widely copied by American artists early in the century, Jesus is kneeling in prayer, facing left, with hands folded on a large table rock (Luke 22:41-42). The original hangs in the Riverside Church in New York City.[16]

Sallman's first change was to turn the Hofmann picture around. Jesus now faces right, praying with folded hands on a table rock further right. The sleeping disciples, Peter, James, and John, are in the background left, not right, and the city of Jerusalem is likewise at the left in the distance. Background olive trees are also shifted over from the right of the Hofmann painting, and gone is the large olive tree Hofmann had behind the table rock. As compensation Sallman brings in a large rock behind Jesus, intended to be "the rock that is higher than I" (Psa 61:2).[17] This symbolizes the saving presence of God, whose very name is "Rock" (Deut 32:4). One sees on it the shadow of a jagged cross, but in Christian theology the cross is salvific. In 1942 Sallman did the same basic painting for the Covenant Congregational Church in Manchester, Connecticut.

Sallman's next painting for Kriebel and Bates was *Christ at Heart's Door* (1942 © K&B 1942), which develops from William Holman Hunt's classic,

The Light of the World. A late version of this famous work hangs on the south side of the nave in St. Paul's Cathedral, London. The original 1854 version is at Keble College, Oxford, and another is housed in the Manchester City Art Gallery. In the Hunt painting a regal Christ, with lighted lamp in hand, knocks at a door overgrown with weeds. The theme derives from Revelation 3:20: "Behold, I stand at the door and knock; if any one hears my voice and opens the door, I will come in to him and eat with him, and he with me." The Hunt picture too was widely known; nevertheless, it was but one of many nineteenth century paintings of Christ knocking at the door (see Appendix III). A version by Zabateri, for example, was reproduced by Sallman for the First Covenant Church in Fort Dodge, Iowa (1947).

Sallman in his rendition turns the Hunt picture around, the same as he did with Hofmann's *Christ in Gethsemane*: Christ approaches the door from the other direction. He comes as friend and guest, and so Sallman depicts him simply in a white garment—resurrection white (cf. Rev 3:5, 18)—and devoid of jewelry. No gold crown is upon his head, nor does he carry a lighted lamp, as in the Hunt painting. The lamp is not needed, says Sallman, because Christ himself is "the light of the world" (John 8:12; 9:5). Light therefore emanates from his person, and, with help from the rounded upper portion of the door, it makes the shape of a heart.

The solid oak door has large ornate hinges on the right, which means the door handle has to be on the left. The figure of Christ blocks this portion of the door, which may then preclude the embellished interpretation that Sallman's door is without a handle because it must be opened from inside. The lattice window shows inner darkness, indicating that whoever is living there much needs the light of Christ. Sallman says regarding the lattice,

> [It] is there so that the individual may see who is at the door. By responding to the knock, he may have a view of the Presence before letting him in. It is just possible that there are many people who have had a glimpse of the Savior from time to time who have not responded in glad recognition. Through this opening, be it ever so tiny, one can see that he is good and kind.[18]

After the *Head of Christ* this picture is second in demand.[19] Sallman did the same painting later for the Covenant churches of Dawson, Minnesota (1950) and Norway, Michigan (1953).

The Lord Is My Shepherd was also done in 1942 (© K&B 1943). At first it was called *Good Shepherd*, deriving its title from John 10:11, 14: "I am the good shepherd." Later it was titled *The Lord Is My Shepherd* after Psalm 23:1. Sallman did the same painting a year later for the Salvation Army Evanston (Illinois) Corps, and, with modifications, for the Bethlehem Covenant Church in

Stephenson, Michigan. Both of these paintings were given the title *The Good Shepherd*. The watercolor, *He Leadeth Me* (1949 © K&B 1951), has Jesus leading the sheep away in the other direction.

Sallman appears to derive his inspiration for this painting from *The Good Shepherd* of Bernard Plockhorst,[20] which was popular at the time and widely available in prints. In the Plockhorst painting Jesus carries a staff in his left hand, and in the right arm holds a small lamb. At his side, on the right, is a mother sheep looking up at her lamb. Visible at the left is the head of one sheep that is black. Sallman, in his rendition, engages once again in reversals: Jesus carries the lamb in his left arm, and in the right hand holds the staff. Other prominent details, however, follow the Plockhorst work, such as the mother sheep looking up at her lamb, and one sheep to the left and behind being black, etc. In the background five or more sheep are lying together near water (cf. Psalm 23:2).

Sallman enriches his background with mountains and a winding stream. The canyon, or else the dark passageway in the mountain at the upper left, suggest the "valley of the deathshadow" through which the shepherd and his sheep have just come (Psalm 23:4). But the shepherd is now in daylight, and after wandering all day has found a grassy meadow where the sheep can graze and drink water from a quiet stream (Psalm 23:2). It is springtime, and the valley is abloom with wild flowers. Still, it is late in the day. The shepherd is heading toward the sheepfold where he must arrive before dark. Sallman wants to tell us in this picture that no path in life is too rough or too long when the Lord is our shepherd.

The next year Sallman did an oil entitled *Peter Matson Praying at a Minnesota Haystack* (1943), which has been housed in the World Missions Office of Covenant Headquarters in Chicago. Peter Matson was a pioneer China missionary, and this painting depicts his moment of commitment to serve the Lord on the mission field.

The Boy Christ, also called *My Father's World* (1944 © K&B 1945), was Sallman's next painting for Kriebel and Bates. The face has similarities to Hofmann's *Christ at 12*. In Sallman's painting continuity is kept with his two previous works. From *Christ in Gethsemane* he retains the large rock with a shadowed cross, and from *The Lord Is My Shepherd* he keeps the lamb in Jesus' arms. Here the lamb is said to have strayed from a flock grazing on a distant hillside.

Sallman's setting, rich in color and symbolism, distinguishes this picture. God's handiwork is everywhere. The picture's earlier title was thus *My Father's World*.[21] The boy Jesus is sitting outside Nazareth in the surrounds of his Father's world. Background detail presages later teachings by Jesus on the Kingdom of God. The village in the upper left is Nazareth—"a city set on a hill [that] cannot be hid" (Matt 5:14). Overhead are "birds of the air," below which grow "lilies of the field" (Matt 6:26, 28). Flowers at the right include yellow blossoms of a mustard plant (Matt 13:31-32; 17:20). Sheaves of wheat grow amidst thorns and thistles (Matt 13:3, 8, 24-30). Clusters of grapes hang from an overhead vine—another image Jesus used to describe the Kingdom of God (Matt 20:1-15; 21:28-32, 33-43; John 15:1-2). The picture is intended to illuminate the "hidden years" of Jesus' youth.[22]

In *Christ at Dawn* (1945 © K&B 1945) Sallman shows indebtedness once again to Johann Hofmann. Hofmann's *Christ on Mount of Olives* is a similar pose and a similar setting. In Sallman's painting, however, Jesus sits on a Galilean hill, just above Capernaum. It is early morning, and he has come out to pray (Mark 1:35). His face is turned heavenward and his hands are folded. The Sea of Galilee lies calm and still below. On the other side of the sea lies the town of Bethsaida, believed by Jesus to remain asleep throughout the day (Matt 11:21).

Jesus, the Children's Friend (1946 © K&B 1947) betrays indebtedness to Plockhorst's *Jesus Blessing the Children*. The inspiration for both paintings is Matthew 19:13-15 (and parallels), where Jesus stops to bless the children on his way to Jerusalem. The traveling party is somewhere near Jericho. The scene, according to the biblical account, is a happy interlude between a hostile encounter with the Pharisees, and a test posed by someone seeking eternal life.

The women and children have come to see Jesus. A golden-haired girl has arrived ahead of the others and stands on a ledge with Jesus' arm around her. A mother at far right wants her child there also, and is lifting her up. Other mothers—with children in arms or standing alongside—press close to Jesus. Disciples Peter (at left) and John (at lower right) attempt to restrain them. But Jesus' extended hand says, "Let the children come..." Peter's extended hand says, "Keep the children back."

All these early oils done for Kriebel and Bates, *Christ in Gethsemane* (1941), *Christ at Heart's Door* (1942), *The Lord Is My Shepherd* (1942), *The Boy Christ* (1944), *Christ at Dawn* (1945), and *Jesus, the Children's Friend* (1946), have identifiable prototypes in nineteenth century religious art. The themes they portray were common fare in Lutheran, Covenant, Methodist, and other Protestant churches, where they appeared in altar paintings, framed prints, or Sunday School and church paper reproductions.

In Rugby, North Dakota, at a reconstructed Pioneer Village, a sampling of this art can be seen in two buildings relocated from the surrounding area: The Zion Lutheran Church (now the All-Faiths Church) and the Norwegian House. Built in 1906, Zion Lutheran originally stood a few miles southwest of Rugby and had a largely Norwegian congregation. In the church is an altar painting of Christ in Gethsemane similar to Hofmann's. Hanging on the sanctuary wall is a print of *Christ the Good Shepherd*. Christ holds a staff and a small lamb while the mother sheep at right looks up at her lamb. A black sheep at left is mixed in with the other sheep—all features of the Sallman rendition. On a wall in the Norwegian House is a Lutheran confirmation certificate, dated 1889, containing four pictures: *Christ the Good Shepherd*; *Christ Knocking at the Door*; *The Last Supper*; and a picture of five small children in a circle. Sallman did renditions of all of them. This artwork then is typical of what could be found in Lutheran, Covenant, and other Protestant churches at the turn of the century.

His Presence, painted in 1946 (© K&B 1947), was particularly well received. This full figure Christ with upraised arms is showing nail-scarred hands to the disciples on the evening of the resurrection (John 20:19-20). The painting builds also on other biblical texts. From the Old Testament Sallman cited for inspiration Exodus 33:14 ("my Presence will go with you..."), and Malachi 4:2 ("the Sun of Righteousness, [risen] with healing in his wings"). The Exodus passage finds a sequel in Matthew 28:20, where the abiding presence of the risen Christ is promised to the church. The other scripture embodied in this painting is Revelation 1:18: "I am the living one; I died, and behold I am alive for evermore."

Sallman's radiant Christ enters here into a dark room, similar to the one in which the disciples were gathered. A bright light surrounds his head, and light emanates from his entire body. The setting is modern, as one can tell even more from the *His Presence* done by Sallman for the Covenant Church of Escanaba, Michigan (1960). Here the room has not only the floorboards, but a door, a door casing, and a baseboard from a turn-of-the-century house. Sallman wishes to convey that the resurrected Christ comes into dark rooms with his radiant presence today. The message is similar to *Christ at Heart's Door*, where the "room" is the human heart.

His Presence was further developed in *I Have Overcome the World*, done for First Methodist Church in Mason City, Iowa (1952), and *Behold He Cometh*, done for First Covenant Church in Rockford, Illinois (1967). In these paintings Christ stands atop the world. *The Triumphant Christ* at the South Jacksonville Presbyterian Church (1965) is another painting developing from *His Presence*. There the hands are lower down, and Christ is standing barefoot on grass.

In the late 1940s and early 1950s Sallman's output for Kriebel and Bates was steady. In 1948 *We Would See Jesus* (1947 © K&B 1948) was ready for distribution, and in the same year *(Mary the) Mother of Christ* (1948 © K&B 1948) and *Follow Thou Me* (1948 © K&B 1949). *We Would See Jesus* shows Jesus teaching in the temple at the time Greeks ask to see him (John 12:21). He is not teaching here, however, at least not at the moment. Sallman has him standing composed and serene, looking silently upward. The reason is that "the hour has come for the Son of man to be glorified" (v 23). A voice has just been heard out of heaven, answering Jesus' prayer that God's name be glorified. It says, "I have glorified it, and I will glorify it again" (v 28). The wonderment expressed by the crowd is their response to this voice (v 29).

(Mary the) Mother of Christ is a profile view of Mary who is wearing a deep blue cape over white. This picture was well-received, not just by Protestants but also Roman Catholics who were familiar with *The Blessed Mother* (1936), a pastel quite similar that appeared on a Scripture Text calendar for 1938. *Follow Thou Me* (1948 © K&B 1949) is essentially the 1940 oil, however, here Christ looks sideward in the other direction. The inspiration for this painting was John 21:22, which was Jesus' words to Peter after the resurrection: "What is that to you? Follow me!"

The next year Sallman did his rendition of *The Lord's Supper* (1949 © K&B 1949). Jesus and his disciples are in the Upper Room, but they are not eating the Passover meal. That has been completed, and now they are standing around the table singing a hymn (Mark 14:26; Matt 26:30). The table is small, already transformed into a communion table with a chalice and two empty plates.

Christ Our Pilot (1950 © K&B 1950) develops a late nineteenth/early twentieth century theme of the Christian life as a seagoing voyage where Jesus is piloting one's individual ship. The song, "Jesus, Savior, Pilot Me" (Edward Hopper 1871)[23] helped reinforce the image among Protestant Christians. The image of a sea pilot behind the wheel was also dear to Scandinavians, particularly Sallman, whose grandfather was a Baltic sea pilot.

Sallman almost certainly modeled *Christ Our Pilot* on an earlier picture very much like it. A glossy print found among surviving Kriebel and Bates materials shows an older seaman standing behind a young sailor boy piloting a ship. Quite possibly, this piece served as a war poster (the sailor boy wears a Navy coat and cap), but its provenance is not actually known.[24] In this picture the boy has both hands on the wheel. The seaman behind has his left hand on the boy's shoulder, and his right hand on the wheel. Water is pouring into the ship on the left. A circle of light, possibly a halo, surrounds the head of the older seaman. The seaman has a generous head of hair and a beard. He also wears a robe with a draped-over sash, and has no sailor's cap. He could well be Jesus.

The boy in the Sallman painting is small, but then so is the boy in this prototype. He holds the wheel with both hands. The Christ behind has the left hand on the boy's shoulder, and the right hand raised, pointing out the direction. Sallman has intentionally kept Christ's hands off the wheel, leaving it to the young pilot to do the actual navigating. The patch of blue overhead is all that remains of a cloudless sky when the voyage began. Black clouds are now threatening. The wind has also stirred up the water, which is about to lap over the side of the boat. Sallman has painted a threat into clouds made pink by the hidden sun. It is the Archenemy, on the prowl like a "roaring lion" (1 Peter 5:8).[25] Sallman rarely depicts Satan, but here he does so very subtly. A more vivid portrayal of Satan can be seen in *It Is Finished* (1958).

Into this picture Sallman has painted his own illness. As a young man he was sailing along on a calm sea, only to meet up with threatening clouds that nearly overwhelmed him. What he learned through this experience was that with Christ as one's pilot, no matter what the danger, one's life will be kept (Psalm 121:7-8); one will be safely led into the harbor of God's eternal Kingdom. *Christ Our Pilot* is third in demand after the *Head of Christ* and *Christ at Heart's Door*.[26]

Sallman was present at the Tenth International Luther League Convention, held at Michigan State in August 1951, to unveil his painting, *Thine Is The Power* (1951), an apocalyptic scene inspired by Revelation 6. Christ here is standing above four horsemen who are riding across a smoke-covered scroll. Behind the horsemen burns the fire of hell; above is a glowing mushroom cloud from a nuclear explosion.

The next painting for Kriebel and Bates was *He Arose* (© K&B 1951), a rendition of Christ ascending from the tomb, which follows the account in Matthew 28:2-7 where the guards are said to have become "like dead men" when the angel descended to roll back the stone. The look on the risen Christ is the typical Sallman look: serious, up and away.

Teach Me Thy Way (1951 © K&B 1952) takes its title from Psalms 27:11 and 86:11, with inspiration perhaps coming also from this hymn text by Frances Ridley Havergal:[27]

O teach me, Lord, that I may teach
The precious things thou dost impart
And wing my words, that they may reach
The hidden depths of many a heart.

Jesus here is sitting with a young boy in the shelter of a rock and the shade of an old olive tree. The setting is much the same as *The Boy Christ* (1944 © K&B 1945), the main difference being that Jerusalem is the background city. One can imagine that Jesus has stopped to rest along the Bethlehem road. Seeing a young boy, he has called him to come over. The boy knows Jesus, and has said to him, "Teach me your way." Now he listens attentively. This picture means to counterbalance the perception that Jesus appeared only before large crowds of adults. Sallman wants the viewer to know that Jesus has time for individuals, especially the young.

The Son of God (1952 © K&B 1952) was initially introduced to the public through the *Chicago Sun Times*, which announced the painting under the title, *Jesus Was a Little Boy*.[28] Pictured here is the small boy Jesus on the lap of his mother. A bright light surrounds his face, reminding the viewer that while this boy is a real child, he is also "the Son of God." Mary, dressed in blue, has a white cape over the head and shoulders. She looks down fondly at her child.

In 1954, Sallman was particularly busy. In addition to supplying Kriebel and Bates with four new oils, Sallman did a portrait of King Gustaf VI Adolf of Sweden, which was presented to the King via Pastor Holmberg of the Swedish Mission Covenant Church. *He Careth for You* (1954 © K&B 1954) was another painting done primarily for children and young people. It too derived inspiration from Sallman's illness, during which time he found great comfort in the words of 1 Peter 5:5-7: "God giveth grace to the humble. Humble yourselves therefore under the mighty hand of God, that he may exalt you in due time; casting all your care upon him, for he careth for you."

In *He Careth for You*, the Christ of antiquity is brought boldly into mid-twentieth century America. Three children—a brother and two sisters—are in the back yard of their home where play has been interrupted by the discovery of a sparrow with a broken wing. The boy holds the sparrow in his hands and is showing it to Jesus, who has stopped to sit with them. The older sister is attentive to her brother, but has a protective arm around her younger sister The younger sister is holding a doll and looking into the face of Jesus. A pet lamb is also there. Jesus, with arms around two of the children, looks not at them nor at the bird. His gaze is into the distance—this time because he is wondering what the children will be like when they are grown. Will they possess the humility and trust they now show in casting their cares upon him? Or will they, like so many adults, become arrogant and self-sufficient?[29] The boy and two girls—also the small girl's doll—wear American clothes of the 1950s. Background houses and a colonial church are also 1950 America. This unconcealed mixing of antiquity and modernity has had its share of critics, although it exists in artwork from all ages.[30]

Resurrection Morn (1954 © K&B 1954) is largely unknown. It develops from Mark 16:1-2, which reports the three women—Mary Magdalene, Mary the mother of James, and Salome—going early to the tomb Easter morning with spices. All three look troubled. At the lower right is the familiar Sallman entrance to the tomb—square, door-like, and bathed in a flood of light.

Jesus, the Light of the World (1955 © K&B 1956) is a full-figure portrait with the classic face of the 1940 oil in three-quarters profile. Jesus is pointing to himself, saying, "I am the light of the world" (John 8:12; 9:5). With his right hand, which is down to the side and slightly extended, he invites people to follow the Light (John 8:12b). Here Jesus wears sandals and is standing on grass.

Madonna and Christ Child (1955 © K&B 1956) is one of Sallman's most popular renditions of Mary with the baby Jesus. Mary is cradling the babe with one hand holding his tiny hand. He is kicking both legs. The two are looking into each other's eyes. The whole is framed by a circle of light, the lighter shades of which make a heart.

The nativity theme continues with *The Little Lord Jesus* (1956 ©K&B 1956), said by some to look like a painting by Correggio.[31] This picture is similar to the watercolor *The Nativity (of Christ)* (1947 © K&B 1948). In the present work Mary and the baby are centered in the Bethlehem stable, with Joseph looking on at upper left. Joseph is not eclipsed here, as in so many nativity paintings of an earlier era; Sallman has him as fully a part of the holy family. To the right are four shepherds, one of whom is a young boy.

Sallman did two Jesus of Nazareth paintings, the second of which Kriebel and Bates marketed under the title *Jesus of Nazareth* (1963 © K&B 1963). Both are head and shoulder portraits of Jesus, who is wearing a blue robe draped over the right shoulder. *Jesus of Nazareth I* (1956 © K&B 1956) makes a halo with fractured light, anticipating *Power and Glory* that Sallman will paint the following year.

A large painting, *Jean Sibelius* (1957) by Sallman, was unveiled at a memorial concert held in Sibelius' honor by the Nordic Philharmonic Society of Chicago on 24 November 1957. The painting was given to North Park College, and now resides in the Covenant Archives. In the portrait, Sibelius sits leisurely in a comfortable chair before his piano. A flag of Finland appears in clouds at the upper right, over which is printed in block letters the title of Sibelius' most famous work, "FINLANDIA."

Power and Glory (1957 © K&B 1958) makes a significant departure from all previous Sallman paintings. In fact, when the work was released, Sallman felt constrained to defend its indebtedness to "modern abstract influence." It does betray modern abstract influence, but that aside, the one earlier painting to which the present work should be compared is *His Presence* (1946), which in all likelihood served as a prototype. Jesus is now standing atop the world, not on floorboards or some other earth surface. The world, says Sallman, has become his footstool (Acts 7:49; cf. Isaiah 66:1). The ascending coil that surrounds the figure of Jesus makes refracted light, giving the painting its modern look. The setting is cosmic. Bright orange circles, seemingly from the sun, are rather light from God's heavenly throne (cf. Rev 21:23). The right hand of Jesus points heavenward. Stars also twinkle in outer space.

With the ascending coil, Sallman intends to create an impression of the "three rings of heaven," alluded to in 2 Corinthians 12:2. The upward ascent of the spiral is Sallman's way of stating that these realms can neither be defined nor measured. Nevertheless, he does say,

> I have proposed the geometric design of three heavenly domains: the first above the earth, the atmospheric heaven; the second, the astronomical heaven; and the third, paradise....up to the throne of God. From thence, the source of pure white light as it descends toward the earth, breaks up into the multicolored refractions, as we see and know

them. All this speaks of God's omnipotence, creative and sustaining power, his majesty and glory.

Christ is portrayed as the "Son" of Hebrews 1:2-3 "…whom [God] appointed the heir of all things, through whom also he created the world. He reflects the glory of God and bears the very stamp of his nature, upholding the universe by his word of power." Sallman continues, "A lamb has been placed in the tender care of our Lord, connoting that Christ himself was the Lamb of God, which taketh away the sins of the world. The sign of the cross with its implications is infused within the whole message."[32]

Sallman concludes his interpretation by citing inspiration received also from Psalm 148:

It was my desire to present, by divine illumination, an allegory of symphonic praise on canvas, unto my Lord and Savior, and to use symbols, materials and techniques to visualize somewhat the hymn of praise found in the 148th Psalm of David:

Praise the Lord!
   Praise the Lord from the heavens
   Praise him in the heights!
Praise him, all his angels
   Praise him, all his host!
Praise him, sun and moon
   Praise him, all you shining stars
   Praise him, you highest heavens…
   Let them praise the name of the Lord
   for his name alone is exalted
   his glory is above earth and heaven…
   Praise the Lord![33]

A chalk of *Power and Glory* was done for Northern Baptist Theological Seminary in 1963.

Abraham Lincoln (1958 © K&B 1958) was done in anticipation of the 150th anniversary of Lincoln's birth, 12 February 1959. Lincoln here is pictured reading his Bible by a window during the Civil War. Explosions light up the background. Sallman said about this painting,

For many years I was familiar with a quote attributed to him [Lincoln] concerning the Bible: "I am now profitably engaged in reading the Bible." After a long, diligent search for the origin and authenticity of this statement, I came upon the published facts with the aid of the librarian at the Chicago Historical Society. In a book entitled *The Soul of Abraham Lincoln* by Wm. E. Barton (Doran, 1920), we came upon this episode. Joshua F. Speed, a long-time friend and confidant of Lincoln, one who had free access to the executive mansion at any time, relates the following experience in one of his lectures on Abraham Lincoln. It happened during the summer of 1864, several months before Lincoln was assassinated: "As I entered the room, near night, he was sitting near a window intently reading the Bible. Approaching him, I said, "I am glad to see you so profitably engaged!" "Yes," said he, "I am profitably engaged!" "Well," said I, "if you have recovered from your skepticism, I am sorry to say I have not." Looking me earnestly in the face, and placing his hand on my shoulder, he said, "You are wrong, Speed; take all of this Book upon reason that you can and the balance on faith and you will live and die a happier man."[34]

The following year Sallman did for Kriebel and Bates *Jesus Our Savior* (1959 © K&B 1959), a contemplative pose of Jesus dressed in a yellow garment with a draped-over robe of rich blue. Hands clasped, he sits prayerfully looking upward, communing with God prior to his arrest (John 17). Sallman did this picture in chalk the same year for the Trinity Covenant Church of Oak Lawn, Illinois.

In 1960 Sallman painted the *Youth Christ* (1960 © K&B 1960), which invites comparison with Hofmann's *Christ at 12*. In the Hofmann work Jesus is older than in Sallman's *The Boy Christ* (1944 © K&B 1945), but not by much. Around the head here is a substantial halo.

Sallman put all his talent in rich backgrounding to work in *The Road to Emmaus* (1961 © K&B 1961), a landscape painting, basically, which portrays Jesus' resurrection appearance to the two disciples on the Emmaus Road (Luke 24:13-35). It is springtime, and Sallman outdoes himself in depicting nature's beauty. The color of the sky, the landscape, the flowers and the tree blossoms are truly extraordinary. Rolling hills conform nicely to reality, a happy change from the Colorado-looking mountains in *The Lord Is My Shepherd*.

If this picture has one shortcoming it is that the figures are too small. Also, quite surprising for a Sallman painting, one cannot be certain which figure is Jesus. The faces cannot be seen, and nothing can be decided by the apparel of the three. The man in the center is dressed in white, but he wears a kaffiyeh (Arab headdress), which is not seen on Jesus in any previous Sallman painting. Respective positions—also hand gestures—scarcely make Jesus any more obvious. About all we can say for certain is that Jesus is not the man on the right, who seems clearly to be extending the invitation to come into the village. If Jesus is the man on the left, then Sallman has portrayed him as the one who "appeared to be going further" (Luke 24:28). But Jesus could be the one in the center, slightly behind the other two, in which case he is in need of coaxing to come into the village (v 29). Sallman also did an unfinished oil of the three men close-up (*Men on Road to Emmaus* n.d.). In the unfinished work, the men are dressed differently, they have different hand gestures, but one still cannot identify Jesus. Of course, this is precisely what the Lucan text wants to report about the incident.

Small figures and rich background also characterize *Abraham on the Plains of Mamre* (1962), a painting in the Anderson University collection that does not seem to have been marketed by Kriebel and Bates. Abraham here is greeting the divine messengers at the "oaks of Mamre" (Gen 18:1-2). A beautiful large oak dominates the center of the painting. This is the only Sallman oil, so far as we know, depicting an exclusively Old Testament theme.

In his last years Sallman did five additional Christ portraits: *Pleading Savior* (1962); *The Smiling Christ* (1962); *Jesus of Nazareth II* (1963 © K&B 1963); *The Just One* (1964 © K&B 1964); and *Portrait of Jesus* (1966 © K&B 1966). Of these *The Just One* and *Portrait of Jesus* are of particular note. *The Just One* portrays Jesus with short curly hair, wearing a robe of lime green. It is the same basic portrayal as *Lord and Master* (1962), which Sallman did in other media.

Sallman's last two oils for Kriebel and Bates, *The Story of Gethsemane* (1964 © K&B 1964) and *Portrait of Jesus* (1966 © K&B 1966), redo his first two. *The Story of Gethsemane* reverts to features of the Hofmann classic, which his own *Christ in Gethsemane* had moved away from. Jesus faces left, once again, although here he looks in the direction of the viewer. The rock on which he leans butts up against a large olive tree. Gone is the "Higher than I" rock, its place being taken by a heavenly angel, present in many earlier Gethsemane paintings.

In Hofmann's *Christ in Gethsemane* and Sallman's own rendition earlier Jesus is praying before a table rock, much as one prays at the side of a bed. Here he lies on a flat rock, on his side. His hands are no longer folded; the one hand holds the other arm at the elbow. Whereas before it was basically Jesus at the rock, now we are given a panoramic view—of the garden, the Kidron Valley, and Jerusalem's wall. Flowers and trees are painted in all their springtime splendor. Details are more distinct than in earlier works. The background is also brightened by the light of the moon. One can clearly see the soldiers and others coming to arrest Jesus. In earlier paintings they were indiscernible. The three disciples behind the large olive tree are also distinctly painted, as are the eight disciples set apart further left (cf. Mark 14:32-35; Matt 26:36-39). In earlier pictures the eight disciples were not shown.

In *Portrait of Jesus* (1966 © K&B 1966) Sallman ends where he began—with a head of Christ. Only the title used is Jesus, not Christ. The face here does seem to be more friendly, more approachable, and more human, and there is even the trace of an emerging smile. Tones continue in brown, but the view in this portrait is frontal.

During Sallman's last years he painted a number of Methodist church leaders. A portrait of Texas Bishop William C. Martin was done in 1962, another of the Reverend Harry Denman, General Secretary of the Board of Evangelism for the Methodist Church, in 1963. In 1964 portraits were also painted of Dr. John Thompson and the Reverend Charles Ray Goff, successive pastors of Chicago Temple. A portrait of the Reverend Robert Bruce Pierce, who succeeded Goff, was done in 1967. At the time of his death, Sallman was working on portraits of Texas Bishop W. Kenneth Pope and Gaston Foote, pastor of First Methodist Church in Fort Worth. Both pieces were left unfinished.

[1] Personal communication from the Reverend Kenneth R. Strom, 19 January 1994.

[2] There is no connection in name between Warner Press and Warner Sallman.

[3] See further note 10.

[4] Letter from Sallman to Anthony Kriebel, 5 December 1940.

[5] Letter from Sallman to T. W. Anderson, President of the Covenant, 22 January 1941.

[6] Ibid.

[7] Letter from Sallman to Warner Press, 18 January 1941.

[8] Letter from Sallman to Kriebel and Bates, 17 December 1941.

[9] Letter from Sallman to T. W. Anderson, 22 January 1941.

[10] In the Kriebel and Bates inventory, now in the Sallman Collection at Anderson University, is a brown pen sketch of *Son of Man* (© K&B 1941) on the left page of an open Bible. Kriebel and Bates planned on using this for a series of "Jesus said" plaques to be produced by the Felsenthal Company of Chicago. These may be the plaques Bates came to discuss with Sallman the day he saw the *Head of Christ* in oil in Sallman's living room. The very fact that Kriebel and Bates went ahead and copyrighted the original—for whatever purpose—would be reason enough for Norstrum to argue the copyright question. In the Anderson University collection are also two reproductions of a small black and white ink sketch entitled *Son of Man* (n.d.). This sketch has Sallman's signature and the date 1924. On one reproduction "The Son of Man" is written in black pen below the picture.

[11] Letter from Sallman to Anthony Kriebel, 27 January 1941.

[12] Letter from Sallman to Anthony Kriebel, 26 October 1941.

[13] Letter from Sallman to Anthony Kriebel, 6 December 1941.

[14] Ibid.

15 David Morgan, "Sallman's *Head of Christ*: The History of an Image," *The Christian Century* 109/28 (7 October 1992): 868; idem., *Icons of American Protestantism*, 6.

16 The painting was a gift to the church from John D. Rockerfeller. It hangs in a chapel off the narthex.

17 The words are embodied also in William Cushing's hymn, "Hiding in Thee", which begins, "O Safe to the Rock that is higher than I...". See *Covenant Hymnal* 1931, #200; *Covenant Hymnal* 1950, #338.

18 Howard Ellis, *Story of Sallman's "Christ at Door"* (Chicago: Kriebel and Bates, 1944) 7.

19 Margaret Anderson, "His Subject Shaped His Life," *The War Cry* Central 2136 (9 December 1961): 8

20 Sallman is said to have had a fascination with the religious paintings of Plockhorst (and Hofmann) from an early age; see Olga Lindborg, "Another Picture of Jesus," *Our Covenant* 17 (1942): 68.

21 Taken from the hymn, "This Is My Father's World" (Malthie D. Babcock, *Covenant Hymnal* 1996, #57).

22 Howard Ellis, *Story of Sallman's "Boy Christ"* (Chicago: Kriebel and Bates, 1945) 5.

23 *Covenant Hymnal* 1950, #290.

24 Professor David Morgan of Valparaiso University, conversation with the author during a visit to the university. The artist is unknown; the print simply says © 1944 Extension, Chicago. For a picture see David Morgan, *Icons of American Protestantism*, 31.

25 Sylvia Peterson, *Story of Sallman's "Christ Our Pilot"* (Indianapolis: Kriebel and Bates, 1951).

26 M. Anderson, "His Subject Shaped His Life," 8.

27 "Lord, Speak to Me," *Covenant Hymnal* 1973, #534.

28 *Chicago Sun Times*, 14 June 1952, 10.

29 Sylvia Peterson, *Story of Sallman's "He Careth for You"* (Indianapolis: Kriebel and Bates, 1955).

30 See further chapter XII.

31 *The Nativity* by Antonio Allegri, called Correggio, was published in *Ladies Home Journal* 27/5 (April 1910): 15.

32 Interpretation supplied with the release of the painting by Kriebel and Bates in 1958.

33 Ibid.

34 Interpretation supplied with the release of the painting by Kriebel and Bates in 1960.

VIII

Sallman Art in Churches, Hospitals, Schools, Benevolence and Correctional Institutions

Sallman spent some twelve to sixteen hours on location doing finishing work. Sallman wasn't satisfied with the sacks lying on the other side of the pool. He just could not get them the way he wanted, and redid them at least three times. Nutter remembered Sallman's big strong hands and his quick movements while working. A cut-off broom handle stabilized his hand, and wads of fresh white bread were used for an eraser. (Completing *The Master Healer*, Thanksgiving 1960)

Over a forty-year period Sallman did commissioned works—large and small—for churches, chapels, hospitals, schools, student centers, reformatories, and homes for children and the elderly. In total, Sallman painted over thirty such works, including those done for the Salvation Army. Sallman also did collective works of glass art, a small one for a university student center, and a much larger one for the chapel of a children's home.

His institutional oils were not murals in the strict sense, for they were not painted directly on a wall. Except for one attempt on glass, and a couple oils on masonite, all were painted on canvas. The canvas was usually mounted on a wood frame, or, less frequently, affixed directly to the wall. Some of those affixed directly to a wall have not survived particularly well, usually because the wall was an outside wall of brick or cement block, which allowed moisture to seep in.

Sallman's earliest institutional paintings were done for Mission Covenant churches, where they were hung on the front wall of the sanctuary. Covenant churches did not have altars. Communion tables stood out in front of a center or corner pulpit, and behind, or to the side, sat the choir. Typically, then, a picture would hang above the choir loft, or else behind the pulpit on the front wall. In later years, when paintings were done for churches of other denominations, and Covenant church architecture underwent its own change, locations elsewhere in the church were selected, usually for oils of smaller size. Also, many Sallman paintings now situated outside church sanctuaries were moved there after the congregation relocated to another building, and in the new facility the painting was found unsuitable for the front of the sanctuary.

Before Sallman did these larger works he would usually make a preliminary visit to look over the setting, and decide how best to use the space available. The painting was then done at home. If it was too large for his attic studio, he would do it in sections, rolling up the finished portion and then painting the portion that remained. For two large church paintings Sallman used the facilities at North Park College. The *Ascension* for South Bend Covenant (1926) was done in a vacant college room during summer recess. But even here the panels had to be done in sections. The 1952 *Ascension of Christ* for Iron Mountain Covenant was painted in Nyvall Hall, the North Park Seminary building. This time school was in session, which allowed students and other interested people to stop by and watch the artist at work, which they did. Sallman worked on this painting an entire month, sometimes late into the night. After completion it was left on display at the school for a couple days, then shipped to Iron Mountain. Sallman's last oil for the First Covenant Church in Rockford, Illinois, *Behold He Cometh* (1967), was done right at the church.

After the painting was completed Sallman would roll up the canvas, place it in a tube, and send it by freight to its destination, or else he would drive it to the location himself. Many paintings were delivered on the top of Sallman's car. Mounting was done on location. Church paintings were typically mounted by the men of the congregation. Mission Covenant churches, comprised as they were largely of Swedes, were rarely without a good carpenter. In the later years Ruth, together with her sister and husband, Ethel and Bert Williams, made the trip with Sallman to deliver paintings. Bert was a contractor, and thus able to see to the details of properly mounting the painting. Sallman also took care to insure his paintings while they were in transit.

If Sallman accompanied the painting, or followed afterwards, he would typically stay just long enough to see that the painting was properly mounted, and then do whatever finishing work was necessary. In most cases only touch ups were required, although some instances demanded considerably more work on location. By the time of the painting's dedication, he was usually back home. If the dedication took place right away, or the location was close to home, he would make an effort to be present. Services of dedication were high moments, with invited guests, talks, special music, and sometimes a dramatic unveiling.

Frank Lloyd Wright believed that buildings must fit their environments, and designed them accordingly. Sallman similarly believed that paintings needed adaptation to the environments into which they were placed. The *Ascension* painted for the Covenant Church in Braham, Minnesota (1934) was done in three stylized panels that matched the other windows in the church sanctuary. Appropriately, Sallman completed for hospitals two paintings depicting Christ's healing ministry: *The Great Physician* (1958), for the Iowa Methodist Hospital in Des Moines, and *The Master Healer* (1960), for the Union Protestant Hospital in Clarksburg, West Virginia. The Des Moines painting also included flowers from outside the hospital. In *The Triumphant Christ* (1965) for the South Jacksonville Presbyterian Church, Sallman painted a foreground of pink azaleas and palm branches, typical of Florida in the spring. In this painting Jesus also stood barefoot on grass. In *Behold I Send You Forth* (1944), done for Bob Jones College, a background factory and mountains recreated the setting in Cleveland, Tennessee, where the college was located prior to 1947. The sky over the factory was appropriately gray.

Sallman's first church painting, so far as we know, was a large oil of the Ascension done in 1926 for the Mission Covenant Church in South Bend, Indiana. The motif was already familiar from earlier church paintings. At least two Chicago Covenant churches had Ascension paintings by other artists. One was in the large South Side Mission Covenant Tabernacle, at 31st and LaSalle, which was painted by the father or grandfather of Ingrid Bergman.[1] Ingrid attended the Tabernacle Sunday School. This was a mural, i.e., it was painted directly on the wall. After the church was sold to a black congregation in 1912, the features of Jesus were painted over and the skin color darkened to make Jesus look Afro-American. Sallman visited the tabernacle shortly before it was torn down, and expressed no disapproval of the alterations.[2]

Another *Ascension* was painted directly on the front wall of the old Grand Crossing Mission Covenant Church at 74th and Cottage Grove, now the St. Mark A. M. E. Zion Church. It was extant until late 1994, and in reasonably good condition. The artist is unknown. The painting bears neither signature nor date, but that could result from the side panels (which contained only scenery) having being painted over in a refurbishing and redecoration of the church for a fiftieth anniversary celebration in 1942. The mural after reduction is approximately 10 feet wide and 15 feet tall in the center. The ascending Christ, with left foot forward and right foot bent back, is enveloped in U-shaped clouds. Outstretched arms bless the eleven disciples, who are clustered below on a slab of rock. Some disciples are standing; some are on one or two knees; and one is bending to the ground. Some have one or both hands in the air. A village (Bethany?) can be seen in the background.

Sallman's painting in South Bend was for the old church located at Monroe and Main. The picture as a whole is similar to the *Ascension* at Grand Crossing. Whether that painting had any influence on Sallman one is not able to say, but the possibility cannot be excluded. The Grand Crossing *Ascension* almost certainly predated 1926, and Sallman would definitely have seen it at one time or another. The figures in the South Bend *Ascension* are Sallman's own; the ascending Christ compares most closely with the ascending Christ at Grand Crossing. But in detail these two paintings differ, e.g., at South Bend the clouds are not U-shaped, the disciples are gathered on a grassy knoll, not a rock, Peter holds a staff, trees at the side are different, and there is no background village.

Sallman's painting draws its primary inspiration from Acts 1:9 where the ascending Christ, surrounded by clouds, is taken into heaven. Onlooking disciples are clustered on a grassy knoll below; some are standing and some are kneeling on the ground. Some have one or both hands in the air. The prominent disciple left of center is Peter, who is holding a staff, for he is now shepherd of the flock. Christ is blessing the eleven with uplifted hands, where the inspiration is from Luke 24:50-51.

The painting was done on three sail-cloth panels, the total dimensions being 23 feet wide and 18 feet high. Originally the panels were divided by two large pillars. In 1959-60, when the painting was transferred to the new church, Sallman came to South Bend and repainted the panels so they would appear as one. The painting is now in the church foyer where large glass windows and after-dark lighting make it clearly visible to passersby.

The dedication and unveiling of the original work took place on Saturday evening, 27 March 1926, at which time Sallman was present to give the main talk. The service was said to be very moving. After a song by the Young People's Aid Society, who had given the painting, and a short talk by the pastor, Paul E. Johnson,

> the suspense became increasingly great.... The luxurious curtains were gently drawn aside and fastened at either side of the arch by a blue silk cord... The effect was marvelous...The greatest and deepest effect was probably produced upon the "Older Pilgrims" who have walked many a happy step, as well as many a weary mile with Christ and who long for his return. Their emotions could no longer be controlled and the fountains of the deep broke forth, and the tears of joy were loosed, and through it all the sunshine of love for him shone forth supreme in all its glorious splendor. It was a scene that is not soon forgotten. It was as one making, for the first time, that sacred acquaintance with him and being brought into sweet Fellowship and Communion.[3]

During the Depression Sallman did an *Ascension* (1934) for the old Mission Covenant Church in Braham, Minnesota. Though vibrantly painted on masonite, this piece shares the three-panel format of the South Bend painting. Differing from other Sallman works, the ascending Christ here resembles an El Greco—the body slender and straight. The face, while similar to the Sallman face of the 1924 and 1940 oils, is more elongated. The eleven disciples cluster together on grass, all standing, except for one who is on his knees. Again Peter stands in the left foreground with only the bottom of his staff visible.

The panels here were stylized to simulate windows matching windows in the church. This contemporized the painting in that one could easily imagine looking through chancel windows at the Ascension taking place outside. When the church relocated to North Braham in 1967, the painting was placed on a foyer wall in the new building, next to the stairs going down into the basement. Currently it is mounted on the back wall of the sanctuary.

A third *Ascension* was done in 1939 for the old Swedish Mission Church in Iron Mountain, Michigan. Though no longer extant, this painting measured 13 feet wide and 7 feet, 9 inches high and hung above the choir loft. Sadly, Swedish Mission Church burned to the ground in January 1950.

Jesus again ascends into clouds with arms outstretched—his figure slender, as in the Braham painting. The disciples looking on from a grassy knoll differ little from earlier renditions—some are sitting, some are standing, and some are kneeling or partially kneeling on the ground. Some have one or both hands in the air. The configuration most closely resembles that in the *Ascension* completed two years later for the Salvation Army meeting hall on 59th Street in Chicago (1941). The disciple third from the left has both hands extended upward. The center disciple has the left hand raised. And the disciple third from the right, who is Peter, holds a staff in the left hand. What Sallman seems to have done—here and in the Salvation Army painting—is to have taken two disciples from the South Bend painting, the one third from the left and the one third from the right, and exchanged them. The center disciple also has the other hand raised.

In 1952 Sallman completed another *Ascension of Christ* for the new Iron Mountain church. Though considerably larger, this painting reproduces the Swedish Mission painting in almost every detail. The main difference is the figure of Christ, which now is more full like the Christ figure in South Bend. The canvas measures 20 feet in width by 23 feet in height—the largest oil painting by Sallman to be found anywhere. Sallman has named the eleven disciples from left to right: James the lesser, Philip, Matthew, Thaddeus, James son of Zebedee, Thomas, John son of Zebedee, Andrew, Simon Peter, Simon the zealot, and Bartholomew.

Not all institutional paintings were large artworks. Already in the mid-1930s Sallman was painting smaller-size oils—portraits, for the most part, of individuals and of Christ—for schools, churches, and later on for retirement centers. In 1935 he did a *Portrait of C. J. Wilson* for North Park, which was presented to the school as a college class gift. Wilson was North Park professor of science. Two years later Sallman did an oil of the *Head of Christ* (1937), on masonite, for the Scandinavian Lutheran Mission Church in Nelson, British Columbia. Then in 1940, the year the classic *Head of Christ* was painted, Sallman did another *Head of Christ* in oil over a 1924 print of *Son of Man*, which is the same picture as the copyrighted version, except for a white background. This oil was a seminary class gift to North Park.

Because of copyright restrictions Sallman could not reproduce his classic portrait at will. Yet he did manage to paint a large *Head of Christ* in 1956 for the refurbished sanctuary of his home church, Edgewater Covenant, after a fire destroyed the church interior. It measures 8 feet by 10 feet, and is the largest of the Sallman Christ heads. Another *Head of Christ* was done in 1967 for Covenant Village in Northbrook, Illinois. It too is the classic picture, except that the face looks the other way.

In 1940-1941 Sallman was busy doing interpretations of Johann Heinrich Hofmann's well-known *Christ in Gethsemane* (1890). He painted this artwork for at least five Mission Covenant Churches: Lund, Wisconsin (1940), South Chicago, Illinois (1940), Red Wing, Minnesota (1940), Fresno, California (1941), and Stockholm, Wisconsin (1941). Sallman noted at the lower right of the Lund painting, "Adapted from Hofmann's Christ in Gethsemane." The other paintings were similarly documented.

Jesus in this picture is portrayed in the Garden of Gethsemane prior to his arrest. He prays, "Not my will, but thine be done" (Luke 22:42). He faces left, kneeling before a table rock with hands folded on the rock. At the left stands a large tree with thorns growing at its base. To the right and in the background three disciples cluster together. Barely visible in the background are Jerusalem and a line of approaching soldiers on the road.

Hofmann paintings of Christ were very popular at the time.[4] His *Christ in Gethsemane* was widely available in prints, published frequently in church and Sunday school papers,[5] and reproduced by artists in churches everywhere. In the old Mission Covenant Church of Stambaugh, Michigan, for example, was a Hofmann *Christ in Gethsemane* painted by an artist named Robert Verme of Minneapolis. Other Hofmann interpretations, not by Sallman, were done for the old Batavia (Illinois) Covenant Church (1937); the Covenant church in Ironwood, Michigan; the Covenant Church in Ridgway, Pennsylvania; as well as the Ebenezer Lutheran Church (Paulina and Foster Avenues) in Chicago.

Sallman interpretations of the Hofmann classic are all quite similar. The greater height of the Lund and Stockholm paintings allow for more of the large olive tree. In the Fresno painting, Jesus has a blue robe over a rose-colored shirt, whereas in the other paintings the shirt is white and the robe a deep purple. The South Chicago painting was nearly lost in a 1979 church fire that badly damaged the 100-year old frame building. The canvas came loose from the wall, and had to be reattached. It was also washed at the time, and touched up by a woman artist currently visiting from Sweden.

Once Sallman had done his own *Christ in Gethsemane* (1941 © K&B 1942), he reproduced this picture for the Covenant Church in Manchester, Connecticut, changing its title to *Christ in the Garden of Gethsemane* (1942). This painting hung above the choir loft in the chancel of the old church on Spruce Street. In the present church it hangs in the narthex.

Sallman completed *The Good Shepherd* in 1943 for the Covenant Church in Stephenson, Michigan. The work differs from the K&B copyrighted version (*The Lord Is My Shepherd* 1942 © K&B 1943) in that the sheep surrounding Jesus are configured differently. They are also approaching the top of a knoll, not walking on level ground.

Two churches received *Christ at Heart's Door* (1942 © K&B 1942): the Covenant Church in Dawson, Minnesota, in 1950; and the Covenant Church in Norway, Michigan in 1953. Both repeat in all essentials the K&B original. Earlier Sallman had done a *Christ Knocking at the Door* (1947), which was a different picture entirely, and an adaptation from Zabateri, duly noted in the lower left of the picture. Purchased for the First Covenant Church of Fort Dodge, Iowa, the Zabateri adaptation depicts Christ facing the door from the other direction. He also holds a staff. No light emanates from his person, but a tiny lattice window shows the same inner darkness as the better-known Sallman work. This door has a handle, and above it a round key lock. The face of Christ closely resembles the 1940 oil. A circle contains the scene with a square outer frame allowing for symbols and decorations in the corners. Originally on the front wall of the old church, this painting now hangs in the present church above the doorway in the fellowship hall.

His Presence (1946 © K&B 1947) was not done for a church until 1960, when Sallman painted it for the Covenant Church of Escanaba, Michigan. Already in 1952, however, an embellished version of this successful full-figure portrait of Christ appeared in *I Have Overcome the World* (1952), presently in the First Methodist Church of Mason City, Iowa, where it hangs in the back balcony of the sanctuary. The painting is actually untitled, but seemingly builds upon John 16:33, which speaks of Christ having overcome the world by his death and resurrection. Sallman revised the painting in March 1959, superimposing, in lighter tones, a cross over the person of Christ. Sallman presented the painting originally to his friend, the Reverend George Truman Carl, who became pastor of First Methodist in 1957. Carl had a particular fondness for *His Presence*, two prints of which hang elsewhere in the church.

The figure of Christ in *I Have Overcome the World* is essentially the figure of *His Presence*. The difference between the works lies in the coloring and refracted light around the head. In *I Have Overcome the World*, the light, besides making a halo, brightens the earth upon which Christ is standing. Gone are the floorboards of *His Presence*. Sallman develops a space motif by portraying planets swirling in space. Many of these features carry over into *Power and Glory* (1957 © K&B 1958), as well as into *Behold He Cometh* (1967), done for the First Covenant Church in Rockford, Illinois.

His Presence, painted for the Covenant Church in Escanaba, differs from the K&B original in that a large halo of yellow, pink, and blue concentric circles surrounds the head and upper body of Christ. Christ stands on floorboards, as in the original, but here one can see a background door and baseboard from a turn-of-the century house. The message remains the same as the copyright version: the Christ of Easter comes with a revealing presence into our houses.

In 1965 Sallman did *The Triumphant Christ* for the South Jacksonville Presbyterian Church in Jacksonville, Florida. This fine painting, which also develops from *His Presence*, is mounted at the front of a prayer chapel in the church. In a message to the congregation, Sallman said, "In this painting I have tried to present Christ with the living realism of the appearance in the Upper Room and a suggestion of the brightness of his glory on the Mount of Transfiguration."[6]

The full body of Christ and the frontal view is much the same as in *His Presence*, but the face is different. The hands also are not raised, but extend outward as in Thorvaldsen's *Come Unto Me* statue.[7] But Christ is not beckoning. He shows his nail-scarred hands and is bestowing peace. Inspiration for this painting comes from John 20:19-20, where the resurrected Christ says to his disciples, "Peace be unto you," and then shows them his hands. The words above the painting are "Peace Be Unto You."

The other major difference between this painting and *His Presence*, is that here Christ possesses a multi-ringed halo, and refracted light surrounds his person, the glory of his transfiguration. We see the halo and refracted light somewhat differently in *I Have Overcome the World*, and the halo only in *Behold He Cometh*. In the Jacksonville painting Christ stands barefoot on grass, not on a wood floor, or a world in space. Deep pink azaleas and palm branches appear in the lower foreground, a familiar Florida sight in early spring. Sallman had seen the azaleas on his first visit to view the chapel.

Behold He Cometh (1967), a third painting evolving from *His Presence*, was Sallman's last commissioned church work. He painted it for the new First Covenant Church of Rockford, Illinois, where it hangs in the foyer. Christ is once again atop the world, in this instance saying, "Behold, I come quickly" (Revelation 3:11).[8] Around his head and upper body are concentric halos, the outer of which make the colors of the rainbow. The rainbow is a reminder of God's promise. Beams emanate downward from the person of Christ, as they do in *I Have Overcome the World*. This painting, however, has no refracted light.

Not all of Sallman's institutional paintings repeat themes of earlier artists, or themes done for Kriebel and Bates. In 1944 Sallman did an oil, *Behold I Send You Forth*, for Bob Jones College, located then in Cleveland, Tennessee. The school now resides in Greenville, South Carolina. Commissioned by the class of 1943 as a gift to the school, the painting develops the missionary text of Matthew 10:16. Jesus stands behind a young boy and girl about to embark on a life of Christian service. His hands rest upon their shoulders. The figure of Jesus, almost transparent except for his face, fades out completely at waist level. Sallman again wants to portray a Jesus who is hidden yet present. The boy and girl carry Bibles. The girl also has a notebook and pen in hand. At the left stands a college building, and in the background right a factory of Cleveland, Tennessee.

Sallman did a most extraordinary painting, *Walk in the Light* (1951), for the All Faith Chapel at the Illinois State Training School for Boys (now the Illinois Youth Center) in St. Charles, Illinois. It is large—about 16 feet in width and 8 feet in height. The chapel at the time was being renovated after a fire, and it was decided that the rededication would be as a chapel for boys of all faiths. A committee consisting of the Assistant Superintendent, the Protestant, Catholic, and Jewish chaplains, and Sallman met to decide on a theme for a new painting, and agreed that the painting would have to be less explicitly Christian than the former one, which was of the Resurrection.

The general theme and setting of the completed work—which is untitled—are reasonably clear. The wooded area is the environs of St. Charles, the Fox River flows in the background, and Chicago lies in the distance. The burning stacks in the background right are either the oil refineries of Whiting, or the steel mills of Gary, Indiana. The boys in the painting are the boys of St. Charles reformatory. A group in the foreground focuses its attention on a light shining through the trees. The boy near the center, both arms uplifted, embraces the light. Though probably the sun, this light is the only suggestion of the divine. In preliminary meetings with the chaplains Sallman had proposed an angel, or simply the head of an angel, but neither was accepted. Some boys are walking the road that leaves St. Charles, passes over a river, and wends its way through green farm land ending finally in Chicago. These boys are returning home. Boys in the picture are both black and white. The man with his arm around one of the boys is a staff member of St. Charles.

Mary and Martha with Jesus (1954) was done for the Bethany Methodist Home in Chicago, located only a short distance from where Sallman once lived on Ashland Avenue. This large oil derives its inspiration from Luke 10:38-42, which records a visit of Jesus to the home of Mary and Martha. Mary listens to Jesus teach from an open scroll on his lap. Martha enters the room with a tray of food and drink. Jesus looks upward, his right hand upraised. There is very little detail in this painting—some flowers in a vase, a jug on the floor, a silver goblet (?) on a background table, and a vine rising on a trellis outside the window. A later Kriebel and Bates watercolor of the same picture (1961 © K&B 1962) has more detail.

Sallman did two large hospital paintings. For the Iowa Methodist Medical Center in Des Moines, Iowa, he did *The Great Physician* (1958). Originally located in an older part of the hospital that has since been destroyed, it now hangs in the hospital chapel. The painting is inspired by Mark 2:1-12, the story of a paralytic who was lowered through a house roof so Christ might heal him. Christ is standing in the foreground right, extending a hand to the paralytic who is coming down on a stretcher. Sallman gives this interpretation:

> The scene is Capernaum, north side of the Sea of Galilee, shown through the doorway at right. The little fishing village of Bethsaida can be seen across the water. There is some uncertainty as to the owner of the house. It may have been Peter's home because of the location on the lake.
>
> I made Peter quite prominent in the foreground [in the center—holding back the crowd and looking left]. He was a rough character, as you can tell by his hair and dress, and he is brown from being outdoors. Immediately above Peter is the owner of the house [the man with outstretched arms looking at Jesus]...disturbed because the roof of his house has been broken.
>
> To the left of the owner is the figure of John, one of the disciples and James' brother. [The brothers were] athletic young men, described in the Scriptures as Sons of Thunder. The young lad to the extreme left is John Mark.[9] The elderly woman between the owner and John is the mother-in-law of Peter.
>
> I have put two Scribes and Pharisees in the lower right hand corner, and two to the left of Christ. The two on the right are really supposed to be seated (Mk 2:6), but I placed them standing very low in the picture so as to be sure the natural line of vision would proceed from the immediate lower figures up to Christ. They are ready to challenge him on his authority to say that the paralytic's sins are forgiven. "Only God can do that," they say.
>
> The extended hand of Christ portrays his assistance to the paralytic, getting him down to the ground, symbolic of the ready and willing hands of Christ to help those who are in distress and pain.[10]

Sallman adds, with respect to the willing hands of Christ,

> This is meant also to symbolize the hospital's readiness to heal and help all who turn to it for care. The dominant element in the picture is the faith of the four men which caused the incident to take place.
>
> I introduced the centurion [man with helmet in the rear of the picture] to bring in another miracle of healing. The centurion had come earlier to Christ, asking him to heal his servant.[11]

There are seventy-two figures in all. Sallman said regarding the assembled, "I have tried to portray people in all walks of life—indicated by their clothing: shepherds, townspeople, rich and poor, merchants, people of all ages."[12] Flowers in the niche are done in pastels, making them barely noticeable.

> They are field flowers, which are so abundant in Palestine. While they are really very colorful, only the pastel shades were used so as not to distract the eye from the direction of the Lord's figure.
>
> Somewhere in the room there would probably be olive oil lamps hanging from the ceiling. I had a chandelier made of seven oil lamps placed between the ceiling beams, with the lights flickering for the purpose of off-setting the straight lines of the beams. Our postman looked at the painting and the lamps caught his eye at once. When my wife, who had been away, saw the picture, she said, "The lamps will have to go. They are too prominent and draw your attention from the figure of Christ." I was completely dejected because I had designed the lamps and spent one and a half days putting them in. But after thinking it over, I took my brush and painted them out.
>
> The hand of the baby being held by its mother [foreground, in front of and to the left of Peter] was originally extended across the man back of the baby [who has both arms outstretched]. But the hand of the baby did not match well with the stripes in the man's garment, which were added later, so I placed the baby's hand on the mother's shoulder.
>
> The stretcher is homemade. The pallet on it is probably stuffed with straw. The ceiling is made of boards. Brush was gathered and used to cover the boards to a certain thickness and clay was added to form a kind of insulation. Tile was placed over the clay. The splintered boards are shown as is the tile, but none of the brush, for, because of its bushiness, that would have detracted from Christ. All lines in the picture lead to Christ.[13]

When Sallman arrived with the painting strapped to the top of his car, Donald Cordes of the hospital was there to meet him. Cordes remembers there being much excitement at the hospital as people gathered to watch Sallman do the finishing work. At one point Sallman turned to Cordes and asked, "What shall I put in the niche in the wall?" Donald said he didn't know. Warner told him to think of something. Donald said, "Well, since the near-by window looks out on the countryside, it might be a good idea to have a vase with flowers." Warner painted a vase with flowers. "What about the sash on Peter's robe?" Warner didn't like it. Did Donald? Donald didn't know. It looked all right to him. But with a few quick strokes Warner went completely over the robe, making the sash lower, where he wanted it. Sallman sought to involve his audience the moment the work was being created.

Sallman painted *Baptized in Christ* in 1960 for the North Side Christian Church (Disciples of Christ) in Chicago. It is attached directly to the wall above the baptistry, which is at the front of the church. The painting, approximately 8 feet wide and 10 feet tall, pictures the resurrected Christ above the Jordan River. The lower part of his garment fades out over the background mountains. Christ stretches out his arms, much as he does in *The Triumphant Christ* (1965). The painting intends to depict Christ as the expectant presider over the place and moment of Christian baptism.

The other large hospital painting was *The Master Healer* (1960 © Union Protestant Hospital 1961), done for the Union Protestant Hospital in Clarksburg, West Virginia, merged since 1971 with St. Mary's Hospital into the United Hospital Center. This 6 feet, 8 inches by 12 feet painting originally hung in the main lobby of the hospital that was newly-built in 1959-1960, but now hangs in the hospital's north wing. Sallman's inspiration here is from John 5:2-9, the story of Jesus healing the man at the Pool of Bethesda. Jesus stands prominently in the foreground, before a lame man sitting by the pool. Both hands are held out to the man—the right hand lifted, beckoning him to get up. The man, on a rumpled garment, looks up at Jesus.

A number of onlookers are variously portrayed—two curious men behind Jesus look on, a man sits on steps across the pool, a mother holds a babe in her arms, and so on. One man across the pool, with his head resting on one arm, looks skeptical. All five pillars of a Roman-looking pool are visible. The area above the pool is open to the sky, where one sees the sun shining through. Sunlight here is of particular significance. Sallman describes the painting,

> In this porticoed place of five porches or alcoves, the sunlight penetrates the surrounding darkness, revealing the assembly of persons with assorted human needs. Also, the sunlight of God's love and compassion is present in the person of Jesus Christ, responding with divine power to their physical and spiritual needs. The lesson portrayed here is that in the midst of misery, agonizing pain, corruption and sin, Christ often invades the premises of individuals, seeking with tender compassion to help, heal and restore life to one of love, joy, and peace in Him.[14]

Before doing the painting, Sallman made a trip to Clarksburg to look over the setting. A month later he returned with the painting 75 percent complete. Cliff Nutter, who was present at the time and had constructed a frame for the painting, estimated that Sallman spent some twelve to sixteen hours on location doing finishing work. Sallman wasn't satisfied with the sacks lying on the other side of the pool. He just could not get them the way he wanted, and redid them at least three times. Nutter remembered Sallman's big strong hands and his quick movements while working. A cut-off broom handle stabilized his hand, and wads of fresh white bread were used for an eraser.

Christ Healing the Blind Beggar (1963) is a small oil (approximately 40 inches by 45 inches) painted for the Belmont Methodist Church in Belmont, Massachusetts, where it hangs over a fireplace in the church lounge. Inspired by John 9, this painting is a side view of Jesus reaching to touch the eye of a beggar sitting along the path to Jerusalem. Jesus' other hand is cupped, probably holding the clay.

Another small oil by Sallman, *Safe in the Arms of Jesus* (1965), hangs in the narthex of Grace Methodist Church in South Bend, Indiana. Here the familiar Sallman face of Jesus is surrounded by the happy faces of children. Even Jesus has a slight smile. The painting was done in memory of Forest Neal "Skippy" Hay, a five year-old boy tragically killed by an automobile. The happy faces of Jesus and the children are a testimony to the Christian hope amidst this and every other human tragedy.

Sallman also worked on glass and in glass. One artwork on glass, *Christ of the Campus* (1946), was painted for the Wesley Foundation at the University of Alabama in Tuscaloosa. This small portrait of Jesus, with supplemental artwork on the surrounding panels, is done against a background of simulated stained glass. Jesus looks upward—similar to *Jesus Our Savior* (1959 © K&B 1959). The face has no resemblance to the 1924 and 1940 portraits. The work looks to be experimental, and Sallman did not, so far as we know, repeat it elsewhere. The portrait was painted before an assembled congregation in February 1946. The panels and corners were done later, and installed the following Christmas. Originally the piece hung in the Sallman Prayer Chapel of the old Wesley Center. Now it is housed in the library of the present building, encased in a box wired for illumination.

More successful were the stained glass windows Sallman designed for an English Tudor-style chapel of the Methodist Children's Home in Detroit, Michigan (1952). Five collective artworks are here embodied in seventeen small and large stained glass windows. The windows depict biblical and devotional scenes, liturgical symbols, and children from around the world. Sallman designed all but one of the major windows, and most likely the small windows containing the liturgical symbols.

The Nativity Scene, a three-sectioned chancel window, depicts the Nativity and the Beginning of Life. In the center is Mary and Joseph with the baby in a manger. At the left are the adoring shepherds, and in the right window the adoring wise men. In the tracery above appears the hand of God on the left; the Agnus Dei (Lamb of God) in the center; and the descending dove on the right. Together these represent the Trinity: Father, Son, and Holy Spirit.

Jesus Blessing the Loaves and Fishes is at the left in a three-sectioned balcony window. Before Jesus stands a young boy. Behind is a man—perhaps Andrew—looking on. The inclusion of the young boy shows that Sallman followed here the John 6:1-14 account, where a young boy figures prominently in providing the food. *Jesus with the Children* is at the right, a somewhat different configuration than in *Jesus the Children's Friend* (1946 © K&B 1947), but inspired by the same Matthew 19:14 text (and parallels): "Of such is the Kingdom." In the center window is the familiar *Christ Our Pilot* (1950 © K&B 1950). This window means to address the departing worshiper with the words: "Savior, pilot me."

On either side of the nave are depicted *The Children of the World*. They are, beginning at the northwest corner: an English choir boy and a Puerto Rican girl; an African boy and an American Indian girl; a French boy; a Dutch girl; a Canadian girl and a Palestinian boy; a Japanese girl and a Chinese boy; and an Indian Nepalese girl. Compare the Joseph G. Reynolds "A little child shall lead..." window in stained glass at the Washington National Cathedral in Washington, DC.

[1] The Tabernacle at 31st and LaSalle was erected in 1877, and it was here that the organizational meeting of the Mission Covenant Church took place on 19 February 1885.

[2] A final service was held there to which Covenanters were invited. Sallman attended the service with the Reverend Ralph Hanson, from whom this recollection comes.

[3] Paul E. Johnson, "Young People Present Mural to Their Church," *The Covenant Companion* Old Series 5/6 (June, 1926): 23.

[4] William F. McDermott, "A Visit to a Cathedral," *The Chicago Daily News*, (6 February 1943), 7.

[5] See e.g., *Covenant Companion* Old Series 6/4 (April 1927): front cover; *Epworth Herald* 41/12 (22 March 1930): 15, with an article by Cecil S. Smith; *War Cry* Central 760 (20 July 1935) with an accompanying article; and *War Cry* Central Easter 798 (11 April 1936): 13.

[6] In a letter written from the Robert Meyers Hotel in Jacksonville, 27 March 1965.

[7] It stands in Vor Frue Kirke in Copenhagen. For a picture see *Our Covenant Youth* 13/35 (28 August 1932): 1.

[8] The inspiration for this painting is not John 16:33, as stated in the caption below the picture accompanying my article, "Warner E. Sallman: A Centenary Tribute to a Covenant Artist," *The Covenant Companion* 81/7 (July 1992): 9.

[9] Thought by some to be the author of Mark's gospel.

[10] From a brochure explaining the painting available at the hospital.

[11] Ibid.

[12] Ibid.
[13] Ibid.
[14] Interpretation on back of a print of the painting available at the hospital.

IX

Crown of Thorns and Other Watercolors and Drawings

Sallman began doing watercolors at an early age, having learned the technique from his father who was practiced in this medium.

A large portion of Sallman's output consisted of watercolors and drawings in various media—pencil, pen, chalk, crayon, and charcoal. Sallman worked largely in pen and ink as a commercial illustrator, and even after he began doing religious artwork in the 1920s through the early 1940s, he worked primarily in these media. Sallman's first sketch of the famous Christ head was in pencil, and the second in charcoal.

The frieze for the Salvation Army at Chicago's Century of Progress was in crayon. There were also the hundreds of chalks or crayons of his *Head of Christ*, or other well-known pictures, which Sallman did before live audiences. Sallman painted in oil during the early years, but these other media dominated.

Some surviving artworks in pencil—also in charcoal, pen, crayon, and watercolor—were preliminary to a more professional work Sallman intended to do later, usually in oil. Undated pencil sketches of *Son of Man* survive, although none is the original. A pencil of *Naming the Salvation Army* [1933], also survives, which was one of the drawings Sallman did for the Salvation Army exhibit at the Century of Progress. A surviving *Christ in Gethsemane* [1942] in pencil may have anticipated the Kriebel and Bates oil (1941 © K&B 1942), or else the painting done for the Covenant Church in Manchester, Connecticut (1942). A pencil and pen sketch of *Thine Is the Power* [1951] survives, the same picture as the oil Sallman did in 1951 for the Luther League Convention at Michigan State. *Teach Me Thy Way* [1951] survives in pencil, and is the same as the like-named oil (1951 © K&B 1952), except that a large tree branch is in the upper right. A surviving pencil of *The Son of God* [1952] is the same as the K&B oil (1952 © K&B 1952), except that Mary and the boy Jesus are facing the other way.

Christ in the Clouds (n.d.) is a pencil sketch of Christ similar to what appears in *His Presence* (1946 © K&B 1947), except that the left foot is slightly forward. Perhaps this was for the 1952 Iron Mountain *Ascension of Christ* painting, but we cannot be sure. Both *The Light That Shineth* (1954 © K&B 1954) and *Ready to Go—Ready to Stay—!* (1954 © K&B 1954) survive in pencil. *The Light That Shineth* differs from the oil only in that there is no cross on the front of the pulpit.

A red pencil of *His Presence* [1960] survives with an overlay. The overlay outlines a doorway in the background, which compares with the oil done for the Covenant Church in Escanaba, Michigan (1960), where a doorway is visible. But the doorways are not exactly the same. The original *His Presence* shows no doorway at all.

A preliminary sketch composition exists for *The Blind Beggar Healed* (1962), an oil done the same year for the Belmont Methodist Church in Belmont, Massachusetts. *Jesus in Gethsemane* [1964] is a pencil of Jesus as he appears in *The Story of Gethsemane* (1964 © K&B 1964). A sketch in pencil survives for *The Triumphant Christ*, a painting done in 1965 for the South Jacksonville Presbyterian Church in Jacksonville, Florida. A photographed sketch survives for *Safe in the Arms of Jesus* [1965], the oil Sallman did in 1965 for the Grace Methodist Church of South Bend, Indiana.

Sometimes Sallman did his preliminarily sketch in charcoal. In the James and Gene Sallman collection is a charcoal *Head of Christ*, 24 inches by 30 inches, dated 1964, which was intended to precede a painting of the same size. Since 1964 was the year Sallman painted the *Head of Christ* in oil for the Salvation Army chapel in Minneapolis, it is possible that this sketch anticipated that painting, which measures 36 inches by 48 inches.

A crayon of *He Careth for You* (1952), done prior to the copyrighted oil (1954 © K&B 1954), survives. This drawing differs in that in the upper right a nurse is holding a baby. This piece was later given to Sylvia Peterson Knudson, as a memorial to Sylvia's husband Ray.

Other preliminary or experimental works Sallman did in watercolor. An unfinished *Jesus, the Children's Friend* (1946), in pencil, watercolor, and gouache, survives. It was done the same year as the oil (1946 © K&B 1947), and like the oil does not show the sandaled foot of Jesus. The oil original contains a rock hiding the foot. A black and white reproduction (with paint) of the same work survives as well, and it includes the sandaled foot, as does the copyrighted print.

A watercolor of *We Would See Jesus* [1947] survives, which is the same basic picture as the like-named oil (1947 © K&B 1948), except that the figures in the crowd around Jesus are different. *The Emmaus Road* (1961) surviving in watercolor and chalk is similar to *The Road to Emmaus* in oil (1961 © K&B 1961), but with less detail: no light shining on the travelers, no tree with blue blossoms, no tree to the left of the travelers, no bird in flight, and no clouds over Jerusalem.

Some well-known K&B pictures survive in pen sketch, such as *Christ in Gethsemane* (1946 © K&B 1946); *Christ at Heart's Door* (1946 © K&B 1946); *The Lord Is My Shepherd/Good Shepherd* (1946 © K&B 1946); *The Boy Christ* (1946 © K&B 1946); and *Christ at Dawn* (1946 © K&B 1946). These were not preliminary sketches, but sketches done after the oils were completed for additional marketing of the prints. Sallman finished the sketch *Go Ye* (1945) and the watercolor *Mary and Martha with Jesus* (1961 © K&B 1962) after the respective oils were completed, in both cases to present the artwork to a different audience.

America's church-going audience—largely, but not exclusively, Protestant— became introduced to the Sallman watercolors and drawings on calendars, church bulletin covers, devotional booklets, and other church promotional material that was marketed largely by Kriebel and Bates. Many watercolors and drawings were originally done for bulletin covers. Others were prepared for post-War evangelistic efforts by the Methodist Church, a planned biography on the Reverend Dwight L. Moody (*D. L. Moody Sketches* [1948]), and for publications such as, *The Family Altar*, *The Christian Advocate*, *The Upper Room*, *The* (American) *Bible Society Record*, and a Chicago political magazine called *Lightnin'*. Often artworks were used for more than one purpose.

A number of extant watercolors and drawings are of unknown provenance. While it is true that the bulk of Sallman artwork was done to fulfill assignments of one kind or another, some artwork was done with no specific purpose in mind. Frequently, Sallman would paint works for his own satisfaction or for experimentation.

Sallman's extant watercolors and drawings vary a great deal. Some of the earliest are portraits, such as the two of Sallman's mother—one a pen sketch (1909), and another a colored chalk (1916). A pen sketch of his brother, LeRoy Sallman (1909), is preserved on a slide. A pen drawing (1922) and pencil sketch [1922] of Sallman's pastor at Edgewater during the 1920s, the Reverend F. O. Kling, are extant. Four undated portraits survive that also appear to be quite early: one of Charles Lindberg in black chalk; one of Abraham Lincoln in charcoal; and two of David Nyvall in black paint. Nyvall was the first president of North Park College.

The poster drawing, *Our Colossus* (1916), is of unknown provenance. It shows a large man straddling the high banks of a canal. A ship approaches through his legs. Apparently a World War I poster, its top reads: "Our Colossus of Roads to Victory." Below the scene reads, "Help US Speed Ships." Three undated sketches survive in which the focus is on war and the military, two bringing to bear the Christian message. It is not known whether they derive from World War I, or World War II when Sallman was doing artworks of this nature for the *War Cry*. A pencil sketch, *Head of Patriot Soldier*, depicts a soldier with a hat and coat like those worn by American patriots during the Revolutionary War. *Military Salutes the Christchild* is a pencil sketch of Mary and Joseph with the Christchild. Saluting men and women in various branches of the American Armed Forces stand behind the threesome. *Christ Extending*

Hand to Soldier, a third sketch in pencil, shows Christ extending a hand to a soldier on the battlefield. Flowers below symbolize Easter and the Resurrection.

Sallman liked bands and parades. *Three Men on Parade* (1918) is a pen sketch from the World War I era. A man in a suit walks with band players on either side. The one on the left blows bagpipes; the one on the right beats a drum.

Sallman's entry into the world of politics was a modest one, yet enter it he did, with cartoons for *Lightnin'*, a political magazine published during the 1920s on Chicago's north side. *Clown with Flag* (1928) is a pen sketch, signed "Elias," featuring a clown racing across stage holding an American flag and a doll of King George. The clown's identity is unknown, but from a billboard in front of the stage and an inside editorial, it would seem that he represents one of Chicago's politicians running on an "America first" platform, and promising to clean up city corruption. But, because he is caught up in the corruption himself, his campaign has become a joke. This cartoon appears on the front of an April Fool's edition of *Lightnin'*, dated April 1928. On page 12 of the same issue are two other sketches hitting at unjust taxes, *Tax Payers Feast and Fast* (1928). These likewise bear the cryptonym, "Elias." The sketches simulate an eyeglass-look into a Chicago hotel at the left, where the rich are feasting, and into a modest city house at the right, where the poor are fasting. *Management and Labor Shaking Hands*, an undated pencil sketch of unknown provenance, shows a worker in bib overalls wearing a hat marked "Labor," shaking hands with a man dressed in a suit. Both figures are smiling.

Sallman produced a number of sketches in support of Bible study, prayer, and family devotional life. A pen sketch *Christian Family Life* (1921) appears on the front cover of *The Family Altar* for May 1921, the issue requested by Sallman's friend, John Meredith. The cartoon shows how church, civil, and social life grow like branches out of Christian family life, which stands as the trunk of a tree. Men with axes and shovels representing contemporary intellectual and cultural forces thought to be destructive attack at the base of the tree labeled "daily family Bible reading and prayer." A whirlwind of "Bolshevism" approaches from behind the tree, threatening everybody.

Another work of unknown origin, the charcoal, *Kneeling Man in Beam of Light* (1933) depicts a barefoot young man—an athlete, perhaps—on one knee looking up into a beam of light. Both his hands extend upward with an open Bible on one knee. Behind stand large city buildings. Whether this sketch had any connection with the Chicago Century of Progress, which was being held that year, is not known. Sallman's poster drawing, *The Bible Speaks Today* (1956), appeared on the front cover of the *Bible Society Record* for October 1956 to support Universal Bible Sunday being sponsored by the American Bible Society. The watercolor, *Abraham Lincoln and Son* (1963), survives in a private collection. Lincoln is again reading his Bible, as in the oil, *Abraham Lincoln* (1958 © K&B 1958), only here his son stands beside him.

Sallman's Salvation Army artwork for the 1933-1934 Century of Progress is not extant. We do, however, possess a pencil of one of the drawings, *Naming the Salvation Army* [1933], which is probably a preliminary sketch.

Sallman began reaching a Roman Catholic audience when he submitted a pastel of his *Head of Christ* (© Messenger Corp. 1935) to the Messenger Corporation for use on a 1935 Scripture Text Calendar. This pastel also circulated in the Covenant and elsewhere—in prints and on bulletin covers. The Messenger Corporation published two other Sallman pastels. *The Blessed Mother / Our Lady of the Atonement* [1936], a picture of Mary similar to the later oil, *(Mary the) Mother of Christ* (1948 © K&B 1948), appeared on a Scripture Text Calendar for 1938. In *Woman, Why Weepeth Thou?* ([1936] © The Messenger Corp. 1937) Mary Magdalene meets Jesus on Easter morning. It anticipates *Rabboni* [1952], in colored pencil, and the watercolor, *Behold the Lord* (1952 © K&B 1953). *Woman, Why Weepeth Thou?* is featured on other calendars and church materials published by the Messenger Corporation between 1939 and 1960.

Some years later Sallman did a chalk and watercolor, *Face of Our Lord in Space* (1959), for a Kriebel and Bates Triumphant Life Calendar. This face has the gentle look of *Portrait of Jesus* (1966 © K&B 1966), only it is completely frontal, with no tilt of the head. The face is set against a green-colored earth, which doubles as a frame. The deep blue expanse of space surrounds the earth as well as other planets, one with a ring (Saturn?), and stars. Used separately, the face, *Face of Our Lord* (1959 © K&B 1961), appeared as a bulletin cover.

Sallman began doing watercolors at an early age, having learned the technique from his father who was practiced in this medium. Here the artist cannot go over his work the way he can an oil. Sallman's watercolors are some of his finest artworks. For these works, Sallman used brushes of sable or camel hair, sometimes in combination with chalk or pen. Pen was used primarily for outlining. One very fine watercolor, *Brass Bowl* (1910), which Sallman did when he was only eighteen, survives in a private collection. Sallman also did a *Self Portrait* in watercolor. It is undated, but must be before 1920, since it shows the artist as a young man.

Two fine watercolors survive from a later period: *Old Covered Bridge and Mill Site-Turkey Run, Indiana* (1940), and *French Bark on Reefs of Brottö at Föglö, Åland-Finland* (1941). The latter Sallman reproduced from an oil his father had done of a stricken vessel offshore his childhood home in Åland. Another fine Sallman watercolor is *Kenora - Canada* (1948).

Sallman's best-known watercolor, done in combination with chalk, is *Crown of Thorns* painted in 1941. Sallman did this piece just after the *Head of Christ* oil had been completed, and amid work on a number of *Christ in Gethsemane* paintings. In 1943 *Crown of Thorns* appeared in the *War Cry*,[1] at which time Sallman took out a copyright on the picture in his own name. In 1956 he turned the picture and the copyright over to Kriebel and Bates, who then sold it in prints and used it on bulletin covers, wallet-size cards, and other marketed items.

This picture of the Crucified portrays Jesus with unopened eyes and a crown of thorns upon his head. Only the top of his light purple robe shows at the neck. Jesus grips the robe with his right hand. On the face, and down the hair and neck, are drippings of blood. Below is written, "'yet when he was afflicted he opened not his mouth' Isaiah 53:7."

Another artistically successful watercolor, also made available as prints, has been the portrait of Mary entitled, *The Annunciation* (1953 © K&B 1953). Here Mary wears a lime green cape. Her right hand touches the cape above the breast. The face is the same as in *Mary and Baby in Manger* (1954 © K&B 1954). Inspiration for the work is said to derive from Luke 1:28.

The bulk of watercolors and drawings in the Anderson University Collection were done originally as bulletin covers, although in some cases—as with *Crown of Thorns* and *The Annunciation*—they were issued as prints, or marketed in some other fashion. Artworks prepared for church bulletins portray seasons in the church year, primarily Christmas and Easter. Sallman's bulletin work also depicts the sacrament of Communion and the church's ministries of evangelism and mission. The theme of Christ's return is present as well. Other themes relate to the biblical story, family life, and church-going.

The Covenant Church placed a special emphasis on missions, designating its Easter offering exclusively for missions. During Ralph Hanson's tenure as Covenant Foreign Missions Secretary (1944-1963), Sallman chaired a committee that planned and prepared promotional material for the Covenant Easter offering—bulletin covers, posters, banners, and brochure illustrations. The committee included artists Walter Ohlson and Birger Sponberg, as well as expert letterer Phil Peterson.

The Nativity (of Christ) (1947 © K&B 1948), a watercolor done for a bulletin cover, closely resembles the oil, *The Little Lord Jesus* (1956 © K&B 1956). Here Sallman's familiar-looking Mary sits on straw in the Bethlehem stable, holding the baby Jesus on her lap. Joseph stands behind her, his head erect and with staff in hand. In the background, behind the animals, three shepherds cluster together. The colors are bright: Mary has a red garment with light green cape; Joseph is dressed in blue; the cloths for the baby are bright yellow. The same picture survives in pencil [1947], where the overhead lamp is missing.

In the exceptional watercolor with paint, *Mary and Baby in Manger* (1954 © K&B 1954) Mary and the baby dominate the center of the picture. It is predominantly in light green, with Mary's garment a complementary deep purple. Two winged-angels hover overhead in flowing gowns. They bend and face each other, making the shape of a heart. Mary looks here as she does in *Mary, the Mother of Christ* (1948 © K&B 1948), *The Son of God* (1952 © K&B 1952), *The Annunciation* (1953 © K&B 1953), and *Madonna and Christ Child* (1955 © K&B 1956). She faces to the right, looking intently at the baby and holding the cloths of the crib. The baby returns her gaze, and has both arms outstretched.

Another watercolor, *Glory to God in the Highest* (1964 ©K&B 1964) depicts the Bethlehem scene and serves in a cropped version as a Christmas bulletin cover. For the bulletin a star, shining as a cross, was added at the upper right. The bulletin frame also contains an open scroll on which reads, "'Glory to God in the highest...' Luke 2:14." In the full picture three shepherds visit Mary, Joseph, and the baby, who lies in a comfortable blanketed manger. Of particular interest is the stable, which is here a house with walls, a doorway, a window, and a slightly pitched roof, though animals are nevertheless present—two lambs in the front, and a donkey in back.

Shepherds Outside Stable (1966), a watercolor and pen sketch, also illustrates a Christmas bulletin cover. The Bethlehem scene here is from the perspective of five shepherds who are grouped outside a thatched-roof stable looking more like an African hut. They peer in through an open doorway, looking at Mary and the Christchild. Joseph is not visible.

Map of Palestine with Christmas Sketches in brown chalk and perhaps brown paint, and *Wise Men and Shepherds Approaching Heavenly Angel* in brilliant watercolor and pen, illustrate Christmas materials or are perhaps more bulletin covers. The former contains sketches of Mary and Joseph going to Bethlehem, shepherds in the field, and wise men coming from the East. The latter artwork depicts wise men and shepherds, with their animals, above which appear hidden and partially-hidden angels. Pen outlining gives this artwork the look of stained glass.

A number of watercolors and drawings portraying the Easter event survive, as well as a lesser number of the Passion. One of Sallman's favorite Easter portrayals was of Mary Magdalene meeting Jesus in the Garden (John 20). One can recognize Mary Magdalene in the Sallman pictures by her long curly hair. *Rabboni* [1952], in colored pencil, is an early version of *Behold the Lord* (1952 © K&B 1953). Both works portray the John 20 encounter of Mary with Jesus. Below the *Rabboni* sketch, for the bulletin cover, is written: "Rabboni; which is to say MASTER John 20:16."

Behold the Lord (1952 © K&B 1953) appears to be a watercolor. In any case, in this beautifully-done picture of Mary greeting the resurrected Lord, a rainbow arcs behind Jesus, made by the bright light that shines down upon him.

Easter lilies and trumpet daffodils grow at the lower left. At the right stands the square entrance to the tomb—a Sallman trademark—and behind Jesus is a large round stone formerly sealing the tomb.

Thine Is the Victory! (1952) is a watercolor and pen done for another Easter bulletin. It reworks a 1920 *Förbundets Veckotidning* ink drawing of the resurrected Christ emerging out of the Crucified Christ. The whole is superimposed on an Easter lily, with coloring making a "V" ("V" for victory). The outstretched arms of the resurrected Christ reach down to grasp the upward extended arms of the Crucified.

Other Easter drawings in the Anderson University collection, some of which were done for bulletin covers, include, *Peace Be Unto You* (1956 © K&B 1956) in color chalk; *Christ on Easter Hill* (1958) in watercolor, chalk, and pen; *Up from the Grave He Arose* (1959) in colored chalk; *The Resurrected Lord* (1961) in colored chalk; *Jesus in the Garden* (1966) in colored chalk; and *He Is Risen* (n.d.) in watercolor.

A lesser number of Passion artworks survive, and some already anticipate the Resurrection. One, the watercolor, chalk, and pen, *It Is Finished* (1958 © K&B 1958), appeared on a bulletin cover. In the center of this work, the resurrected Christ, with hands uplifted, rises behind three men on crosses. The man to the left looks up at the resurrected Christ. The man to the right is eclipsed, his face not showing. The rent veil of the temple frames the whole scene. Below, in the narrow portion of the rend, appears a winged serpent in tones of red. This sketch has similarities to *Christ Rending the Veil* (1929), done earlier for *Förbundets Veckotidning* (26 March 1929).

Not My Will But Thine (1961), in watercolor and chalk, portrays Jesus' passion in the Garden. The picture resembles the well-known *Christ in Gethsemane* in oil (1941 © K&B 1942). *Pilate Offering Jesus to Mob*, an undated work of unknown provenance, consists of two pen sketches framing a center poem entitled, "The Crucifixion of Jesus." In the top sketch Pilate gestures with his hand toward Jesus, who stands at his right partially robed, bound, and wearing a crown of thorns. The bottom sketch shows seven angry men calling for Jesus' death.

The Carpenter of Nazareth/Jesus the Carpenter (1948 © K&B 1948 & 1951), in watercolor and chalk, shows Jesus as a young adult—perhaps in his early 20s—in the carpenter shop making a plow. To the right, in an adjoining room, Mary works at the loom. The bearded man under the archway is Joseph, also a carpenter. In the foreground two young children, a boy and a girl, look on. They are said to be listening to a story Jesus is telling them about his heavenly Father. Mary too listens from the other room. The head of Jesus here survives also in an undated red pencil sketch. *He Leadeth Me* (1949 © K&B 1951) is a watercolor/colored chalk similar to *The Lord Is My Shepherd* (1942 © K&B 1943), only Jesus leads his sheep in the other direction—away from the viewer.

For a communion bulletin Sallman did *In Remembrance of Me* (1956 ©
K&B 1956), a charcoal of Jesus behind a communion table with a plate of bread
in one hand, and a chalice in the other. On the table is an open Bible. The same
artwork, in color, exists in a reproduction, where it appears in a blue frame
(1956). *The Holy Communion* (1958 © K&B 1958), in watercolor, chalk, and
pen, illustrates another Sunday communion bulletin cover. Its square top and
oval bottom form the shape of a parament, red in color. A thorn-crowned Jesus
is at the top, positioned at the intersection of a cross. Directly below is a gold
chalice, and below it a gold communion plate with wafers. The chalice is particularly striking. Its close detail is suggestive of the *Chalice of Antioch* displayed at
the Century of Progress,[2] only that chalice had a slightly smaller pedestal.
Sallman may have seen the chalice when he was doing the Salvation Army and
American Bible Society exhibits at the fair.

Springs of Grace are Streaming (1959), another beautiful colored chalk,
appeared either on a communion Sunday or Easter bulletin cover. A sheep and
lamb bound through the grass in this spring scene of flowering fruit trees. To the
right a tree sprouts leaves. On the tree branch sits a robin. Three empty crosses
can be seen on a distant hill. Below are words of a communion hymn, "Springs
of grace are streaming, from the cross of Christ."[3]

One of Sallman's last sketches, *Christ Blessing Young People* (1967) pictures
Jesus in a clerical robe above a boy and girl with his hands over their heads.
Each holds a Bible. Palm branches and flowers appear at the bottom. A Gothic
church window frames the entire scene. At the bottom is written "GRACE."
The sketch is long and narrow, which would seem to preclude its use on a bul-
letin cover. The artwork suggests a number of celebrative events in the life of the
church—baptism, confirmation, a wedding, or, because of the palm branches,
Palm Sunday.

Some Sallman art for bulletin covers promote church-going. *Colonial
Church* (1942), in watercolor and possibly chalk, shows two people standing
outside a colonial-style church. *Let's Go to Church* (1947), in watercolor, pictures
nicely-dressed adults and young people entering the narthex of a church, where
they pass by a Sallman Head of Christ in stained glass (*Head of Christ in
Simulated Glass* 1946 © K&B 1946). In *People Approaching Colonial Church*, an
undated watercolor, people again walk to a colonial-style church. At the back of
the procession, two young people frolic.

A number of extant watercolors and drawings focus on prayer. Their origins
are largely unknown. In an extraordinary charcoal surviving from Sallman's personal collection, *Christ at Prayer* (1957 © K&B 1958), folded hands appear in
the foreground, unconnected to the praying Christ behind. The face of Christ is
the one in *Christ in Gethsemane* (1941 © K&B 1942) and *Our Redeemer* (1941
© K&B 1942). The watercolor *Girl at Bedside Praying* (1957) portrays a small

girl kneeling at her bed praying. Above the girl's head, in an oval frame, hangs a picture of *Madonna and Christ Child* (1955 © K&B 1956). A doll and kitten are also present. The girl resembles the Canadian girl in one of the stained glass windows of the Children's Chapel at the Methodist Children's Home in Detroit (*The Children of the World* 1952).

Boy at Bedside Praying is an undated collage in brown chalk. A cut-out of *Christ our Pilot* (1950 © K&B 1950) hangs in an oval frame above the boy's head. A model ship sits in the window. *Christ at Prayer on Globe* (1961) is a watercolor and chalk resembling *Christ in Gethsemane* (1941 © K&B 1942), only here a globe replaces the table rock on which Jesus prays. On the globe, at a number of points, appear to be nuclear explosions. But a ray of light descends upon Jesus. In its beam is a shadowed cross. *We Ought to Pray* (1963 © K&B 1963) is a crayon and paint sketch of three sets of hands. Those in the foreground right are folded; those at the upper left are together, but unfolded; and those in the background center are open and uplifted. Different modes of spirituality are thus offered to people wanting to pray. An undated colored pen sketch *O Lord Our God*, measuring approximately 20 inches by 20 inches, depicts folded hands with a supporting a verse from 1 Chronicles 29:16. Two other undated pencil sketches of folded hands also survive in a private collection.

For Sallman evangelism went hand in hand with youth ministry, which resulted in artworks combining the church's commitment to youth and its mandate to bring Christ to the world. Covenanters and Methodists, the primary audience of this artwork, defined mission broadly, that is, extending beyond evangelism to included a whole range of benevolent ministries to the sick, the needy, and the hungry. Mission was understood as transforming the culture as well as the individual. In *Missionary Doctor and Nurse*, a pencil sketch of unknown date and provenance, a doctor and nurse examine patients in what appears to be an African mission hospital.

In the mid-1940s Sallman did artwork in support of Methodist outreach efforts. One such work, a watercolor (and possibly an oil), *The Crusading Christ* [1944], was done for a Methodist Crusade for Christ. It depicts Christ passing with haste through a world ravaged by war. Amidst bombed-out churches and destroyed houses, hurting people—including mothers with children—watch as Christ passes through the scene. This picture appeared on the front of the *Christian Advocate* for 14 December 1944, accompanied by a statement of the Federal Council of Churches which concludes that "the cross of Jesus Christ demonstrated the power of God to overcome evil in its very moment of victory."

Another pen (and possible charcoal) sketch, *The Compassionate Christ* (1944), appears on the front cover of the *Christian Advocate* for 15 February

1945. This picture also illustrates a poster advancing the Methodist crusade. Here a thorn-crowned Christ looks down on a globe swirling in space. Below this image, a hand carries the Christian flag. *Christ of the Harvest Fields* (1946), possibly a watercolor, also supports Methodist evangelism. The figure of Christ, much same as in *The Crusading Christ* [1944], is depicted here above a field filled with bales of hay. The picture also served a decade later to advance Covenant youth programs, including the 1954 Covenant Quadrennial held at Mission Springs in California.

Jesus and the Children of the World (n.d.), a watercolor with an overlay, meant to precede an oil Sallman planned to paint for a Methodist crusade. Probably used in a post-War crusade for which the other artwork was done, the work illustrates the cover of a leader's manual. Sallman's interpretation, written in his own hand on the overlay, calls for both evangelism and foreign aid to help victims of war:

> Christ is down on one knee, enfolding within his right arm, close to himself, the children of...the world here typified. His left hand, extended toward the onlooker, [is] appealing to all to give themselves and their money to help in his cause.
> EVANGELISM—suggested by stretcher-bearers bringing in their sick and wounded pal to the Savior. Sunday School and Child Evangelism suggested by children within his arms.
> FOREIGN RELIEF AND REHABILITATION—by wounded soldier, the children of all nations, stretcher bearers, and refugee mother or soldier's widowed wife and child (in lower right). The hope and comfort of the cross on the grave of the soldier who did not die in vain. Attainment of eternal peace through faith in Christ. Devastation of homes and churches revealed against the radiance of hope from heaven.

Feed My Sheep (1950) illustrated the front cover of the *Upper Room* for May-June 1950. Jesus, standing at the left of this picture, stretches one hand toward a crowd of people who are behind him, the other hand beckoning the viewer. Storm clouds—symbolizing sin and evil in the world—overshadow the multitude. But a beam of light shines upon Jesus.

In the undated pen sketch *Young People with Flags*, young people stand on a church platform holding flags. Arrayed in the dress of different countries, they carry flags of the United States, four Scandinavian countries (flags with crosses), Turkey (flag with a crescent and star), Japan (flag with the rising sun), Germany (flag with three stripes), and other countries. *Jesus Walking with Boy and Girl*, another pencil of unknown date and provenance, depicts Jesus walking with a young boy and girl, holding their hands. He is in the center. The girl on the left carries a Bible.

Forward with Christ (1956 © K&B 1956), a watercolor, illustrates a 1957 bulletin cover. Young people are here again marching with flags—an American flag at the left; a flag with the 1924 *Head of Christ* and John 3:16 in the center; and a Christian flag at the right. Other flags contain evangelistic slogans. Over the top is written, "His Banner Over Us Is Love." This picture also survives in pencil (*Forward with Christ* [1956]).

The undated (and unfinished) brown sketch *And the Books Were Opened* focuses on the return of Christ and serves as a bulletin cover. At the top a finger points to Revelation 21:27 in an open Bible. This verse, together with words from a hymn, "Is My Name Written There?"[4] appear below and to the right.

Some watercolors and drawings were done for Kriebel and Bates booklets. Between 1944 and 1962 Kriebel and Bates published a series of seventeen or more booklets to introduce the Sallman oils, beginning with the *Head of Christ*. These booklets contain devotional interpretations by Howard W. Ellis, Sylvia E. Peterson, F. Martin Bates, and others.

The booklet, *Story of Sallman's "Boy Christ,"* by Howard Ellis, includes nine pen sketches from *The Boy Christ* painting (1944 © K&B 1945). All of the sketches survive (*Boy Christ Sketches* © K&B 1945). *Road to Emmaus*, written by F. M. Bates, introduces Sallman's *Road to Emmaus* painting (1961 © K&B 1961). This booklet's sketches were not from the painting, but were rather illustrations to go along with a recounting of Luke 24 in its entirety (*Road to Emmaus Sketches* 1961 © K&B 1961). The final sketch, *The Ascension at Bethany*, is the last-mentioned event in the chapter (Luke 24:50-51). Four of these sketches, in pencil, are also extant (*Road to Emmaus Sketches* [1961]).

A brown pen sketch of *Lord and Master* (1962 © K&B 1962), perhaps the most rugged-looking Sallman portrait of Christ, appeared on the cover of *Survival Power*, a booklet on the Lord's prayer by F. Martin Bates (1962). It later appeared in a marbleized frame (© Warner Press 1964). A subsequent printing of *Survival Power* used Sallman's watercolor *Lord and Master* (1962 © K&B 1962).

Kriebel and Bates also prepared a booklet on Sallman's *Story of Gethsemane* (1964 © K&B 1964). Five unfinished and incomplete pen sketches for this booklet survive (*Story of Gethsemane Sketches* [1964]). These sketches illustrate a story that builds on the events leading up to and following Jesus' prayer vigil in the Garden. Sketch #1 depicts Jesus and his disciples leaving the Upper Room. In Sketch #7, Roman soldiers lead Jesus away. The final sketch—if eight were planned—is not extant.

Passion-Easter Sketches (1966), another incomplete and unfinished series of pen sketches for a K&B booklet, consists of only four sketches. The accompanying story, in which Mary Magdalene figures prominently, begins with Jesus' arrest and trial (in sketch #2, Pilate washes his hands with Jesus behind him).

Mary, who is present at the crucifixion, sees Jesus also after his resurrection (John 20). This booklet seems to pick up where the *Story of Gethsemane* booklet leaves off. A colored pen sketch of *Portrait of Jesus* [1967] also survives, similar to, but not exactly the same as the like-named oil (1966 © K&B 1966). It was used on the cover of K&B 1968 catalogue.

Two sketches, with accompanying poetry by F. M. Bates, may have been intended for more devotional booklets. The one, *Bright Stars in the Darkness* (1966), is a blue watercolor or chalk portraying a nocturnal landscape. A farmhouse sits in between trees. Clouds cover the sky, except at the upper left, where stars are shining brightly and a hidden moon gives the clouds a silver lining. On the back of the original Sallman has written, "The beauty of the stars would be lost, if it were not for the darkness—F. M. Bates." Underneath he adds, "High above the darkening clouds, the stars are shining bright."

A Tree (1968), a black pen sketch with whiting, surrounds another Bates poem entitled, "A Tree." The picture shows a campus building and a log cabin. Prominent once again are trees, one at the right tall and filled with leaves, and in front of it a smaller tree felled to the ground. At the bottom of the original is noted 1 Peter 2:24, which speaks of Christ bearing our sins on a tree. The date '68 on this sketch indicates that it was one of Sallman's last before his death.

Some sketches were done for various Kriebel and Bates marketed items. We recall that when Fred Bates came to Sallman's home and first saw the *Head of Christ* in oil, he intended to make arrangements for using *Son of Man* on plaques. The brown pen sketch of *Son of Man* (© K&B 1941), which survives in the Anderson University collection, is possibly what Sallman gave him. The 1924 Christ head is shown here on the left page of an open Bible. On the right page, written at the top, is "Jesus said—." A blank space is underneath. This artwork was intended for plaques to be produced by the Felsenthal Company of Chicago. A black and white *Head of Christ* (© K&B 1964)— perhaps a photocopy—also survives in the Anderson collection. This picture, in a cardboard frame with a circular cut-out, resembles the 1940 oil. Written below, in Sallman's hand, is "suggestion for medallion."

Sallman gave away as gifts some particularly fine watercolors and drawings. A *Head of Christ* in pastel, done over a sepia print, was a Christmas gift in 1947 to his son and wife, James and Gene Sallman. An extraordinary watercolor of the same picture, the classic *Head of Christ* (1952), was given to Newell and Gladys Johnson as a wedding gift. Gladys was Sallman's niece.

In 1959 Sallman did seven portraits of Edgewater pastors in charcoal. One was of the Reverend C. V. Bowman (1959), pastor of Edgewater Covenant Church (1917-1920) and later President of the Covenant. A second was of the Reverend Frederic E. Pamp (1959), student pastor of Edgewater Covenant and later pastor of the Covenant Congregational Church of Boston. A third was of the Reverend C. J. Andrews (1959), pastor of Edgewater Covenant (1914-16), Superintendent of Swedish Covenant Hospital (1921-1932), and the pastor who married Warner and Ruth Sallman. The remaining four were of the Reverend F. O. Kling (1959), the Reverend K. K. Jacobson [1959], the Reverend Paul F. Erickson [1959], and the Reverend Arthur N. Johnson [1959], all former pastors of Edgewater Covenant.

[1] *The War Cry* Central 1164 (17 April 1943): front cover.

[2] For a picture see the *The War Cry* Central 710 (4 August 1934): 16; also *Fortune* 33/1 (January 1946): 133.

[3] Carl A. Stenholm, "Hälsokällan flödde," trans. E. Gustav Johnson, *Covenant Hymnal* 1950, #434; 1973, #510.

[4] Mary A. Kidder and Frank M. Davis, "Lord, I Care Not for Riches," *Covenant Hymnal* 1950, #262.

X

Recognition Around the World

...at the name of Jesus every knee should bow, in heaven and on earth and under the earth, and every tongue confess that Jesus Christ is Lord, to the glory of God the Father (Phil 2:10-11).

Sallman was clear about his need for an audience. He wanted people to be impacted by his art so they might come to a living faith. "I'm not in this for myself," he said, "I believe the Lord has given me a job to do—of pointing people to Christ through the medium of art."[1] If people were already believers, Sallman's depictions of Christ would then be to edify them in their Christian walk.

Sallman worked with the largest possible audience in mind. At the same time he had no idea his *Head of Christ* would have the impact it did. In a personal message to sixth graders in weekday church schools of the St. Paul, Minnesota Council of Churches, penned in 1948, Sallman said,

> Twenty-four years ago when I made the first charcoal sketch and later when I painted it on canvas with oil paints, I never dreamed this *Head of Christ* would reach out around the world in prints of many forms. I am happy to know that my God-given talent has been used to serve and magnify our Lord. Also I am pleased to hear that St. Paul boys and girls will use it in their study of the life of Jesus. I pray that you will learn to know Him, to love Him, and to serve Him all the days of your life.[2]

Sallman received much affirmation during his lifetime. Part of the reason—but only part—was his own generosity in affirming others. The Reverend Charles Goff gives the following account of what Sallman told him concerning the role that Goff played in the drawing of the Christ head:

> When I came to the [Chicago] Temple, I was searching for a great picture for this place, believing that in the throngs that come and go it would do an immense amount of good. Appealing to a preacher-artist friend for suggestions, he told me of Sallman's *Head of Christ* and agreed to write Mr. Sallman for an interview. When I went to his studio I was completely surprised to see my friend of years gone by. When I said to him, "You did not paint that picture, did you?" he replied,

"No, I have been waiting all these years to tell you that you gave me that picture." When I asked him how that could possibly be, he replied, "But you gave Christ to me!"[3]

Some believe Goff was given too much credit for the Sallman Christ head, misinterpreting the words, "you gave me that picture." Sallman himself explained what he meant, saying, "[I]n the Bible class of many years ago, [Goff] gave me the precious gift of Christ's presence in the classroom." Others feel that Goff himself took too much credit, but that rests upon a similar misunderstanding. Goff went on to say, "Perhaps I was one link in a long chain. I know this, that if I had anything to do with this painting, it is no different from the thousands of important things that are being done by all of us right along without our full knowledge."[4]

As mentioned earlier, the first-year distribution of the Christ head in oil was very successful. Sales took off immediately. Kriebel and Bates reported totals for 1941 of one million prints, and for 1942 another three million. Soon the Sallman picture began appearing in churches, Sunday School rooms, hospitals, and an array of other public places. In 1943, Swedish Covenant Hospital of Chicago received a large Sallman print, and later placed smaller prints in every room.[5] Other hospitals followed suit. Sallman prints, for example, could be found in every room of the Methodist Hospital in Philadelphia, Pennsylvania. In some cases, individuals who had seen the Sallman picture in their own hospital room, or who had been given a small picture of the Sallman Christ head by a hospital chaplain, financed campaigns to place a Sallman Christ head in every hospital room. The picture made its way as well into military chapels. By 1954, it was said that in almost every armed forces chapel in the country displayed at least one Sallman picture.

While the Sallman Christ head was being distributed across America, American missionaries and men and women in the American Armed Forces were carrying it around the world. As early as 1942 the *Head of Christ* reached others through the USO, thanks to distribution efforts by the Salvation Army and the YMCA. Ironically, World War II contributed as much to a world-wide distribution of the Sallman Christ head as the American Missionary Movement of the mid-twentieth century.

Carl H. Duning of Richmond, Indiana, played a particularly important role in distributing the Sallman picture at home and abroad. His program, which went by the name, "Christ in Every Purse," distributed wallet-sized prints of the Sallman Christ head. Duning was a semi-retired furniture executive, who, prior to World War II, had sold religious pictures in his furniture store. The Sallman *Head of Christ* had become his favorite. The program of distributing the prints began very simply. Duning, as superintendent of the Sunday School at St. John

Lutheran Church in Richmond, wanted to keep in touch with seventy-six boys from his church who were in the service, three of them his own. He, together with other members of the congregation, decided to write the boys letters. In each letter they enclosed a couple of wallet-sized Christ head pictures. With these went the admonition "Keep these handy in your purses. If and when the going gets tough, they will help your thinking, always reminding you of His presence." On the back was a statement that the picture should not be treated as a lucky pocket-piece, but serve instead as a reminder to love and worship the Christ it presented. In a booklet written later to accompany pictures sent out in quantity, Duning reiterated the point that carrying a picture of Christ was intended only to facilitate genuine devotion. He wrote, "Worship of the picture of Sallman's Christ is idolatry, but worship of Christ is true Christianity."

Letters came back. One from a soldier named Don, who was hospitalized in Italy, read, "Very happy to get the pictures. Would you send me some more that I may share them with my buddies in the hospital."[6] More pictures went out. Paul Marshall of the Salvation Army recalls writing for pictures while he was stationed with an anti-aircraft unit in the Fiji Islands: "I wrote home to my parents and said I must have a packet (I don't remember how large a quantity) to give out to missionary friends and to servicemen in my outfit. I was the chaplain's assistant. And so I received a goodly number of small prints."[7]

Some weeks after a packet had been sent to Don in Italy, Don's mother came into Duning's office with a letter from her son. "This you must read," she said. The letter told about Don's buddy who was in the hospital bed next to him. He claimed to be a "toughy," but his boasting only covered up his fear. His wounds were superficial, and he knew once they were healed he would be back in action. Don read to him from the New Testament. He also showed his buddy the Sallman picture and talked to him about Jesus. The witness bore fruit. The young soldier made his peace with God, and was baptized by the chaplain. A week later he was ordered back into action, and was killed. But he left behind a testimony that was now an inspiration to Don. The letter closed with this question, "Why doesn't everybody carry this picture in their wallet? It would help them in their thinking!"[8] The words set Mr. Duning to thinking.

Other experiences caused Duning to think further about whether his modest program might be expanded. Once he met a runaway woman at Union Station in Detroit and gave her a Sallman print. A home-town acquaintance, this woman spoke of "ending it all."[9] In another instance, Duning gave a picture to a drunk man on a fishing boat tossing wildly in turbulent seas out of Miami. This fellow was running away from a wife and two children, and now had a woman in Miami.[10] In both instances the picture-assisted witness bore fruit. The individuals decided to return to their families. These encounters convinced Duning that the distribution of Sallman picture cards could well reach larger numbers of men and women away in the military, as well as individuals floundering amidst crises at home.

Duning then launched his Christ in Every Purse project. He admits being inspired in part by current publicity about "card-carrying" Communists. "Why not have card-carrying Christians?" he thought. In his booklet he wrote, "All of us carry money, valuable papers, and identification cards in our purse. We are watchful so as not to lose them. If Christ is our most treasured possession, why not carry His likeness in our purses?"

Within two years the Christ in Every Purse project had spread over much of the United States, and into five foreign countries. When the workload of filling orders became too great, Duning solicited help from young people in Luther Leagues, Lutheran brotherhoods, Kiwanis clubs, the Salvation Army, the Gideons, and Alcoholics Anonymous. Distribution was assisted by Methodist, Baptist, Presbyterian, and other church groups. Millions of pictures were sent out. Five thousand alone went to the International Lutheran Conference in Oslo, Norway. Another one hundred thousand prints were distributed after a December 1954 article on the project appeared in *Guideposts* magazine. In 1955, distribution was said to be running about twenty thousand pictures a month. If groups wanted quantities in the hundreds or thousands, Dunning requested payment of three cents a picture. Otherwise they were sent out free.

The Christ in Every Purse project elicited broad support. By 1955 more than fifty foreign missionaries were said to be using the Sallman prints, and its boosters included Norman Vincent Peale, Elton Trueblood, Governor Wayne Guthrie of Indiana, J. Edgar Hoover of the FBI, and President and Mrs. Eisenhower. Duning traveled the country, making an estimated one hundred speeches to churches, service groups, high schoolers, lodges, and Alcoholics Anonymous groups in support of his project.

Stories soon began to filter back, telling what impact the Sallman picture was having. A Head of Christ sent by a Sunday school in Massachusetts to a mission church in Japan helped bring together a Japanese and American soldier during World War II. This American soldier from Newton Centre had been captured by the Japanese and feared for his life, as three of his buddies had been killed and he together with the other three, were being marched off at bayonet point.

...He began to repeat the words of the 23rd Psalm.

Still gripped by fear, he repeated the psalm a second time...After repeating the psalm for the third time, the fear seemed to leave him. He became very calm. He then began to hum quite softly a familiar hymn tune. He had a strange feeling that someone else was humming the tune with him, but could not be sure. His voice broke off in the middle of it, and, sure enough, another voice carried it on.

He was amazed to discover that it was the Japanese soldier whose bayonet was prodding his back, who was joining in the singing of the hymn. He turned around to look. And the Japanese soldier said to him in understandable English, "You are a Christian?" And when the American replied that he was, the Japanese said, "Me Christian too"...

When they got out of earshot of the others, the Japanese soldier said, "Some of us know that we are not going to win this war. We are tired of fighting. I know where there are six other fellows who are Christians, who would be willing to surrender to you, if you will lead us back to the American lines."

After the six had surrendered they were being interrogated by American intelligence officers and were asked where they came from. The boy from Newton Centre was standing by. One of the Japanese named a town in Japan, which struck a chord of memory in the mind of the boy from Massachusetts. He remembered that his Sunday School had once sent a package to a mission church in that town, and he said, "Why, our Sunday school sent a gift to your town once, and I had a part in making it possible. In it, we had a picture of Sallman's *Head of Christ*." And the Japanese soldier said, "Well, I decorated the altar on the Sunday that picture was dedicated."[11]

Charles Goff received this letter on 7 October 1945 from one of the boys in his church away at war:

I was on an island in the south Pacific when it was being unmercifully shelled from the sea by the Japanese Navy. I sought refuge in a cave and found when I entered that it was filled with GI's on their knees praying. Someone had built a rustic altar on which was placed a cross and two lighted candles. Behind the cross and the candles was a large copy of Sallman's *Head of Christ*. Before this altar we all knelt in prayer. It was a precious hiding place during the fury of the storm, and the experience is unforgettable.

Countless other stories have been told about how the Sallman *Head of Christ* inspired soldiers and sailors during World War II. The following, relating to a sailor, was published originally in the *Augustana Quarterly*:[12]

A chaplain was inspecting some of the sailors' lockers. In one of the lockers, he says, I saw another picture—beside that of his wife—Sallman's picture of the head of Christ, that magnificent work that pictures Him as one whom real men can follow. I stopped to tell the seaman how I have always been inspired by that picture and how I noticed it in his locker. "Yes, Chaplain," he told me, "He's my shipmate."

Theodore Adams of First Baptist Church in Richmond, Virginia, also sent the Sallman picture to service men and women during the war. After the war he decided on a project closer to home. Plaques of the *Head of Christ* were offered to business men and women of Richmond for display on their desks. The plaques cost Adams thirty cents each, but he gave them away free if the recipient would promise to keep the picture continually in view. According to *Newsweek*, Adams succeeded in distributing four hundred reproductions of the *Head of Christ* in this manner. One woman claimed it helped her keep her "redheaded" temper in check. A man reported it controlling the tempers of others. "No one has cursed in my office," he said, "since the picture has been on my desk." [13]

The goal of Ora O'Riley was to get the Sallman Christ head displayed in public places—first in Durant, Oklahoma, where she lived, then elsewhere in the state, and finally in the nation's capitol. Her effort led to Durant being designated "the city of the Christ head picture." During the 1950s this woman, who was a full-blooded Chataw Indian princess and a devout Roman Catholic, literally flooded schools, stores, banks, lawyers' offices, courts, service organizations, and governmental buildings with 16-inch by 20-inch framed prints of the Sallman Christ head, exacting in each case a simple promise only that the print be hung in a prominent place.

One year as a Christmas gift to the people of Durant, O'Riley saw to it that a large 30-inch by 40-inch Sallman Christ head was hung prominently on the outer wall of city hall. Above the picture were the words, "Put Christ Back into Christmas." O'Riley succeeded in securing acceptance of Sallman pictures by a number of political and civic leaders.[14] In the early 1950s Oklahoma Governor Johnston Murray accepted a large print of Sallman's *Christ at Heart's Door* in a televised ceremony from the state capitol.[15]

O'Riley's project received broad support from Catholic bishops and area-Protestant churches. The Reverend Eugene J. McGuinness, bishop of Oklahoma, was particularly fond of the Sallman Christ head, and asked for a 30-inch by 40-inch print to be hung in a new Catholic preparatory seminary under construction in Oklahoma City. He had just seen a Christ head being presented to then-Governor Raymond Gary.[16] In 1957 Sallman visited Governor Gary in the state capitol, and the next year sent him a print of his newly-completed *Power and Glory* (1957 © K&B 1958).

When O'Riley extended her campaign to the nation's capitol, House Whip Carl Albert from Oklahoma received a print of the Sallman Christ head, for which he sent a kind letter of thanks. The city of Durant presented a Sallman print to Vice President Lyndon B. Johnson. Sallman signed each of these pictures at O'Riley's request.

Similar to O'Riley, Mae Maust took it upon herself to distribute Sallman prints to public officials. Maust had attended a banquet at the Mission Covenant Church in Los Angeles, and become so impressed by a *Head of Christ* hanging above the speaker's table, that she began giving away prints. By 1954 she had sent off more than five hundred prints to well-known people, such as the Queen of England, General Douglas MacArthur, the Mayor of Los Angeles, and others. She is said to have received personally-written notes of thanks from over forty-seven governors and fifty-eight senators.[17]

Sallman sent out countless signed prints himself. In 1959, for example, he sent a bunch, including his recently-completed *Abraham Lincoln* (1958), to his friend the Reverend G. T. Carl, Pastor of First Methodist Church in Mason City, Iowa. Carl in turn distributed them to Methodist pastors at the North Iowa Methodist Annual Conference. Carl wrote back to Sallman, "I had such a good time—giving autographed prints to younger ministers in struggling, difficult, churches. I saw the light of heaven in their eyes. I even gave a couple to aged servants of the Lord and they walked with a firmer step."[18]

In the post-war years distribution of the Sallman picture abroad continued unabated. Covenant missionaries took the *Head of Christ* to the Ubangi region of the Belgian Congo. By 1947 the Sallman Christ head had also arrived at Monieka, a Congo mission station on the Busira River run by the Disciples of Christ. *Life* magazine reported it being used there in religious pageants. The magazine included a picture of one such pageant of the Last Supper, where the Sallman Christ head was placed on the center of the table to symbolize Jesus' presence.[19]

In 1949 Sylvia Peterson presented two prints of the Christ head to E. Stanley Jones for his Ashram in Sattal, India. One was put in the Ashram proper, and the other in the chapel. By 1952 Covenant President Theodore W. Anderson was able to write in a letter of tribute to Sallman on his 60th birthday the following:

> In the jungles of Africa and in high offices in our national capital, in the snow and ice of Northern Alaska and in the torrid heat of the Philippines, in the strategic lands of Japan and Formosa in the Orient and in various countries in Europe, I have seen copies of your *Head of Christ*.[20]

Goff reported much the same thing after a round-the-world trip. He said in every one of the twenty-two countries he visited he saw the *Sallman Head of Christ*. Virginia Ohlson, another personal friend of Sallman's who directed the public health nursing program in occupied Japan (SCAP), and worked in other capacities for the American and Japanese governments after the war, presented a large print of the *Head of Christ* in 1954 to the YWCA Headquarters in Tokyo, before returning home.

I recall seeing the Sallman *Head of Christ* in a Maronite Catholic bookstore in Beirut in 1964, and a framed print in Kenya in 1981, when on a speaking tour that year to Central and East Africa. I was visiting my friend, the Reverend Benson O'tieno, bishop of the Episcopal Church of Africa, in his home village near Kisumu. I had just entered the modest house in which he was living, with no electric lights and no running water, sat down at the table, only to look up and see above the doorway through which I had just passed, the Sallman picture. My host, and the other African pastors present, were indeed surprised when I told them the story behind the painting, and that the artist had been my good friend and neighbor in Chicago.

In May 1990, not quite a year after the conflict in Tiananmen Square, Ernie and Vivian Johnson with friends made a visit to the former Covenant Field in China where Vivian grew up as a young girl. Her parents, Oscar and Ruth Anderson, were China missionaries before the Communist revolution. Oscar had, in fact, endured a long captivity at the hands of Mao's forces. When the group visited the Protestant Church of Guling (formerly Kuling), which is located in the Lushan Mountains of Kiangsi Province, Vivian saw to her surprise three Sallman pictures on the wall: *Christ at Heart's Door*, the *Head of Christ*, and *The Lord Is My Shepherd*. It is doubtful whether these predate the Cultural Revolution of 1965-1966. More than likely they have been imported more recently from Taiwan or Korea, where the Sallman pictures have become quite popular.

It was a great day of celebration in 1991 when the Sallman Christ head came to Föglö, in the Åland Islands, where Sallman's father was born, and from where he emigrated to America. The weekend was 29-30 June, when the St. Maria Magdalena Kyrka in Föglö was celebrating its 750th anniversary. Sallman's son, Richard, and his wife Marion, were invited to be present, and arrangements had been made for Richard to present a large print of the Sallman Christ head to the church. It was the first time a member of Elias Sallman's family had returned to Åland. After the worship service Richard presented the *Head of Christ* to the congregation, and Marion presented two smaller prints of *Christ at Heart's Door* and *Christ Our Pilot* to the Sunday School.

[1] Bruce Baylor, "A Man's Artist," *Sunday School Promoter* (May 1943): 26.

[2] Letter from Warner Sallman to sixth grade boys and girls of the Weekday Church Schools of the St. Paul Council of Churches, St. Paul, Minnesota, 21 September 1948.

3 Taken from the leaflet *The Story of Warner Sallman's "Head of Christ"* by Charles R. Goff distributed at the Chicago Temple.

4 Ibid.

5 "Artist Donates Painting in Oil," *Covenant Weekly* 32/50 (10 December 1943): 1. This article says that a "large oil" was given to the hospital and "prints" were placed in every room. Actually the large picture was also a "print," which hung for many years in the hospital's board room. This print, 18 inches by 24 inches, in a gold oval frame with a date of 16 November 1943, is extant, although it is no longer on display. My thanks to Allan Anderson of Covenant Benevolent Institutions for locating the picture.

6 Carl Duning in a letter to Sylvia Peterson, 12 April 1955.

7 Paul Marshall in a letter to the author, 19 November 1987.

8 Carl Duning in a letter to Sylvia Peterson, 12 April 1955.

9 Ibid.

10 Ibid.

11 This story was told by Peter Marshall in a sermon on World Communion Sunday 1945 in the New York Avenue Presbyterian Church of Washington, DC. An excerpt of the sermon under the title, "Blest Be the Tie That Binds," appears in the *Covenant Weekly* 35:4 (25 January 1946): 1. The story originated with James Berkeley of Andover-Newton Theological School.

12 *Augustana Quarterly* 25 (1946): 186.

13 *Newsweek* 30/1 (July 7 1947): 79.

14 For a picture of Ora O'Riley and Oklahoma District Judge Sam Sullivan, see *Covenant Weekly* 39/12 (24 March 1950): 1.

15 Johnston Murray was governor of Oklahoma from 1951-1955.

16 Raymond Gary was governor of Oklahoma from 1955-1959.

17 Dorothy C. Haskin, "The Man Who Painted a Manly Head of Christ: Warner Sallman" in, *Christians You Would Like to Know*, (Grand Rapids: Zondervan Publishing House, 1954) 71.

18 Reverend G. T. Carl to Warner Sallman, 7 July 1959.

19 Donald Burke, "Congo Mission," *Life* (2 June 1947): 108. Photograph by N. R. Farbman.

20 Theodore W. Anderson in a letter to Warner Sallman, 25 April 1952.

XI

Warner Sallman 'Live'

Even as Warner Sallman carefully adjusted his easel to catch the right lighting, and prepared his drawing board for a coloured crayon replica of the Christ portrait, perhaps four or five times life size, the atmosphere was electric…

(Paul Marshall, Salvation Army)

Over a forty-year period Sallman made countless public appearances before church groups of various denominations, minister's groups, children's groups, Salvation Army groups, YMCA groups, Kiwanis Clubs, and other gatherings. He would begin by giving a personal testimony, telling about his "thrilling vision" and the events leading up to the famous Christ head drawing. The rest of the time was spent doing a chalk, crayon, or charcoal of one of his pictures, usually the *Head of Christ*. Sometimes he would do cartooning before drawing his Christ head.

While Sallman drew, someone would play the piano, or else a soloist, a choir, or an entire congregation would sing hymns of faith. In Calumet Park, Chicago, the church choir gave a concert while Sallman drew. Drawing the head of Christ took anywhere between thirty minutes and an hour, usually about forty minutes. After it was finished, Sallman would blow on a clear lacquer to fix the picture and keep it from smearing. The fumes, unfortunately, gave him later respiratory problems.

Sallman was not comfortable speaking in public. He once remarked,

I've done this many times now, but I'm still tremulous. I can paint much better than I can talk. Often, when appointments draw near, I wish I could cancel them. The reason I speak so often is that folks make their arrangements far in advance when the prospect of addressing a big congregation doesn't seem so bad.[1]

Sallman began his illustrated chalks early. He recalled doing his first one before the Keystone Club at the Waveland Avenue Congregational Church, while still in his teens. Before doing colored chalks of the head of Christ he apparently did charcoals, which, of course, was the medium of the original. A note attached to the templet over one surviving charcoal of the *Head of Christ* (1927) reads, "Sketched about 1927–used as a templet for my early chalk talks. Warner '62."

In 1932 Sallman did a colored chalk, *Gustavus Adolphus efter Van Dyke* (1932), for the tercentenary celebration of Gustav Adolphus' death, held at Moody Church.[2] But most frequently he drew his *Head of Christ*, particularly during the 1920s and 1930s.[3] A 1939 *Head of Christ* in colored chalk survives from the Edgewater Covenant Church. During the 1940s through the 1960s, Sallman continually appeared before live audiences, drawing his *Head of Christ*, or, less often, other well-known pictures, in colored chalk, crayon, pastel, and occasionally watercolor.[4]

The first color chalk of the *Head of Christ* before a live audience is said to have been before a young people's meeting at the Mission Covenant Church of Evanston, Illinois. It came about quite spontaneously, according to the report that survives.

> After he [Sallman] had drawn two or three pictures, which was all that he had planned to do, and was about to lay aside his chalk, someone spoke out, "Warner, could you draw the portrait of Jesus that you did in charcoal for The Covenant Companion?
>
> "It has been some time since I did that picture," Mr. Sallman said, "and I have never tried it in color. I don't know how long it might take, for I have made no preparation to paint the picture in pastel."
>
> However, his congregation was willing and eager to see him sketch the picture, so he went to work, enlarging his picture from memory.[5]

The drawing took about an hour.

By the early 1950s Sallman was fulfilling speaking engagements all across the country. Second to his *Head of Christ*, the picture most often requested was *Christ Our Pilot* (1950 © K&B 1950). Sallman did a large watercolor and chalk of *Christ Our Pilot* in three colors–brown, black and white–for the West Suburban (Rich Port) YMCA in La Grange, Illinois in 1964. He drew another in chalk on Easter Sunday 1952, at Polytechnic Methodist Church in Fort Worth, Texas. *Christ Our Pilot* was also done at First Covenant Church, Jamestown, New York; Austin Methodist Church, Chicago; Bethesda Covenant Church, Rockford, Illinois; and elsewhere. For each work in the latter four churches, a preliminary pencil sketch also survives.

Other Kriebel and Bates pictures done by Sallman in chalk, crayon, or charcoal for public audiences include: *Mary the Mother of Christ* (1948 © K&B 1948), for the Seminary Wives at North Park Seminary in May 1950; *Follow Thou Me* (1948 © K&B 1949), for Polytechnic Methodist, Fort Worth, Texas in 1951 and First Methodist, Mason City, Iowa in 1962; *Jesus Our Savior* (1959 © K&B 1959), for Trinity Covenant, Oak Lawn, Illinois in 1959; and *Power and Glory* (1957 © K&B 1958) in brown and white chalk for the Women's Auxiliary at Northern Baptist Theological Seminary, Lombard, Illinois in 1963.

Other chalks and charcoals done before public audiences, *Christ in Gethsemane* (1941 © K&B 1942), *Teach Me Thy Way* (1951 © K&B 1952), *The Son of God* (1952 © K&B 1952), and *Portrait of Jesus* (1966 © K&B 1966), now reside in private collections.

Sallman would occasionally create an original work while in front of an audience. The brown chalk, *Christ Looking Down* (1948), done for Neighborhood Nite, 12 February 1948, at the North Park Covenant Church is, as far as we know, one of a kind. Other surviving drawings of unknown provenance include two charcoals entitled, *Face of Christ above Mary and Christchild* [1964], and two color chalks entitled, *Thorn-crowned Christ above Mary and Christchild* (1964). The former is a preliminary sketch of the latter, without the crown of thorns.

For many years, Sallman was featured in the Christmas program at Edgewater where he drew to music by the church choir. A few pieces from these programs have survived: *The Holy Family* (1948) a fine chalk 7 feet by 4½ feet done for the Christmas program in 1948, now in the James and Gene Sallman private collection; *God Is Love* (1960) done for the Christmas program in 1960, now in Covenant Archives; and some works of unknown date such as *The Flight into Egypt*, *Mary and the Baby*, and *Mary with Baby in Cloak*, which survive in private collections.

During 1948-1951 Sallman accompanied the Reverend Ralph Hanson on what were called "Missionary Blitz Tours." These tours sought to highlight Covenant mission work and raise money for missions. The traveling group, in addition to Hanson and Sallman, consisted of two or three Covenant missionaries, a musician or singer, and a Covenant leader from the conference or the denomination. Four or five churches normally went together to sponsor the rally. If one of the sponsoring churches was large enough, the rally would be held there. Otherwise a larger church, a high school gym, or, in the case of the rally planned for Oakland, California, a civic auditorium was rented.

The rally began with a presentation by one of the missionaries. Then Sallman would draw his *Head of Christ*, with vocal or instrumental music providing the background. At the end of the evening the picture would be auctioned off to the person making the largest contribution to missions. A general offering was also taken. Quite expectedly, a significant amount of money was raised for missions. In Turlock, California the chalk alone brought in $10,000, a considerable sum in those days.

Sallman appeared before crowds of all sizes. Sometimes one hundred or less would be present, other times two hundred or three hundred. At an Easter Sunday Evening service at Polytechnic Methodist in Fort Worth, Texas, in 1952, a crowd of more than eight hundred saw Sallman draw his *Christ Our Pilot*. A crowd of six hundred was on hand at Emmanuel Lutheran in Rockford, Illinois to see Sallman draw in 1956. In 1959, Sallman did a chalk *Head of Christ* for delegates and friends of the General Assembly of the Presbyterian Church US, held in the large Druid Hills Presbyterian Church in Atlanta, Georgia. This showing was arranged by his boyhood friend, Carl Olson, a member of Druid Hills Presbyterian. In June 1961 Sallman did a chalk *Head of Christ* for sixteen hundred people at an evening service in the Park Place Church of God in Anderson, Indiana.

Because Sallman could not fulfill all requests that came for a personal appearance, a color film entitled *Son of Man* was made in 1954 with the aim of reaching a larger audience. The film was jointly sponsored by North Park College, Swedish Covenant Hospital, and the Mission Covenant Church. At the beginning Sallman did a chalk of the *Head of Christ* in a church, and from that a dramatic story unfolded, showing what impact the living Christ had on a young man and woman about to embark on their careers. The filming took place in the North Park Covenant Church, with choral music provided by the North Park College Choir.

After filming, Sallman retained the chalk. Later he presented it to Ethel and Wally Cederberg of Attleboro, Massachussetts, in appreciation for a Stinson airplane the Cederbergs had donated to the Covenant for missionary work in Alaska. When the Cederbergs moved to Florida, they gave the picture to the Covenant Church of Attleboro, where it now hangs.

In 1966 Sallman came to the Salvation Army Officers' School in Chicago for what turned out to be one of his last public appearances. The crowd was large, and the event a memorable one. Sallman could no longer speak while drawing, as the chalk dust was causing serious problems to his lungs. His appearance on this particular occasion was a compromise of sorts. The doctor had told him to discontinue all chalk drawings, but he had found a dustless pastel crayon he thought he could use. However he still had to refrain from speaking. Paul Marshall, who was present for the evening, gives the following account:

> Even as Warner Sallman carefully adjusted his easel to catch the right lighting and prepared his drawing board for a coloured crayon replica of the Christ portrait, perhaps four or five times life size, the atmosphere was electric... Warner briefly told the story of how the drawing of the Christ head had come about, after which he turned to the Salvationists and said: "I shall be gratified if you will be kind enough to give me atmosphere and inspiration as I draw for you. While I work, please sing about Jesus."

Marshall continued,

Warner Sallman 'Live' 147

There was a moment's silence. Then a voice began, "Jesus, Jesus, Lily of the Valley, bloom in all Thy beauty in the garden of my heart," and soon it was a full-throated chorus. "Jesus, Jesus, Jesus, sweetest name I know," started another. Then, "Jesus is real to me." For nearly two hours the Salvationists sang about Jesus, as the artist portrayed Him... Skillful lines and bold colors sprang from the drawing to tell of a Christ, loving in heart and mighty in power; and when the group sang "Jesus, Thou art everything to me," the artist had already declared it in his portrait. Rarely, it would seem, could the unseen but real Christ have so deeply moved the hearts of His followers. He was present. He spoke, He blessed. He drew the company unto Himself with infinite compassion in an experience of abounding joy. When the artist finished his work, he bowed his head. So did everyone else.[6]

Marshall added that Sallman seemed to have trouble that night getting the eyes right. He worked and worked on them. Earlier Ruth had confided to him that as Warner got on in years, she was afraid one day he would start a chalk and not be able to bring it to a successful conclusion. It was, of course a classic portrait, and she realized as Warner did that while the picture may be completed, the possibility was a real one that it might not turn out just right. Marshall commented,

Many times a congregation would watch the work progress while glancing unconsciously from time to time at a large framed print of the original oil–comparing. He was stuck with an inflexible standard. "Does it look like the original?" Consequently, every performance had to be something of a home run.[7]

Marshall's recollections were echoed by others in attendance that evening.[8] The chalk drawn on this occasion has been preserved in the museum at the Salvation Army School for Officers' Training in Chicago.

[1] Carl F. Henry, "Sallman Made the Deadline," *Power* 19 (19 September 1943): 5.

[2] The occasion and where it took place is recorded in Sallman's hand on the back of the picture.

[3] Already in 1943 Sallman said he had "reproduced this picture for close friends, for preachers' groups, and for children hundreds of times...in crayon, in watercolor, and in oil." See T. Otto Nall, "He Preaches As He Paints," *Our Covenant Youth* 24/49 (5 December 1943): 4.

[4] One will find these artworks displayed all across the United States and Canada. Framed originals can be found in the following churches, schools, and

campus centers: Evangelical Covenant, North Mankato, Minnesota; First Covenant, Marinette, Wisconsin; Covenant Congregational, Boston, MA; Easton Covenant (=Bridgeport), Connecticut; Pilgrim Covenant, Brooklyn, New York; Beverly Evangelical Covenant (=Redeemer), Chicago, Illinois; First Covenant, Rockford, Illinois; First Covenant, Moline, Illinois; Turlock Covenant, Turlock, California; Berkeley Covenant, Berkeley, California; Emmanuel Lutheran, Rockford, Illinois; First United Methodist, Mason City, Iowa; Polytechnic United Methodist, Fort Worth, Texas; First United Methodist, Chicago (Chicago Temple); (New North) Austin United Methodist, Chicago; Lyonsville Congregational, Burr Ridge Illinois; Park Place Church of God, Anderson, Indiana; First United Methodist and the Wesley Foundation, Tuscalossa, Alabama; and the Salvation Army Officers Training School, Chicago. There are many, many more—including some now existing in private collections.

[5] Howard Ellis, "Art with a Message III," *Covenant Youth Today* 3/3 (17 March 1957): 2.

[6] Paul Marshall, "An Evening with Sallman." *War Cry* Toronto 4249 (30 April 1966): 2.

[7] Paul Marshall's notes on Warner Sallman in the author's possession.

[8] Margaret Troutt, "Gospel Artist," *War Cry* 101/5 (31 January 1981): 5.

Protestantism...has spawned an immense but largely ignored popular visual culture. This genre has influenced how millions of Protestants think and feel about Christ. In this respect we can speak of Sallman's work as a popular classic...A popular classic is the representation embraced by the nonelite. (David Morgan, Valparaiso University)

Two years after prints of the Sallman Christ head in oil were first offered for sale, in June 1943, William McDermott wrote in the *Chicago Daily News* about religious pictures selling in the gift shop of the Cathedral of St. John the Divine in New York City. He said,

> The famous work by Hofmann is the most popular. There are several by living artists, but the one by far most sought after is that by a Chicago commercial artist and religious lay reader, Warner Sallman...I have long been an admirer of it. But when I discovered that it was accepted by cathedral visitors from the world over–most of them religious-minded and of discriminating taste–I realized that it must have merit of unusually high order.[1]

McDermott expressed the hope that some day "proper recognition may come to the local artist for his work." By 1943, critical comments about the Sallman pictures–particularly the *Head of Christ*–began surfacing, and they continued in the years following World War II. Sallman art, it seems, had now come to the point where it merited critical attention.

In 1943 an art professor at Wheaton College (Illinois), DeWitt Jayne, questioned the originality of Sallman's famous work, noting a similarity to Christ's head and upper body in L'hermitte's *Friend of the Humble* (1892). This work hung in the Boston Museum of Fine Arts. Jayne added insult to injury by saying later, "Sallman didn't even have the draftsmanship to make a good copy of it."[2]

Houghton College (New York) Art Professor H. Willard Ortlip agreed about the indebtedness to L'hermitte, but he at least gave credit to Sallman for borrowing the lighting and shading around the head.[3] More recently, Professor David Morgan of Valparaiso University has concluded much the same, deciding that Sallman must have used the L'hermitte painting to "flesh out his midnight sketch." Morgan says, "The shape and attitude of the head and the patterns of

light on Christ's forehead and brow strongly suggest that Sallman had the reproduction of Lhermitte's picture in front of him as he created the 1924 charcoal
version."[4]

Sallman never saw the L'hermitte original. What he did see was a picture of
Friend of the Humble on a magazine cover. Our one and only source for this
information is Margaret Anderson, who interviewed Sallman and reported the
following in a 1961 *War Cry* article:

> ...as a child, [Sallman] spent many hours poring over copies of Gustave
> Dore's illustrated Bible pictures. Later he was drawn to Munkacsy's
> *Christ Before Pilate*. When he saw L'hermitte's *The Friend of the Lowly*
> used as a *Ladies Home Journal* cover, he had it framed and gave it to his
> mother.[5]

There is a problem, however, in that no picture of L'hermitte's *Friend of the
Humble / Friend of the Lowly*, ever appeared on a *Ladies Home Journal* (*LHJ*)
cover. Sallman must therefore have taken the picture from another magazine
cover, or from inside a *LHJ* issue, or else from another source entirely.

A print of *Friend of the Humble* did appear inside a *LHJ* issue dated
December 1922. David Morgan assumes that this is the picture Anderson
reports Sallman as having seen. With a publication so close in time to Sallman's
own sketch—only one year earlier—Morgan concludes that the picture would be
readily at hand for Sallman's use, and that he did use it.

Such a reconstruction, however, is quite unlikely. First of all, it ignores the
context of the L'hermitte sighting in the Anderson article. The prior experiences
cited by Anderson, both of which are well-known, can easily be dated. Sallman
pored over the Doré pictures when he was about four. The impression made by
the Munkacsy painting in the Lake View Mission Church also came early. Sylvia
Peterson says it was when he was "yet a very small boy."[6] It had to be before
confirmation, because after confirmation Sallman began attending the
Waveland Avenue Congregational Church. These early years are then the proper
context for his giving the L'hermitte picture to his mother, the mention of
which completes the Anderson paragraph. The next paragraph refers to
Sallman's enrollment at Moody Bible Institute prior to January 1914, which
gives us a *terminus ad quem* for the incident in question.

According to the Morgan reconstruction Sallman finds the L'hermitte and
gives it to his mother between 1922 and 1924, at which time he is thirty or
more years old, married for six or more years, and living with his wife Ruth in
their own home over in North Park. An unlikely scenario, to say the least, not to
mention that the alleged dates extend well beyond the *terminus ad quem*.

Sallman's reply to the charge of influence from L'hermitte also deserves
another look. Sallman said, "I don't wonder that people say the L'Hermitte

painting influenced my drawing. Isn't everything we create a composite of what we have subconsciously stored through the years?"[7]

What does "subconsciously stored through the years" mean? Can it mean that Sallman copied from the L'hermitte work in direct fashion as Morgan and others imagine? Hardly. The L'hermitte sighting—like pivotal life experiences he so often cited in this connection[8]—influenced his drawing *subconsciously*, which all but precludes the Morgan interpretation. Also, the plain meaning of "through the years" is that the L'hermitte viewing was well in the past.

In another account Sallman says about the completed 1924 Christ head in charcoal, "Strangely enough, it was almost precisely what I had seen in my dream. All I did was to reproduce as faithfully as I could what I had seen in my dream."[9] Sallman goes on to refer to the many life experiences that went into the preparation of the picture, but does not mention the L'hermitte piece. Jim Sallman cannot remember his father ever talking about the L'hermitte painting, another indication that the experience of seeing it was long in the past and had no direct impact on the charcoal drawing of 1924.

Arguments then for direct dependence of the Sallman Christ head on the L'hermitte picture rest solely on a comparison between the two works. How close are they? How different? The Sallman picture, when held up against the original as I did with a staff member of the Boston Museum of Fine Arts some years ago, does not look that similar. But, of course, the likeness is said to be between the Sallman drawing and a *published picture* of the L'hermitte. Here the similarity is admittedly greater. But more than that one cannot say.

One would do better to compare the 1924 sketch with faces of Christ Sallman drew earlier for *Förbundets Veckotidning* such as *Resurrected Christ Rising from Crucified Christ* (1920, published in *FV* 359, 30 March 1920: 1). The work presents a frontal view of Christ's face, but there are similarities, all the same, to the 1924 Christ head. There are also similarities in the profile of Christ appearing in *A Thank Offering?* published just two months before the 1924 sketch (*FV* 500, 27 November 1923: 1).

Another criticism made of the Sallman Christ focused on its "strength" and "manliness." Already the Sallman charcoal of 1924 had evoked responses that this Christ looked "strong and manly," unlike earlier depictions that were weak, emaciated and effeminate. Sallman himself made the claim. Now not everyone agreed. A 1948 *Time* article reported the emotional reaction of a certain Alan Devoe, who had written a piece in the *American Mercury* in which he said he was scandalized because Sunday school teachers and parents, in using the Sallman picture, were presenting to children "a distorted, sissified impression of Christ." This picture, said Devoe, showed Christ as

> ...a pale and posturing person with immoderately long, silky hair...who clutched a kind of diaphanous drapery gracefully about him

with an expression of simpering vapidity. It was into this hand, so unmistakably the limp and clammy hand of an effeminate curate, that little boys were to put theirs trustingly...This was the pietistic poseur—the very spit of every disgusting little 'teacher's pet'...that we were to take as the earthly evidence of what The Everlasting God is like.

Devoe felt that the New Testament tells us enough about Christ's "manner of speech and the habits of his days" so we can be sure "he was not frail, not pale, not piously smirking, not actorishly barbered and finical. He was one who spoke homely and strong."[10]

Lutheran scholar Paul Roth voiced a similar criticism a decade later. His remarks focused on what he called the "calendar art of the unsophisticated:" "In Sallman's *Head of Christ* we have a pretty picture of a woman with a curling beard who has just come from the beauty parlor with a Halo shampoo, but we do not have the Lord who died and rose again."[11]

The same year, in 1958, Harold Ehrensperger who was professor of religion and creative arts at Boston University School of Theology, said regarding the Sallman Christ head, "The most famous picture of Jesus makes him look weak and effeminate. You present this famous picture of Jesus on some of our mission fields, and the people say, 'Your God looks weak.'"[12]

Interestingly enough, Homiletics Professor William Stidger of the same school stated earlier that the Sallman picture, in his view, was genuinely creative, and he embraced it with enthusiasm.[13] Among the art critics, then, there seems to be no consensus as to whether the Sallman Christ head looks masculine or feminine, strong or weak. It should be pointed out, however, that these criticisms all predate the return to long hair among men in the 1960s, and the gender debates of the 1970s and 1980s.

The criticism that Sallman's Christ looks too weak and effeminate is similar to another argument that says the portrayal is not "rugged" enough. Devoe objected to Sallman's Christ being "actorishly barbered;" Roth didn't like what looked to him to be "a pretty picture." Yet if one looks at other contemporary Christ pictures, for example the *Jesus of Nazareth* done by the Hungarian-American painter Louis Jambor (1949), which was widely-acclaimed in the 1950s and said to project Christ's spiritual greatness as well as his physical strength, the hair, eyes and other facial features are scarcely different from Sallman's Christ.[14] Perhaps the question being asked here is whether or not the Sallman portrayal of Christ is, in fact, too nice-looking.

Yet a beautiful Christ does not strike everyone as necessarily bad. Bernt Opsal, after looking at a colored chalk of the Sallman Christ head hanging in the lobby of the Minneapolis Lutheran Bible Institute, made this comment:

As I stand in front of this portrait, I realize that this is not an actual photograph of our Lord. This is Sallman's interpretation or his understanding of what Christ must have been like at a certain time during His life. I appreciate this interpretation. As I look and ponder, I am reminded of that wonderful hymn, "Beautiful Savior." But I appreciate other interpretations too...[15]

Opsal goes on to express appreciation–particularly during Lent–for pictures of Christ not so beautiful–of "Christ on the cross, suffering and dying for our sins." Sallman, it should be noted, did pictures of the suffering Christ, one of the most extraordinary being the watercolor, *Crown of Thorns* (1941 © K&B 1956), which depicted Christ as the Suffering Servant of Isaiah 53.

Morgan, to return to the 1940 Christ head, accents the genial virtues that the image conveys:

The features of Sallman's Christ reveal the gentle, compassionate, approachable savior whom believers desire. Christ's countenance in this image promises a relationship with the savior to those who seek to understand him in an essentially pastoral and intimate way.[16]

By 1962 Sallman's *Head of Christ* had made *Christian Century*'s list of things "on the way out,"[17] a backhanded concession of sorts that for a time, at least, the picture had been considered "in." It certainly was "in" for one critic who called it "an evangelical icon,"[18] putting the picture on a par with the art form in Eastern Orthodoxy that Protestants–and before them Roman Catholics–judged to be idolatrous.

To some extent, Sallman's *Head of Christ* fell out of fashion because of a long-standing elitist attitude that art becomes cheapened by reproduction, especially mass reproduction. The Sallman *Head of Christ* and other Sallman pictures appear on book marks, stationery, witness cards, funeral cards, key chains, plaques, and illuminated clocks in book stores, department stores, and trinket shops across America. Many who buy the reproductions–not to mention the many who disdain the same–know nothing of oil originals, or other Sallman originals in oil, watercolor, charcoal, pen, and other media. The *Mona Lisa* and Leonardo daVinci's *Last Supper* have also been much reproduced, but here, at least, the originals are known.

In the 1960s and 1970s anti-WASP (White, Anglo-Saxon, Protestant) sentiments surfacing in the wake of Civil Rights included a strong reaction against Sallman art. The *Head of Christ* was now said to be "too white," "too Western-looking," "too Northern European," etc. While still a seminarian at North Park in 1967, I overheard a friend make a disparaging remark about the Sallman *Head of Christ* that was hanging on the wall in Isaacson Chapel. I asked him why he didn't like it. He said, "It's a white Christ; looks too Swedish!" I asked him if he would object to a black-faced Christ. "Oh, no," he said, "I'd have no problem with that." When asked what made one painting acceptable and the other one not, he responded that he did not know. I've asked the same question many times since, and almost without exception the answer has been along the same lines. Individuals who recoil at the Sallman picture because it looks too white, or too Nordic, will embrace—with no critical judgment whatever—a Christ painted to look Afro-American.

Anti-WASP sentiment was likely behind the reaction to a Sallman picture, about this same time, at Northern Baptist Theological Seminary in Lombard, Illinois. Sallman did a *Power and Glory* (1957 © K&B 1958) in chalk for the Seminary Women's Auxiliary in 1963, but a few years later it had to be taken down because of student opposition. The dean told me the picture was "hidden" for a number of years in a closet. Later it was restored to the student commons, where it now hangs.

There has also been a disproportional uneasiness about Sallman's juxtaposition, in certain pictures, of an ancient-looking Christ with American people and American settings in the 1940s and 1950s. The most oft-cited example is *He Careth for You* (1954), where Christ has a first-century Palestinian look—long hair and wearing a robe—while everything else is contemporary America. The three American children—also the American doll—all wear the clothes of the 1950s. The background is rural America of the same period—a country house and a neo-colonial church in the distance. If this painting were known abroad, which it is not, one wonders how people in different cultures would assess it, whether they would respond as negatively as do many Americans who knew and lived through America of the 1950s.

Perhaps what we want is art a bit more stylized. When I saw the painted altar reliefs of Bror Hjorth (1894-1968)—whose dates correspond almost exactly to those of Sallman—in the Jukkasjärvi Church near Kiruna in northern Sweden, I had no objection to seeing Sami (=Lapp) people—and Jesus too— portrayed in native Sami dress. In fact, it struck me as charming. Why? I'm not sure. These people, of course, look differently than Americans. But my positive assessment could be to Hjorth's stylized art. Hjorth studied in Paris during the 1920s, where he came under the influence of the Cubist Movement.

Actually, it has long been considered acceptable in religious paintings to blend the ancient with the contemporary. Early frescos of Mary and the baby Jesus in the catacombs of Rome depict the babe as a young Orpheus in a Phrygian dress, and Mary as a Roman matron both in type and costume.[19] The Renaissance masters likewise depicted biblical figures in types and costumes corresponding to their own day and country,[20] as did the Middle Ages painters preceding them. The Spanish, German, Flemish, and Dutch painters all did the same. One notes, for example, monastic dress and an abbey setting in Dieric Bouts' (1410/20-1475) *Christ in the House of Simon the Pharisee*; the same in Thierry Bouts' (1415-1475) *Last Supper*; a contemporary church chancel in B. Furtmeyr's *Abendmahl* (1482); contemporary dress and a contemporary house in Jacob van Oostsanen's *The Adoration of the Christ Child* (circa 1520); contemporary dress of the three men and a foreground chair from the time in Caravaggio's (1573-1610) *Supper at Emmaus*; contemporary dress of the two men and a contemporary table setting in Valázquez' (1599-1660) *Christ and the Pilgrims of Emmaus*; contemporary dress of the three men and a contemporary table and chairs in Rembrandt's *Les pèlerins d'Emmaüs* (1648); contemporary dress and a contemporary house with shutters in Renesse's *La parabole du Bon Samaritain* (circa 1650); contemporary formal dress of the assembled men, a contemporary banquet table, and contemporary chairs—indeed contemporary decor of the entire banquet room—in Jean Béraud's *La Madeleine chez le Pharisien* (1891); contemporary peasant dress and a contemporary setting in L'hermitte's *Friend of the Humble* (1892), also his *(Christ) Among the Poor in Heart* (1905); etc. As one critic has said, these "innocent anachronisms shocked no one."[21]

On the subject of Christ's portrayal being time- and culture-conditioned Billy Graham has said,

> Artists through the centuries have tried to depict Christ as they imagined him to be. He has been painted as a Dutch burgher, a Norwegian workman, a German peasant, an Oriental, and an American. Each century has painted him in the frame of its particular mood or experience. Warner Sallman's *Head of Christ* probably is more satisfying to Americans than the more ancient conceptions which portrayed Christ as weak and emaciated. Perhaps the reason why we have no likeness of Christ is that he desired to be seen in the lives of his disciples. The Bible says, "As we have borne the image of the earthly, we shall also bear the image of the heavenly" (1 Cor 15:49).[22]

The question of genre—also quality—of the Sallman art was raised in somewhat crude fashion by Jerry Adler in a *Newsweek* article of 1979.[23] Sallman, said Adler, perpetuates the "saccharine vision" of nineteenth century religious art—that devitalized sentimentality, which was a kind of backwater between the high art of the Renaissance that depicted Jesus as unmistakably human, and serious twentieth century religious art that gives "realistic" portraits of Christ, more or less. To make his point a Rembrandt portrait of Christ was juxtaposed to Sallman's *Look unto Me* (1958)—a work virtually unknown, and one that was never successfully marketed. The caption below said: "from Rembrandt to schlock" (Yiddish for "trash, something cheap"). Adler then repeated the disdain expressed earlier by Roth for mass-produced calendar art.

More recently, however, "calendar art" has been appraised positively. There are, for example, the highly-acclaimed calendars of Norman Rockwell paintings, the popular calendars of paintings by the Swedish artist Carl Larsson (1853-1919), and the now-classic Americana Calendar, which contains paintings on early American life by the Polish-American artist Charles Wysocki. One could mention others. Warner Press, in recent years, has issued calendars of the Sallman paintings.

Elitist criticism of the Sallman Christ head sunk to a new low when Martin Marty said a few years ago in a published remark that this picture had to be "as ugly as a rented bowling shoe." He embellished the comparison saying, "It's so banal and insipid that, like rented bowling shoes, it tempts no one to steal it." "With it," Marty assures his readers, "you can keep church doors open."[24] This criticism, unlike most for which Marty has become known over the years, hones in on nothing.

Renewed attention to the Sallman art has forced the needed question whether popular religious art does, in fact, have a rightful legitimacy. Morgan raises this question forthrightly:

> Protestantism…has spawned an immense but largely ignored popular visual culture. This genre has influenced how millions of Protestants think and feel about Christ. In this respect we can speak of Sallman's work as a popular classic…A popular classic is the representation embraced by the nonelite.[25]

Morgan recognizes that much of the criticism made of the Sallman art originates in intellectual and upper class circles. Roth talked about the "calendar art of the unsophisticated." Sallman, perhaps anticipating this judgment nearly fifty years ago, said, "Of course, the *Head of Christ* is not intended for scholars or theologians. It is intended to present the Master so that he who runs may see and understand."[26]

Richard Leet, Director of the Charles H. MacNider Museum in Mason City, Iowa, thinks the Sallman art should be compared with the art of N. C. Wyeth, Remington, and Russell who painted the American West, as well as Norman Rockwell, who said of himself that he was an illustrator, basically.

Sallman was an illustrator. He did not work through art dealers, but with religious publishing firms who were in the business of producing inspirational literature. David Morgan correctly states that "[Sallman's] chosen vocation was not 'fine artist' but illustrator; his preferred audience was not the cultured elite of the art world but devout Christians."[27]

Where then does Sallman fit into the modern art movement? Perhaps nowhere. If so, he may still be in good company. The following has been said of Norman Rockwell:

> In 1913, when the great Armory Show introduced modern art to New Yorkers, Norman Rockwell was busy doing one hundred ink drawings for the *Boy Scouts Hike Book*. What part has our most popular artist played in the upheavals which have made us a major power in the art world? Absolutely none. He—and all those other artists with publishers instead of galleries—are the "meanwhile back at the ranch" branch of modern art.[28]

Olga Lindborg, too, remarked back in the 1920s, "America has developed a class of artists known fundamentally as *illustrators*, of which the world may well be proud, and of which the world may well admit: they are unsurpassed–except by themselves."[29]

Lindborg cited the pictures of W. L. Taylor, Harold Copping and O. A. Stemler as splendid examples of art used to illustrate Bible stories–better than any Raphael, daVinci, or Rubens. In her view, "Great pictures frequently are not illustrative! They are simply works of art."[30] Lindborg later added the pictures of Warner Sallman to her list of extraordinary illustrative art.

Morgan agrees that the works of the "Old Masters" have not had impacted twentieth century American Christians the way Sallman art has "…Sallman's images have done more to inform the imagination of twentieth-century American Christians than images by such venerable 'Old Masters' as Raphael, Michaelangelo, or Rubens."[31] Jane Lauber, having arrived at the same conclusion, urged therefore that church publishing houses make more use of the great masterpieces in the teaching materials they produce.[32]

Morgan in recently published articles has provided other insights into the Sallman art, some of which merit further discussion. For example, he has pointed out how Sallman's *Head of Christ* reflects contemporary photographic art:

> The darkened definition of eyes, nose and lips, which also stand out by virtue of their pigmentation (pink- colored lips and blue eyes), combined with blurred contours and soft lighting, recall the retouched studio photographs that replaced portrait painting in the late nineteenth and early twentieth centuries. The head and shoulders format of the image further hints at commercial studio photography.[33]

The *Head of Christ* certainly does look like a studio photograph, particularly with its "head and shoulders format." Perhaps there was some family influence here. Sallman's cousin, Evelyn Sallman, was a professional photographer who owned the Sallman Studios on North Clark Street in Chicago. But influence is certainly much broader than this, coming indeed from the larger American culture, where, for a century or more, portraits of every description have appeared before an American public highly responsive to visual images.[34]

Morgan also develops the point that Sallman's Christ images have become religious "icons." They are so in two distinct senses. First, they are icons in the traditional sense, i.e., pictures such as those in the Eastern Orthodox tradition that create for the believer "a special linkage to Christ himself—whether by virtue of ontological metamorphosis or actual resemblance confirmed by mystical vision."[35] Morgan cites two examples of people who reported miraculous happenings from the picture, one where the picture secreted a red substance from the right eye of Christ.[36] Many other similar happenings have been reported.

The pictures are also "Protestant icons," says Morgan, in the sense that they are "images that poignantly visualize to Protestant believers the world of social relations (rather than celestial persona) that characterize their lives."[37] Morgan expands this definition:

> In accord with the Protestant imperative of transforming daily life, Sallman's art has been most widely deployed in the everyday world—in the home, hospital, office, workplace, and purse—in hopes of influencing practical conduct by visualizing a properly Christian social order.[38]

Individuals attest to Sallman's *Head of Christ* having given them an immediate sense of the "presence" of Christ, the testimony basically of Paul Marshall after seeing a chalk Christ head done "live." Yet, as Morgan says, "the picture remains a picture," which spares it the charge of being idolatrous.

Morgan continues to say Sallman art reflects American Protestant middle class values of family, gender, rural life, etc. Citing *He Careth for You* (1954 © K&B 1954), he says, "Humility, obedience, and security—all are the features of a patriarchal ethos of conservative Protestantism in America that admirers of Sallman's work have found especially appealing."[39]

My own observation, after examining a Sallman inventory that currently numbers over five hundred original works, is that Sallman art

a) is international in scope, and includes depictions not only of Anglo-Americans but also of American Indians, Alaskan Eskimos, and other ethnic groups;

b) is evenly balanced in presenting women and men, children, young people and adults;

c) is urban as well as rural, and after 1950 develops in a number of artworks the motif of space;

d) addresses social issues—including the rich and the poor—besides promoting the family and a personal devotional life;

e) presents war—including apocalyptic scenes—as well as pastoral and other peaceful scenes;

f) depicts a thorn-crowned and suffering Christ as well as a Christ risen and victorious.

From the very beginning Sallman's art had a global view. This perspective largely originated from his interest in and support of Christian missions. His faces of children are the faces of children from around the world, not just white, Protestant, middle class children. See, for example, *A Mirror for the Soul* (1929), and *The Children of the World* in stained glass (1952). A number of Sallman works also depict native American Indians and their culture. The most extensive was the frieze done for Cherokee Hall at Camp Shagbark in 1934, but see also *American Indian and the US Capitol* (1920), and *Indian Trail Tree* (1949).

Evangelism posters commonly picture the globe, e.g., *World for God Campaign* (1935); *Thorn-crowned Christ on World* (1942); and *An Army on the March* (1942). See also the globe on *The Compassionate Christ* (1944). The motif of space—which develops naturally from earlier global and cosmic scenes—appears in *I Have Overcome the World* (1952); *Power and Glory* (1957 © K&B 1958); *Face of Our Lord in Space* (1959); and *Behold He Cometh* (1967).

Whatever may be concluded from *He Careth for You* about Sallman reflecting the "patriarchal ethos" of conservative Protestant America, it is nevertheless the case that in Sallman pictures women as well as men teach Bible classes, young women stand alongside young men as they study or prepare for full-time Christian service, and children are not eclipsed by adults when the sum of Sallman artwork is examined. His emphasis on the family, no doubt, had much to do with this. But the church, for Sallman, was the entire "household of God" (Eph 2:19).

Sallman admittedly did a number of pastoral scenes. One might even say that landscape painting took over on some of his religious works such as *The Road to Emmaus* (1961 © K&B 1961). Like all artists, he loved nature and painted it with relish—in religious as well as non-religious works. He also had, from early childhood, a fascination with the Wild West. But Morgan errs in saying that "Sallman never painted the modern urban world in his religious work, but depicted only nostalgic rural towns and biblical cities."[40] The city may not be prominent in *Walk in the Light* (1951), but it is present. Sallman did a poster for the Best Seller Publicity entitled, *Christ Looking at the City* (1957). City buildings can also be seen in *Family Altar of the American Home* (1923) and *Kneeling Man in a Beam of Light* (1933).

Sallman art does accent the devotional side of the Christian life. It also addresses social issues, beginning with posters Sallman made for the Temperance Movement while he was still a teenager. Temperance movements in nineteenth century Sweden and early twentieth century America, were responses to serious social maladies. The problem of inequality between the rich and poor comes forth strongly in the political cartoon, *Tax Payers Feast and Fast* (1928).

Devotional themes ought also to be juxtaposed to missionary themes, themes of giving to missions and other benevolences, and themes of liberation for service to Christ and humankind. All are well represented in the total Sallman output. A related theme one sees often in Sallman art, and a very important one, is the ministry of healing in both its biblical and modern setting. This too is but another expression of genuine social concern.

Much of Sallman's artwork during World War II, particularly that done for the Salvation Army, focuses on the hurt of war and humanity's longing for peace. The ravages of World War II appear vividly in *The Crusading Christ* [1944]. Earlier, during World War I, Sallman did two illustrations on war and peace for *Förbundets Veckotidning: Frid på jorden* (1918) and *Hope for the New Year* (1918). Two pictures from the post-World War II era depict nuclear explosions: the apocalyptic *Thine Is the Power* (1951) and *Christ at Prayer on Globe* (1961).

Finally, while we see in Sallman art many depictions of the Christ risen and victorious, depictions of the suffering Christ are not wanting. There is *Crown of Thorns* (1941 © K&B 1956), done in watercolor, and the many oils done during 1940 and 1941 of Christ in Gethsemane. Likewise, the suffering Christ can be seen in *Thorn-crowned Christ* (1926); *Thorn-crowned Christ on the World* (1942); *Christ Carrying the Cross* (1942); *Pilate and the Angry Crowd* (1943); *The Compassionate Christ* (1944); and *Thorn-crowned Christ above Mary and Christchild* (1964). The extraordinary chalk *Christ Looking Down* (1948), is likewise not the victorious Christ, but the one known rather as "Man of Sorrows."

[1] William F. McDermott, "A Visit to a Cathedral," *Chicago Daily News*, 6 February 1943, 7.

[2] Carl F. Henry, "Evangelical Piety and Christian Art," *Christianity Today* 11/11 (3 March 1958): 26.

[3] Ibid., 32.

[4] David Morgan, "Sallman's *Head of Christ*: The History of an Image," *The Christian Century* 109/28 (7 October 1992): 869-870.

[5] Anderson, "His Subject Shaped His Life," 8.

[6] Sylvia Peterson, "The Ministry of Christian Art," *The Lutheran Companion* 55/14 (2 April 1947): 10.

[7] Ibid.

[8] See earlier chapter V.

[9] Nall, "He Preaches As He Paints," 3.

[10] "Not Frail, Not Pale," *Time* (22 November 1948), 70.

11 Robert Paul Roth, "Christ and the Muses," *Christianity Today* 11/11 (3 March 1958): 9.

12 Henry, "Evangelical Piety and Christian Art," 32.

13 Letter from William L. Stidger to Warner Sallman, 26 January 1949.

14 It was published in the *Chicago Sunday Tribune Grafic Magazine* (10 April 1949): 8; also in the *Sunday Tribune's Grafic Magazine* (24 February 1952): 7. See in addition the *Christian Advocate* 126/10 (8 March 1951): front cover; and *(Covenant) Youth Today* 7/8 (1 August 1954): part 1, 4.

15 Bernt C. Opsal, "The Many-Sided Christ," *The Bible Banner* 39/4 (July-August 1963): 2-3.

16 Morgan, "Imaging Protestant Piety: The Icons of Warner Sallman," 34-35.

17 "'In' and 'Out,'" *The Christian Century* 79:23 (6 June 1962): 731.

18 Jane W. Lauber, "Are We Losing Our Artist Heritage?" *Christianity Today* 10/23 (2 September 1966): 24.

19 Lindborg, "Choosing Pictures That Illustrate Bible Stories I," *The Teacher's Companion* 2/4 (September 1923): 6.

20 Ibid.

21 Maurice Hamel, *The Salons of 1905*, trans. Paul Villars (Paris and New York: Goupil & Co. [Manzi, Joyant & Co.], 1905), 13.

22 Printed in the *Chicago American* during the summer of 1957, and quoted by Sallman in a talk before the Union League Club on 4 November 1957.

23 Jerry Adler, "The Faces of Jesus," *Newsweek* (24 December 1979): 51.

24 [Martin Marty], "As Ugly As a Rented Bowling Shoe, "*Context* (15 February 1990): 4.

25 Morgan, "Sallman's *Head of Christ*:: The History of an Image," 869

26 Nall, "He Preaches As He Paints," 4. The final words appear to paraphrase Habakkuk 2:2: "Write the vision; make it plain upon the tablets, so he may run who reads it."

27 Morgan, "Imaging Protestant Piety: The Icons of Warner Sallman," 30.

28 Thomas S. Buechner, *Norman Rockwell: A Sixty Year Retrospective* (New York: Harry N. Abrams, 1972) 7.

29 Lindborg, "Choosing Pictures That Illustrate Bible Stories II," 6.

30 Lindborg, "Choosing Pictures That Illustrate Bible Stories I," 5.

31 Morgan, "Imaging Protestant Piety: The Icons of Warner Sallman," 30.

32 Lauber, "Are We Losing Our Artistic Heritage?" 24.

33 Morgan, "Sallman's *Head of Christ*:: The History of an Image," 868.

34 This point was well made by Professor Neil Harris of the University of Chicago in a response given at the conference on the art of Warner Sallman held at the Divinity School, the University of Chicago, on 4 March 1994.

35 Morgan, "Imaging Protestant Piety: The Icons of Warner Sallman," 32-35. This first sense, however, applies only to the Eastern Orthodox tradition, not to

both Eastern Orthodox and Roman Catholic traditions as Morgan states. The Eastern and Western Church split on the use of icons centuries ago.

36 Ibid., 33.

37 Ibid., 32.

38 Ibid., 34.

39 Ibid., 39.

40 Ibid., 39.

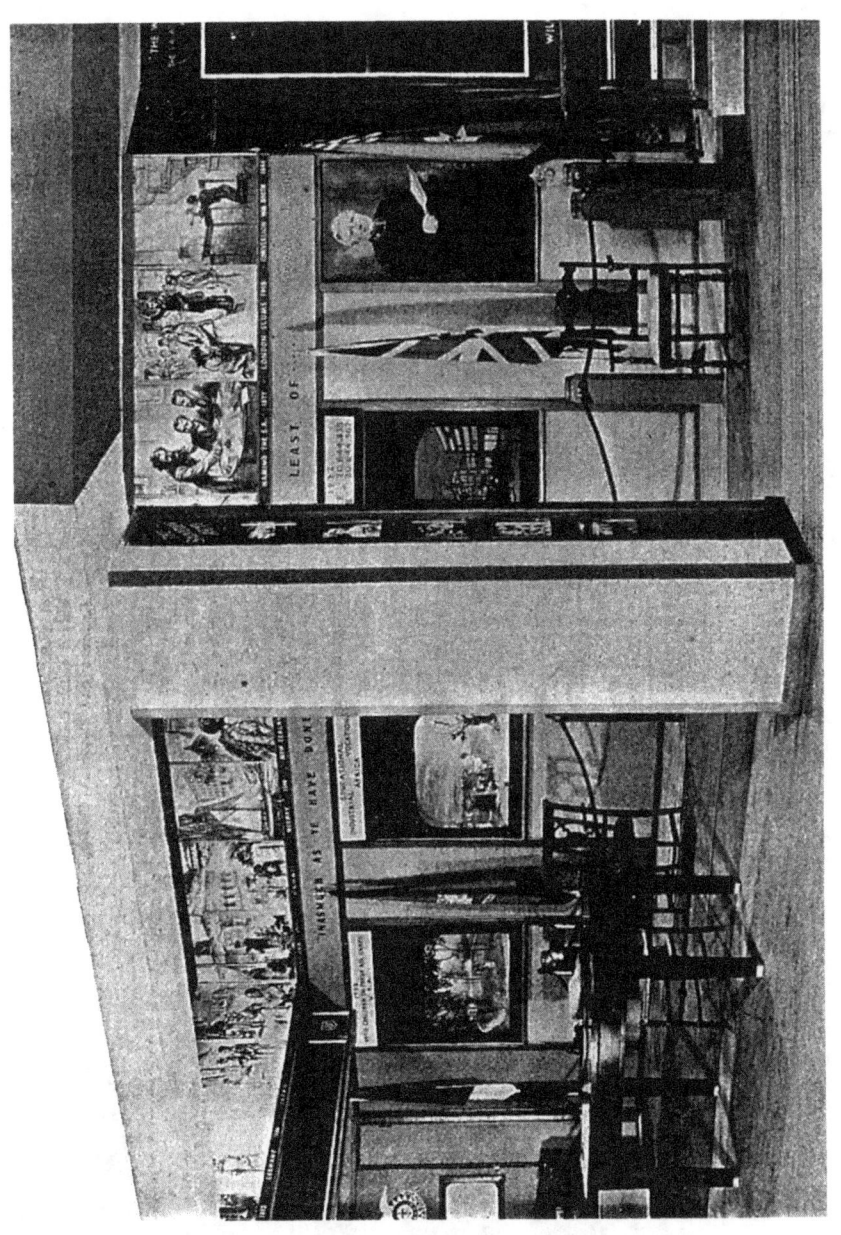

Salvation Army Frieze (1933-34) at the Chicago Century of Progress.

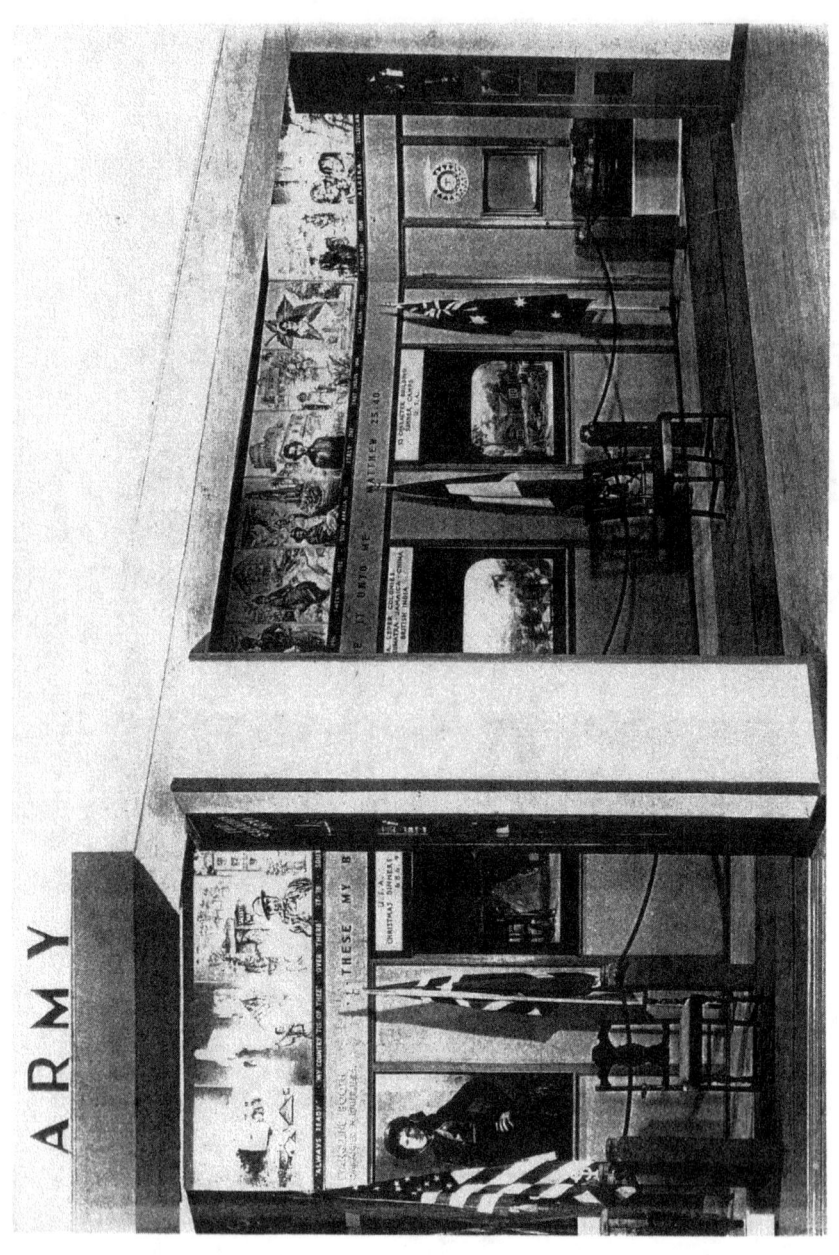

Salvation Army Frieze (1933-34) at the Chicago Century of Progress.

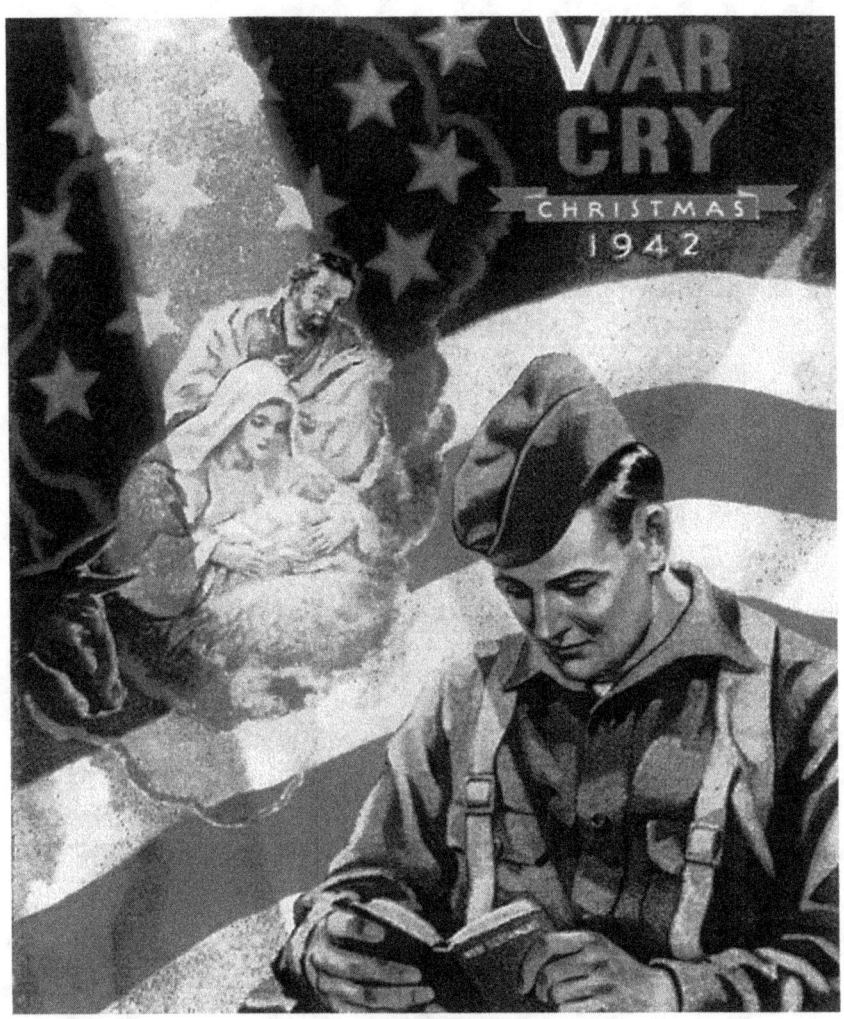

The Christmas Story (1942) medium unknown. Printed in *The War Cry*.

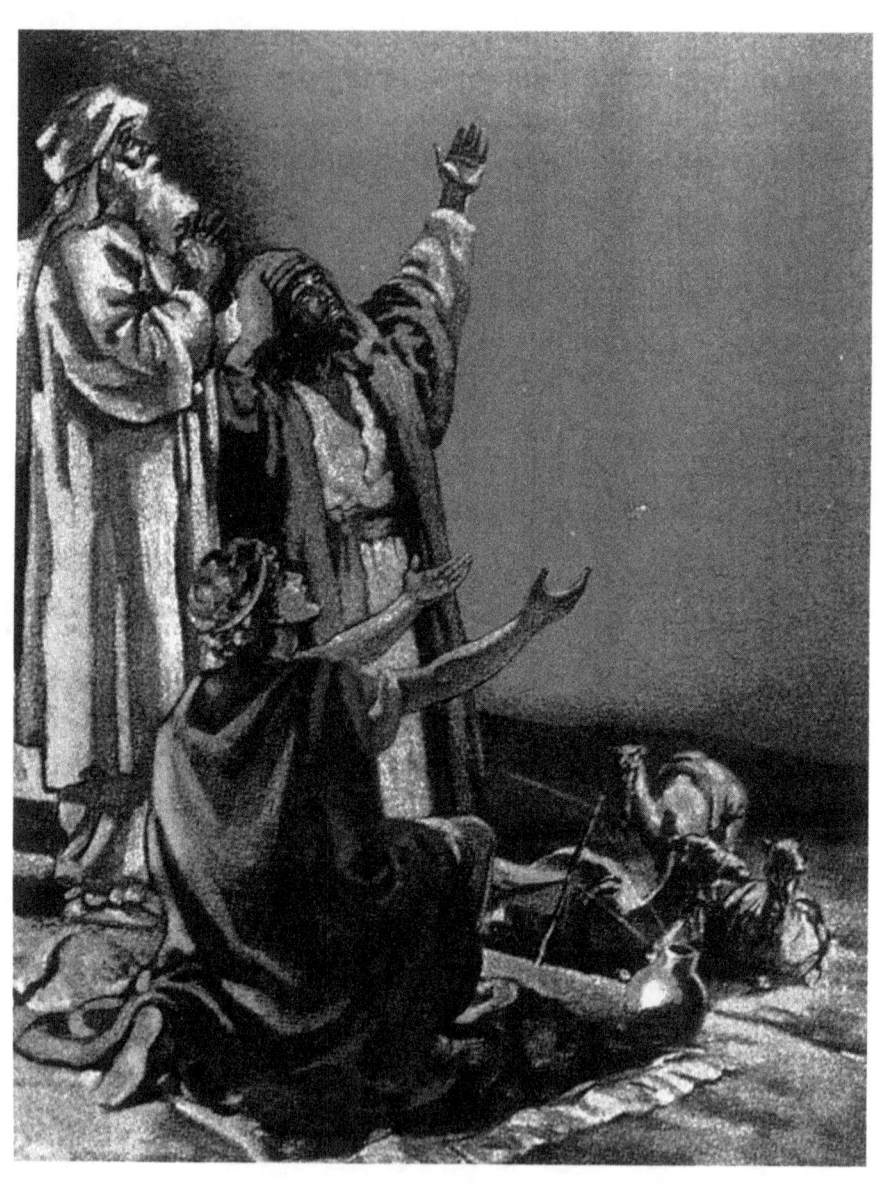

The Wise Men (1942) oil. Printed in *The War Cry*.

The Evangelistic Note

Volume I   CHICAGO, ILL., MARCH, 1921   Number 2

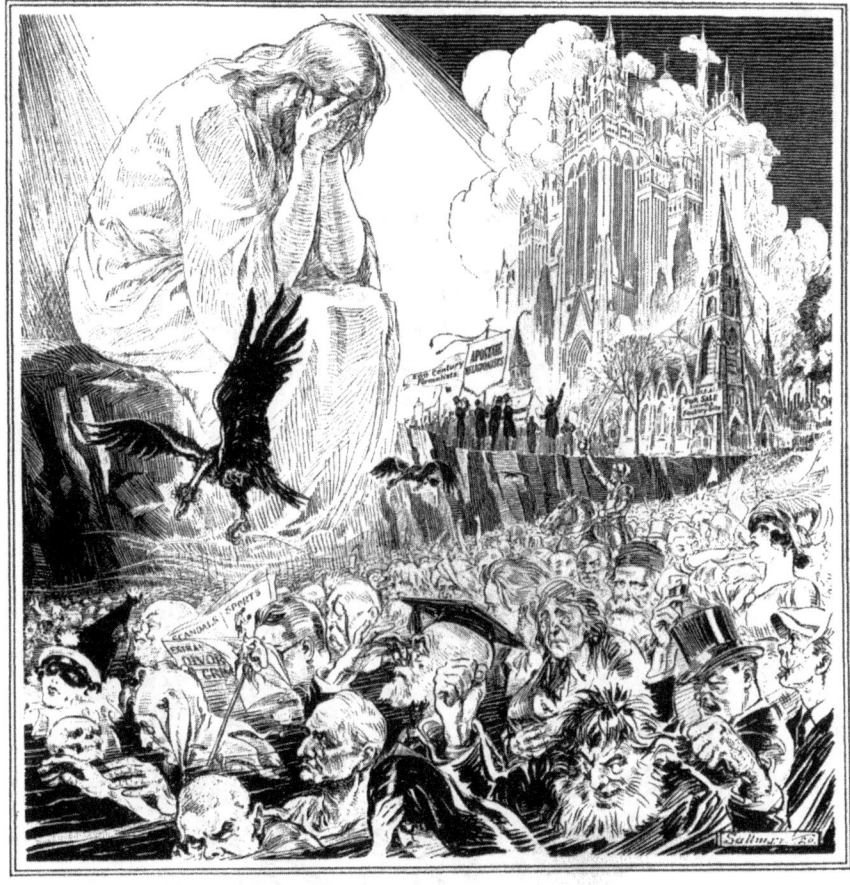

OH! JERUSALEM, JERUSALEM, HOW OFT.... BUT YE WOULD NOT—JESUS

Apostate Religionists (1920) pen. Printed in *The War Cry* and *The Evangelistic Note*

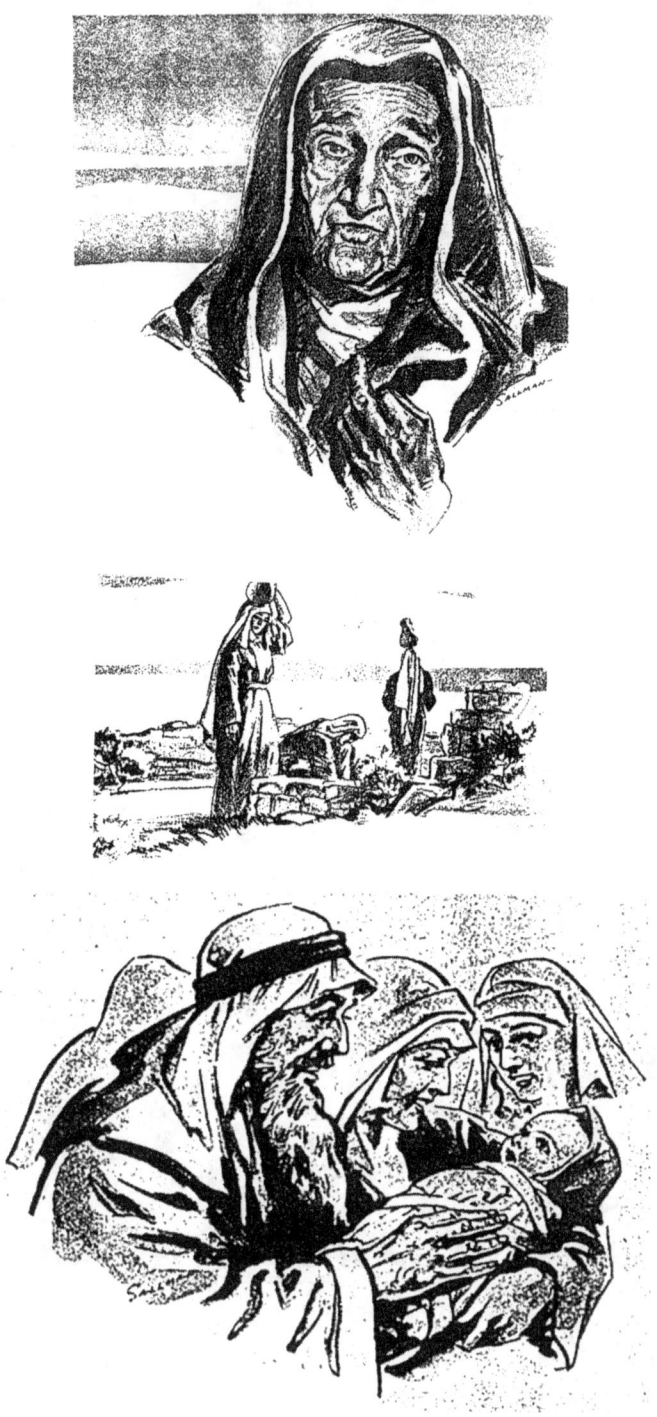

Woman at the Village Well (1940) medium unknown.
Printed in *The War Cry*.

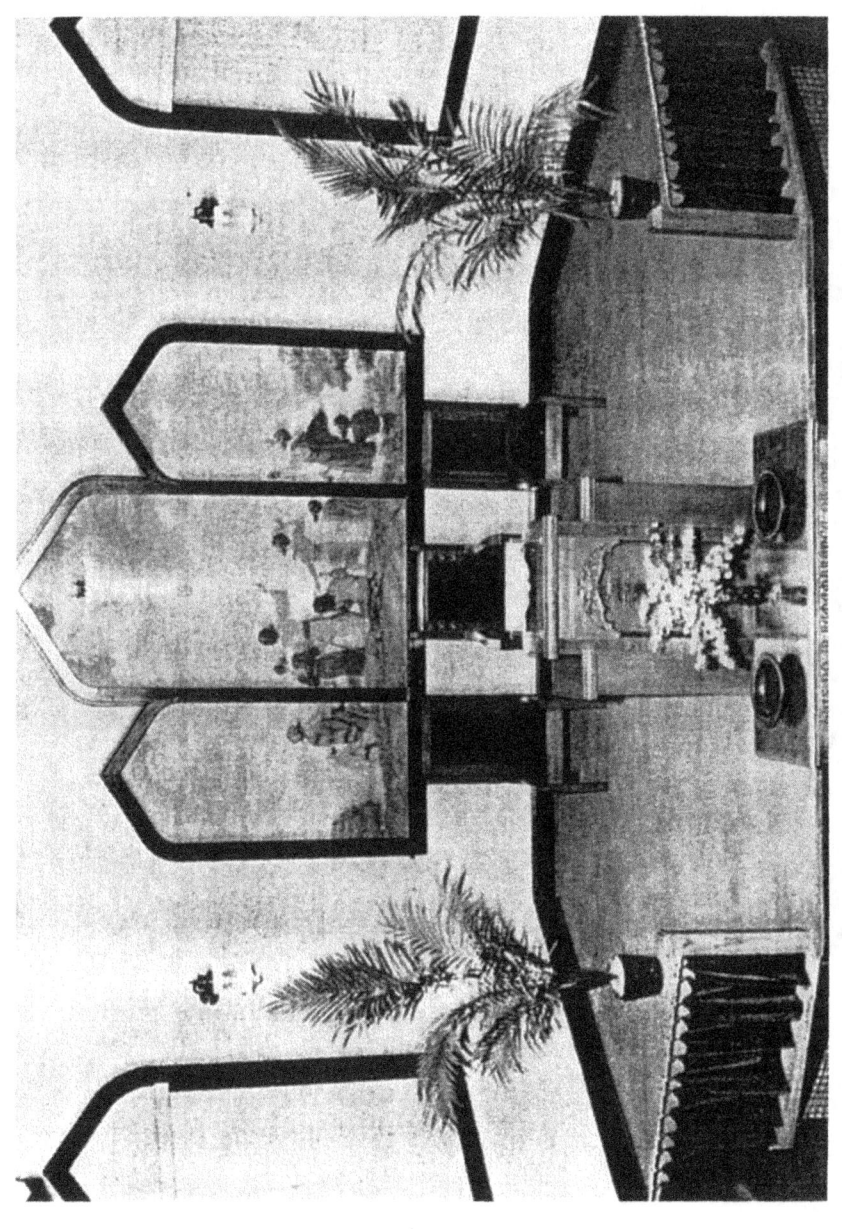

The Ascension (1934) in the old Mission Covenant Church, Braham, MN

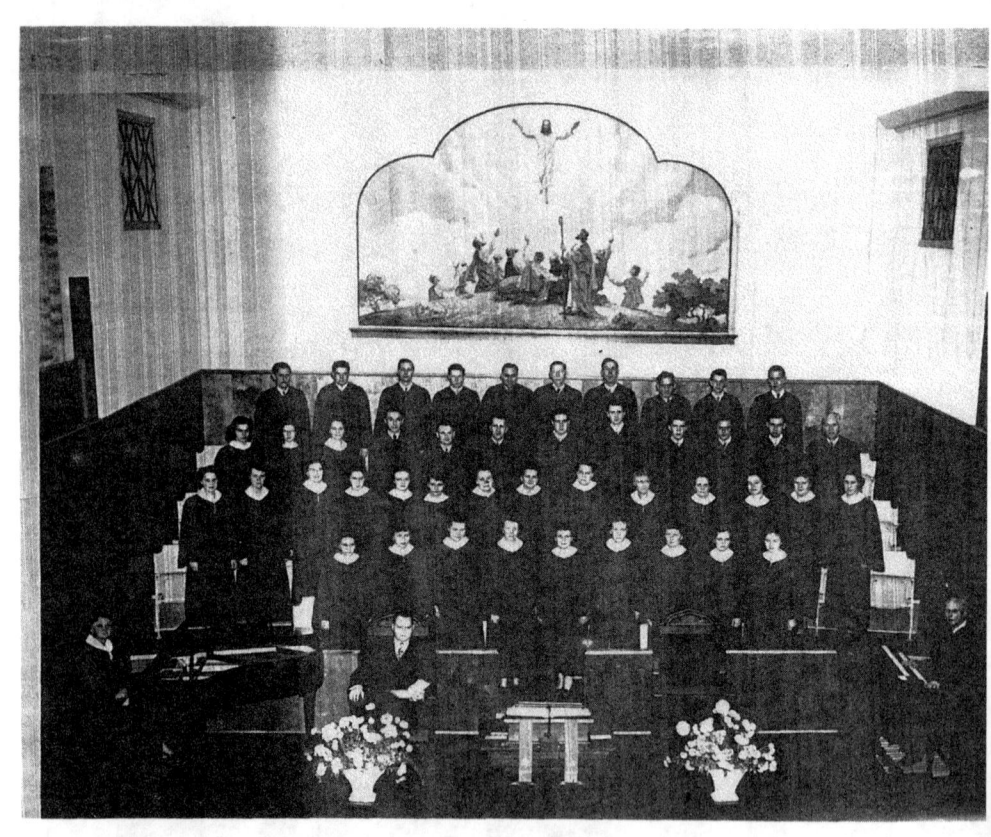

The Ascension (1939) in the old Mission Covenant Church, Iron Mountain, MI

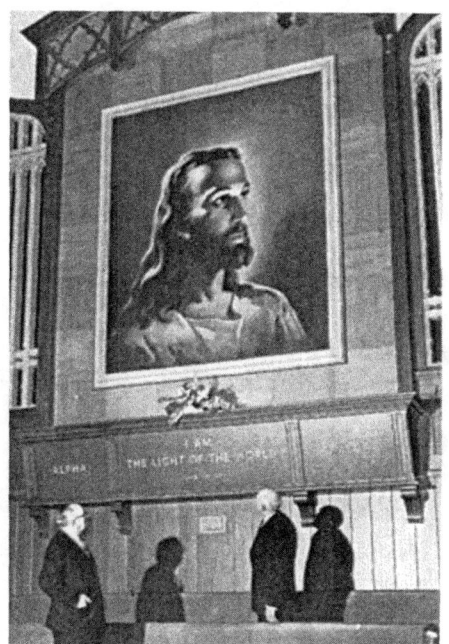

Large *Head of Christ* (1956) in the
Edgewater Covenant Church, Chicago

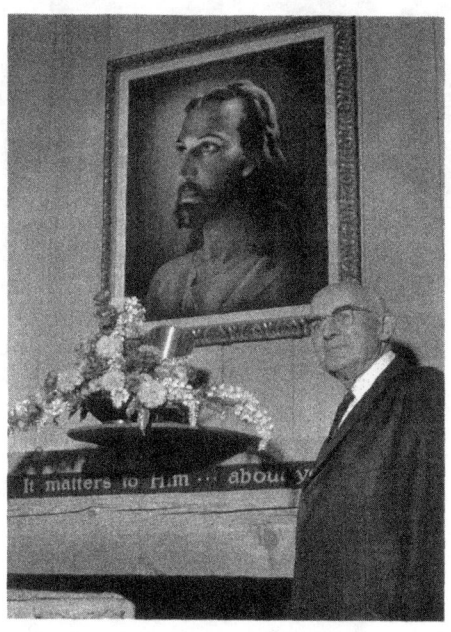

Warner Sallman before *Head of
Christ* at Covenant Village,
Northbrook (1967)

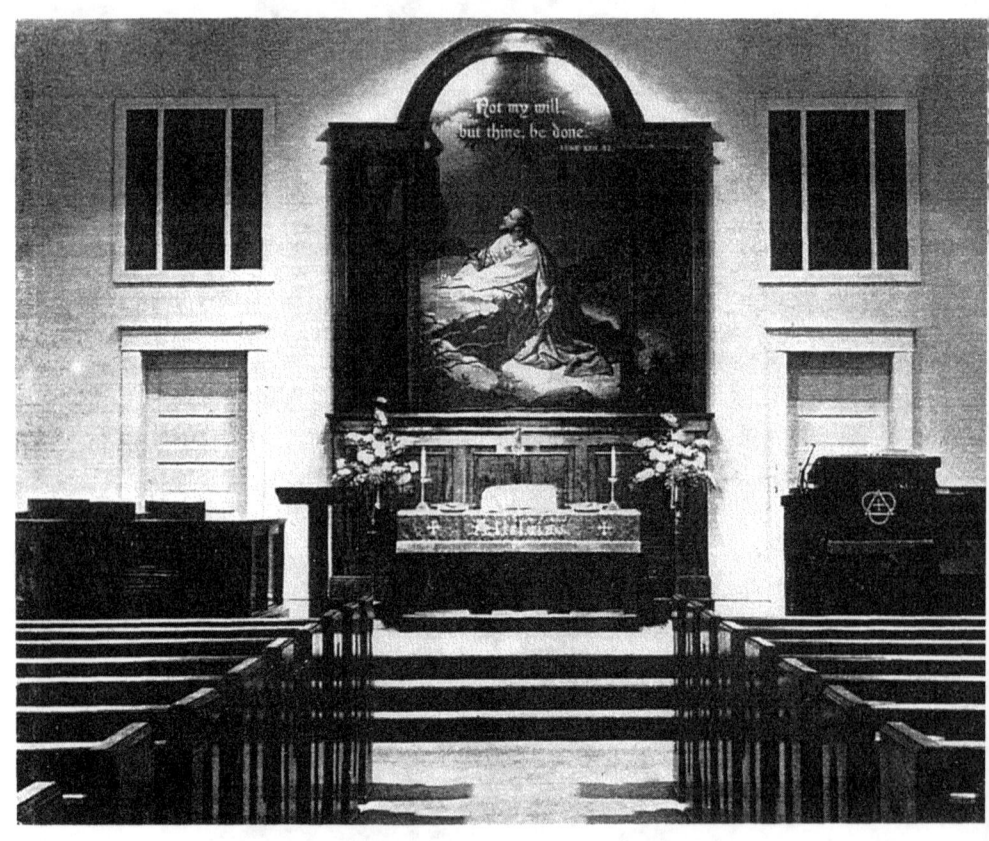

Christ in Gethsemane (1940) in the old First Covenant Church, Red Wing, MN

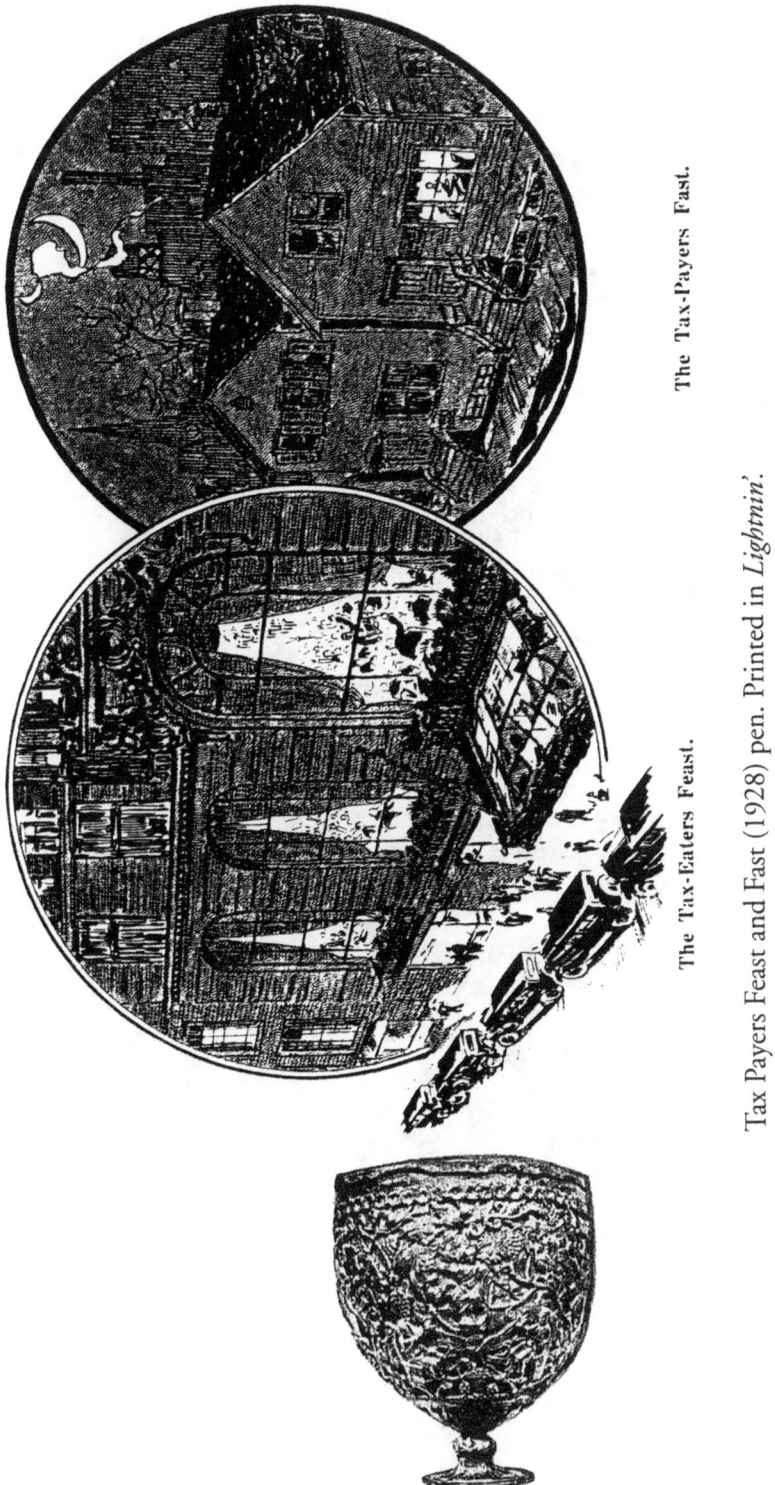

The Tax-Payers Fast.

The Tax-Eaters Feast.

Tax Payers Feast and Fast (1928) pen. Printed in *Lightnin'*.

"Chalice of Antioch," displayed at the Chicago Century of Progress, 1933-34

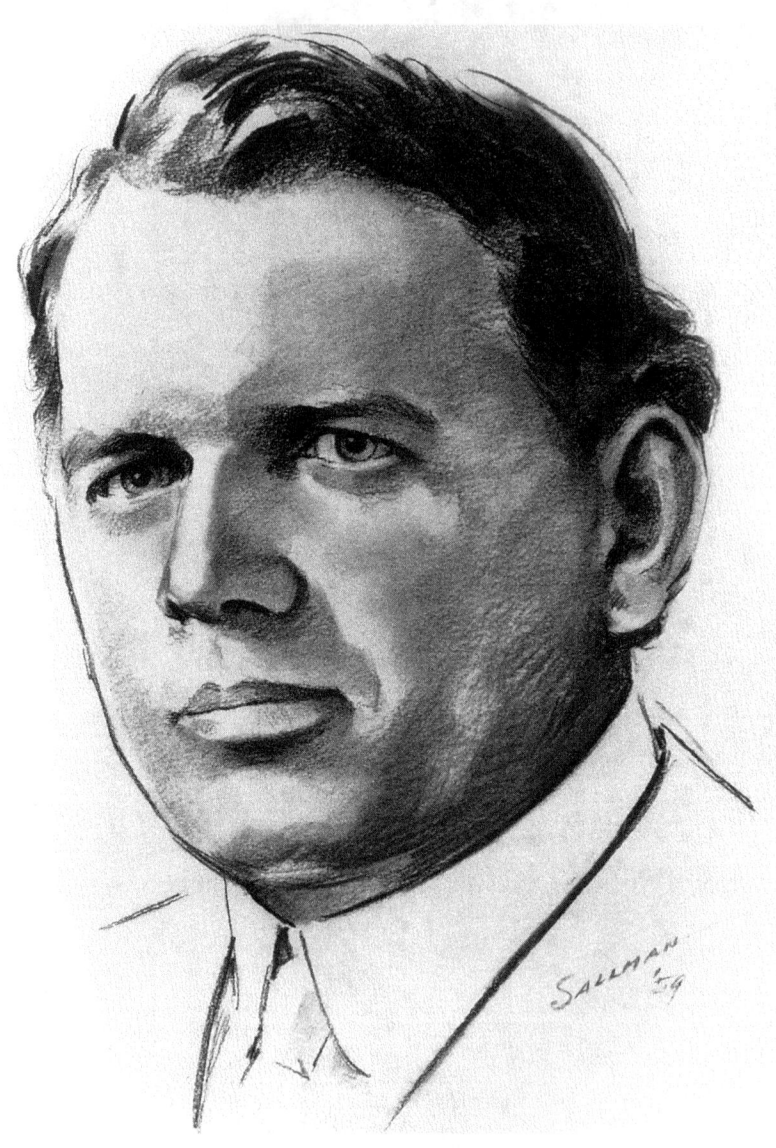

Portrait of the Rev. C.J. Andrews (1959) charcoal.

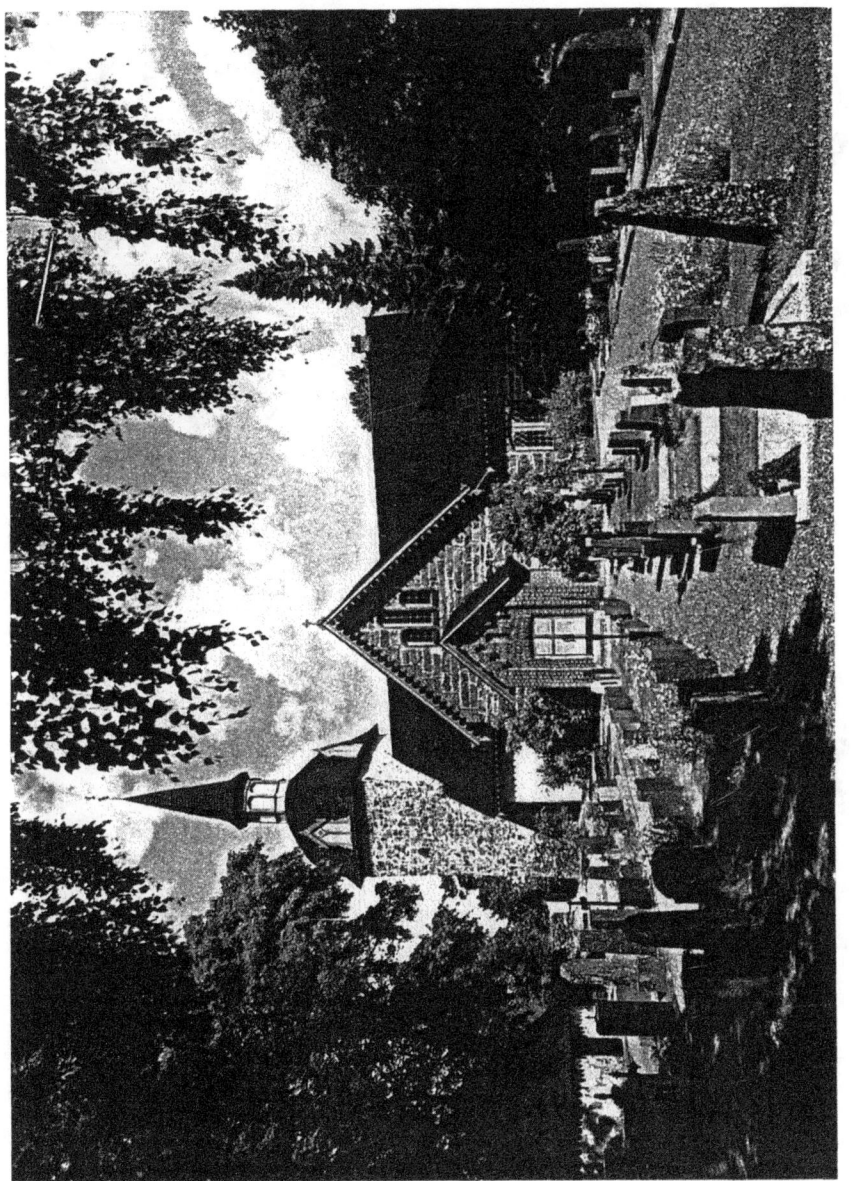

Saint Maria Magdalena Kyrka in Föglö, Åland

ILLUSTRATED LECTURE

By the Well-Known

WARNER SALLMAN

FROM

CHICAGO, ILLINOIS

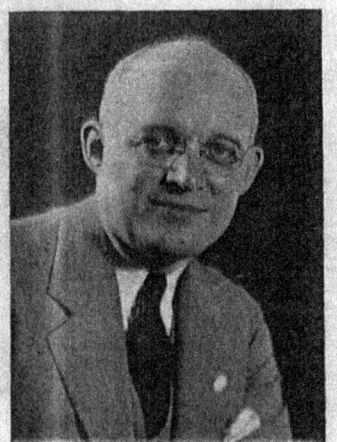

Who Will Again Sketch His Famous

Head of Christ

in the

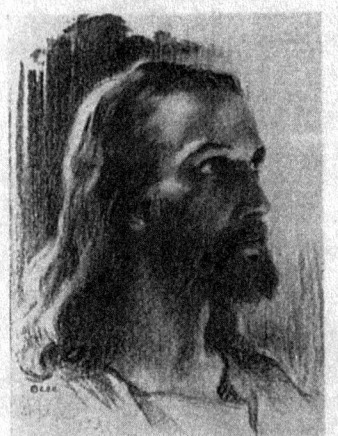

Swedish Pilgrim Church
415 Atlantic Avenue
Brooklyn, N. Y.

SUNDAY, JUNE 5

at 7.30 p. m.

Sponsored by the Sixth District of the Eastern
Missionary Association; Also Featuring
A Large United Chorus Choir

Everyone Cordially Invited and Heartily Welcome!

Announcement for a Warner Sallman illustrated lecture

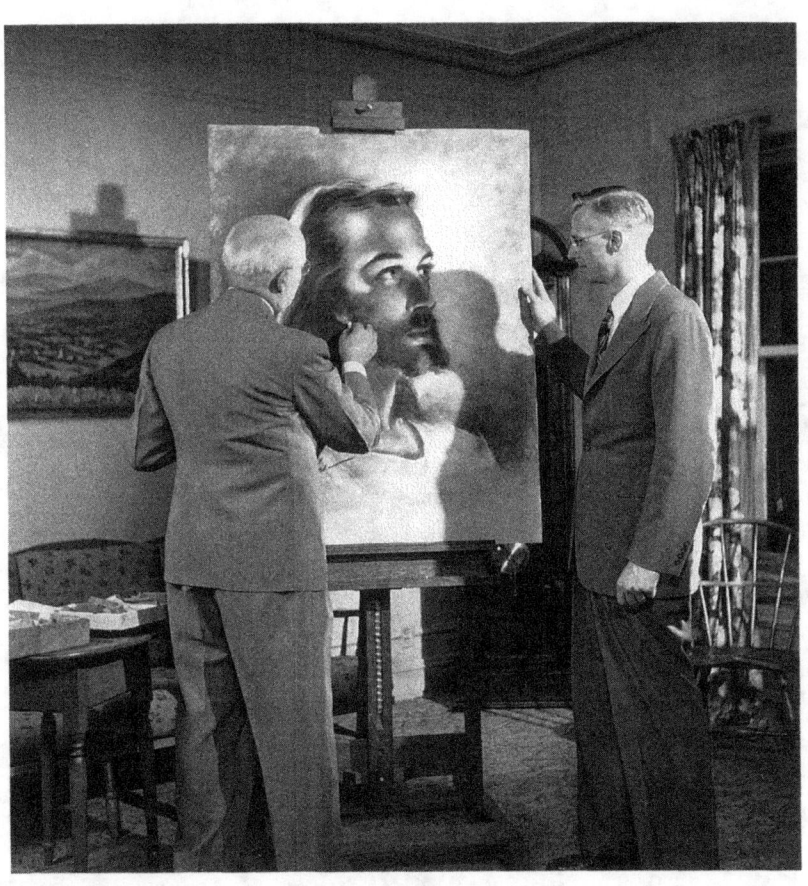

Warner Sallman completing a chalk of his *Head of Christ* at North
Park College, with Kenneth Strom looking on

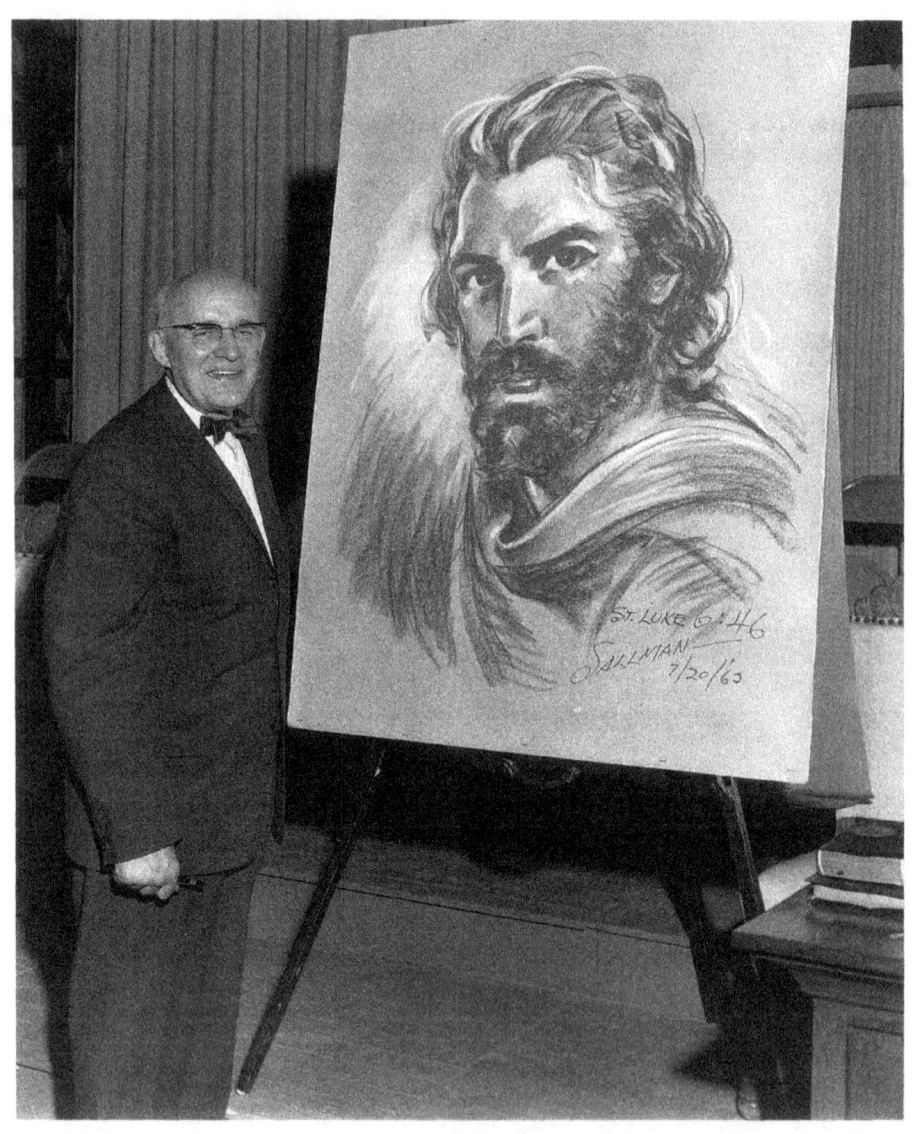

Warner Sallman standing beside a recently completed chalk of his *Lord and Master*

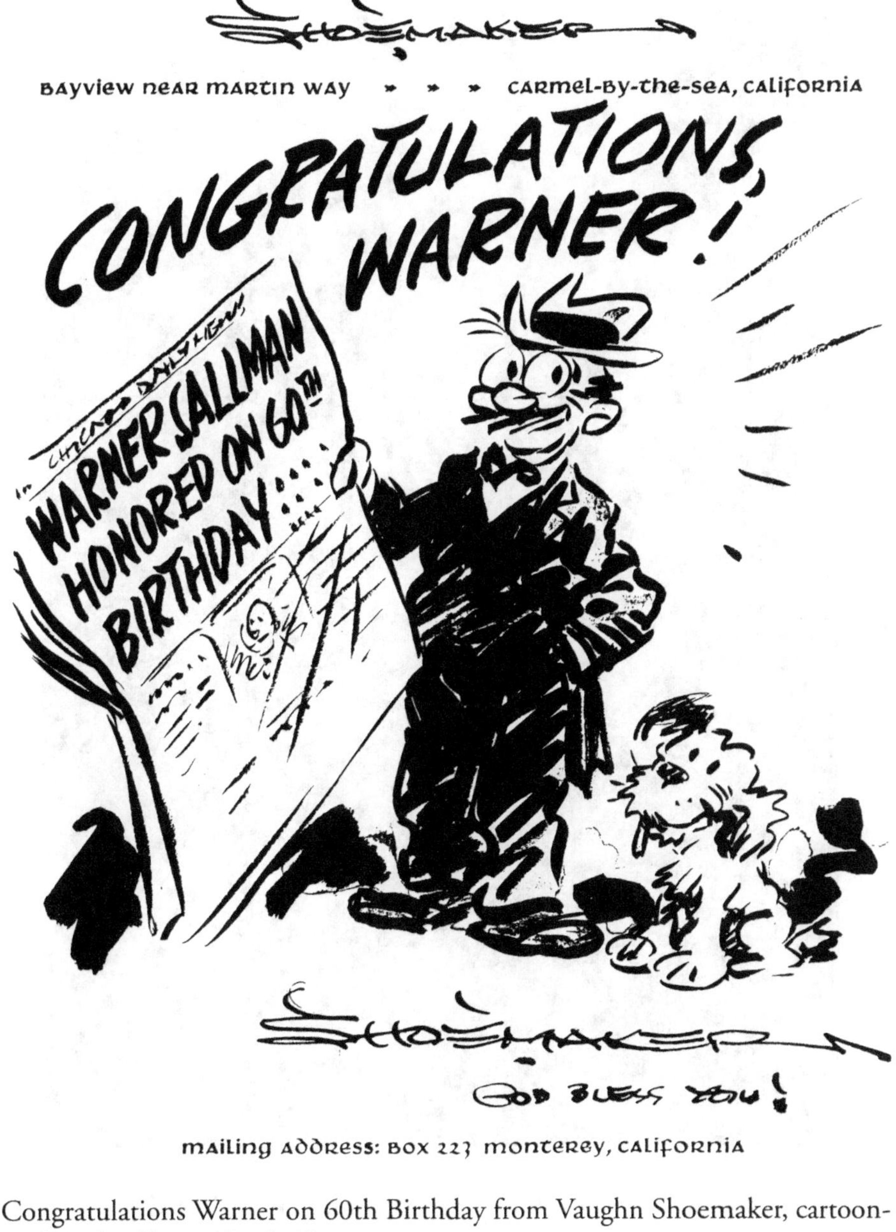

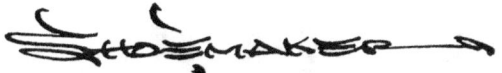

Congratulations Warner on 60th Birthday from Vaughn Shoemaker, cartoonist for *The Chicago Daily News.*

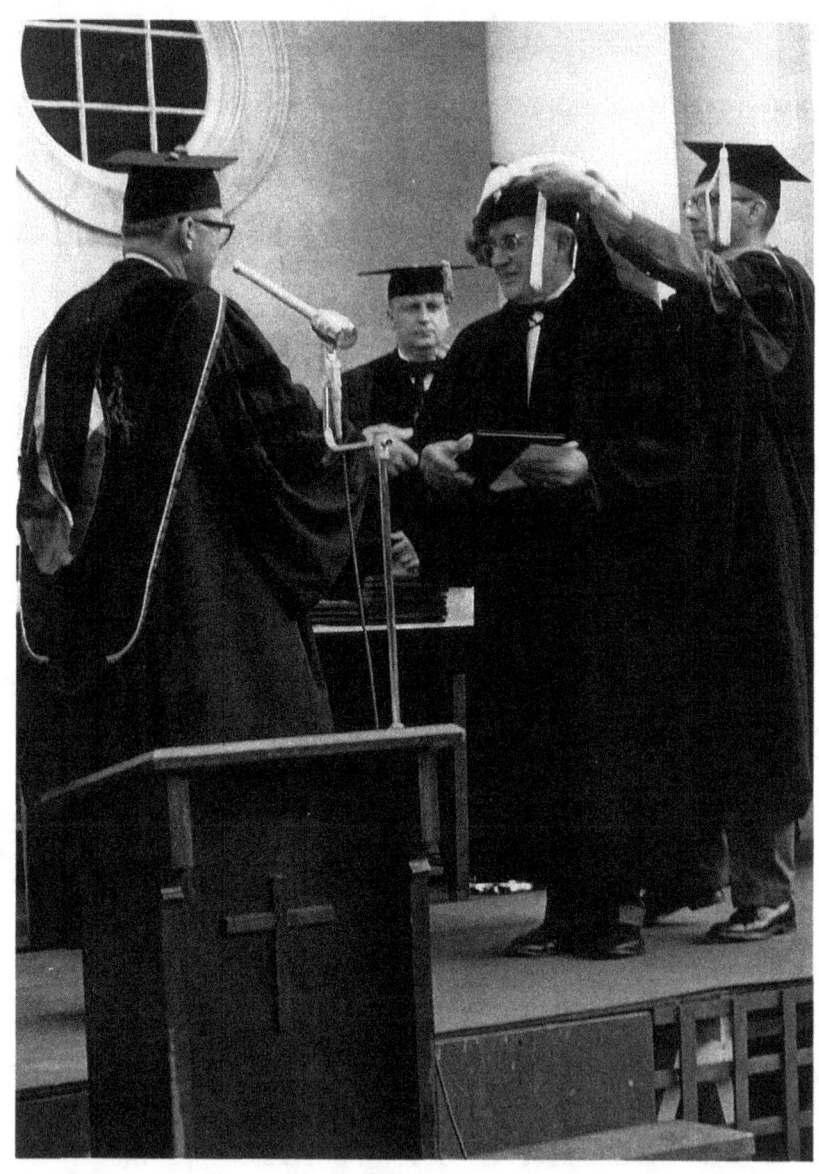

Warner Sallman receiving honorary Doctor of Humanities degree
from West Virginia Wesleyan College, Buchhannon, WV, in 1962.

West Virginia Wesleyan College

To all who read these presents, Greeting

The Trustees of the College by the authority vested in them
have conferred upon

Warner Sallman

the degree of

Doctor of Humanities

with all the rights, privileges and honors which everywhere
pertain thereto.

In Testimony Whereof, let this diploma, duly signed and
sealed, bear witness. This the 27th day of May, nineteen
hundred and sixty-two.

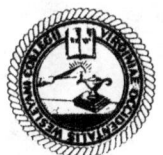

President of the College

President, Board of Trustees

Honorary degree from West Virginia Wesleyan College

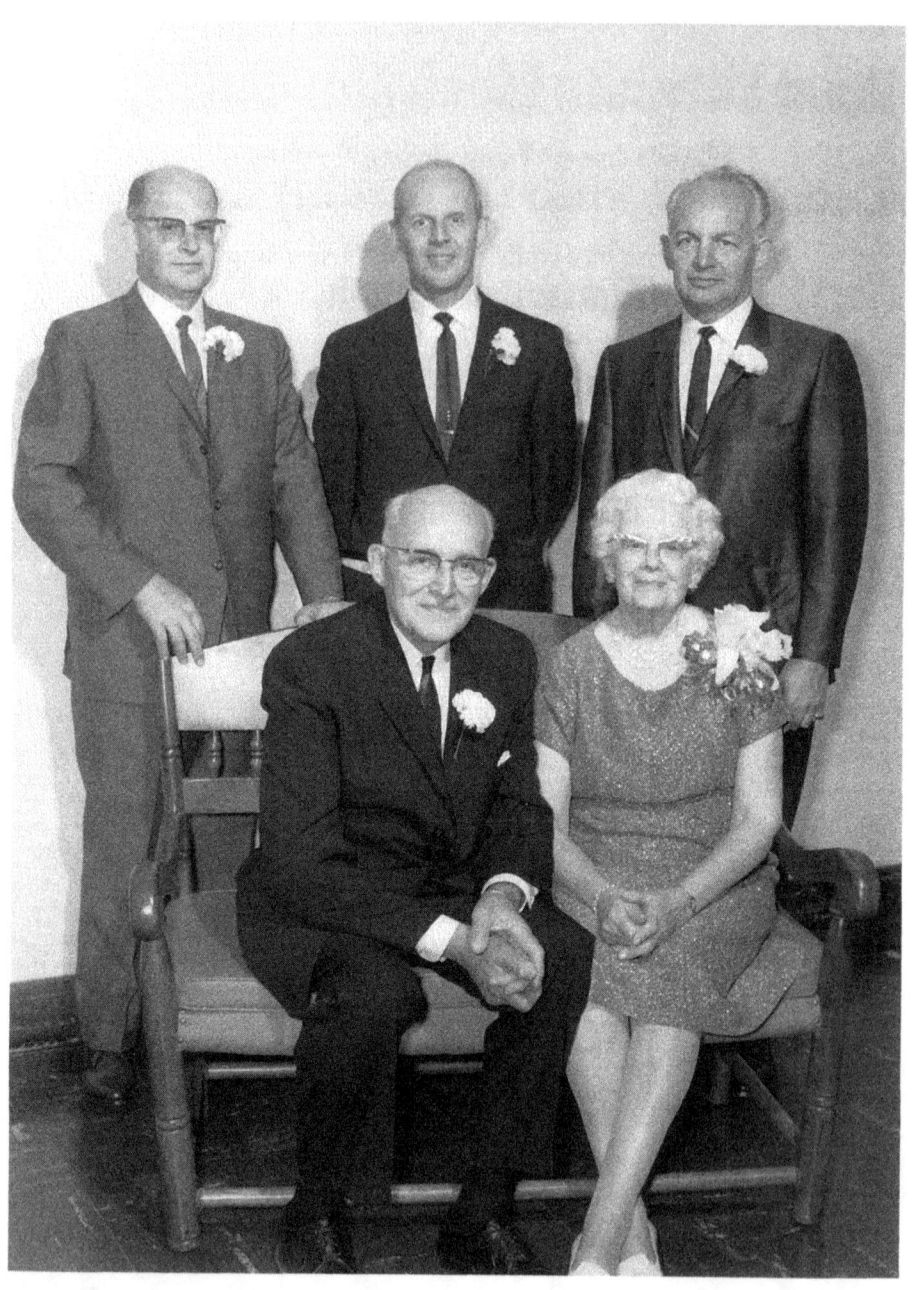

Warner and Ruth Sallman, with Everett, Richard and Jim behind them, at the Sallman's 50th wedding anniversary, held at North Park Theological Seminary, May 31, 1966

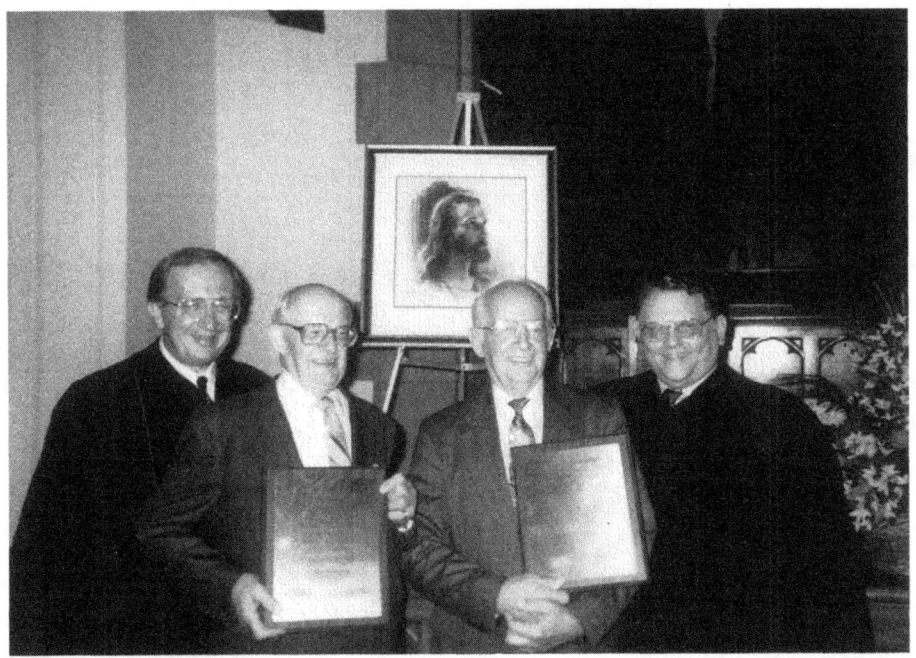

100th Anniversary of Sallman's birth, Covenant Central Conference Annual Meeting, May 1, 1992, North Park Covenant Church. L-R: Rev. Herbert Freedholm, Central Conference Superintendent, Everett Sallman, James Sallman, Dr. Jack Lundbom

XIII
'Well Done, Good and Faithful Servant'

His master said to him, 'Well done, good and faithful servant; you have been faithful over a little, I will set you over much; enter into the joy of your master' (Matt 25:21).

In his later years Sallman received a steady stream of appreciative letters from individuals telling what impact his artwork had upon them as well as others they knew. These came from people in all walks of life, the educated and uneducated, men and women, young and old, public figures and ordinary folk.

A lady in Nebraska wrote to tell him how she was mounting and framing Heads of Christ from greeting cards and giving them to children in the neighborhood. She wanted Sallman to know particularly about a nine year old girl who stopped to pick up the pictures on her way home from school, and how "her eyes beamed in thanks."[1]

Peter Homburger wrote to Sallman from Japan, "To me, a converted Jew, your two pictures *Head of Christ* and *Christ at the Door* have always meant a lot. Both of them tell the Gospel in such a vivid manner." Homburger enclosed in his letter a picture painted by a Japanese Christian girl who had learned about the gospel and been helped by these pictures. Homburger closed by saying that Sallman was engaged in nothing short of missionary work.[2]

A letter from Vachel Davis in Eldorado, Illinois read:

As an artist, I have always been a profound admirer of your *Head of Christ* painting. I consider it the greatest portrayal of the Savior by any artist of any time! Every time I look upon it, I am held spell-bound by its appeal and sacred charm. You have given the world a masterpiece of religious art that will be a never-ending inspiration to humanity.[3]

Davis' art consisted largely of paintings of coal miners. He lived all his life in the coal fields, and spent fourteen years working in the mines.

The Reverend Maurice S. Sheehy from the Catholic University of America in Washington, DC, wrote the following in a letter sent to Fred Bates: "Sallman's concept of the *Head of Christ* is sublime. It grows on one. Nothing complimentary or derogatory can add to or subtract from this precious work of art."[4] Sallman derived great joy in seeing fruit from his labors. For him it was confirmation that God was using him to his honor and glory.

Warner and Ruth celebrated their Silver Wedding Anniversary with a host of family and friends at the Edgewater Covenant Church on 3 June 1941. The couple received many telegrams and other expressions of good wishes, including a cartoon of congratulations from Sallman's good friend, Vaughn Shoemaker, cartoonist for the *Chicago Daily News*.

Sallman also received a number of honors, one of the first being his initiation, in February 1948, into the Alpha Chapter of Pi Tau Chi, a national honor society of the Wesley Foundation at the University of Alabama, Tuscaloosa. This was in appreciation for his *Christ of the Campus* done for the Wesley Foundation in 1946.

On 1 May 1952, for Sallman's 60th birthday, a large number of friends held a party and banquet at Edgewater Covenant for the artist. Nils W. Lund of North Park Seminary noted that Sallman made his first appearance on the day when the people of the north celebrate the coming of spring. He said, "There has always been about you that exuberant vitality, enthusiasm, and joy which is characteristic of Spring." Lund continued, "Your warm heart has radiated friendliness and helpfulness to all men. Your consecrated art has enriched our homes and our churches, and so you have left us a trail of light...to Him who is Himself The Light of the World."[5]

Dean Eric Hawkinson of North Park Seminary, in a letter signed by him and his wife Lydia, commented on Sallman's friendship and unspoiled character. He said their friendship remained secure "because you have not allowed the fortunes of fame to take you away from us." Hawkinson continued, "We honor you today because you are so unspoiled in a world full of vanity and pride, despite your many opportunities to be otherwise. Not a little of your Masterpiece is reflected in the living warmth of yourself, so dear to all of us."[6]

In a similar vein the Reverend Fred Pamp, after recalling the days when he was student pastor at Edgewater and Warner joined the church, became active there, and found his wife Ruth in the congregation, spoke of a friendship that had endured the years and a character that was unspoiled by success. Pamp said,

> The friendship that began in those happy days has continued strong. How happy we have been in your success. Still more have we rejoiced that this success and popularity has not changed you. God has given you grace to remain the same humble man that we knew back there in those early years.[7]

Covenant President Theodore W. Anderson, although present, conveyed the sentiments of an entire church along with his own in a letter, which read,

> We recognize that you belong to the entire Christian church but also recall that the Mission Covenant is your spiritual home. Our commu-

nion thanks God for the fact that you are one of its sons. To many of us your personal friendship is a cherished and priceless possession.

It is not only your professional skill but also your humble and earnest personality that has made us love you and esteem you so highly. The very traits of strength and tenderness that you have depicted in Christ are reflected in your own character.

Someone has said that where genius and faith meet miracles occur. Your career as a portrayer of the living Lord exemplifies this truth.[8]

President Anderson correctly perceived that Sallman belonged not just to the Mission Covenant, but to the whole church. He also correlated, as did Lund and Hawkinson, Sallman's picture of Christ with the artist himself, recognizing that Sallman had succeeded in combining Christian faith with his God-given talent of art—the very task that lay before him over thirty years ago. The result was nothing short of a miracle. Sallman's son Jim said that the life of his father more than complemented his artwork. "My father's greatest work," he said, "was his portrait of a godly life through the artistry of living."[9]

Gerard Johnson summed up the festive evening by noting the outpouring of affection for Sallman from friends and admirers, and the gracious acceptance shown by the honoree. He wrote,

Anyone knowing the artist knows also the secret of his popularity, for Mr. Sallman is generous beyond all measure—on a moment's notice he is ready to extend any favor great or small and to do it with such genuine friendliness that joy overflows wherever he goes. One day a very surprised left hand is going to discover what the right hand has been doing.[10]

This occasion was a high point for Sallman. Soon after, unfortunately, he developed an asthmatic condition that forced him to cutback his work. This condition persisted over the next five years. He made reference to this in a talk before the Union League Club on 4 November 1957, saying that only now was he fully recovered and back to feeling a hundred percent.

In his last decade of life, Sallman received numerous other awards, citations, and honors—including an honorary doctors degree—in recognition of his artwork and also for the Christian statesman that he was. On 5 June 1954, the North Park Alumni Association awarded him a lifetime honorary membership. In October 1957, Sallman was given the Upper Room citation designating him Man of the Year. The *Upper Room* is a Methodist devotional guide used worldwide. The association gives this citation annually to some person in the United States who has made an outstanding contribution to the Christian church world-wide. Editor J. Manning Potts said in announcing the award for 1957 that Sallman had been selected because of artistic leadership in "helping bridge the gap between different denominations and bringing them closer in a world Christian fellowship."[11]

The citation was given at a dinner held at the National Press Club in Washington, DC. Over eleven hundred invitations went out to an array of government and religious leaders. Major General Charles Carpenter, chief chaplain of the United States Air Force, served as toastmaster for the evening. Greetings were sent by the President and Vice President of the United States. Among Sallman's Methodist friends in attendance was the Reverend Charles Ray Goff, who gave the main address. The citation presented by Dr. Potts reads,

> Warner E. Sallman
> The one person selected to represent the United States in the World Christian Fellowship Number.
> Student of the Bible and art, artist, illustrator, painter and art editor; modest, humble and devoted follower of Christ. He has so painted the Christ that his works have inspired millions of Christians around the world to a fuller understanding of the message of the Savior; the world has honored this artist by the acceptance of his interpretation of Christ. He is beloved by countless people, who have placed copies of his pictures in their churches, hung them in their homes, or carried them in their pockets and purses. His is an extraordinary contribution to World Christian Fellowship.

The next month Sallman received honorary membership in the Nordic Philharmonic Society of Chicago for his painting of Jean Sibelius, who died in 1957. The award, signed by the director of the orchestra, the president and secretary of the society, and the consul of Finland in Chicago, reads,

> The Nordic Philharmonic Society of Chicago awards its honorary membership to Warner Sallman in recognition of his contributions to American art and culture and particularly for his painting the portrait of Jean Sibelius, the Finnish composer, unveiled at the memorial concert held by the Nordic Philharmonic Society, November 24, 1957.

In 1960 Methodists honored Sallman with another citation, this one at their Summer Assembly in Des Plaines, Illinois. It once again recognized "his significant contribution to World Christianity" by realistically portraying the Christ, citing in addition his ability as an artist and his being a true disciple of Jesus Christ.

Two years later, in March 1962, the Greater Chicago Churchmen, the laymen's unit of the Church Federation of Greater Chicago, cited Sallman along with John Mulder and Norman Ross as "laymen of the year." Mulder was a lawyer and prominent Presbyterian lay leader, Ross a television-radio commentator and newspaper columnist. The three were presented with copies of the New English Bible at a March dinner meeting of the Greater Chicago Churchmen, held at the Chicago Bar Association in downtown Chicago.

Two months later, on 27 May, Sallman was made an honorary member of the Rho Alpha Christian Fraternity of America, sponsor of the Arts-for-Christ Crusade. The citation, issued by the Southwestern Conservatory of Fine Arts in Dallas, Texas, reads,

> Warner Sallman
> Having made distinct and laudatory contributions to the field of The Arts, thus distinguishing himself and his field of American culture.

A third honor came during 1962. West Virginia Wesyleyan College, Buckhannon, West Virginia, awarded Sallman an honorary Doctor of Humanities at a 27 May commencement. A former president of West Virginia Wesyleyan was Roy McCuskey DD, the father of physician John F. McCuskey in whose memory Sallman did *The Master Healer* (1960) at Union Protestant Hospital in Clarksburg, West Virginia

Honors at this point now began to accumulate not by the year, but by the day. In the same mail that brought word of the honorary doctorate voted by West Virginia Wesyleyan came a handbook from Pi Tau Chi, the Honor Society of Religion at the University of Alabama, which had granted Sallman membership back in 1948. Inside was Sallman's picture and a statement dedicating this handbook to the "world-famous Christian artist and illustrious member of Pi Tau Chi." In 1964 West Suburban YMCA gave Sallman a Life Membership, the year he did the watercolor of *Christ Our Pilot* for the YMCA.

Warner and Ruth celebrated their 50th wedding anniversary on 29 May 1966. A reception was held for them in Nyvall Lounge at North Park Seminary, with a host of family and friends in attendance. Then a couple weeks later a citation for "outstanding contributions to the field of religious art" was presented to Sallman from the Evangelical Covenant Church at its June Annual Meeting. Covenant President Clarence A. Nelson made the presentation.

Warner Sallman's penultimate festivity was a 75th birthday party held 30 April 1967, which occasioned a tribute in the *Covenant Companion*.[12] A year later Sallman suffered a severe heart attack. Ruth and he had just returned from a trip to the East Coast. This first of two attacks did not seem that serious, but from the second he never recovered. Sallman died 25 May 1968 at Swedish Covenant Hospital. He was seventy-six. Speaking at the funeral service was Sallman's pastor at Edgewater, the Reverend Wesley D. Morris, and Covenant

President Emeritus Theodore W. Anderson. Burial was in Memorial Park Cemetery in Chicago.

His last and most important reward had now been given. Commenting on his passing, long-time friend Sylvia Peterson Knudson said that Warner Sallman "went to meet his Creator who had endowed him with such rich gifts, and to receive from him the reward Warner coveted most, 'Well done, good and faithful servant.'"[13]

A dedicatory Christmas concert was held in December at the Edgewater Covenant Church. It was a fitting tribute, coming as it did in his home congregation, where, for the past twenty-five years Warner Sallman and Christmas choir concerts were well-nigh synonymous. The church choir, small groups, and an array of soloists sang. The main tribute was given by Church Chairman Edgar E. Swanson Jr. Swanson recalled the disastrous church fire of 1955, and how Sallman's encouragement and wise counsel prevailed at a time when many in the congregation wanted to sell and move out. Swanson, thirty-four at the time, had just been elected to a first term as church chairman. Swanson said,

> Warner put his hand on my shoulder, told me not to become discouraged, counselled the seeking of God's will, and then labored hard and long with many of the rest of us to remake this building [into] an even more effective instrument. His great contribution to our restoration was the large Head of Christ which you see before you. It is a testimony to his faith and love for his Christ. To those of us who knew and loved Warner, it is also a symbol of his compassion and concern for this church.

Swanson concluded with a word about the Christmas concerts:

> Over the years, Christmas at Edgewater and Warner Sallman became an institution. Season after season, while the choir sang and rejoiced over the long expected Messiah, Warner depicted the same theme through his artistry and his chalks. He meticulously sketched scenes of the babe in his mother's arms, the lonely and lowly manger on a hill side, the wise men coming from the east, the great diffused light from the hallelujah chorus, the single strong glow of the great star—all these themes and many more were indelibly impressed on our hearts and minds. This was Christmas at Edgewater.[14]

[1] Letter from Mrs. B. M. Underberg to Warner Sallman, 29 March 1950.
[2] Letter dated 3 August 1951.
[3] Letter dated 30 July 1955.
[4] Letter dated 17 December 1948.

[5] N. W. Lund to Warner Sallman, 30 April 1952.

[6] Eric and Lydia Hawkinson to Warner Sallman, 21 April 1952.

[7] Frederic E. Pamp to Warner Sallman, 25 April 1952.

[8] Theodore W. Anderson to Warner Sallman, 25 April 1952.

[9] Gerard Johnson, "Friends Fete Artist on Sixtieth Birthday," *Covenant Weekly* 41/20 (16 May 1952): 3.

[10] Ibid.

[11] Reported in an unknown newspaper following the dinner.

[12] Ben Bankson, "Happy Birthday, Mr. Sallman!" *The Covenant Companion* 56/8 (21 April 1967): 8-9, 26.

[13] Sylvia Knudson Larson, *Warner Sallman and His Ministry of Christian Art* (a pamphlet published privately for the Sallman Exhibit at Covenant Village, Northbrook, Illinois in January 1984).

[14] Edgar Swanson, "A Tribute to Warner Sallman," distributed with the program of the Dedicatory Christmas Concert at Edgewater Covenant Church, 8 December 1968.

Epilogue

Ruth Sallman lived to be over ninety, residing her last years at Covenant Village in Northbrook, Illinois. In honor of her 90th birthday, on 2 January 1984, an exhibit of twenty-nine Sallman artworks, on various subjects and in various mediums, was held at Covenant Village 11-29 January. It was also the 60th anniversary of the original charcoal, *Son of Man*. The exhibit was sponsored by the North Park College Arts Guild, headed by committee chairperson Helen Fredrickson. A reception for 250 invited guests was held on 8 January. The day was an emotional one for Ruth. She said, "This is the first time I've seen [the paintings] all together like this. I've only seen them one at a time and forget some then."[1]

In 1987 Anderson University, Anderson, Indiana and Warner Press purchased the entire Kriebel and Bates collection, containing well-known oils and an assortment of other Sallman originals, totaling over 140 artworks. Prior to their purchase, sixteen of the best-known artworks were displayed for the first time during June 1986, in connection with the annual convention of the Church of God of Indiana, in Anderson. In the summers since selected Sallman artworks have been put on exhibit at the university during the church convention. The Sallman Collection at Anderson University is presently housed in the Jessie C. Wilson Galleries.

Just one day after Sallman's 100th birthday, the 1992 Covenant Central Conference Annual Meeting held a centenary tribute to Warner Sallman at a special service on May 1, at the North Park Covenant Church. I was privileged to be the speaker that evening,[2] and two of Sallman's sons, Everett and James, were present to receive commemorative plaques from the conference. Richard Sallman, seriously ill in Texas, was unable to attend. Word came later that Richard had died while the service was in progress. Jim and Gene Sallman arranged for a large exhibit of Sallman's pictures–both originals and prints–in the church parlors after the service.

On 4 March 1994, the Divinity School of the University of Chicago held a public conference entitled, "Icons of American Protestantism: The Art of Warner Sallman." The program consisted of papers by five scholars specializing in art history, popular culture and church history, ranging over a variety of topics dealing with the Sallman art: "Evangelical Theology and the Art of Warner Sallman," by Betty A. DeBerg of Valparaiso University; "Personal Lord and Savior: Christology and the Devotional Image," by Leonard I. Sweet of United

Theological Seminary; "'Would Jesus Have Sat for a Portrait?': The Likeness of Christ in the Popular Reception of Sallman's Art," by David Morgan of Valparaiso University; "Interchangeable Art: Warner Sallman and the Critics of Mass Culture," by Sally Promey of the University of Maryland, College Park; and "Marketing Jesus: Warner Press and the Art of Sallman," by Colleen McDannell of the University of Utah. Responses and a general discussion followed. There was also a public exhibit of Sallman originals and prints. This exhibit appeared subsequently at Valparaiso University and at the Institute for Sacred Music, Worship and the Arts at Yale Divinity School, Yale University. For a published verson of the conference essays, see David Morgan (ed.), *Icons of American Protestantism: The Art of Warner Sallman* (New Haven and London: Yale University Press, 1996).

[1] Susan Eckhardt, "Covenanters Celebrate the Sallman Legacy," *Covenant Companion* 73/3 (March 1984): 40-41.

[2] The talk was published as "Warner E. Sallman: A Centenary Tribute to a Covenant Artist," *The Covenant Companion* 81/7 (July 1992): 8-11, 40.

Appendix I
Sketches In Covenant Church Papers

The following list chronicles Sallman artwork in various Evangelical Covenant church papers: *Förbundets Veckotidning* (*FV*), *The Covenant Companion* Old Series (*CC* Old Series), *The Covenant Weekly* (*CW*), *Our Covenant Youth* (*OCY*), *Our Young Covenanters* (*OYC*), *Covenant Youth Today* (*CYT*), *Our Juniors* (*OJ*), *Our Covenant Little Folks* (*OCLF*), *The Children's Friend* (*CF*), *Missions-Förbundets Ungdomstidning* (*MFU*), *Missions-Vännen* (*MV*), and *The Children's Hour* (*CHo*). Reprints occasionally noted are not exhaustive. Titles not in italics are works without titles or works that were at one time titled, but whose titles are now unknown. Dates in square brackets are assumed dates.

FV 263 (24 December 1918): 1; two sketches dated 1918:

a) *Frid på jorden* (*Peace on the Earth*). The sketch shows Jesus with arms outstretched behind a star sending down a beam of light over Bethlehem. In the foreground American soldiers of World War I stand behind flags, one of them the American flag. Caption below: Frid på jorden!

b) *Mänskorna ett gott behag* (*Goodwill to the People*). A man here walks in snow carrying a Christmas tree, with a dog trailing behind. A Swedish church and a snow-covered house stand in the background. A caption below the scene reads, Mänskorna ett gott behag!

FV 264 (31 December 1918): 1; one sketch dated [1918]:

Hope for the New Year. This piece depicts Humanity as a huddled woman and War as a soldier. "Old man 1918" attempts to restrain War, who carries a chewed-up sickle. Background light floods incoming 1919, and a soldier with a Union shield stands behind Humanity looking toward the light. At the base of the light, on the horizon, a small cross is visible.

FV 315 (23 December 1919): 1; three sketches, the center one dated 1919:

a) *Winter in Sweden.* In this winter scene of a house behind a picket fence, a man shovels snow out back, and birds eat off of a shock of corn from the light post in front of the house. Birds are also eating off the path. To the right stands a snow-covered pine tree. Below the picture is a poem by Josef Rosenius. Originally given as a gift to Elmer L. Anderson and his wife, the piece now resides in the James and Gene Sallman private collection.

b) Angels Blowing Trumpets. Two sketches of winged angels blowing trumpets, one at the right and one at the left. Both sketches have churches in the background. The caption of one reads, "Ära vare Gud" ("Glory be to God"), the caption of the other, "Frid på jorden" ("Peace on the earth").

The three sketches are reprinted in *FV* 557 (23 December 1924): 3, 6; the first sketch appears again by itself in *FV* 869 (16 December 1930): 1; *OYC* and *OJ* 4/51 (23 December 1934): 2; *CW* 24/1 (1 January 1935): 1; *OYC* 6/51 (20 December 1936): 1; *OYC* 8/51 (18 December 1938): 1; *OCLF* 7/2 (11 January 1942): 1; etc. The latter two sketches reappear in *FV* [870][1] (23 December 1930): 1; *FV* 1026 (19 December 1933): 1; and *CW* Swedish 25/51 (22 December 1936): 1.

FV 315 (23 December 1919): 4; one sketch dated [1919]:
Christmas Tree with Snow-covered House. Candles and ornaments decorate a Christmas tree, below which are children's toys. Above the scene is a poem entitled "Jul" by Paul Nilsson. Reprinted in *FV* 503 (18 December 1923): 5; and *FV* 765 (18 December 1928): 3. Top part only reprinted in *OYC* 10/52 (29 December 1940): 1; *OCLF* 9/52 (28 December 1941): 1; *OYC* 12/52 (27 December 1942): 1; *OYC* 14/52 (24 December 1944): 1.

FV 359 (30 March 1920): 1; one sketch © W. E. Sallman 1920:
Resurrected Christ Rising from the Crucified Christ. The resurrected Christ, framed in an Easter lily, rises out of the crucified Christ. The frontal view of Christ's face is similar to that of *Son of Man* (1924). Below is written, "Den sanna Påskliljan" ("The True Easter Lily"). Reprinted in *FV* 520 (15 April 1924): 1; *FV* 884 (31 March 1931): 1; and *OYC* 8/16 (17 April 1938): 1; also in a collage in *FV* 410 (22 March 1921): 1 *CC* Old Series, SS Teacher's Edition 7/4 (April 1928): front cover; and *CW* 23/13 (27 March 1934): 1. A slightly modified watercolor, *Thine Is the Victory!* (1952), was used later as a bulletin cover.

FV 393 (23 November 1920): 1; one sketch dated 1920:
Tacksägelse (Thanksgiving). A bearded man sits alone at a table, his hands folded on an open Bible. Food and a pitcher are on the table. The title above is "Tacksägelse," and below are three verses from the Swedish hymn, "Tack, O Gud" ("Thanks to God").[2] A charcoal with whiting—perhaps the original—hangs in the Covenant Archives.

FV 397 (21 December 1920): 1; one large sketch dated 1919:
Tell Me the Old, Old Story. A family sits before the hearth at Christmas. The father reads from the Bible. Smoke from the fire makes a cloud in which

appears sketches of the Christmas story. At the left is the angel appearing to Mary; in the center are shepherds arriving at the stable; and to the right are wise men following the star to Bethlehem. At the bottom are four verses of a Swedish poem, and possibly a hymn text, "Var hälsad, du himmelska gåva." This sketch appeared also on the front of *The Family Altar* 13/12 (December 1921), and was used in 1921 and 1959 for the Sallman Christmas card. On the 1959 card was printed a musical score and the words to "Tell Me the Old, Old Story, of Jesus and His Love" (Katherine Hankey).[3]

FV 406 (22 February 1921): 1; one sketch dated 1920:

Here Am I, Lord, Send Me. A man seen from behind carries a suitcase and looks at a sign calling for "5 Mission-Spirited Men" to take charge of five government schools for Eskimos on the Covenant field in Alaska. Holding the sign are two women—the one on the left named "Covenant," and the one on the right named "Columbia." Below is printed, "Here am I, Lord; send me" (Isaiah 6:8).

FV 409 (15 March 1921): 4; one sketch dated [1921]:

Eskimo Child. A verse from Romans 10:14 here frames an Eskimo child in a parka. The sketch is signed only with an "S." Reappears in *OYC* and *OJ* 1/5 (1 February 1931): 1; *CW* 23/4 (23 January 1934): 1; 23/31 (31 July 1934): 2; *OYC* 6/5 (2 February 1936): 2; *OYC* 9/28 (9 July 1939): 4; *OYC* 15/51 (23 December 1945): 4; *OCLF* 17/7 (16 February 1947): 1; etc.

FV 410 (22 March 1921): 1; one sketch, a collage, dated 1921:

Self-Denial, Self-Indulgence. The top sketch is the aforementioned *Resurrected Christ Rising from the Crucified Christ* (1920), printed in *FV* 359 (30 March 1920): 1 and reprinted in *FV* 520 (15 April 1924): 1 and *FV* 884 (31 March 1931): 1. The sketch on the left depicts a husband and wife at a table, with the husband writing a check for their Easter offering and the wife holding a bank for the world's children, who are sketched in the background. In the sketch at the right, a crying child walks ahead of fashion-clad parents "going their worldly way." The title above is "Supreme Sacrifice"; the title below is "Self-Denial—Self Indulgence." An Easter message at the bottom concludes with a quote from Romans 12:1. This collage was reprinted in *CC* Old Series SS Teachers' Edition 7/4 (April 1928): front cover; *OYC* and *OJ* 3/16 (16 April 1933): 1; and *CW* 23/13 (27 March 1934): 1.

FV 449 (20 December 1921): 1; one large sketch dated 1921:

Memories of Julotta. In the foreground four parishoners—one a child—sit in a candle-lighted church for the Christmas morning "Julotta" service. Outside horse-drawn sleighs are bringing others to church. Over the distant church steeple a star shines down. A winged angel blows a trumpet in the sky overhead. With the right hand the angel touches the star shining on the church steeple. The light from the star forms a cross. Below is written, "Dyrbara minnen (Julottan)" ("Dear memories of Julotta"). This sketch is reprinted in *FV* 713 (20 December 1927): 2; and, without the angel and the star, on the front cover of *CC* Old Series 9/29 (22 December 1930). The Sallmans used this picture for their 1922 Christmas card.

FV 464 (11 April 1922): 1; one sketch dated 1922:
   Mother Reading the Easter Story. An aged mother sits at a table with her finger pointing to the Easter story in John 11:25-26. On the table is a coffee cup, coffee bread, and a potted Easter lily. Compare sketches of *Mother* (1909) and *Mother Knitting* [1913]. The work is reprinted in *CC* Old Series 5/4 (April 1926): front cover.

FV 451^4 (19 December 1922): 1; one sketch dated 1922:
   Hallelujah Scroll. A winter scene and trumpet-blowing angels frame an open scroll on which is written a Christmas message beginning, "Hallelujah, He is the King of Glory...." Reprinted in *FV* 713 (20 December 1927): 5; *CC* Old Series SS Teacher's Section 7/15 (12 December 1928): 1; and *OYC* 9/52 (24 December 1939): 1.

FV 465 (27 March 1923): 1; one sketch dated 1923:
   Christ Holding an Easter Lily. Christ holds an Easter lily in his left hand, his right hand lifted up. The face is young, in contrast to the face of *Son of Man*, which Sallman will draw a year later.

FV 500 (27 November 1923): 1; one cartoon sketch dated [1923]:
   A Thank Offering? This cartoon is of a materialistic-minded man loaded down with a horn of plenty, an automobile, and a sack of money, walking away from a church pulpit signifying "Treasury, Lord's Work." A dollar sign appears on the smoke of his cigar. Behind the pulpit is Jesus, hidden but nevertheless present, looking on. His profile looks very much like that of *Son of Man*, which Sallman will draw two months later. Above is written Psalm 107:8. Below is the title "A Thank Offering?" The portion of the cartoon showing Christ behind the pulpit is reprinted in *CW* Swedish 28/41 (10 October 1939): 1, used there together with John 8:12, 20.

FV 503 (18 December 1923): 4; one watercolor? dated 1923:

Snow-Covered Pines. This winter scene features snow-covered pines with a house in the distance. Reprinted in *CC* Old Series 11/50 (10 December 1932): front cover, over the title "Nature's Peace in Advent"; also in *OYC* 10/4 (28 January 1940), 1; *OCLF* 13/3 (17 January 1943): 1; *OYC* 17/1 (5 January 1947): 1; *CHo* 2/6 (6 February 1949): 1; and *CW* 40/2 (12 January 1951): 1.

FV 557 (23 December 1924): 1; one sketch dated [1924]:

Christmas 1924. Three angels—one playing the harp, one blowing the trumpet, and one emitting stars—make a border along with a winter scene of a house and a church for a poem entitled "Änglabudskapet" by Anna Preluitz. The title above reads "Christmas 1924." Reprinted in *FV* 609 (22 December 1925): 5 with text of Luke 2:9-14 in Swedish; *OYC* 11/1 (5 January 1941): 1; *OCLF* 12/51 (20 December 1942): 1; and *OCLF* 15/50 (16 December 1945): 1.

FV 572 (7 April 1925): 1; one drawing dated 1925:

Jesus Leaving Gethsemane. Roman soldiers and Jewish leaders lead Jesus from Gethsemane. Jesus' hands are bound. The branch of an olive tree is seen at the upper right. Men carry torches and have raised fists. Reprinted in *OYC* 13/16 (18 April 1943): 1.

FV 609 (22 December 1925): 1; one drawing unsigned and undated, but doubtless by Sallman [1925]:

Snow-Covered Pines and Bells. Pine trees and two large bells appear above the poem "Julklockorna" by Felicia. A title states, "Jul, Jul, Signade Jul!"

FV 777 (12 March 1929): 1; one sketch signed "Elias" dated [1929]:

Young Man Kneeling on Jesus. A young man with hands folded kneels in the lap of Jesus. A cross stands behind them. Below is a poem entitled, "A Man." Reprinted in *OYC* and *OJ* 6/7 (16 February 1936): 1; *OYC* 6/37 (13 September 1936): 1; and *OYC* 8/12 (20 March 1938): 1. An adaptation of a nineteenth-century European painting, a copy of which, prior to 1978, stood as the altar painting of the Månsarp Kyrka in Sweden. The theme is "Come to me all who labor and are heavy laden, and I will give you rest" (Matthew 11:28). Publication of the well-known painting appears on the front page of *MFU* 3/9 (5 May 1914) under the caption "Den bäste vännen" ("The best friend"); and in *OYC* and *OJ* 2/17 (24 April 1932): 3; *OYC* and *OJ* 3/4 (22 January 1933): 3; *OYC* 5/40 (6 October 1935): 1; *OYC* 9/10 (5 March 1939): 1; and *OYC* 12/4 (25 January 1942): 1.

FV 778 (19 March 1929): 1; one sketch signed "Elias" dated 1929:

The Lamp of My Life. A man sits before an open Bible looking up at a picture of the Crucified. A lighted lamp is on the table. Done originally to accompany a poem of the same title by the Reverend T. J. Bach. The sketch was later reprinted in *WC Central* 664 (16 September 1933): 16.

FV 779 (26 March 1929): 1; one sketch signed "Elias" dated 1929:
    Christ Rending the Veil. The resurrected Christ ascends in a flood of light, with the thief on his left seen through the rent veil of the temple. The other thief is not seen. Below is a man's face and a portion of a serpent. Similar to the drawing, *It Is Finished* (1958 © K&B 1958). Below is written, "In Him was life; and the life was the light of men. Spread the message far and wide, Jesus lives:—Jesus reigns."

FV 780 (2 April 1929): 5; one cartoon signed "Elias" dated 1929:
    Waldenström on the Radio. Dr. P. P. Waldenstrom, with "Mission Covenant Friends" written on his sleeve, holds a *Förbundets Veckotidning* in his hands and is speaking into a radio microphone labeled "Central Board." His words are,

> Let love be without hypocrisy. Abhor that which is evil; cleave to that which is good. In love of the brethren be tenderly affectioned one to another; in honor preferring one another; in diligence not slothful; fervent in spirit; serving the LORD. Romans 12:9-11

FV 781 (9 April 1929): 1; one sketch signed "Elias" (in upper left) dated 1929:
    Look and Live. King David—or possibly Isaiah—holds a ram's horn and is pointing to a cross rising out of a mountain. The cross says,

> Which is of most importance, the age of the rocks or the ROCK OF AGES—our origin or our end?—"Except a man be born again he cannot see the Kingdom of God." CHRIST offers a new heredity to ALL, even though born bad and reared worse they can have the bad job rectified by being born again.

At the lower right men are digging into the ground with picks. Each man in the scene is named: Evolutionist, Atheist, Agnostic, Higher Critics, and Modernist. Below is a quotation of Isaiah 51:1, then these words:

> A materialistic age seeks to justify its Christless philosophy by searching for life in prehistoric graveyards. In this they are getting down pretty low and their progress is backwards. They need to look up, not down; forward, not backward. "Lift up thine eyes unto the hills from whence cometh thy help," sings the psalmist.

Compare *Christian Family Life* (1921).

FV 789 (4 June 1929): 9; one sketch, a collage, signed "Elias" dated 1929:
Turn the Radio On. This ad for KFLV in Rockford, Illinois, accompanies a picture of the station's founder, the Reverend A. T. Frykman. A man and woman sit in chairs listening to the radio. The man holds an open Bible. Over the radio waves comes "Tryggare kan ingen vara, Än Guds lilla barnaskara" ("Children of the Heavenly Father…").[5] Above are two radio towers with a house in-between. Printed also in *MV* 55/23 (4 June 1929): 8.

FV 791 (18 June 1929): 7; four sketches unsigned and undated but doubtless by Sallman [1929]:
Radio Audiences. Another ad for KFLV in Rockford, Illinois, this sketch is of the station's four listening audiences: two women in the hospital; a mother at home with children; a man playing pool; and three men out of doors. Warner E. Sallman is listed as one of four members of the Radio Publicity Committee.

FV 814 (26 November 1929): 1; one sketch signed "Elias: dated 1929:
Pilgrims on Their Way to Church. An early colonial-looking family of father, mother, daughter and son are on their way to church. Their house stands in the background. The father carries a Bible. Four lines of poetry are printed below. Reprinted in *OYC* and *OJ* 2/47 (20 November 1932): 1; *OYC* 6/47 (22 November 1936): 1; *OYC* 9/48 (26 November 1939): 1; *OYC* 14/48 (26 November 1944): 1, where it bears the title "The Pilgrims on Their Way to Church"; *OCLF* 15/47 (25 November 1945): 1; *OCY* 27/47 (24 November 1946): 1.

CC Old Series 3/2 (February 1924): front cover; one charcoal dated 1924 © Covenant Book Concern 1941:
Son of Man. This piece is the original Christ head by Sallman. Reprinted on the front cover of *CC* Old Series 9/5 (3 March 1930); also on the front cover of *CC* Old Series 11/24 (11 June 1932). Later reprinted on the front cover of *WC* Central 661 (26 August 1933); *WC* Central 887 (25 December 1937): 12; *WC* Central 893 (5 February 1938): 9; *WC* Western 3106 (12 April 1941): 4; and *WC* Central 1187 (25 September 1943): 3. Also reprinted on the front cover of *the Expositor* 45/2 (February 1943).

CC Old Series 3/4 (April 1924): front cover; one watercolor? dated 1924:
Up from the Grave. Christ ascends from the grave while Roman soldiers lie stricken in the foreground. A winged angel with right arm uplifted and left arm pointing toward the empty tomb is at left. There is light in the grave from

which Christ has come. In the background one sees women approaching, and behind them lower portions of three crosses on top of the hill. Compare *The Christ Triumphant* (© The Salvation Army 1943) and *He Arose* (© K&B 1951).

CC Old Series 3/9 (September 1924): front cover; one sketch dated 1924:

Saved for Service. Men and women study at desks. The teacher up front looks with the class at the theme written on the board: "Saved for Service, Study to shew thyself approved unto GOD, a workman that needeth not to be ashamed, rightly dividing the word of truth. II Timothy 2:15."

CC Old Series 3/10 (October 1924): front cover; one watercolor? dated 1924:

Harvest Time. A horse-drawn wagon in the field is filled with hay; farmers are piling on more hay. A farm is in the background. Reprinted in *OYC* and *OJ* 3/34 (20 August 1933): 1; *CW* 24/29 (16 July 1935): 1; *OYC* 10/31 (4 August 1940): 1 and *OYC* 11/34 (24 August 1941): 1.

CC Old Series 3/11 (November 1924): front cover; one sketch dated 1923:

Family Altar of the American Home. Here a family of four prays around a chair; at the sides are large neo-classical pillars, and in the background tall city skyscrapers. A quote from Calvin Coolidge at the right states that "the true civic center of our municipalities will be found… around the family altar of the American home." Reprinted in *CC* Old Series 12/2 (14 January 1933): front cover.

CC Old Series 4/1 (January 1925): front cover; one sketch in brown and white dated 1923:

Snow Covered Tree and Bush. A winter scene in brown and white of snow-covered tree and bush branches shows a distant house tucked in the mountains. Reprinted in *OYC* 9/4 (22 January 1939): 1; *OYC* 10/6 (11 February 1940): 1; *OYC* 15/3 (21 January 1945): 1; and *CW* 39/3 (20 January 1950): 1.

CC Old Series SS Teacher's Section 8/8 (17 April 1929): front cover; one sketch dated [1929]:

The Benediction of Christian Education. This title appears below a sketch of an older man teaching a group of young people. An outstretched resurrected Christ is outlined in the background. The teacher holds a book—presumably the Bible—on his lap and with the left hand points to Christ. Reprinted in *OYC* and *OJ* 2/26 (26 June 1932): 1.

CC Old Series SS Teacher's Section 8/25 (9 December 1929): front cover; one pen sketch dated [1929]:

A Mirror for the Soul. A hand mirror over a poem is superimposed on a cross. In the four corners are heads of people representing all ages and nationalities. Below is cited Mark 10:45. Reprinted in *OYC* 9/39 (24 September 1939): 1 and *OYC* 16/5 (3 February 1946): 1.

CC Old Series 12/3 (21 January 1933): front cover; one pen sketch dated 1928:
Prayer of an Aged Minister. An aged minister kneels before a chair in his living room praying. Over the fireplace is a vision of his younger self preaching. Below is a poem entitled, "The Aged Minister's Prayer." The minister is praying not be forsaken when he is old. Reprinted in *OYC* 4/32 (12 August 1934): 2. The minister kneeling before his chair is reprinted in *CW* 24/17 (23 April 1935): 4; *CW* 28/40 (3 October 1939): 1; and *CW* 29/9 (27 February 1940): 1. The younger self preaching is reprinted in *OYC* and *OJ* 6/41 (11 October 1936): 3 and *CW* 28/41 (10 October 1939): 4.

CW 24/25 (18 June 1935): 1; one cartoon sketch dated 1935:
Four Covenant Presidents. Four Covenant presidents and their place in Covenant history are sketched in this work. C. A. Björk represents the "Pioneer Days"; E. G. Hjerpe's tenure is labeled "Institutional"; C. V. Bowman's tenure is "Transitional"; and T. W. Anderson represents the "Present and Future." Done for the Mission Covenant Church Golden Jubilee in 1935. Reprinted in *OCY* 22/40 (5 October 1941): 3; and *CYT* (20 March 1955): 6-7.

CW 29/7 (13 February 1940): 3; one pen sketch signed "Elias" dated [1940]:
He Loved the Sheep. The boy Jesus is shown with sheep and a sheepdog. An accompanying article is entitled, "The Hidden Years" (Luke 2:52). Below the sketch it says, "He Loved the Sheep." Reprinted in *OYC* 11/52 (28 December 1941): 3; *OCLF* 12/25 (21 June 1942): 1; *CHo* 2/31 (31 July 1949): 3; etc.

OCY 16/46 (17 November 1935): 1; one charcoal? dated 1935:
Talking about Sunday School. A teenage brother and sister talk in the living room about the big day next Sunday in Sunday School. The brother, who is sitting in a chair, has something in his lap. The sister is reclining on a couch. Picture accompanies an article by Olga E. Lindborg entitled, "Good Stewards."

The following artworks from *Our Young Covenanters* (*OYC*) 1931-1937, appeared also in *Our Juniors* (*OJ*) for the same date:

OYC 1/7 (15 February 1931): 1; one pen sketch signed "Elias" dated 1930:
Riding the Pony Express. An early American settler riding the post route is being chased by Indians. Arrows are flying by at the head. Reprinted in *OYC*

7/21 (23 May 1937): 4 and *OYC* 13/35 (29 August 1943): 2 with an accompanying article entitled "When Dave Rode the Pony Express." Printed in *OJ* for the same date. Reprinted in *OJ* 7/20 (16 May 1937): 4; *OYC* 7/21 (23 May 1937): 4; and *OYC* 13/35 (29 August 1943): 2.

OYC [1/14] (19 April 1931): 1; one pen sketch signed "Elias" dated 1930:
    Chinese Boy Working on Model Airplane. A boy sits at a table full of working materials. An accompanying article is entitled, "Friendship on a Non-stop Flight." Printed in *OJ* for the same date.

OYC 2/24 (12 June 1932): 1; one charcoal or watercolor dated 1929:
    Japanese Woman Carrying Baby. A Japanese mother carries a baby on her back. In this first printing the work appears above an article entitled, "Little Folks in China." Printed in *OJ* for the same date. In a later reprinting it accompanied an article, "Little Nurse" in *OYC* and *OJ* 4/12 (25 March 1934): 3, where the young woman was Japanese. The work was reprinted again as "Japanese Mother and Her Baby" in *OYC* and *OJ* 5/32 (4 August 1935): 2, and used in subsequent Covenant papers to illustrate stories about the Japanese.

OYC 2/33 (14 August 1932): 1; one charcoal signed "Elias" dated 1932:
    Gypsy Girl. In this sketch, a gypsy girl with headband and full skirt stands by a tree. A tent is in the background, and a cooking pot lies behind the girl on the ground. An accompanying story by Helen A. Larson is entitled, "Betty and the Gypsies." Printed in *OJ* for the same date. The original is in the Helen Larson private collection.

OYC 3/28 (9 July 1933): 1; one charcoal signed "Elias" dated 1932:
    A Birthday Party. Four children—three girls and a boy—sit together with a dog. The boy holds a Chicago softball; one girl has a book in her lap; another girl wears roller skates; the third girl listens to the others talk. The accompanying article is entitled, "A Birthday Party." Printed in *OJ* for the same date. Reprinted in *OCLF* 15/21 (27 May 1945): 1.

OYC 6/14 (5 April 1936): 1; one charcoal signed "Elias" dated 1934:
    Palm Sunday. Jesus rides a donkey with his right hand partially raised. Hands holding palm branches and throwing flowers appear at the sides. The caption is "Palm Sunday." Below are four verses of "Ride on! Ride on in Majesty."[6] The face is quite different from the 1924 *Son of Man*. Printed in *OJ* for the same date. Reprinted in *OYC* 8/15 (10 April 1938): 1 over the title "The Triumphant Entry" (Matthew 21:1-9); also in *CHo* 2/15 (10 April 1949): 2; and *CW* Swedish 40/11 (16 March 1951): 1.

OYC 7/38 (19 September 1937): 4; one pen sketch; stylized "S" perhaps for "Sallman" dated [1937]:

Woman with a Dog. A woman wearing a bib apron stands in front of a farm house telling her dog to put down the stick in its mouth. Underneath it is written, "Whenever we chide her for wrongdoing, she picks up a stick." Illustration for a short story. Printed in *OJ* for the same date.

OYC 15/45 (11 November 1945): 1; one pen and charcoal? dated 1944:

The Compassionate Christ. A thorn-crowned Christ looks down upon a globe swirling in space. Below and to the left of the globe is a hand carrying a Christian flag. Opposite the face of Christ is a verse from Frank Mason North's, "O Master of the Waking World."[7] The Methodist Church used the artwork as a poster to advance a 1946 Crusade for Christ. It was published earlier on the front cover of *the Christian Advocate* 120/7 (15 February 1945). Reprinted in *OYC* 15/45 (11 November 1945): 1; and *CW* 40/13 (30 March 1951): 1.

OCLF 12/14 (5 April 1942): 1; pen sketch signed "Elias" dated 1930:

Behold I Am Alive. Christ rises with hands outstretched from a darkened grave. Easter lilies are in the foreground. Three crosses stand on a hill in the background. Reprinted in *OCY* 25/15 (9 April 1944): 1; *OCLF* 15/13 (1 April 1945): 1; and *CHo* 1/13 (28 March 1948): 4. The original is in the Marion Sallman private collection.

OCLF 16/16 (21 April 1946): 1; one pen sketch dated [1946]:

Tis Easter, Tis Easter. A boy and girl look at a large Easter lily growing among tulips. Below is printed, "'Tis Easter, 'tis Easter!' the flowers say."

OCLF 16/32 (11 August 1946): 1; one pen sketch signed "Elias" dated [1946]:

The Children's Friend. In this sketch Jesus in outline stands behind five small children sitting or lying on the ground. Jesus' arms are outstretched with palms face down, signifying care for the children. Below is printed, "Jesus, the Children's Friend."

CF 32/2 (July 1949): 1; one charcoal and pen sketch; dated 1943:

Girls Bible Class. A woman is teaching a girls' Bible class out of doors. The setting appears to be the Covenant East Coast Conference camp in Cromwell, Connecticut. They sit on a hilltop, with Bibles and notepads in their laps. In the background are hills and a small winding river. The teacher points towards a clouded sky. Clouds at top of the picture contain a cross, in front of which is a line of flags.

CHo 3/20 (14 May 1950): 1; one charcoal dated 1950:
Mother Holding Baby. A mother holds her baby. This issue is for Mother's Day. Below is a two-verse poem taken from the *Gospel Messenger*.

[1] Running number is 869, which appears to be an error.

[2] August Ludvig Storm, "Thanks to God for My Redeemer," trans. Carl E. Backstrom, *Covenant Hymnal* 1996, #657.

[3] *Covenant Hymnal* 1996, #527.

[4] An inconsistency in the running numbers of *Förbundets Veckotidning* begins with the 22 August 1922 issue. The 15 August issue is numbered 483 and the 22 August issue 434 (instead of 484). The mistake was never corrected. The running numbers therefore continue from 434 in subsequent issues.

[5] Lina Sandell, "Children of the Heavenly Father...," trans. Ernst W. Olson, *Covenant Hymnal* 1996, #87.

[6] Henry Hart Milman, *Covenant Hymnal* 1996, #229.

[7] *Covenant Hymnal* 1973, #547.

Appendix II
Artwork for the Salvation Army

The following is a listing of surviving Sallman artwork for the Salvation Army. The frieze from the Century of Progress Exhibit is not extant, nor are the murals and stage work in Shagbark's Cherokee Hall, with the exception of two free-standing Indian cut-outs that have survived in storage. There are two lists: 1) pen sketches, crayons, charcoals, pastels, watercolors, and oils published in the *War Cry* (*WC*); and 2) oils done for two Chicago-area meeting halls, and one rehabilitation center in Minneapolis.

Titles not in italics are untitled works, or works that were at one time titled, but whose titles are now unknown. Dates in square brackets are assumed dates.

Art work in *The War Cry*

WC Central 661 (26 August 1933): front cover; one charcoal dated 1924 © Covenant Book Concern 1941:

Son of Man. The original Sallman Christ head published on the front cover of the *Covenant Companion* Old Series (February 1924). Reprinted (in burnt orange) in *WC* Central 887 (25 December 1937): 12; *WC* Central 893 (5 February 1938): 9; *WC* Western 3106 (12 April 1941): 4; and *WC* Central 1187 (25 September 1943): 3.

WC Central 664 (16 September 1933): 16; one sketch signed "Elias" dated 1929:

The Lamp of My Life. A man reads at a table by lamplight looking up to a picture of the crucified Christ. Reprinted from *FV* 778 (19 March 1929): 1.

WC Central Christmas 678 (23 December 1933): front cover; one watercolor dated [circa 1910]:

Christmas Light in Children's Eyes. Two wide-eyed children—a boy and a girl—are pictured here amidst a decorated Christmas tree and Christmas toys. At lower right it reads, "Christmas light in children's eyes is like a glimpse of paradise…"

WC Central 732 (5 January 1935): front cover, 4; two cartoons dated 1934:

Sunday School Kickoff. On the front cover a 1935 helmeted football player, who is only a baby, kicks off a campaign to lift the 1935 Sunday School membership to fifty thousand. At the bottom of the page two young kickers kick a ball over a goal post sketched at the top. The cover cartoon was reprinted on the front cover of *WC* Central 784 (4 January 1936).

WC Central 761 (27 July 1935): back cover; one cartoon in pen and watercolor dated [1935]:

On to 50,000 Campaign. Poster drawing for a Salvation Army "On to 50,000" campaign. In the foreground a young boy, with a banner declaring "On to 50,000!" is at the back of a large company of Salvationists marching toward a distant sunrise where a cross is rising. Reprinted in *WC* Central 845 (6 March 1937): 8; and *WC* Central 944 (28 January 1939): 8.

WC Central 770 (25 September 1935): 8; one pen sketch and watercolor? dated [1935]:

World for God Campaign. This work was used on a poster for a "World for God" campaign led by Evangeline Booth. Booth, with Bible in hand, preaches here to a vast multitude. At right a couple banners are aloft. At left are clouds and a flash of lightning. Behind Booth, Christ stretches out his arms, and behind Christ stands a cross. In the distance is a target board of concentric circles. At the lower right Matthew 28:19 is quoted, "Go Ye…make disciples of all the Nations." Reprinted in *WC* Central 816 (15 August 1936): 15; *WC* Central 827 (31 October 1936): 9; *WC* Central 845 (6 March 1937): 8; and *WC* Central 944 (28 January 1939): 8.

WC Central Christmas issue 782 (21 December 1935): 10-11; two watercolors dated 1935:

Christmas Morning. A young girl here arrives downstairs on Christmas morning. She stands at the foot of the stairs. Across the page, an old man hastily departs. These watercolors illustrate a Christmas story, "The Truce of God," by Mary Roberts Rinehart.

WC Central Easter issue 798 (11 April 1936): 4-5; one watercolor dated 1936:

Roman Soldiers and Barabbas. Painted only in purple and green, this watercolor depicts Roman soldiers raising the sword against Barabbas as a young woman looks on. The piece illustrates an Easter story, "The Healer," by Margaret E. Sangster.

WC Central Christmas issue 834 (19 December 1936): 18-19; two illustrations in an unknown medium dated 1936:

Horse Riders at Bethlehem. The artwork consists of two sketches: men riding horses, with a star over Bethlehem in the background; and a thorn-crowned Jesus with one of the two crucified thieves. Both works illustrate the story, "Rugged Road," by Elizabeth Chisholm.

WC Central Easter issue 848 (27 March 1937): 4-5; two crayons or charcoals dated 1937:

Girl Praying. An illustration of a young girl lying in bed with her hands folded and a collage comprised of angels, an Easter lily, a church, and trumpets serving here to illustrate the story, "Easter Sunrise," by Elsie Singmaster.

WC Central Easter issue 903 (16 April 1938): 10-13; five charcoals and two watercolors dated 1938:

Miracle and Menial Tasks. Five charcoals illustrate an article on the mission of the Salvation Army entitled, "Christ of the Miraculous and the Menial," by P. LeRoy DeBevoise: a) a pair of hands extend from a burst of light (at top); b) a beam of light streams into the open tomb, with three crosses on a distant hill and an Easter lily in the foreground; c) outstretched hands of the risen Christ; d) a plate of fishes; and e) the hands of Jesus wash a disciple's feet.

The Centurion of Faith. Two watercolors illustrate the story, "The Mantle of the Master," by Orlo Choguill: a) Roman soldiers leave the cross, but are looking back; and b) a lone centurion looks up at Jesus on the cross.

WC Central Christmas issue 939 (24 December 1938): 22-23; one watercolor dated 1938 and one simulated pen etching dated 1920:

The Innkeeper. In this watercolor, a bearded innkeeper of Bethlehem looks out the window, with extended hands, saying he has no room.

Apostate Religionists. In this pen etching images of a weeping woman, a cathedral being picketed by people carrying banners that say "apostate religionists," and another cathedral posted with a sign saying, "For sale, suitable factory site" form a collage. In the foreground crowd one person reads in the newspaper about divorce, crime, and scandals. Vultures hover overhead. This artwork was published earlier on the cover of the *Evangelistic Note* 1/2 (March 1921), with the caption below, "Oh! Jerusalem, Jerusalem, How oft…but ye would not—Jesus."

Both artworks illustrate a Christmas story, "No Room in the Inn," by Albert Linn Lawson.

WC Central Easter issue 1004 (23 March 1940): 10-12, 18; three sketches dated [1940]:

Woman at the Village Well. Three pictures here illustrate an Easter story, "The Mother," by Margaret E. Sangster: the face of an old woman, women with water jugs at the village well, and a woman holding a baby while a man and woman look on.

WC Western Easter issue 3106 (12 April 1941): 6-7, 18; three watercolors dated 1941:

Women Talking in a Garden. Two watercolors here show a dejected-looking boy coming down the walk toward two women who are sitting in a garden. The women are sewing and talking about the trial of Jesus.

Puppy in a Basket. Here a puppy dog in a basket is held by a hand from above. A picture with a prominent thorn branch is in the background.

All three watercolors illustrate an Easter story, "Blessed Souvenir," by Margaret E. Sangster.

WC Western Easter issue 3106 (12 April 1941): 14-15, 22; three charcoals or crayons dated 1941:

Salvation Army Woman Selling Flowers. A man buys flowers from the woman as two children look on.

Down the Cellar Passageway. Two children, a boy and a girl, lead a Salvation Army woman down a cellar passageway.

Telling the Easter Story. A Salvation Army woman is telling children the Easter story. In the background a Salvation Army doctor gives medicine to a bed-ridden woman.

These works illustrate an Easter story, "Out of the Dark," by Grace Livingston Hill.

WC Central 1087 (October 25 1941): front cover; one charcoal dated 1941 © K&B 1942:

Our Redeemer. The face on the oil of *Christ in Gethsemane* (1941 © K&B 1942).

WC Central 1089 (8 November 1941): front cover; one charcoal dated 1941 © Warner Sallman 1941:

Christ on the Clouds. Framed by the rent veil of the temple. Below are explosions on earth. An accompanying poem speaks of Christ's return.

WC Central Christmas issue 1095 (20 December 1941): front cover, 10-11, 14, 15; back cover; six artworks total—four oils, the media of the others unknown—dated 1941; three oils © The Salvation Army 1941:

The Prince of Peace. 1941 © Salvation Army 1941. This oil painting, on the front cover is a close-up of the baby Jesus sleeping in the stable. Hands surround the baby, indicating he is being held. To the right are hands of a shepherd on his staff. The head of a donkey is at the left. The baby's head is bathed in light. An advance announcement, with picture, appears in *WC* Central 1084 (4 October 1941): 11. Reprinted in *WC* Central Christmas issue 1200 (25

December 1943): 2; used on a Salvation Army Christmas card in 1987; and reprinted again in *WC* 109/10 (13 May 1989): 5. The original hangs in the Salvation Army National Headquarters, Alexandria, Virginia. This painting is not to be confused with *Prince of Peace* (© K&B 1950).

A Bethlehem Shepherd. Illustrating the Christmas story, "The Light on the Hilltop," by Margaret E. Sangster, these three artworks—the second said to be an oil—depict the following scenes: a) a shepherd with sheep sitting at night on a hillside, holding his staff; b) a beam of light piercing the clouds over Bethlehem, while shepherds watch from a hillside (the possible oil); and c) a stranger greeting a shepherd boy perched on a rocky ledge above; behind the pair, a star beams over Bethlehem.

The Boy Jesus. 1941 © The Salvation Army 1941. In this oil, on page 15, the boy Jesus stands next to his father, Joseph. Joseph sits on a carpenter bench with outstretched arm, his other arm around the boy. The boy rests folded hands on his father's knee. A hammer sits on the bench at left. The face of the father is a recognizable Sallman face, although not the Christ face of 1924 and 1940. Sallman did this painting at Will Rogers Camp Shagbark, Camp Lake, Wisconsin. Reprinted in *WC* 109/10 (13 May 1989): 6. The original resides in the Lieutenant Colonel Don Rose private collection.

The Flight into Egypt. 1941 © The Salvation Army 1941. In this oil, on the back cover, Mary, Joseph, and baby Jesus travel by night to Egypt (Matthew 2:14). Mary, riding a donkey, holds Jesus in her arms as Joseph walks alongside. His right hand secures a sack slung over the shoulder. In his left hand he holds a pouch and a walking stick. Two pyramids are seen in the distance. Mary and the baby look much the same as other Sallman renditions of just Mary and the baby. Reprinted in *WC* Christmas issue 101/51 (19 December 1981): 20–21, also in *WC* 109/10 (13 May 1989): 5. A chalk done for an Edgewater Covenant Christmas program (*The Flight into Egypt*, n.d.) differs only slightly in that Joseph looks to the side. Compare Hans Lietzmann's painting, *The Flight to Egypt*, printed on the back cover of *WC* Central 757 (29 June 1935); also Eugene Girardet's *The Flight into Egypt*, printed in Maus, *Christ and the Fine Arts*, 66. The original of Sallman's *Flight into Egypt* hangs at the Salvation Army's National Headquarters in Alexandria, Virginia.

WC Central 1097 (3 January 1942): front cover; one watercolor and nine pen sketches dated 1941:

Achieving with Christ. Nine pen sketches of the work of the Salvation Army surround a near-full figure of Christ in watercolor. Christ has his right hand lifted up and his left hand extended sidewards. The pen sketches, clockwise from upper right, depict numerous examples of the Salvation Army's work: a) a band playing; b) a choir singing; c) scouts carrying a tray of food to the needy;

d) a woman teaching Sunday School; e) a man praying with two other men; f) a nurse reading to a sick woman in bed; g) a man giving a homeless man a bed; h) a nurse tending babies in a hospital nursery; and i) a man visiting another man in prison. The collage appears again on page 5 accompanying an article, "Achieving with Christ," by E. I. Pugmire. Sketches d), e), f) and g) are reprinted in *WC* Central 1246 (11 November 1944): 3.

WC Central Easter issue 1110 (4 April 1942): front cover, 10-11, 16; back cover; five artworks total—one a probable oil, three watercolors, and one a confirmed oil—dated 1942; the probable oil © Warner E. Sallman 1942; the confirmed oil © The Salvation Army 1942:

Head of Christ. 1942 © Warner E. Sallman 1942. Medium unknown, but likely an oil. A Christ head that looks very much like *Jesus of Nazareth I* (1956). It is not the classic picture of 1924 and 1940. Printed on the front cover. Reprinted in *WC* 109/10 (13 May 1989): 4.

A Mother's Reflection. Three watercolors on page 10-11 and 16 illustrate an Easter story, "Quiet Streets," by Margaret E. Sangster: a) Mary with folded hands and a pensive look reflects back on the birth of Jesus; b) Mary walks through the streets of Jerusalem; and c) a young mother holds a baby.

Consider the Lilies. 1942 © The Salvation Army 1942. This oil, on the back cover, takes its theme from Matthew 6:28. Walking with three disciples, Jesus points out lilies, daffodils and other flowers growing at the side of the path. In the background are rolling hills, and, most likely, the Sea of Galilee, only a small portion of which can be seen. In his left hand Jesus holds what appears to be a lily of the valley. Reprinted in *The Young Soldier* (5 April 1947): 16, and *WC* 109/10 (13 May 1989): 6.

WC Central 1139 (24 October 1942): front cover; one crayon and watercolor? dated 1942:

Thorn-crowned Christ on the World. A thorn-crowned face of Christ, with drops of blood, is set in front of planet earth. The face of Christ is done in brown, and the earth in blue and white. A musical score and the words of a hymn, "Take Jesus to all the World, He will put things right!" appear above and below. Reproduced later in the same issue in brown with white shadows.

WC Central 1142 (14 November 1942): front cover; one watercolor dated 1942:

An Army on the March. Here a long winding train of Salvationists marches down a road that traverses a globe showing North America. The title appears beneath the scene.

WC Central Christmas issue 1147 (19 December 1942): front cover, 6-7, 18, 19, 31; six artworks total—two oils, three crayons or charcoals, and one unknown medium dated 1942; the three oils © The Salvation Army 1942:

The Christmas Story. 1942 © The Salvation Army 1942. Printed on the front cover. A preview of the present issue, together with the picture, appears in *WC* Central 1134 (26 September 1942): 14. In this oil a serviceman reads his New Testament against the background of the American flag. To the left, and slightly above, is a Bethlehem scene consisting of Joseph, Mary holding the Christ child, and an onlooking donkey. A heavenly beam shines down upon the open Testament and lights the entire scene. The drawing of Mary, Joseph, and the baby resembles their depiction in the watercolor, *The Nativity (of Christ)* (1947 © K&B 1948), except that in the present painting Joseph has no staff and his head is tilted left. The portrayal of Mary, Joseph, and the baby in the oil, *The Little Lord Jesus* (1956 © K&B 1956), is also similar, only there Mary faces the other way. The present picture is reprinted in *WC* 109/10 (13 May 1989): 7.

Servant of the Bethlehem Inn. Three crayons or charcoals illustrate a Christmas story, "The Ragged Cloak," by Margaret E. Sangster: a) Mary and Joseph enter the Bethlehem inn, with the innkeeper watching his servant prepare a bed of straw; b) the young servant peers out a slightly opened door to see upward-gazing people outside; and c) a renewed servant, stands tall with animals in the foreground.

The Wise Men. 1942 © The Salvation Army 1942. In this oil, three wise men—two standing and the other on one knee—greet the "star over Bethlehem." The star is not seen, although its light shines from the upper right. Two of the wise men extend their hands; the other has folded hands. In the background three camels rest at their stopping place for the night. Reprinted (in black and white) in *WC* Central 1247 (18 November 1944): 12; also in *WC* 109/10 (13 May 1989): 5.

Faithful unto Death. 1942 © The Salvation Army 1942. In this picture of unknown medium, a soldier lies upon the ground, close to death. He smiles as he looks up to a robed Christ surrounded by a flood of light. Christ extends his right hand, beckoning the soldier; his left hand shields him from another burst of light, which comes from the explosions of war. Below the scene are three verses of a poem, "Faithful unto Death," by Thomas Curtis Clark. Reprinted in *WC* 109/10 (13 May 1989): 7.

WC Central 1164 (17 April 1943): front cover; watercolor and chalk dated 1941 © Warner E. Sallman 1943; © K&B 1956:

Crown of Thorns. This artwork depicts the face of Christ with a crown of thorns. The work's publication here was its first; in 1956 it was copyrighted by K&B, who thereafter distributed prints.

WC Central Easter issue 1165 (24 April 1943): front cover, 9, 10, 16, back cover; five artworks total —a pastel dated 1942, two pictures in an unknown medium and two watercolors dated 1943; the pastel © The Salvation Army 1943; the two pictures in an unknown medium © The Salvation Army 1943:

The Christ Triumphant. 1943 © The Salvation Army 1943. Christ dominates this front-cover piece of unknown medium. Having risen from the grave, Christ is about to pass over stricken Roman soldiers who lie face-up in the foreground. A winged angel is behind at the left. Behind, and to the left, a blinding light can be seen above the horizon. On a background hill, three empty crosses are silhouetted against a dark sky. Reprinted in *WC* Central Easter issue 1266 (31 March 1945): 24; and *WC* 109/10 (13 May 1989): 6. The painting resembles *He Arose* (© K&B 1951). Compare also a picture on the front cover of *CC* Old Series 3/4 (April 1924).

Christ Carrying the Cross. 1942 © The Salvation Army 1943. In this pastel on page 9, Jesus carries his cross up a modern Golgatha. Rockets and canon fire light up the background. Below is a poem, "A Soldier's Prayer," by Joyce Kilmer. Reprinted in *WC* 109/10 (13 May 1989): 7.

Pilate and Claudia. Two watercolors on pages 10 and 16 illustrate an Easter story, "The Green Branch," by Margaret Sangster: a) Pilate walks away from Claudia in the Roman palace, Claudia's head buried in her hands; and b) Claudia throws a palm branch "at the feet of the Master."

The Unseen Easter Guest. 1943 © The Salvation Army 1943. This back cover work in an unknown medium depicts a hidden yet present Christ, with hands behind his back, overseeing an Army chaplain who is standing before a group of soldiers on a South Pacific beach. The chaplain's right hand points upward. He reads from a pocket Testament. A small boat appears some distance out in the water. At the top of the picture a palm tree serves as a canopy. Reprinted in *WC* 109/10 (13 May 1989): 7.

WC Central Christmas issue 1200 (25 December 1943): front cover, 10-11, 12-13, back cover; six artworks total—two in unknown mediums and four watercolors dated 1943; the two in unknown media © The Salvation Army 1943:

Thoughts at Christmastime. 1943 © The Salvation Army 1943. In this front-cover picture of unknown medium, a helmeted soldier, carrying his rifle, looks up to a star-studded sky where he sees, at the upper right, his wife tenderly holding their young daughter. A wreath, brightly lighted against the night sky, frames the wife and daughter. Reprinted in *WC* 109/10 (13 May 1989): 7.

Pilate and the Angry Crowd. These two watercolors on page 10-11 illustrate a story, "Upon His Shoulder," by General Evangeline Booth: a) the angry crowd; and b) Pilate offering to free a bound and thorn-crowned Christ.

Woman Journeying to Bethlehem. Two watercolors on page 12-13 illustrate a Christmas story, "The Long Road," by Margaret E. Sangster. The woman carries a sack.

A Home Away from Home. 1943 © The Salvation Army 1943. In this back-cover picture of unknown medium, servicemen at a Salvation Army post drink coffee and listen to carolers. One caroler plays the accordion. The room is decorated with paper chains and a Christmas tree. On the wall, in the background, is a picture of wise men on camels going toward the beam of light shining over Bethlehem. A Salvation Army insignia is at the left. At the top is the theme, "A Home Away from Home." Reprinted in *WC* 109/10 (13 May 1989): 7

WC Central Christmas issue 1252 (23 December 1944): front and back covers; two oils dated 1944 © Warner Sallman 1944; the second oil © The Salvation Army 1944:

Lest We Forget. 1944 © Warner Sallman 1944. This painting on the front cover is of a young boy and girl standing before a Christmas candle. The girl holds a doll. A decorated Christmas tree stand in the background upper right. Above the candle light, and to the right of the tree, hangs a flag with one star, signifying that a son of the family has lost his life in the war. Reprinted in *WC* 109/10 (13 May 1989): 4.

Madonna and Child / Babe of Bethlehem. 1944 © Warner Sallman 1944; © The Salvation Army 1944? This picture, introduced on the back cover as "The Babe of Bethlehem," is one of many Sallman paintings of Mary and the Christchild. It should not be confused with *Madonna and Christ Child*, a Kriebel and Bates © oil of 1956, which has Mary looking the other way. Reprinted under the title *Madonna and Child* in the Christmas issue of *WC* 104/51 (22 December 1984): 11; also (in black and white) on the front cover of the *Southern Spirit* (*WC* Southern) 5/7 (14 December 1987); and in *WC* 109/10 (13 May 1989): 5. The original is at Salvation Army National Headquarters, Alexandria, Virginia.

WC Easter issue 105/14 (6 April 1985): front cover; one oil dated 1946 © K&B 1947:

His Presence. In this full-body portrayal, the risen Christ extends his hands with palms upward. Reprint of an oil © 1947 by K&B.

WC 107/23 (7 November 1987): front cover; one oil; dated 1950 © K&B 1950:

Christ Our Pilot. Christ stands behind a boy piloting a ship. Reprint of the 1950 oil © by K&B.

WC 109/10 (13 May 1989): front cover; one oil; dated 1940 © K&B 1941: *Head of Christ.* Reprint of the classic *Head of Christ* © by K&B.

Paintings for Salvation Army Halls

The Ascension
1941. Originally at Scandinavian Corps #16 of the Salvation Army, 1140 W. 59th Street, Chicago, Illinois. Presently at Mt. Greenwood Corps of the Salvation Army, 11355 S. Central Park Avenue, Chicago, Illinois. This beautiful painting of the Ascension is later than the Ascension paintings done for the old South Bend, Indiana (1926), Braham, Minnesota (1934), and Iron Mountain, Michigan (1939) Covenant churches. It is slightly smaller than the Iron Mountain painting, with which it has the most affinity. In the lower left corner is the date, 1 November 1941, and Sallman's signature. Across the bottom, in block letters, is inscribed the verse from Acts 1:11: "This same Jesus which is taken up from you into heaven, shall come in like manner as ye have seen him go into heaven."

Clustered together in different postures and with different hand movements are eleven disciples on a grassy knoll watching Jesus ascend into the clouds. The Christ figure, with a face much like the face on the Christ head of 1924 and 1940, is exceptionally well done. The painting was remounted at the front of the chapel of the Mt. Greenwood facility in 1971.

The Good Shepherd
1943. Salvation Army Evanston Corps, 1403 Sherman Avenue, Evanston, Illinois. This painting hangs at the front of an upstairs auditorium. It is a large oil on canvas, mounted on a frame, about 9 foot square. Very similar to *The Lord Is My Shepherd* done for K&B a year earlier (1942 © K&B 1943), also *The Good Shepherd* (1943), painted for the Covenant Church in Stephenson, Michigan. Because the present painting is square, top and bottom portions of the K&B version are missing. The painting is not as bright and vivid as the K&B oil, from which it differs only in minor details.

Sallman can be seen working on this painting in Bruce Baylor's, "A Man's Artist," *Sunday School Promoter* (May 1943): 27. Completion was on 21 April 1943, and that date appears together with the Sallman signature at the lower right. A picture of the painting appeared in *WC* Central 1170 (29 May 1943): 16; another on the front cover of *The Evangelical Beacon* 13/4 (26 October 1943), although there, unfortunately, it appears in reverse.

Head of Christ

1964 © Messenger Corp. 1935. Salvation Army Central Territory Headquarters, 10 W. Algonquin Road, Des Plaines, Illinois. This oil, measuring 36 inches by 48 inches and painted on masonite, was done originally for the chapel of the Salvation Army Adult Rehabilitation Center (earlier the Rehabilitation Center for Homeless Men), 900 N. Fourth Street, Minneapolis, Minnesota. It has a white background. The face reproduces the color pastel of 1935 done for the Messenger Corporation, whose copyright is noted. Relocated to Central Territorial Headquarters in Des Plaines, Illinois in 1992.

Appendix III
The Head of Christ and Other Oils

The following list contains all the oils discussed in chapter VII. Included as well are other oils done for Kriebel and Bates, special events, select individuals, and audiences no longer known. Some oils Sallman did with no particular audience in mind. If a work has gone by more than one title, the better-known title is given first. Titles not in italics are untitled works, or works that were at one time titled, but whose titles are now unknown. Dates in square brackets are assumed dates.

Bouquet of Lilacs
    1913. Everett Sallman private collection. From the Sallman yard at 5111 N. Ashland Avenue, Chicago.

Santa Claus
    1913. Marion Sallman private collection. Sallman did this painting of Santa with rosy cheeks, a white beard, and no hat, when he was at the Art Institute.

Red Swedish Church
    1916. Everett Sallman private collection. The separate bell tower of the church in this painting was modeled on the bell tower of the Bottnaryd parish church in Sweden, taken from a postcard. Originally in the possession of Myrtle and Evelyn Anderson, this painting was given to Everett Sallman in October 1986.

American Indian and the US Capitol
    1920. Marion Sallman private collection. This sketch in black paint depicts an Indian in full headdress set against the US Capitol Building. In front of the capitol is an automobile; to the right are walking two men.

Portrait of Dr. T. W. Anderson
    1934. Covenant Archives. This portrait was presented to Mrs. Theodore W. Anderson by Mission Covenant boards, pastors and friends at a reception and welcome for Dr. Anderson to Chicago on 2 October 1934, held at the Bethany Mission Church. In 1933 Dr. Anderson came from Minneapolis to Chicago to

assume the office of president of the Mission Covenant Church. See *CW* 23/41 (9 October 1934): 1.

Portrait of Signe Lund

1934. Mildred Lund private collection. Signe Lund was the first wife of Nils W. Lund, Dean of North Park Seminary, who died in 1943. An inscription on the painting says, "With gratitude and appreciation to my good and true friend, Nils W. Lund. March, 1934[1]. Warner. 2 Corinthians 4:6."

Head of Christ

1935. Location unknown. This large oil on a silver background was done for the Covenant Golden Jubilee of 1935, held on the North Park College campus. The painting was later given as a gift to Dr. Charles F. Weigle from the North Park Covenant Church, Chicago.

Portrait of the Rev. C. A. Björk

1935. Covenant Archives. Björk was a pioneer preacher and later president of the Mission Covenant Church. Here he sits in a chair, holding a Bible in one hand and his spectacles in the other. Sallman may have reproduced an earlier work, for a painting of Björk in the same pose appeared in *FV* 153 (7 November 1916): 1.

Portrait of the Rev. F. M. Johnson

1939. Covenant Archives. The Reverend Frederick M. Johnson (1857-1931) was a pastor and prominent leader in the Mission Covenant Church. This painting was presented originally to his son, Fred M. Johnson, by the Edgewater Mission Covenant Church Sunday School on 24 September 1939.

Portrait of the Rev. Otto Högfeldt

1939. Don and Kay Olson private collection. Högfeldt was a Mission Covenant pastor, and for fifty-seven years edited the church paper *Missions-Vännen*. This painting was commissioned by the board of *Missions-Vännen* to mark the 50th anniversary of Högfeldt's tenure as editor.

Head of Christ

1940 © K&B 1941. Wilson Galleries, Anderson University, Anderson, Indiana. The classic oil of the 1924 *Head of Christ*, entitled *Son of Man*, done in brown tones. The view is the same 3/4 profile as the earlier sketch, and the look remains "up and away." Jesus has a beard and shoulder-length hair. Compare *The Christ Head* by Hofmann, said to be printed for the first time in color in *LHJ* 35/3 (March 1918): title page.

Green Forest with Lake II

1940. James and Gene Sallman private collection. A woman in a Swedish costume walks at the edge of the woods in this landscape painting. Another person is bending down at the water's edge. This painting was originally a gift from Sallman to Dr. Carl Anderson. Compare smaller oil of the same name (*Green Forest with Lake I* 1924), which is without people.

Christ in Gethsemane

1941 © K&B 1942. Wilson Galleries, Anderson University, Anderson, Indiana. In this adaptation of Hofmann's *Christ in Gethsemane*, but which is nevertheless Sallman's own, Jesus kneels in prayer with hands folded on a large table rock (Luke 22:41-42). He faces right. The sleeping disciples, Peter, James and John, are in the background left of center, below two large olive trees. In the distance the city of Jerusalem reflects the moon's light.

Jesus wears a deep red-purple robe over a white garment. Sallman paints here the familiar head and face of the 1924 and 1940 Christ head, although the look is upward and troubled, and the hair disheveled from perspiration. Around Jesus is a slight halo. Ominous thorn branches are at the right of the picture, just above the praying hands. Two large olive trees stand in the background.

Behind Jesus is a large rock ("the Rock that is higher than I" of Psalm 61:2). Shadowed on the rock is a cross, which in Christian theology is a symbol of salvation. The rock serves also to hide Jesus from the disciples' view. His communion is with God alone. Yet the viewer can see him.

Sallman has painted in this picture a beautiful garden. He wants the viewer to know that, despite Jesus' suffering, God and nature are not against him.[2] Behind the thorn branches are flowers in full bloom. An olive sapling grows between the rocks, and another grows in the foreground right. The painting as a whole strives for balance: thorns and flowers, physical anguish and quiet strength, human suffering and God's abiding presence—metaphors articulating the mysterious way in which God brings about the salvation of the world.

Sallman painted this picture again the following year for the Covenant Congregational Church in Manchester, Connecticut (*Christ in the Garden of Gethsemane* 1942). Sallman also did a later K&B painting, *The Story of Gethsemane* (1964 © K&B 1964), which is a different work entirely. Compare Hofmann's *Christ in Gethsemane*, a picture of which appears in Maus, *Christ and the Fine Arts*, 285; also W. L. Taylor's *Man of Sorrows*, where Christ is similarly portrayed—praying on a large rock. The latter work appears in *LHJ* 18/2 (January 1901): 13, and was reprinted in *LHJ* 23/12 (November 1906): 60, and 24/1 (December 1906): 54.

Christ at Heart's Door

1942 © K&B 1942. Wilson Galleries, Anderson University, Anderson, Indiana. This painting was inspired by Revelation 3:20: "Behold, I stand at the door and knock; if any one hears my voice and opens the door, I will come in to him and eat with him, and he with me." Sallman's Christ head and face are again the head and face of the 1940 oil. Christ wears a simple white garment. The door of the house is narrow, rounded at the top, and has a lattice window at eye level. Bright-colored flowers grow together with thistles and thorns along the path leading up to the door. Yet the garden is neglected, as it is also in Holman Hunt's *The Light of the World*, where fallen apples lie on the ground. The viewer is to imagine an earlier garden that was well tended and more beautiful.

Christ comes to the door as Friend and Guest. He knocks with the right hand having a nail print still visible. Light emanates from Christ's entire person, because he is himself "The Light of the World" (John 8:12; 9:5). This light, aided by the rounded upper portion of the door, makes the shape of a heart. Sallman did this same painting later for the Covenant churches of Dawson, Minnesota (1950) and Norway, Michigan (1953).

The Hunt picture, which the present work develops along different lines, was well known in Sallman's time and much reproduced. It was printed in *LHJ* 27/16 (1 December 1910): 11; *EH* 40/40 (5 October 1929): 9; 42/12 (21 March 1931): 6; *OCY* 21/13 (31 March 1940): 1; *OCLF* 12/21 (24 May 1942): 1; etc. It appeared also in the 1941 Christmas issue of the *War Cry*, to which Sallman contributed.[3] See also Maus, *Christ and the Fine Arts*, 660.

There were actually a number of famous nineteenth-century paintings of Christ knocking at the door: Ludwig Richter's woodcut *Der anklopfende Heiland* (1855); W. H. Fisk's *The Guest* (circa 1867); C. G. Pfannschmidt's *Der anklopfende Christus* (1872); Joseph Ritter von Führich's *Christi Einkehr bei der glaübigen Seele zum heiligen Abendmahl* (1875); and W. Rainey's *Christ Before Thy Door Is Waiting* (circa 1883).[4] Johann Hofmann had a rendition, as well, which was printed on the front cover of *WC* Central 1140 (31 October 1942). Another sketch of Christ knocking at the door appeared in Covenant papers during the 1930s; see *OYC* 6/46 (15 November 1936): 1; *OYC* 9/13 (26 March 1939): 3; *OYC* 9/46 (12 November 1939): 1; etc. A *Christ Knocking at the Door* (1947), which is a Sallman rendition of Zabateri's work, is at the First Covenant Church in Fort Dodge, Iowa.

The Lord Is My Shepherd / Good Shepherd

1942 © K&B 1943. Wilson Galleries, Anderson University, Anderson, Indiana. This painting was at first called *Good Shepherd*, the title deriving from Jesus' words in John 10:11, 14: "I am the good shepherd." Later it was titled *The Lord Is My Shepherd* after Psalm 23:1. Sallman's shepherd is here leading a flock of more than twenty sheep. In the left arm he carries a small lamb, and in the right hand he holds his staff. The foreground contains flowers and half-hidden rocks; in the background are imposing mountains and a mountain stream. The face of Jesus is the familiar Sallman face of the 1940 oil. His robe is white, like the robe in *Christ at Heart's Door*, but the cut is different.

The mountains are supposed to be Galilean,[5] but they go straight up like the mountains of Colorado. Galilee—and Palestine generally—has rolling hills. However, photos available at the time did show shepherds and sheep on sharp mountain cliffs, near Jerusalem.[6] For mountains more typical of Palestine, see Sallman's later painting, *The Road to Emmaus* (1961 © K&B 1961).

The following year Sallman did this same painting for the Salvation Army Evanston Corps in Evanston Illinois (1943), and, with modifications, for the Bethlehem Covenant Church in Stephenson, Michigan (1943). The Salvation Army painting contains only minor changes. The painting in Stephenson, Michigan clusters the sheep differently. Also, both shepherd and sheep are approaching the top of a knoll. Sallman also did a watercolor, *He Leadeth Me* (1949 © K&B 1951), which has Jesus leading the sheep away from the viewer in the other direction.

Compare *The Good Shepherd* painting by Bernard Plockhorst, a picture of which appears in *CHo* 8/12 (4 December 1955): 1, and is also in Maus, *Christ and the Fine Arts*, 541. W. L. Taylor's, *The Lord Is My Shepherd*, was printed in *LHJ* 24/1 (December 1906): 7.

Peter Matson Praying at a Minnesota Haystack

1943. Covenant Headquarters, 5101 N. Francisco Avenue, Chicago. Located in the World Missions Office. This small oil depicts Peter Matson, pioneer Covenant missionary to China, in his moment of commitment to serve the Lord on the mission field. Matson crouches in prayer next to a large bale of hay. Other bales dot the field behind him. His rake lies on the ground, and his pitchfork stands upright. Behind him lie his coat and farmer's hat. The year was 1888. A reproduction is in Covenant Archives.

(The) Boy Christ / My Father's World

1944 © K&B 1945. Wilson Galleries, Anderson University, Anderson, Indiana. Jesus here is pictured outside Nazareth, sitting in the surrounds of his Father's world. The earlier title of the work was thus *My Father's World*. Rich contextual detail seeks to illuminate the hidden years of Jesus' youth, more specifically to presage later teachings he gave on the Kingdom of God.

Compare Hofmann's *Christ at 12*. Sallman did a later K&B painting, *The Youth Christ* (1960 © K&B 1960), which is a head and shoulders profile of a somewhat older Jesus.

Christ at Dawn

1945 © K&B 1945. Wilson Galleries, Anderson University, Anderson, Indiana. In this picture Christ sits on a Galilean hill just above Capernaum. The sun rises in the east and a morning star is in the sky. He has come out to pray (Mark 1:35). Around him are rose-colored flowers, a near-match to his slightly-darker robe. On the hillside below is a flock of sheep. The Sea of Galilee, calm and still, also lies below. A fishing boat at the far right turns in the direction of home. On the other side of the sea lies the town of Bethsaida.

A black and white *Christ at Dawn* appears in Maus, *Christ in the Fine Arts*, 545. Compare Hofmann's painting, *Christ on Mount of Olives*.

Jesus, the Children's Friend

1946 © K&B 1947. Wilson Galleries, Anderson University, Anderson, Indiana. This painting derives its inspiration from Matthew 19:13-15 (and parallels), where Jesus stops to bless the children on his way to Jerusalem. The traveling party is somewhere near Jericho. The sun is overhead and the sky is filled with fluffy white clouds. The hills are bare, however, with only sparse growth visible on the rock at the right. From a small background village women and children are coming to meet Jesus. Other mothers with children press close to Jesus, while two disciples—Peter at the left and John at the lower right—try to keep them back. But Jesus' extended hand says, "Let the children come..."

Jesus' white garment resembles that in *The Lord Is My Shepherd* (1942 © K&B 1943), only here the sash crosses the other way. Sallman's next two pictures for K&B, *His Presence* (1946 © K&B 1947), and *We Would See Jesus* (1947 © K&B 1948), have the same garment. The original oil does not show the sandaled foot of Jesus, containing a rock that hides the foot.

Compare Plockhorst's *Jesus Blessing the Children*, a picture of which appeared in *OYC* 3/43 (22 October 1933): 3; and 4/19 (13 May 1934): 1; also in Maus, *Christ and the Fine Arts*, 136. Compare as well Rembrandt's *Christ Blessing the Children*, printed in Maus, *Christ and the Fine Arts*, 622, and Harold Copping's *Jesus and the Children*, printed in Maus, *Christ and the Fine Arts*, 137.

His Presence

1946 © K&B 1947. Wilson Galleries, Anderson University, Anderson, Indiana. This full-figured post-resurrection Christ has arms extended upward, not outward as in Thorvaldsen's famous *Come Unto Me* sculpture. *His Presence* builds on a number of biblical texts: John 20:19-20 ("He showed them his hands..."); Exodus 33:14 ("my Presence will go with you..."; cf. Matthew 28:20); Malachi 4:2 ("the Sun of Righteousness, [risen] with healing in his wings"); and Revelation 1:18 ("I am the living one...").

The setting in this piece, however, is modern. Christ enters a dark room in which only the floorboards are visible. He wears no shoes. He comes—as he did to the disciples on resurrection evening—with a radiant presence. Sallman noted in John 20:20 that the disciples "were glad" when they saw Jesus, an indication that the darkness had been pierced. The face here is a frontal version of the 1940 oil. Marketed separately, this artwork was titled, *Portrait of Christ*. The white robe is the same as in *Jesus, the Children's Friend* (1946 © K&B 1947), and *We Would See Jesus* (1947 © K&B 1948).

A large color picture of *His Presence* appeared on the front page of the *Miami Daily News* for 13 April 1952. The painting was also printed on the front cover of *WC* Easter 105/14 (6 April 1985), with an interpretation on a later page. Sallman did this painting again for the Covenant Church in Escanaba, Michigan (1960), where one can see slightly more of the room in the house.

His Presence was developed further in *I Have Overcome the World*, done for First Methodist Church in Mason City, Iowa (1952), and *Behold He Cometh*, done for First Covenant Church in Rockford, Illinois (1967). In these paintings Christ stands atop the world. *The Triumphant Christ*, done for the South Jacksonville Presbyterian Church (1965), also develops from *His Presence*, but there the hands are lower down and Christ is standing barefoot on grass.

Lewis Keeler earlier did a Christ with outstretched arms for the cover of *WC* Central 734 (19 January 1935).

We Would See Jesus
1947 © K&B 1948. Wilson Galleries, Anderson University, Anderson, Indiana. Inspiration for this painting comes from John 12:20-36, where Jesus is teaching in the temple. Greeks, who are in the city for Passover, have asked to see him (v 21). Disciples figuring in this story are Philip and Andrew. At the moment Jesus is not teaching; he is standing composed and serene as he and the others present are listening to the heavenly voice (v 28). The varied group—some of whom cannot be seen in K&B prints that crop the original—consists of the following, moving clockwise from the upper left:
Three unhappy-looking scribes and Pharisees
Youthful Ethiopian with short hair
Unidentified man to the left of the Ethiopian
Two women to the right of Jesus
Two merchants with red and white turbans
Young curly-haired child with a smile
Roman soldier
Shepherd with green headdress
Unidentified man with hand on merchant's shoulder,
Wealthy Arab in front with green robe and yellow kaffiyeh

Hindu with white turban
Disciples Philip, who wears a headdress, and Andrew
Bald philosopher with a scroll
Philosopher's younger companion in blue, holding a staff
Three unidentified men at upper right
Jesus' robe is the same as *His Presence* (1946 © K&B 1947)—white with a sash.

(Mary, the) Mother of Christ

1948 © K&B 1948. Wilson Galleries, Anderson University, Anderson, Indiana. In this profile view of Mary, she wears a cape of deep blue over white. Sallman often repeated this very popular picture in chalk, one of which he did for the North Park Seminary Wives in 1950. Compare Sallman's portrayal of Mary in *The Son of God* (1952 © K&B 1952).

Follow Thou Me

1948 © K&B 1949. Wilson Galleries, Anderson University, Anderson, Indiana. This painting is essentially the oil of 1940, with Jesus looking sideward in the other direction. He almost—but not quite—looks at the viewer. Around his head is a generous amount of light, carried over, perhaps, from *His Presence* (1946 © K&B 1947). The inspiration for this painting is Jesus' words to Peter in John 21:22: "What is that to you? Follow me!"

A nice chalk of *Follow Thou Me* was done in 1951 for the Polytechnic Methodist Church, Fort Worth, Texas, and another in charcoal and colored chalk for the First Methodist Church, Mason City, Iowa, in October 1962.

The Lord's Supper

1949 © K&B 1949. Wilson Galleries, Anderson University, Anderson, Indiana. This Upper Room painting differs from others in that Jesus and the disciples are standing around the table singing (Mark 14:26; Matthew 26:30). The table is substantially smaller than the one in Leonardo daVinci's *Last Supper*; here one sees only a chalice and two empty plates. It has already become a communion table.

Jesus stands in the center, wearing a white robe without a sash. He gazes up and away in communion with his Heavenly Father and his hands are folded. Still, he sings with the others. Similar to *His Presence* (1946 © K&B 1947), light floods about Jesus' person. The disciples are arrayed in clothes of various colors. Only eleven disciples stand around the table; Judas can be seen descending the stairs at the far right. John stands next to Jesus, on his right because he is thought to be the "Beloved Disciple." As one might expect, Peter occupies the other place of prominence, at Jesus' left.

Christ Our Pilot

1950 © K&B 1950. Wilson Galleries, Anderson University, Anderson, Indiana. In this painting, Christ stands behind a small sailor who is piloting his ship through stormy seas. Sallman intended the picture for youth. The boy, wearing neither coat nor hat, stands erect with a forward gaze. His face is without trace of worry or fear—instead it has a look of trust, courage, and quiet determination. The shadowy Christ standing behind is the boy's help (cf. Psalm 121:2). His left hand rests on the boy's shoulder; with his right hand he points out the course ahead. Christ's hands are intentionally kept off the wheel so the young pilot can do the actual navigating. Sallman wants the viewer to know that with Christ as one's pilot, no matter what the danger, one's life will be kept (Psalm 121:7-8); one will be safely led into the harbor of God's eternal kingdom. Into a cloud made pink by the hidden sun, Sallman has outlined the Arch-enemy, who lies close like a "roaring lion" (cf. 1 Peter 5:8).

Sallman did this picture many times in chalk, and in 1952 it was reproduced in stained glass for a balcony window of the Children's Chapel at the Methodist Children's Home in Detroit, Michigan. A fine watercolor was also done in 1964 for the West Suburban (now Rich Port) YMCA in La Grange, Illinois.

Prince of Peace

© K&B 1950. Location unknown. Another portrait of Jesus, not to be confused with an oil of the Christ child entitled, *The Prince of Peace* (1941 © The Salvation Army 1941). This painting is similar to *Pleading Savior* (© K&B 1962). It was also modified for a Roman Catholic audience in *Sacred Heart of Jesus* [© K&B 1950].

Sacred Heart of Jesus

[© K&B 1950]. Location unknown. This portrait of Jesus very much resembles *Prince of Peace* (© K&B 1950), except that a bleeding heart with a cross and a torch have been added in watercolor. The present painting was printed on the front cover of *Cor* 23/6 (June 1951), a publication of the Sacred Heart Monastery of Hales Corners, Wisconsin.

He Arose

© K&B 1951. Location unknown. In this probable oil, Christ ascends from an open tomb on Easter morning. Soldiers guarding the tomb lie in the foreground "like dead men" after an angel of the Lord has come to open it (Matthew 28:2-7). The angel is not seen. Nor are any of the women seen. Jesus wears the same white robe with a sash appearing in *Jesus, the Children's Friend* (1946 © K&B 1947), *His Presence* (1946 © K&B 1947), and *We Would See*

Jesus (1947 © K&B 1948). Here the sash blows behind him. On a background hill are three empty crosses. Morning light is just beginning to appear over the hills. White clouds fill the sky. The look of Jesus is the typical Sallman look: serious, up and away.

Compare a similar picture that appeared on the front cover of *CC* Old Series 3/4 (April 1924); also Sallman's painting, *The Christ Triumphant*, done for the Salvation Army (1943 © The Salvation Army 1943).

Thine Is the Power

1951. Covenant Archives. The scene here is apocalyptic—from Revelation 6—where Christ is standing above four riding horsemen on a smoke-covered scroll. The rider of the lead horse, which is white, carries a bow. Next comes the red horse whose rider wields a great sword. On the black horse following, a rider holds a balancing scale. Last is the pale horse whose rider's name is Death. He is the reaper and carries a large sickle in hand. Behind the horsemen burns the fire of Hades; above is a glowing mushroom cloud from a nuclear explosion.

The resurrected Christ holds a lamb in his left arm, as he does in *The Lord Is My Shepherd* (1942 © K&B 1943). The lamb is said to represent the power of love. The right hand is lifted up in a sign of peace. Behind the right hand, a bolt of lightning emanates from a stylized cloud with colored, irregular rings. This, perhaps, is the power of Heaven. The sky is a night sky, yet one can see the sun rising on the horizon. Behind Christ stand the crosses of Golgatha, and below them is the door of the empty tomb. The figure of Christ is framed by the rent veil of the temple, which Sallman portrayed also in *Christ Rending the Veil* (1929) and *It Is Finished* (1958 © K&B 1958). The picture teems with displays of power, nevertheless, the message here is that ultimate power belongs forever to Christ (Matthew 6:13).

This painting was done originally for the 10th International Luther League Convention at Michigan State College and entitled *The Christ of Power*. A picture of the painting appears on the front cover of *The Lutheran Standard* 109/37 (15 September 1951).

Teach Me Thy Way

1951 © K&B 1952. Wilson Galleries, Anderson University, Anderson, Indiana. Jesus here is sitting with a young boy in the shelter of a large rock. Olive branches hang overhead. An arm is around the boy, and a hand is over the boy's hands. The setting is on the road to Bethlehem, with Jerusalem's walls visible in the background. Barely visible are two mothers walking in the distance with their children. Jesus wears a white garment with a blue-purple robe draped over the left shoulder. The boy wears a rose-colored robe with cap to match.

Compare *Christ in Gethsemane* (1941 © K&B 1942) and *The Boy Christ* (1944 © K&B 1945), both of which have the large background rock, also *Jesus, the Children's Friend* (1946 © K&B 1947), which has the rock and the same ledge.

The Son of God

1952 © K&B 1952. Wilson Galleries, Anderson University, Anderson, Indiana. This painting portrays a curly-haired Jesus sitting on the lap of Mary, his mother. It is evening and the two are on a grassy hill overlooking Jerusalem. Jesus wears a white garment and is sitting with hands folded. Mary is dressed in blue with a white cape over the head and shoulders. The bright light surrounding Jesus' face is to remind the viewer that while he is a real child, he is also "the Son of God."

Compare *Mary, the Mother of Christ* (1948 © K&B 1948), where the portrayal of Mary is similar. The same picture in chalk was titled, *Behold My Mother* (1953). This picture was printed on the Warner Press 1995 calendar.

Portrait of Otto Schnering

1953. A framed oil approximately 30 inches by 36 inches. Ann Schnering private collection. Otto Schnering was president of the Curtis Candy Company, makers of Baby Ruth and Butterfinger candy bars.

Portrait of King Gustaf VI Adolf

1954. Drottningholm Palace, Stockholm, Sweden. This painting was presented to the King via Pastor Holmberg of the Swedish Mission Covenant Church. A letter of thanks, dated 26 November 1954 and signed by C. F. Palmstierna, Private Secretary to H. M. The King, was received by Sallman.

He Careth for You

1954 © K&B 1954. Wilson Galleries, Anderson University, Anderson, Indiana. This painting has a modern setting. Jesus, and three young children— a brother and two sisters—are in the back yard of the children's home. Behind them are flowering trees and bushes. A sparrow looks out from the tree. Beyond lies their town, and further back high mountains meet a blue sky with white clouds.

The children's play has been interrupted by the discovery of a sparrow having a broken wing. The boy holds it in his hands, and shows it to Jesus, who has stopped to sit with them. Jesus, however, looks neither at the bird nor at the children. He gazes into the distance, , wondering this time what these children will be like when they are grown. Will they possess the humility and trust they now show in casting their cares upon him? Or will they become like so many adults—arrogant and self-sufficient?

Following *Christ Our Pilot* (1950 © K&B 1950) and *Teach Me Thy Way* (1951 © K&B 1952), this picture was intended primarily for children and young people. Another done for young people the same year was *Ready to Go—Ready to Stay—!* (1954 © K&B 1954).

Resurrection Morn

1954 © K&B 1954. Wilson Galleries, Anderson University, Anderson, Indiana. This painting derives its inspiration from Mark 16:1-2, which reports the three women—Mary Magdalene, Mary the mother of James, and Salome—going early on Easter morning to the tomb with spices. The three are approaching the tomb at the left of the picture. The one behind carries two flasks. All the women look troubled. One has her hand to her brow. A very large rock dominates the picture in the center and at the right. At the lower right is a square door-like opening to the tomb—in a flood of light. Spring blossoms hang over the door. Bright-colored flora are also at the lower left, in front of the women. On a hill, in the background, stand three empty crosses. It is dawn, and brightness lights the horizon. Done for a bulletin cover.

The Light That Shineth

1954 © K&B 1954. Wilson Galleries, Anderson University. In this oil, also done for a bulletin cover, a white-robed Christ stands behind a pulpit on which sits an open Bible. The hands hold the pulpit in preacherly-style. The pulpit and background are done in browns. A white cross is on the front of the pulpit. The Christ head is a cut-out of the 1940 oil. At the upper right, against a background of light shining through stained-glass windows, is written the text of John 12:46: "I am come a light into the world, that whosoever believeth on me should not abide in darkness."

Ready to Go—Ready to Stay—!

1954 © K&B 1954. Wilson Galleries, Anderson University. Christ in this picture stands with supportive hands on the shoulders of two young people, one a boy and one a girl. Both are contemplating full-time Christian service. Will they go out as foreign missionaries, or will they remain at home? The boy carries a Bible in his right hand; the left hand is extended forward. The girl's hands are folded prayerfully. This oil was done for another bulletin cover, and a cut-out of the 1940 Christ head was again used for the face of Jesus.

Jesus, the Light of the World

1955 © K&B 1956. Wilson Galleries, Anderson University, Anderson, Indiana. Like *His Presence* (1946 © K&B 1947), this too is a full figure of Jesus, however, in detail it has a number of differences. The face, instead of being a frontal view like *His Presence*, is an exact copy of the 1940 oil. The arms and hands are not raised. Pointing with the left hand to himself, Jesus is saying, "I am the light of the world" (John 8:12; 9:5). With the right hand, which is down to the side and slightly extended, he invites people to follow the Light (John 8:12b). Jesus' white garment in this picture has a blue sash draped over the left shoulder, which Sallman repeats later in *The Master Healer* (1960), done for the United Hospital Center in Clarksburg, West Virginia. Jesus is wearing sandals and standing on grass. More light surrounds him than in *His Presence*, but that is because here he is depicted as the Light of the World.

Madonna and Christ Child

1955 © K&B 1956. Wilson Galleries, Anderson University. One of Sallman's most popular renditions of Mary with the newborn Jesus, known earlier as *The Baby Jesus*. It is meant to develop the text of Matthew 1:21. Mary is cradling Jesus, who is wrapped in a white cloth. With her right hand she takes hold of his tiny hand. He is kicking with both legs, and has a slight smile. The whole is framed by a circle of light, the lighter shades of which make a heart. This picture, in an oval frame, appears also in Sallman's watercolor, *Girl at Bedside Praying* (1957).

The Little Lord Jesus

1956 ©K&B 1956. Wilson Galleries, Anderson University. Mary and the baby are here centered in the Bethlehem stable. The baby is wrapped in white cloths lying on straw. Joseph looks on at the upper left. The head of an onlooking donkey is seen just below, and closer into the foreground is the head of an onlooking ox. A portion of this painting shows similarities to the Nativity scene, which appears in a beam of light in *The Christmas Story* (© The Salvation Army 1942), only there Mary faces the other way. To the right are four shepherds: The shepherd at the back, looking over Mary's shoulder, carries a staff; the young boy next to him has his hands cupped together; the shepherd at the far right has the left hand extended, and in the right hand a staff; and the shepherd in the foreground right is bowing to the ground. This stable is a partially-open structure. In the background, at the upper right, one can see a house and doorway. The horizon over the distant hills is lighted just slightly.

This picture was used on a bulletin cover. It is quite similar to the watercolor and chalk, *The Nativity (of Christ)* (1947 © K&B 1948).

Jesus of Nazareth I

1956. © K&B 1956. Wilson Galleries, Anderson University, Anderson, Indiana. This painting differs little from *Jesus of Nazareth II* (1963 © K&B 1963), which K&B marketed under the title, *Jesus of Nazareth*. Both portraits show a blue robe partially visible on the right shoulder. The faces are also similar, although here the face is more elongated and not as frontal. It is closer to the 1940 Christ head. The neckline, with a ripple in the white garment, is the same as what appears on the 1940 Christ head. Fractured light gives this painting a halo.

Compare the refracted light in *Power and Glory* (1957 © K&B 1958). The present painting looks very similar to the *Head of Christ* (1942 © Warner E. Sallman 1942) that Sallman gave to the Salvation Army for the front cover of *WC* Easter issue 22/1110 (4 April 1942).

Jean Sibelius

1957. Covenant Archives. Sibelius is here sitting leisurely in a comfortable chair before his piano. Partly visible, on the top of the piano, is sheet music with a violin and bow. Pink flowers are next to the piano. A flag with a lion on two legs at the center of the cross is in the clouds at the upper right, over which is printed in block letters, "FINLANDIA." The painting was unveiled at a memorial concert held by the Nordic Philharmonic Society of Chicago on Sunday afternoon, 24 November 1957, at Lane Technical High School. It was given to North Park College in 1965. Compare the sculptured head of Sibelius printed in *OCY* 21/16 (21 April 1940): 3.

Power and Glory

1957 © K&B 1958. Wilson Galleries, Anderson University, Anderson, Indiana. Earlier titles for this painting were *Thine Is the Kingdom* and *Thine Is the Power*. With its refracted light, this painting departs from previous works, although Sallman had been experimenting with refracted light in *I Have Overcome the World* (1952) and *Jesus of Nazareth I* (1956 © K&B 1956). The real prototype of the present work, however, is *His Presence* (1946 © K&B 1947). But now Jesus is standing atop the world. The ascending coil is to create an impression of the "three rings of heaven" (2 Corinthians 12:2), although Sallman concedes these cannot be ultimately defined or measured. Bright orange circles above are light from the heavenly throne (cf. Revelation 21:23). Jesus' right hand points heavenward.

The face is the face of the 1940 oil, which Sallman had just used on *Jesus, the Light of the World* (1955 © K&B 1956). The lamb in Jesus' left arm was carried over from *The Lord Is My Shepherd* (1942 © K&B 1943) and *Thine Is the Power* (1951). *I Have Overcome the World* (1952), done for the First Methodist Church in Mason City, Iowa, has Jesus is standing atop the world with stars and planets swirling about in space. Other works developing the post-war fixation on space include: *Face of Our Lord in Space* (1959); *Christ at Prayer on Globe* (1961); and *Behold He Cometh* (1967), done for the First Covenant Church in

Rockford, Illinois. A picture of *Power and Glory* (called *Thine Is the Power*) was printed in *Together* magazine (October 1959: 3).

In 1963 Sallman did a *Power and Glory* in brown and white chalk for Northern Baptist Theological Seminary in Lombard, Illinois.

Look unto Me

1958 © K&B 1958. Wilson Galleries, Anderson University, Anderson, Indiana. Inspiration for this painting, which is another head and shoulders portrait of Christ, is said to come from Hebrews 12:2. Here the look is almost right at the viewer. A flood of light surrounds the head, and over the left shoulder is a rose-colored robe.

Abraham Lincoln

1958 © K&B 1958. Wilson Galleries, Anderson University, Anderson, Indiana. Lincoln is pictured here reading his Bible by a window during the Civil War. In the background fires are burning. The painting is dated 7 August 1958. 1959 was the 150th anniversary of Lincoln's birth.

Cedars of Lebanon

1958. Charles Bates private collection. This oil was a Christmas gift from the Sallmans to Fred Bates and his wife. For them Sallman painted the Bsherreh Cedar Grove in Lebanon, behind which rise the snow-covered peaks of Dahr el Kohîb. He used for the painting a picture in a book.[7]

Jesus Our Savior

1959 © K&B 1959. Wilson Galleries, Anderson University. Inspiration for this painting comes from John 17, where Jesus communes with God prior to his arrest. The face is not the classic Sallman face, nor is the color of Jesus' dress what we are accustomed to seeing. Here he wears a deep blue robe over a yellow garment. He is sitting, with hands clasped, prayerfully looking upward. The contemplative upward look appeared earlier in *Christ at Dawn* (1945 © K&B 1945).

Sallman did *Jesus Our Savior* in chalk for the Trinity Covenant Church in Oak Lawn, Illinois (1959). Compare Louis Jambor's *Jesus of Nazareth* (© 1949 Augsburg Publishing House),[8] also the Jesus painting by Valerius.[9]

Portrait of the Rev. D. L. Moody

1959. Moody Bible Institute, Chicago. This was done from a painting of Moody by G. P. A. Healy. The occasion was a Founder's Week exhibit at Moody Bible Institute in February 1959.

Study to Show Thyself Approved

1960 © K&B 1960. Wilson Galleries, Anderson University, Anderson, Indiana. The title is from 2 Timothy 2:15. A boy and girl in this painting pause from their study to look up at a Christ figure ringed with halos. The right hand of Christ is lifted up, and the left hand extended out. The boy is sitting at a desk and the girl standing to his left. In her arm she holds a book. Before him lies an open Bible. On the desk are papers, books, a lamp, a globe, a clock, a microscope, and a T-square on a drawing board. In the background hangs a model airplane. Behind the girl is a bookend, which possibly bears the head of Abe Lincoln. This picture was reprinted on a 1995 Warner Press calendar.

The Youth Christ

1960 © K&B 1960. Wilson Galleries, Anderson University, Anderson, Indiana. This head and shoulders profile of the young Christ depicts him older than *The Boy Christ* (1944 © K&B 1945), but not much. A flood of light surrounds the head. Jesus has long black hair and wears a simple blue-colored garment.

Head of Christ

1960 © K&B 1941. Northbrook Evangelical Covenant Church, 2737 Techny Road, Northbrook, Illinois. An oil—possibly over a print—on masonite of the well-known *Head of Christ*. The painting was originally a gift from Sallman to Paul Brandel. Bernice Brandel gave it to the Northbrook Covenant Church in 1989. It hangs in the church foyer.

The Road to Emmaus

1961 © K&B 1961. Wilson Galleries, Anderson University. A painting inspired by the resurrection story of Luke 24:13-35, where Jesus appears to two disciples on the Emmaus road. The view is southeast looking towards Jerusalem, which one sees in the distance atop a large hill. Sallman recreates the setting well, with rolling hills conforming nicely to reality. But the figures are too small. One cannot be sure which of the travelers is Jesus.

It is late in the afternoon, and the sun has just set. The sky and much of the landscape are bathed in various shades of pink. Flowers in the foreground are also pink, with one foreground tree boasting blossoms of light blue. A large olive tree is at the left. The tall tree at the right partially hides the village. The road forks where the disciples have slowed their walk. They are inviting their fellow-traveler to come into the village and spend the night. A dove flies overhead.

A color reproduction of this painting appeared on the cover and overleaf of *Together* Easter issue 6/4 (April 1962), also on the front cover of *The Standard* 54/7 (30 March 1964). Compare Rembrandt's *Christ at Emmaus* (1648) in the

Louvre, which was printed in *OCY* 21/12 (24 March 1940): 3, and on the front cover of the *Christian Advocate* 125/13 (30 March 1950). Plockhorst's *On the Way to Emmaus* appeared on the front cover of *EH* 38/37 (10 September 1927).

Portrait of Bishop William C. Martin

1962. Location unknown; presented originally to Texas Wesleyan College, Fort Worth, Texas. William C. Martin was a bishop in the Methodist Church in Texas. Here Bishop Martin is holding a Bible in hand, and behind him is a drawing of the state of Texas. Benefactors of the portrait were Mr. and Mrs. Johnnie Johnson. It was unveiled at a banquet held 2 April 1962 at Texas Wesleyan College. A picture appeared on the front page of the *Texas Methodist* for 13 April 1962.

Abraham on the Plains of Mamre

1962. Wilson Galleries, Anderson University, Anderson, Indiana. A beautiful large oak dominates the center of this painting, which shows Abraham greeting the divine messengers at the "oaks of Mamre" (Genesis 18:1-2). In the right foreground one can see the opening to Abraham's tent. Another less distinct tent is in the background. Abraham is out in front of his tent, welcoming the approaching visitors with outstretched arms. The messenger in the center carries a staff. The figures here are again too small, as in *The Road to Emmaus*. Yellows and pinks for the ground make the impression of sun reflecting on sand. Mountains are in the distance.

Pleading Savior

1962. Wilson Galleries, Anderson University, Anderson, Indiana. Similar to *Prince of Peace* (© K&B 1950) and *Sacred Heart of Jesus* [© K&B 1950], although in this painting the face is closer to the 1940 Christ head. The blue overgarment appears on both shoulders, not just the left. Jesus' hands are folded, and he is looking left.

The Smiling Christ

1962. Marion Sallman private collection. A Christ head painting very similar to *Jesus of Nazareth I* (1956 © K&B 1956) and *Jesus of Nazareth II* (1963 © K&B 1963). Here, however, the shirt has no blue overgarment on the right shoulder, and the face shows a very slight smile, like *Portrait of Jesus* (1966 © K&B 1966). The painting is slightly damaged. Compare *The Smiling Christ* by Ivan Pusecker, printed on the front cover of the *Chicago Sunday Tribune Grafic Magazine* for 24 February 1952.

Jesus of Nazareth II

1963 © K&B 1963. Wilson Galleries, Anderson University, Anderson, Indiana. This painting was the one marketed by K&B under the title, *Jesus of Nazareth*. It is similar to the earlier and lesser known *Jesus of Nazareth I* (1956 © K&B 1956). Jesus wears a white garment with a blue robe over the right shoulder. The view is almost, but not quite, frontal.

Portrait of Harry Denman

1963. The Upper Room Chapel and Museum Building, Nashville, Tennessee. Harry Denman was a Methodist lay preacher and General Secretary of the Methodist Church General Board of Evangelism during the years 1938-1965. Here he sits at a table with hands folded on a Bible open to Isaiah 52-54. A copy of *The Upper Room* is also on the table. Above his head is a bright opening in what appear to be dark clouds.

The Just One

1964 © K&B 1964. Marion Sallman private collection. This portrait of Jesus with short curly hair is the same basic picture as *Lord and Master* (1962 © K&B 1962) done in other media. The robe is lime green.

The Story of Gethsemane

1964 © K&B 1964. Wilson Galleries, Anderson University, Anderson, Indiana. This is Sallman's second portrayal of Gethsemane, a more panoramic view of Jesus, the garden, and background Jerusalem than in *Christ in Gethsemane* (1941 © K&B 1942). In this painting Jesus is reclining on a flat rock butted up against a large olive tree, which dominates the center of the picture. Gone is the large "Higher than I" rock of Sallman's earlier rendition, its place now being taken by a heavenly angel. The same robe of the earlier paintings appears, except that the color is rose instead of red-purple. Compare the robe in *Look unto Me* (1958 © K&B 1958).

Portrait of Dr. John Thompson

1964. First United Methodist Church (Chicago Temple), Chicago. Thompson was pastor of Chicago Temple from 1920-1941.

Portrait of the Rev. Charles Ray Goff

1964. First United Methodist Church (Chicago Temple), Chicago. Goff was pastor of Chicago Temple from 1942-1961. He is pictured here holding an open Bible.

Portrait of Jesus

1966 © K&B 1966. Wilson Galleries, Anderson University, Anderson, Indiana. This is Sallman's last painting for K&B, another head of Christ in brown tones. The view is frontal and Jesus has a smile about to break forth. Compare *The Smiling Christ* (1962); also Ivan Pusecker's *The Smiling Christ*, printed on the front cover of the *Chicago Sunday Tribune Grafic Magazine* for 24 February 1952. *Portrait of Jesus* was used on the front cover of an inspirational booklet by Kriebel and Bates entitled, *Sustaining Grace*.

Portrait of the Rev. Robert Bruce Pierce

1967. First United Methodist Church (Chicago Temple), Chicago. The Rev. Pierce was pastor of Chicago Temple from 1961-1980.

Portrait of Bishop W. Kenneth Pope

1968. Bridwell Library, Perkins School of Theology, Dallas, Texas. Unfinished. The Rev. Pope was a Methodist Church bishop in central Texas. A Gothic church is in the background right. A picture of the presentation to Bishop Pope at a Central Texas Methodist Conference Meeting appears in the *Fort Worth Star-Telegram* for 27 May 1970.

Portrait of Dr. Gaston Foote

1968. Fred L. Foote private collection. Unfinished. Dr. Foote was pastor of First Methodist Church, Fort Worth, Texas. A communion-table cross is at the left of the portrait. A picture of the presentation to Dr. Foote at a Central Texas Methodist Conference Meeting appeared in the *Fort Worth Star-Telegram* for 27 May 1970.

Works of Unknown Date

Going to Julotta

Everett Sallman private collection. This large unmounted oil on canvas, 6 feet by 8½ feet, looks something like *Memories of Julotta* (1921), done for *FV* 449 (20 December 1921): 1. A Swedish-looking church is alight early on Christmas morning. The moon shines above the mountains. A Swedish-dressed woman is walking up the steps, and others are arriving by sleigh.

Boathouse on a Lake

Everett Sallman private collection. Woods go up from the lake in this early landscape painting. A rowboat sits in front of the boathouse, and another is in the foreground. A large boat on the land has three people in it. The painting has a tear.

Men on Road to Emmaus

Patsy Needham private collection. This unfinished oil is a close-up of the three men in *The Road to Emmaus* (1961 © K&B 1961), although there are differences in detail from the copyrighted work. The present work looks to be experimental. Two of the men—the one on the left and the one behind—are wearing turbans. The man on the right wears a kaffiyeh, and carries a stick in the left hand. The man on the left has both arms extended. One cannot be certain who Jesus is, which is also true in the well-known version. Here he may be the one on the right. The road in this picture is seen straight on. At the left, instead of a large olive tree, is the village. The feet of all three travelers are unfinished. A picture of Sallman next to this painting appeared in William McDermott, "The Miracle Picture," *Christian Life* 24/11 (March 1963): 27.

[1] The day is illegible.

[2] Howard Ellis, *The Story of Sallman's "Gethsemane"* (Chicago: Kriebel and Bates, 1944), 5-6.

[3] *The War Cry* 1095 (20 December 1941): 5. See also *The War Cry* Central 744 (6 April 1935): 8, which printed this painting and had an accompanying article on Hunt. The similarity between the Hunt and Sallman paintings has also been noted by David Morgan in "Imaging Protestant Piety: The Icons of Warner Sallman," 43.

[4] I am indebted to David Morgan for pointing out these works.

[5] Howard Ellis in *Story of Sallman's "Good Shepherd"* (Chicago: Kriebel and Bates, 1944) assumes the hills are Judean.

[6] See those taken by the American Colony in Jerusalem, which were printed in *Our Covenant Youth* 20/4-12 (22 January-19 March 1939).

[7] Colonel Wilson, ed., *Picturesque Palestine I* (New York: D. Appelton & Co., 1881), 475.

[8] See *Chicago Sunday Tribune Grafic Magazine* (10 April 1949): 8, 18; also *Chicago Sunday Tribune Grafic Magazine* (24 February 1952): 7.

[9] A pseudonym of a 19th c. Swedish female artist.

Appendix IV
Institutional Oils and Glass Art

What follows is a descriptive summary of thirty-eight known Sallman art-works done for churches and other institutions: thirty-two oils, and six works of glass art, five of which comprise a single collection in stained glass. Not included are three oils done for Salvation Army halls, which are described in Appendix II. Some oils located presently in churches and other institutions, including portraits, are listed in Appendix III.

Titles not in italics are untitled works, or works that were at one time titled, but whose titles are now unknown. Dates in square brackets are assumed dates.

The Ascension
1926. Evangelical Covenant Church, 3025 East Edison Road, South Bend, Indiana. The first of more than thirty Sallman oils in churches and other institutions, this one done originally for the old Mission Covenant Church at Monroe and Main. Painted on three sail-cloth panels, the whole measures 23 feet by 18 feet. Two large pillars originally divided the panels. For pictures see *CC* Old Series 5/6 (June 1926): front cover; *CW* 23/20 (15 May 1934): 1; *OYC* 4/27 (8 July 1934): 1; *OYC* 12/29 (19 July 1942): 1; *CW* 32/23 (4 June 1943): 1; *OCY* 25/20 (14 May 1944): 1; etc. Sallman did the painting at North Park College, during the summer recess. After the work was hung, Sallman painted over the panel seams to make them invisible. The unveiling and dedication took place on 27 March 1926, on which occasion Sallman was present to give the main talk.

The painting draws its inspiration from Luke 24:50-51 and Acts 1:9. White clouds in a blue sky surround the ascending Christ. His right foot is pulled back, and outstretched arms bless the eleven disciples, who are clustered below on a grassy knoll. Some disciples stand while others kneel on the ground. Some have one or both hands raised in the air. The prominent disciple at left center, Peter, holds a staff. To the left and right, in the corners, stand small leafy trees.

The painting was transferred to the new church building in 1959-1960. It was first cleaned, then peeled from its arched recess and cut to fit the rectangular wall of the new church foyer, where it was then hung. Sallman came to South Bend and repainted the panels so they would appear as one. A picture of him doing this work appears in the *South Bend Tribune Magazine* (17 April 1960): 8-10. The painting compares with an *Ascension* done by another artist in the old Grand Crossing Mission Covenant Church at 74th and Cottage Grove in Chicago.

The Ascension

1934. Evangelical Covenant Church, 508 Broadway Avenue North, Braham, Minnesota. This fine oil, like the earlier *Ascension* in South Bend (1926), consists of three panels, only it is painted on masonite. The ascending Christ differs from the South Bend painting, but resembles the Christ of the first *Ascension* painted for the Covenant Church in Iron Mountain, Michigan (1939) in that the body appears uncommonly slender and straight. Christ's hands are outstretched. Nailprints are observable in both hands and feet. The face, while resembling the Sallman face of 1924 and 1940, has a look of its own. Barely-observable light beams emanate from Christ's face. All eleven disciples stand, except one who is on his knees. Some have outstretched arms. Continuity with the earlier work is kept by placing Peter in the left foreground, except that here only the bottom of his staff is visible. Like the other Ascensions, a small tree is at either side.

Eleanor Bondeson of the Young People's Society saw a picture of the *Ascension* Sallman did for the church at South Bend in a Covenant paper, and decided that the Braham church should have a similar painting. She helped initiate a fund-raising drive, and contact was made with Sallman to do the work. The Young People's Society raised $100.00, to which the congregation added another $50.00. It was the Depression, and Sallman did the painting for $150.00.

Sallman completed he painting in Chicago and then sent it to Braham. A local contractor, G. William Carlson, supervised the construction of a frame and the mounting in the front of the church. Men of the congregation helped. The panels were stylized to match other windows in the church, with the tops pointed, but gently rounded. The painting was completed by Christmas 1934, and dedicated at a Christmas service. Bondeson and a friend were given the honor of unveiling. Special pulleys were constructed to bring down a white cloth that covered the painting.

The painting was moved to the new church building in North Braham in 1967, and hung for many years on a foyer wall, next to the stairs going down to the basement. A new oak frame was made and protective glass was placed over the panels. Now the painting hangs on the back wall of the sanctuary.

Portrait of C. J. Wilson

1935. Wilson Hall, North Park University, 3225 West Foster Avenue, Chicago, Illinois. This painting was a 1935 college class gift to North Park; see *CW* 24/25 (18 June 1935): 8. Wilson was a North Park science professor. Sallman therefore includes a microscope to the left of the portrait.

Head of Christ

1937. Evangelical Covenant Church, 702 Stanley Street, Nelson, British Columbia. Painted on masonite for the Scandinavian Lutheran Mission Church in Nelson, this early oil of the Christ head measures 22 inches by 27 inches. The portrait is essentially the same as the 1924 charcoal and the 1935 pastel, and differs from the oil of 1940 only in tone, having blues and white, instead of brown. The background contains light blue sky with pink clouds. The Rev. Earl E. Lindgren, a friend of Sallman's and the church's pastor, requested the painting.

Covenant President T. W. Anderson presided over a service of dedication and unveiling. Anne Busk,[1] a young girl in the congregation, sang "Turn Your Eyes upon Jesus." The painting was given to the church by Esther Lindgren, wife of the pastor, in memory of her mother, Anna Burklund. Originally it hung at the front of the old church on Baker and Hendrix Streets, in a frame made of rough-hewn yew wood native to the area. When the church relocated, a decision could not be reached on where to hang the painting. Currently the painting is in storage.

The Ascension

1939. Swedish Mission Church, East Ludington and Iron Mountain Streets, Iron Mountain, Michigan. This painting, which measured 13 feet in width and 7 feet 9 inches in height, hung for ten years at the front of the old Iron Mountain Mission Covenant Church. It is no longer extant, having been destroyed when the church burned to the ground on 18 January 1950.[2]

Sallman competed the painting in Chicago, and then shipped it to Iron Mountain. A committee of three, composed of Oscar Olson, Gust Peterson and Carl Larson constructed a frame, and hung the painting on the front wall of the church, above the choir loft. The unveiling and dedication took place on 30 November 1939, at an evening service.[3] Lloyd Bastien, on behalf of the Men's Fellowship League, presented the painting to the church. Over a period of two years, the Men's Fellowship League had raised money for the painting. The pastor of the church at the time was J. H. Lundgren.

Inspiration for the painting was again from Luke 24:50-51 and Acts 1:9. Jesus appeared lifted up into the clouds, with arms outstretched. His figure was straight and slender, as in the Braham *Ascension* (1934), but the right foot was drawn back, as in the *Ascension* at South Bend (1926). The sky contained fluffy white clouds. Disciples clustered on a grassy knoll, with small trees to the right and left. The cluster differed little from the South Bend painting—some were sitting, some standing, while others were wholly or partially kneeling. Some disciples had one or both hands raised in the air. Now the shepherd of the flock, Peter, stood prominently in the foreground, staff in hand.

In 1952 Sallman completed another *Ascension of Christ* for the new church. Though larger, it reproduces the earlier painting in almost every detail.

Head of Christ

1940. Covenant Archives, 3225 West Foster Avenue, Chicago, Illinois. This oil, painted over a 1924 print, was given to North Park College and Seminary from the seminary class of 1940. Except for a white background, it is almost identical to the well-known oil given to Kriebel and Bates in 1940.

Christ in Gethsemane

1940. Lund Mission Covenant Church, County Road CC, Lund, Wisconsin. This front-wall painting is not the familiar Kriebel and Bates copyrighted version, but an interpretation of Johann Heinrich Hofmann's *Christ in Gethsemane*. Sallman did at least five Hofmann interpretations before painting his own *Christ in Gethsemane* in 1941. In this painting Sallman notes in the lower right, "Adapted from Hofmann's Christ in Gethsemane." The painting is taller than it is wide—approximately 6 feet by 8 feet.

This artwork portrays Jesus in Gethsemane just prior to his arrest. He prays, "Not my will but thine be done" (Luke 22:42). Jesus faces left, the same direction as in the Hofmann original. Though the face here is not the familiar face of the 1924 and 1940 *Head of Christ*, one can recognize that it is Sallman's. Jesus wears a purple robe over a white shirt. His hands are folded on a table rock, to the left of which stands a large olive tree with thorns growing at its base. To the right, and some distance back, are the three disciples., Jerusalem is barely visible in the background, and on the road one sees soldiers and others approaching.

The congregation held an unveiling and dedication for the painting on 19 May 1940, at a 2:30 service in the afternoon. See *CW* 29/20 (May 14 1940): 7. During the 1940s it was moved back with the front wall when the chancel underwent expansion. Since 1956 the painting has had a frame of light oak.

Christ in Gethsemane

1940. Painted for the South Chicago Evangelical Covenant Church, 10023 South Avenue L, Chicago, Illinois., where it has hung for nearly sixty years. Presently it is in the possession of the Central Conference of Evangelical Covenant Church, following the closure of the South Chicago Church in 1997. This painting is similar to the *Christ in Gethsemane* in Lund, Wisconsin, only the shape is different. Beveled side edges helped create a perfect fit in the small apse of this 100-year-old frame building. The painting was affixed directly to the wall. Above, in a cloud, appeared the words, "'Not my will but thine be done' Luke XXII, 42." The shape allows for less olive tree than in the Lund painting, also a less-erect posture for Jesus, but other details remain the same. At the lower right of the painting is written, "An interpretation of Hofmann's 'Christ in Gethsemane' by Sallman 1940."

The Men's Brotherhood presented the painting to the church on Father's Day 1940. A fire in 1979 badly damaged the church building, and the painting was nearly lost. The canvas came loose from the wall and had to be reattached. It was also washed and touched-up slightly by a visiting artist from Sweden. A picture of the painting appears in *CW* 29/24 (11 June 1940): 7; *The Expositor* 43/3 (March 1941): cover; and *CW* 30/15 (11 April 1941): 1.

Christ in Gethsemane

1940. First Covenant Church, 2300 Twin Bluff Road, Red Wing, Minnesota. This work is Sallman's third interpretation of the Hofmann *Christ in Gethsemane*. The date 17 November 1940 appears at the lower right, where Sallman has also written, "An interpretation of Hofmann's 'Christ in Gethsemane.'" In the old church, located on Sixth Street and West Avenue, the painting was attached directly to the front wall of the sanctuary. There it had a dark wood frame. Since 1978 it has hung in a room off the new church sanctuary. The top, which contained the words, "'Not my will, but thine be done' Luke XXII, 42," had to be cut when the painting was fit into the new space. Now the words hang separately above. This same verse is above the *Christ in Gethsemane* painting done for South Chicago. The painting now has an attractive frame of dark oak, also a protective railing in front.

Few changes are made from the Lund and South Chicago paintings. The shape is like South Chicago—more width than height. A rock, absent in both the Lund and South Chicago paintings, has been added in the center foreground. The painting was presented to the church by the Ladies' Aid Society at the time of a church redecoration. The congregation held a service of dedication 17 November 1940, on which occasion Theodore W. Anderson, president of the Covenant, was present as the main speaker.

Christ in Gethsemane

1941. First Covenant Church, 2727 North First Street, Fresno, California. The fourth painting by Sallman interpreting the well-known *Christ in Gethsemane* by Johann Hofmann. The lower right bears the date 18 April 1941, as well as Sallman's note, "An interpretation of Hofmann's Gethsemane by Warner Sallman." The painting hung originally on the front wall of the old downtown church on Divisidero and P Streets, where drapes flanked it on either side. Now it hangs in the narthex of the present church building.

The painting measures approximately 6 feet by 4 feet, similar in shape to the paintings done for South Chicago and Red Wing, which are wider than they are tall. Because of the shape, only a portion of the olive tree at the left is visible.

The sleeping disciples are more distinct than in earlier paintings. Instead of Sallman's common white shirt and purple robe, Jesus here wears a rose-colored shirt and blue robe. Also, in this painting one notes drops of blood on Jesus' face (Luke 22:44).

John and Esther van Natta gave the painting as a memorial to the church. Paul Anderson, pastor of the church, made the arrangements with Sallman. The painting was done in Chicago and sent to Fresno after completion.

Christ in Gethsemane

1941. Calvary Covenant Church, 105 E. Second Street, Stockholm, Wisconsin. This interpretation of Hofmann's *Christ in Gethsemane*, the fifth in two years, hangs in a well-preserved frame church overlooking Stockholm and Lake Pepin. Like the painting in nearby Lund, this one is greater in height than in width, measuring approximately 4 feet by 7 feet. Its beautiful wood frame has been done over in gold leaf. The painting has hung for the past fifty-five years on the front wall of the sanctuary, moved only once for the installation of new paneling. Sallman worked on the piece entirely in Chicago and shipped the painting to Stockholm.

Perhaps the most noticeable difference from other Hofmann interpretations is the very large olive tree now standing behind Jesus. The shape of the painting allowed the larger tree to be in a more prominent position. Of the three disciples in the distance, two are particularly distinct. Brightly-colored dots along the road from Jerusalem, no doubt, are soldiers and others coming with torches.

The children of Mr. and Mrs. Carl E. Erickson gave the painting as a gift to the church in memory of their parents. Sallman over his signature has inscribed, "An interpretation of Hofmann's Gethsemane, 1941." The painting was dedicated at a service on 22 June 1941. See *CW* Swedish 30/24 (13 June 1941): 10; *CW* Swedish 30/25 (20 June 1941): 10; and *CW* Swedish 30/26 (27 June 1941): 10. Neighboring Covenant pastors and the conference superintendent, Jacob Elving, attended the dedication. An offering taken at the service helped fund extension work in the Northwest Conference.

Christ in the Garden of Gethsemane

1942. Trinity Covenant Church, 302 Hackmatack Street, Manchester, Connecticut. This oil is essentially the same painting as *Christ in Gethsemane*, done the year before for Kriebel and Bates (1941 © K&B 1942). It hung originally in the chancel of the old church on Spruce Street, behind the choir loft. For a picture there see *OYC* 13/3 (17 January 1943): 4. In the new church building the painting hangs in the narthex.

Originally at the bottom was an inscription reading, "Not my will, but thine be done," followed by Matthew 26:39. The wording actually derives from Luke 22:42, however, and was later corrected. The inscription is now folded under and cannot be seen. The picture was also shortened when hung in the new church building.

An unveiling and dedication occurred on 12 April 1942, commemorating the 50th anniversary of the church. Leander Carlson's six children donated the painting in memory of their father.

The Good Shepherd

1943. Bethlehem Covenant Church, Church Road, Stephenson, Michigan. This painting, on the front wall of a beautiful 100-year-old frame building in the open country of Michigan's Upper Peninsula, strongly resembles both *The Lord Is My Shepherd*, painted for Kriebel and Bates (1942 © K&B 1943), and *The Good Shepherd*, painted for the Salvation Army Evanston Corps (1943). The work's dimensions are approximately 6 feet by 9 feet. Inspiration for the painting—as well as for the better-known versions—derives from John 10:11, 14 and Psalm 23.

This painting, like the one in Evanston, lacks the detail of the K&B original. The mountain at the upper left does not have a dark passageway, and the winding river through the mountains is not visible. There is no waterfall and no flora—just green grass. The face of Jesus is also more elongated. A more significant difference is that the sheep surrounding Jesus are approaching the top of a grassy knoll, not walking on level ground. They cover the entire width of the canvas. No sheep are in front of Jesus, as in the K&B original, which makes visible Jesus' sandaled feet and the bottom of his staff. The background sheep, however, are the same. And a black sheep is to Jesus' left, also a mother sheep on the right, straining to see her lamb in Jesus' arm.

Pastor Paul A. Nygren went to Chicago to request the painting from Sallman. The cost was said to be about $200.00, which the church had difficulty raising. The painting was completed 21 May 1943, just in time for 60th anniversary services, which took place the weekend of 21-23 May. At the Friday evening service the painting was unveiled, and two ladies sang "The Lord Is My Shepherd." Sallman came to the church on two subsequent occasions—once shortly after the dedication, and once in 1952—to do touch-up work and wash the painting. A picture of the painting appeared in *CC* 81/7 (July 1992): 10.

Behold I Send You Forth

1944. Bob Jones University, 1700 Wade Hampton Boulevard, Greenville, South Carolina. Among the many fine artworks at Bob Jones University is this oil by Sallman, commissioned by the class of 1943 as a gift to their school. The oil measures approximately 5 feet wide and 3 feet tall.

The title comes from Matthew 10:16. Jesus stands behind a young boy and girl who are ready to embark on a life of Christian service. His hands rest upon both their shoulders. The face of Jesus—similar to but not the same as the 1940 oil—appears in full, though Jesus' robed body is nearly transparent, fading out entirely lower down. The boy and the girl carry Bibles. The girl also has a notebook and pen in hand. She extends her left hand forward. At the left of the picture is a college building with neo-classical pillars. The boy and girl stand next to a path leading away from the building. In the background, at the lower right, lies a factory with mountains further distant. The gray sky is Cleveland, Tennessee where Bob Jones College was located prior to 1947.

The frame partially hides the date on the painting, 3 April 1944. The unveiling took place on 7 April when the donor class met for a reunion in the campus snack shop. On the old campus the painting hung in the college parlor in Old Main. Now it hangs in the Student Services Office in the student center. This picture was printed on the cover of a 35th anniversary booklet of the Edgewater Young People's Society in 1945. A year later, North Park College received a slightly different black and white sketch of the same picture, entitled *Go Ye* (1945).

Christ of the Campus

1946. The Wesley Foundation, University of Alabama, Tuscaloosa, Alabama. This small portrait of Jesus, with supplemental artwork on surrounding panels, hung originally in the Sallman Prayer Chapel of the old Wesley Center. It is now in the library of the present building, encased in a box wired for illumination. The roughly-square portrait with panels is about 3 feet square.

The portrait is a side view, set over against a background of simulated stained glass in red, blue and purple. Compare the simulated stained glass on *Let's Go to Church* (1947), a watercolor done a year later for a bulletin cover. Jesus in the present work has reddish-brown hair and an off-white garment. His face has no resemblance to the 1924 and 1940 portraits. Jesus looks upward—similar to *Jesus Our Savior* (1959 © K&B 1959), only facing the other way.

Sallman painted this portrait in the presence of an assembled congregation in February 1946. The panels and corners were done later and installed the following Christmas. In the lower left corner, a lighted Herodian lamp sits on top of papers and a book, possibly the Bible. In the upper left corner, a hand holds an ancient scale, behind which are two tablets of the Decalogue. In the upper right corner, two serpents coiled on a winged pole symbolize the medical profession. In the lower right corner is a neo-Roman citadel with towers on both the right and left. Palm leaves with ribbons appear in the side panels; the top panel bears a center flower with leaves going right and left. The bottom panel carries the title: "Christ of the Campus."

Sallman visited Tuscaloosa in 1946 and 1952 during the time William Graham Echols was pastor of First Methodist Church. In 1952 he came to conduct an art seminar. While in town, Sallman also visited the Kiwanis Club. Three chalks from these visits hang in the church, and three more in the Wesley Foundation.

Christ Knocking at the Door

1947. First Covenant Church, 831 A Street, Fort Dodge, Iowa. This painting is not the well-known *Christ at Heart's Door* done for Kriebel and Bates (1942 © K&B 1942), and repeated later for the Covenant churches in Dawson, Minnesota (1950) and Norway, Michigan (1953). It is an adaptation from Zabateri, noted by Sallman at the lower left, where his signature and the date appear. The painting hung originally on the front wall of the old Fort Dodge church. Now it hangs above the doorway in the fellowship hall of a building completed in 1965. A member of the congregation, Lloyd Elg, made its beautiful mahogany frame. Like other paintings of Christ knocking at the door, this one derives its inspiration from Revelation 3:20.

Compared with *Christ at Heart's Door*, Christ faces the door from the other direction. Over his white garment he wears a robe of bright rose, whereas the robe in *Christ at Heart's Door* is completely white. No light in this picture emanates from Christ. But the tiny lattice window shows the same inner darkness as the well-known version. Here, however, the door has a handle, and above the handle a round key lock. Christ holds a staff. His face resembles the 1940 oil. The house, like the one in *Christ at Heart's Door*, is made of hewn stone. A circle contains the entire picture, with a square outer frame allowing for symbols and decorations in the corners. In the lower left corner is a crown of thorns around a cross; in the upper left a flower with leaves; in the upper right a bunch of grapes with leaves; and in the lower right leaves of holly.

Sallman apparently did the painting some years prior to its purchase and presentation to the Fort Dodge Church. It was given to the church in the late 1950s in memory of Mr. and Mrs. Gust W. Lundgren by their daughter.

Christ at Heart's Door

1950. Dawson Covenant Church, County Road 3, Dawson, Minnesota. This oil, in a small country church nine miles southwest of Dawson, duplicates the Kriebel and Bates *Christ at Heart's Door* (1942 © K&B 1942) almost exactly. Sallman has therefore noted in the lower right, "copy of copyrighted painting— not for reproduction." The work measures approximately 3½ feet wide and 6 feet tall, larger than the K&B painting. Nicely framed, it hangs in the apse of the church. A carpenter from the congregation, Walter Swenson, made the frame and affixed the canvas to masonite before mounting. The painting was given to the church by the children of Charles and Frieda Erlandson. A service of dedication was held on 18 June 1950. A picture of the painting appears in *CC* 81/7 (July 1992): 11.

Walk in the Light

1951. All Faith Chapel, Illinois Youth Center (formerly Illinois State Training School for Boys), Route 38, St. Charles, Illinois. This large oil painting hangs on the front wall of the All Faith Chapel at the school and stands 8 feet tall and 16 feet wide. The painting is untitled, and no interpretation from Sallman survives.[4]

At the right of a wooded foreground a group of young boys focus attention on a bright light shining through the trees. The one boy, near the center, has both arms upraised to embrace the light. Most of the other boys also look up, some with intense expression. In the background, a road passes over a river, winds through green farm land, and leads to a large city off in the distance. To the right are stacks with fires burning out the top. Boys walk on the road toward the city—some wear overalls, others dress more nicely. On a grassy hill descending from the woods to the road, a man stands with his right arm raised toward the light; his left arm is around one of the boys. Two boys head toward the road; one boy carries a suitcase while another carries what appears to be a bedroll under his arm.

The setting and general theme of the painting are clear enough. The wooded area is the environs of St. Charles, the river is the Fox, the city with tall buildings is Chicago, and the burning stacks are either the oil refineries of Whiting, or the steel mills of Gary, Indiana. The boys are the boys of St. Charles reformatory. Some are remaining at the facility; others are walking towards Chicago, on the road they traveled when they came to St. Charles. The road is also "the road of life." The light shining through the trees is divine light, not just the sun, and it shines on everyone—those remaining at St. Charles and those returning home. Its rays go in all directions. Boys in the picture are both black and white. The man with his arm around one of the boys is a staff member of St. Charles.

In a preliminary drawing Sallman placed an angel where the light now appears. One of the chaplains objected, so the figure was reduced to the head of an angel. There was still objection, so Sallman settled finally on a burst of light. Curtains were installed at the sides so the painting could be covered during communion. The painting cost $5000.00 and appeared in the *Elgin* (Illinois) *Daily Courier-News* for 5 May 1951. Among the invited guests at the chapel rededication on May 6th was Illinois Governor Adlai Stevenson.

The Ascension of Christ

1952. First Covenant Church, 125 E. H Street, Iron Mountain, Michigan. This large oil was done for the new church after the old church building, containing a smaller Sallman *Ascension* (1939), was destroyed by fire. The canvas of this painting measures 20 feet wide by 23 feet high—the largest oil painting by Sallman to be found anywhere. Sallman worked on the painting an entire month, sometimes late into the night, in Nyvall Hall at North Park Seminary, Chicago.

The painting was done in two sections. A seam goes horizontally across the middle, with a V cut in the bottom half so as not to divide the figure of Jesus. As soon as it arrived in Iron Mountain the men of the church, working from a chart furnished by Sallman and following his instructions, began attaching the canvas to the front wall, made of cement block. Problems quickly developed, and Sallman had to be contacted. Warner and Ruth drove to Iron Mountain a week later. After fitting the canvas to the wall, Sallman painted over the seam where the panels met. The Sallmans remained for the dedication, which took place on 25 May 1952.

As in the earlier painting, Sallman again derives inspiration from Luke 24:50-51 and Acts 1:9. With arms outstretched and right foot drawn back, Jesus ascends into heaven in a circle of white clouds bathed in a bright light. Nail prints can be seen in the hands and in the left foot. The face closely resembles the Sallman face of 1924 and 1940, more than in any of the other Ascension paintings. One can also see a similarity to *Face of Our Lord in Space* (1959). Jesus looks down, however, and his eyes are not visible. Fluffy white clouds fill the sky. The disciples below cluster on a grassy knoll. Small trees grow on the right and left, similar to the South Bend *Ascension* and exactly like the *Ascension* (1939) done for the old church. Peter again stands prominently in the foreground, with staff in hand.

Sallman can be seen working on this painting in *CYT* (13 May 1956): 6-7. The *Chicago Daily News* reported on the painting's display at North Park.[5] Sallman can also be seen doing final touch-up work, perched high atop a 20 foot scaffold, in the *Iron Mountain News*.[6]

This beautiful painting has unfortunately not fared well over the years. Bubbles in the canvas developing early are still visible. Also, moisture penetrating what was originally the outside wall of the church has taken its toll, particularly at the seam. Some years ago a local artist touched up the work.

I Have Overcome the World

1952. First United Methodist Church, 119 S. Georgia Avenue, Mason City, Iowa. Though an untitled work, this painting builds on John 16:33, which speaks of Christ having overcome the world by his death and resurrection. *Behold He Cometh* (1967) of the First Covenant Church in Rockford, Illinois, is similar. The present painting is 5 feet wide and 7 feet tall and bears the date 24 September 1952. In March 1959, Sallman superimposed, in lighter tones, a cross over the person of Christ. In this year the painting was given to the church in memory of Elvin G. Johnson (1902-1959). It hangs in the back balcony of the sanctuary.

Sallman originally presented the painting to his friend, George Truman Carl, who became pastor of First Methodist in 1957. The painting develops from *His Presence* (1946 © K&B 1947), which was a favorite of Carl. Two prints of *His Presence* hang elsewhere in the church. One, at the back of the Wayside Chapel, has been touched-up with paint and redated in 1959, the year the chapel was dedicated.

The figure of Christ—with a frontal view of the face, nail-scarred hands lifted upward, feet partially visible, and a draping robe—is essentially that of *His Presence*. What is different here is the coloring and refracted light making a halo around Christ's head. Also, the world—not a house floor—is under his feet, with planets swirling in space. Many of the these features appear later in *Power and Glory* (1957), and in *Behold He Cometh*. The blue and yellow refracted light becomes more refined in *Power and Glory*. On the globe one can see an outline of North America.

The Nativity Scene

1952. Children's Chapel, Children's Village, Methodist Children's Home Society, 16645 W. Six Mile Road, Detroit, Michigan. This artwork, and the four following, appear in seventeen small and large stained glass windows beautifying a sixteenth century English Tudor-style chapel at the children's home. Built with money from the Kresge Foundation, the Children's Chapel was dedicated the week of 21-28 September 1952. The windows depict biblical and devotional scenes, liturgical symbols, and children from around the world. Sallman designed all but one of the major windows, and possibly the small windows containing the liturgical symbols.

The three-sectioned chancel window depicts the Nativity and the Beginning of Life. In the center are Mary and Joseph with the baby in a manger. Above them, a cross sends down light from a star, and below is the monogram IHC, an old form of the first three Greek letters in the name Jesus. The left window contains the adoring shepherds, below which is a cross with dove's wings—signifying peace on earth. In the right window are the adoring wise men, below which is a five-pointed Epiphany Star. The smaller windows above present yet other religious images: the hand of God on the left; the Agnus Dei (Lamb of God) in the center; and the descending dove on the right. Together these represent the Trinity: Father, Son, and Holy Spirit.

Jesus Blessing the Loaves and Fishes

1952. Children's Chapel, Children's Village, Methodist Children's Home Society, 16645 W. Six Mile Road, Detroit, Michigan. This left window of a three-sectioned balcony window in the chapel shows Jesus blessing the loaves and fishes before feeding the five thousand. Before Jesus stands a young boy. Behind Jesus, a man—perhaps Andrew—looks on (John 6:1-14).

Jesus with the Children

1952. Children's Chapel, Children's Village, Methodist Children's Home Society, 16645 W. Six Mile Road, Detroit, Michigan. Here in the right section of the balcony window, Jesus sits with the children. The configuration differs from that in *Jesus the Children's Friend* (1946 © K&B 1947), but the inspiration comes, nevertheless, from Matthew 19:14 (and parallels): "Of such is the Kingdom." These words appear over the door of the Administration Building at the Village.

Christ Our Pilot

1952. Children's Chapel, Children's Village, Methodist Children's Home Society, 16645 W. Six Mile Road, Detroit, Michigan. In the center section of the balcony window appears the familiar *Christ Our Pilot* (1950 © K&B 1950). This window means to address the departing worshiper with the words: "Savior, pilot me."

Below the main pictures in each of the three balcony windows, angels at left and right blow trumpets. A center angel sings from an open songbook. The message here is that there is joy serving the Lord in music and in song. Above the panels, in small windows completing the upper arch, are a radiating cross at the left; an anchor cross in the center, and at the right, a heart with rays emanating outward in four directions. In the small window at the very top is a fleur de lys, meant to symbolize purity.

The Children of the World

1952. Children's Chapel, Children's Village, Methodist Children's Home Society, 16645 W. Six Mile Road, Detroit, Michigan. Here on either side of the chapel nave are depicted children of the world. The figures represent a number of nationalities. They are, beginning at the northwest corner: an English choir boy and a Puerto Rican girl, an African boy and an American Indian girl, a French boy, a Dutch girl, a Canadian girl and a Palestinian boy, a Japanese girl and a Chinese boy, and an Indian Nepalese girl. The figure of a Canadian girl praying resembles Sallman's watercolor, *Girl at Bedside Praying* (1957). Completing the series is a Norman Rockwell Boy Scout reproduction.

Christ Knocking at Heart's Door

1953. Evangelical Covenant Church, 730 Brown Street, Norway, Michigan. This unframed painting is recessed and centered in a small apse at the front of the church. The Christ figure stands over 6 feet high in this large work. In all essentials it repeats the Kriebel & Bates *Christ at Heart's Door* (1942 © K&B 1942). Over the top of the door, however, hangs a bare branch, and flora on both sides of Christ differ slightly from the copyrighted version. Otherwise details remain the same, even down to the arched thorns in the lower fore-ground. Sallman painted another version of the same painting for the Covenant Church of Dawson, Minnesota (1950).

The painting was requested in anticipation of the church's seventy-year jubilee. A refurbishing of the church sanctuary began in October 1951, but Sallman's poor health, prevented him from completing the painting until August 1953. The congregation, in fact, feared he would be unable to do it. His response was "Be patient!" The picture carries a date of August 1953, one month after the Jubilee. Sallman delivered the painting himself, and stayed long enough to supervise its hanging. He was not present, however, for the dedica-tion, which took place on 8 November 1953.

Mary and Martha with Jesus

1954. Bethany Methodist Home, 4950 N. Ashland Avenue, Chicago, Illinois. This large painting draws its inspiration from Luke 10:38-42, which records a visit of Jesus to the home of Mary and Martha (cf. John 11:1). In this work, Mary sits before Jesus, listening as he teaches from an open scroll on his lap. The face of Jesus is the familiar face of the 1940 oil. Jesus looks upward, and he raises his right hand. Behind Mary, Martha enters the room with a tray of food and drink. The house interior has plastered walls and exposed ceiling beams. Behind Jesus is an open window, outside of which a vine rises on a trel-lis. The room behind has a smaller window. There is very little detail—some flowers in a vase, a jug on the floor, and a silver goblet (?) on a background table.

This painting was done when Bethany Home opened its new facility on 1 November 1954. Sallman was present a week before to supervise its hanging and do final touch-up work.

A watercolor of the same title was done by Sallman in 1961 (© K&B 1962). Here a different-looking Jesus directs his gaze downward and extends his right hand toward Mary. There is more detail in this work—both inside the house and out. Compare a Jesus with Mary and Martha painting printed in *CHo* 3/38 (17 September 1950): 3; also the Gramstorff Brothers (Malden, Massachusetts) painting of Mary and Martha with Jesus, printed on the front cover of *WC* Central 1204 (22 January 1944). There Martha carries a tray of fruit, and Jesus sits in a chair. A picture of Hermann Seegar's *Mary Hath Chosen the Better Part* also appears in Maus, *Christ and the Fine Arts*, 177.

Head of Christ

1956. Originally done for the Edgewater Covenant Church, Bryn Mawr and Glenwood Avenues, Chicago, Illinois., where it hung on the front wall until the church building was sold and the painting moved in 1994. Currently the painting is owned by the Central Conference of the Evangelical Covenant Church and is on loan to the Broadway Covenant Church, 3525 Broadway, Rockford, Illinois. This painting, the largest of the Sallman 1940 Christ heads, measures 8 feet by 10 feet and replaced an earlier work destroyed in a 1955 church fire. The canvas stretches over a half-inch plywood frame. The date on the painting is 23 September 1956. It was given to the church by Sallman's good friend, Fred Johnson, in memory of Johnson's wife who died a year earlier. Sallman did the painting in his home studio. A picture appears in *CC* 56/8 (21 April 1967): 9.

The Great Physician
1958. Iowa Methodist Medical Center, 1200 Pleasant Street, Des Moines, Iowa. This large oil painting hangs in the hospital chapel; originally it hung in an older part of the hospital that has since been destroyed. Inspiration derives from Mark 2:1-12, the story of a paralytic being lowered through a house roof so Christ might heal him. Christ stands in the foreground right, extending his hand to the paralytic who comes down on a stretcher. Four friends lower the paralytic. Sallman has given a detailed interpretation of this painting containing no less than seventy-two figures (see chapter VII). The date on the painting is 11 May , 1958. Cost was $5,000.

A full-page picture of Sallman doing final touch-ups appears in the *Des Moines Tribune*, 10 May 1958, 14. A picture in color appears also in *Together* magazine (October 1959): 2. Compare Hans Lietzmann's *Christ Healing the Paralytic*, which appears in *WC* Central 749 (4 May 1935): 16.

For God So Loved the World
1960. Woodlawn Baptist Church, 6207 University Avenue, Chicago. This artwork, most likely an oil, was done for a multi-racial congregation at the time the church sanctuary was remodeled by a work team of Papagos Indians. It contains a cross superimposed on a globe, with John 3:16 printed on both sides at the bottom. Placement was on the front wall of the church. A picture of the painting appears in the *Chicago Daily News* for 5 May 1960, 2S.

Baptized in Christ
1960. North Side Christian Church (Disciples of Christ), 1507 W. Sunnyside Avenue, Chicago, Illinois. This good-sized oil attaches directly to the wall above the baptistry at the front of the church. About 8 feet wide and 10 feet tall, it portrays the resurrected Christ above the Jordan River. The surrounding area is lush green. The river is a rapids, as one can tell by the sparkling water passing over two small falls. Rocks line the river on both sides. To the left is a palm tree, and to the right a tree looking like a small live oak. The lower part

of Jesus' garment fades out over the background mountains. His arms are further down, as in *The Triumphant Christ* (1965) done for the South Jacksonville Presbyterian Church in Jacksonville, Florida. Nail prints are visible in the hands. Jesus gazes downward, his eyes not seen.

The painting's dedication occurred on Palm Sunday, 3 April 1960, in memory of Arthur Holmberg Jr., by his parents. Arthur, who had recently died unexpectedly, was the first person to be baptized in the old church next door. Grandson Arthur Holmberg III did the unveiling. Sallman attended the dedication and spoke a few words. Later, on 12 January 1963, he returned to sign the painting.

The Master Healer

1960 © Union Protestant Hospital 1961. United Hospital Center, Route 19 South, Clarksburg, West Virginia. Sallman painted this large oil originally for the Union Protestant Hospital, which has since merged with St. Mary's Hospital into the United Hospital Center. The painting hung originally in the main lobby of a hospital newly-constructed in 1959-1960. Now it has a choice location in the hospital's north wing.

Inspiration comes from John 5:2-9, the story of Jesus healing a man at the pool of Bethesda. There are twelve figures in all. Jesus stands in the foreground, before a lame man who sits by the pool. The figure of Jesus, with a large blue stole draped over a white robe, is the same as in *Jesus, the Light of the World* (1955 © K&B 1956). He holds out both hands toward the man—the right hand beckoning him to get up. The man, sitting on a rumpled garment, looks up at Jesus. Behind the man are a couple of jars, a rumpled cloth, and a cushion or pillow.

Two old men at the right of the painting look on. One holds a cane. In the background, at the left, a man helps another out of the pool. In the background center, a man sits on steps at the pool's edge, his feet almost touching the water. Behind him, a mother holds a babe in her arms. To the left, another man lies before the pool with his head resting on one arm. He looks skeptical. Many of the onlookers—but not all—gaze toward Jesus and the lame man. Five pillars stand about this Roman-looking pool. Sunlight shines through the open area above the pool.

Two hundred and fifty people attended the painting's unveiling and dedication on 8 January 1961. The work hangs as a memorial to John F. McCuskey MD by his family and friends. McCuskey had initiated the original contact with Sallman, and it was his desire that Sallman paint for the hospital a picture portraying one of the healing miracles of Jesus. Then on 30 October 1958, shortly after McCuskey had spoken with Sallman by telephone, he was tragically killed in an automobile accident.

Relocation took place when the hospital underwent expansion in 1978. A picture of the painting appears in the *Sunday Exponent-Telegram* of Clarksburg for 27 March 1960, 12, as well as in W. McDermott, "The Miracle Picture," *Christian Life* (March 1963): 27.

His Presence

1960 © K&B 1947. Sallman originally painted this artwork for the Evangelical Covenant Church in Escanaba, Michigan, The painting was transferred to the United Evangelical Covenant Church, 305-307 S. Ninth Street, Gladstone, Michigan in 1995 following a merger of the two congregations. In 1998 it was hung at the back of the newly-constructed sanctuary of the Gladstone Church. This oil, approximately 6 feet by 10 feet, essentially enlarges the well-known *His Presence* (1946 © K&B 1947). In the Escanaba Church it hung on the front wall of the church. The work differs from its prototype in that there is a large halo of yellow, pink, and blue concentric circles around the head and upper body of Christ. Sallman also includes halos in *The Triumphant Christ* (1965) and *Behold He Cometh* (1967), two other paintings developing from *His Presence*. In the present work, Christ wears a robe of melon green, somewhat like that in *Behold He Cometh*. Christ stands on floorboards, as in the original, with a door and baseboards of a turn-of-the century house slightly visible in the background. The message—like in the earlier work—is that the risen Christ comes to reveal his presence in our houses, just as he did in the house of the disciples on Easter evening (John 20:19-20).

The Escanaba Ladies Aid initiated the plan to get this painting, and raised the $800.00 cost. The church at the time was being redecorated. Mabel Crebo and Marion Lundeen went to Chicago to meet with Sallman and make the arrangements. Sallman completed the painting in Chicago and shipped it to Escanaba. A carpenter in the congregation, Herman Carlson, made a frame and supervised the mounting. Originally drapes hung at each side, but these were later removed. For a picture of the painting see Everett L. Wilson, "And This Is How It Was," *CYT* 11/3 (18 July 1965): 1-7.

Christ Healing the Blind Beggar

1963. Belmont United Methodist Church, 421 Common Street, Belmont, Massachusetts. Inspired by John 9, this small oil, about 40 inches by 45 inches, hangs above a fireplace in the church lounge. Jesus, seen in a side view, wears a bright blue robe and reaches with one hand to touch the eye of a beggar sitting along a path. He cups the other hand, perhaps to hold clay. The beggar sits on a blanket with arms outstretched. Behind him a shoulder-high stone wall parallels a path that turns and winds toward Jerusalem. Jerusalem's walls and an arched gate are visible in the distance. Above the wall, in the upper left of the painting, grows a large olive tree. In the background upper right, some distance behind Jesus, are well-dressed onlookers.

This painting was dedicated in memory of Walter and Frances Bruton on 31 March 1963.

The Triumphant Christ

1965. South Jacksonville Presbyterian Church, 2137 Hendricks Avenue, Jacksonville, Florida. Approximately 8 feet to a side, this fine painting beautifies a chapel of prayer and meditation in the church. The painting affixes directly to the wall at the front of the chapel. Next to his signature and the date, Sallman has written, "To the Glory of God."

The full body of the resurrected Christ and the frontal view strongly resemble that in *His Presence*, (1946 © K&B 1947) but the face differs as does the draping of the robe. Likewise, Jesus does not raise his hands as he does in *His Presence*. Rather he extends them outward as seen in Thorvaldsen's *Come Unto Me*. Christ, however, does not beckon; he shows his hands to bestow peace. Inspiration for the painting comes from John 20:19-20, where the resurrected Christ says to his disciples, "Peace be unto you," and then shows them his hands. The words above the painting are "Peace Be Unto You."

The other main difference between this painting and *His Presence* is the background. Here Christ has a multiple-ringed halo and refracted light completely surrounding his person. He also stands barefooted on grass, not on a wood floor, as in *His Presence*. In the lower part of the picture grow deep pink azaleas and palm branches, a familiar Florida sight in early spring.

The painting was done in Chicago, and after completion Warner and Ruth, together with another couple, possibly Ruth's sister and her husband, drove it to Jacksonville. At the church Sallman supervised the installation and did some finishing work around the edges. Ruth particularly liked this painting, saying she thought it was one of Warner's finest. Sallman came to Jacksonville a year or so later to apply a protective coating. Since then the painting has suffered minor water damage, but touch up work has largely remedied the problem.

Safe in the Arms of Jesus

1965. Grace United Methodist Church, 3012 S. Twyckenham Drive, South Bend, Indiana. This small oil painting of Jesus surrounded by the faces of happy children, displayed prominently in the church narthex, honors the memory of Forest Neal "Skippy" Hay, a five year-old boy tragically killed by an automobile. Jesus smiles slightly. The title of the painting derives from a Fanny Crosby hymn.[7]

Compare Reynold's *Angel Heads*, which has the faces of small children in a circle. The Reynold's painting appears in *LHJ* 32/12 (December 1915): 3. A picture of the heads of small children in a circle appears also on a Norwegian Lutheran confirmation certificate, dated 1889, displayed in the Norwegian House at Pioneer Village, Rugby, North Dakota.

Head of Christ

1967. Covenant Village, 2625 Techny Road, Northbrook, Illinois. This painting of the Christ head is very similar to the oil of 1940, except that the face looks the other way. But Christ is not looking over his left shoulder, as in *Follow Thou Me* (1948 © K&B 1949). The basic profile and upper portion of the robe are the same as the classic picture.

The painting hung originally over the fireplace in the dining room, but it was later moved to the wall of the main lobby, just inside the entrance. Since the eyes look toward the door, village residents like to say Christ is welcoming those coming in.

Behold He Cometh

1967. First Evangelical Covenant Church, 316 Wood Road, Rockford, Illinois. Sallman painted this last commissioned church artwork at the church, where it hangs presently in the foyer. An unveiling took place on Easter Sunday 1967.

The painting, which is about 5 feet wide and 7 feet high, develops from *His Presence* (1946 © K&B 1947), as well as *I Have Overcome the World* done for First Methodist Church in Mason City, Iowa (1952). Christ here stands atop the world. With nail-scarred hands extended and lifted up, he says, "I am coming soon" (Revelation 3:11). He wears a light green robe. Concentric halos, the outer one painted with colors of the rainbow, surround his head and upper body. The rainbow reminds the viewer of God's promise. Beams emanate downward from the person of Christ, as they do in *I Have Overcome the World*. Originally there were seven stars for the seven churches of Revelation, but these were painted out at the insistence of the architect. A picture of this painting appears in *CC* 63/1 (1 January 1974) 4; and *CC* 81/7 (July 1992): 9.

[1] Anne later married Covenant pastor Daniel Ericson. After serving the pastorate of the Mission Covenant Church in Thomaston, Connecticut, Dan and Anne went out as missionaries to the Belgian Congo (later Zaire; now again Congo).

[2] *Covenant Weekly* 39/6 (10 February 1950): 8.

[3] *Iron Mountain News*, 29 November 1939, 2.

[4] Amos Reed, the assistant Superintendent who met with the Protestant, Catholic and Jewish chaplains, and Sallman to select a theme, has provided some help with the interpretation.

5 *Chicago Daily News*, 26 April 1952, 10.
6 *Iron Mountain News*, 24 May 1952, 1.
7 *Covenant Hymnal* 1950, #358.

Appendix V
Watercolors and Drawings

Listed here are Sallman's surviving pencil, pen and charcoal sketches; chalks, crayons and pastels, and watercolors. Not included are the many heads of Christ in chalk and crayon, for which no inventory exists. Literally hundreds of these exist across the country, of which are unlocated. They too represent an important part of the total Sallman output. No attempt has been made either to locate even a portion of the sketches Sallman did as a commercial artist in downtown Chicago studios. Only a few surviving originals or reproductions are included here. Watercolors and drawings for Covenant papers are listed in Appendix I; the same done for the Salvation Army's *War Cry* appear in Appendix II.

Titles not in italics are untitled works, or works that were at one time titled, but whose titles are now unknown. Dates in square brackets are assumed dates.

Mother
1909; pen sketch; James and Gene Sallman private collection. Christine Sallman, Warner Sallman's mother, is sitting here at a table with her head down, and resting on one hand.

LeRoy Sallman
1909; pen sketch; location unknown. LeRoy Sallman was Warner Sallman's brother. A slide of this sketch is in the Sallman Collection at Valparaiso University.

Nudes
[1913]; Ten pencil drawings on white paper; James and Gene Sallman private collection. These nude women and nude men were drawn for a life class at the Chicago Art Institute. Some could be earlier, possibly from 1908-1909 or 1910-1911.

Mother
1916; color chalk; Marion Sallman private collection. Small sketch of Sallman's mother.

Our Colossus

1916; poster drawing; location unknown. A large man straddles the high banks of a canal with an approaching ship about to pass through his legs. At the top of the drawing reads, "Our Colossus of Roads to Victory." Below it says on the left, "Help U. S. Speed Ships." A World War I poster. A slide is in the Sallman Collection at Valparaiso University.

Three Men on Parade

1918; pen sketch; Marion Sallman private collection. A fashion plate of a man in a suit with band players on either side. The man tips his top hat and carries a cane in the left hand. The player on the left plays Scottish bagpipes; the one on the right beats the drum. The date (if correct) is stylized to look like a hanging Christmas tree ornament.

Cable Midget Upright

1920; pen sketch; location unknown. An advertisement for a Cable Midget upright piano, Style A, manufactured by the Cable Company, Chicago. A center picture shows a young girl playing the piano at home. A chair with a doll is in the foreground, and a teddy bear sits against one leg of the piano bench. An open book lies on the floor. The frame surrounding the picture is made to look like a house window. To the right of the reproduction in Sallman's hand, is a signature and a date reading, "about 11/20."

Pianos in Walnut

[1920]; pen sketch; location unknown. An advertisement for Martin Bros. Piano Co., home of Cable-made pianos in Springfield (Illinois). Above a promotional piece on walnut pianos, which are said to have been unavailable during the war, is Sallman's drawing of a well-dressed family with a walnut baby grand in their living room. The piano top is raised. A girl sits on the piano bench with one hand on the keyboard, but she is not playing. Father at the left and mother at the right look on. Behind mother is an elegant living-room chair. A floor lamp can be seen in the background, in front of French-style living room windows.

Christian Family Life

1921; pen sketch; location unknown. A cartoon showing how church, civil and social life grow like tree branches out of a Christian family life, which is the tree trunk. Attacking the base of the tree—which is "daily family Bible reading and prayer"—are destructive cultural and intellectual forces, represented by men with ax and shovel. A whirlwind of "Bolshevism" coming up behind the tree threatens everyone. Printed on the front cover of *The Family Altar* 13/5 (May 1921). Compare *Look and Live* (1929).

Mother Reading the Easter Story

[1922]; charcoal sketch; location unknown. This artwork is little different from a pen sketch of the same name, published in *FV* in 1922. A photocopy of the present sketch exists in the Marion Sallman private collection.

Portrait of the Rev. F. O. Kling I

[1922]; pencil sketch; James and Gene Sallman private collection. Same as the portrait of the Rev. Kling in pen (1922).

Portrait of the Rev. F. O. Kling I

1922; pen drawing; Covenant Archives. Kling was pastor of the Edgewater Covenant Church, Chicago from 1922-1927.

Only Mother

1923; sketch probably in charcoal; location unknown. A young mother sits in her modest home (studs and rafters are visible) with a large garment on her lap. She is perhaps mending it. Flowers are on the furniture at the right. The picture appears in the *Sunday School Friend* 9/4 (22 January 1928): 1.

Son of Man

1924; two small black and white reproductions of pen sketches on cardboard; Wilson Galleries, Anderson University. Both contain a signature and the date 1924; one reproduction has "The Son of Man" written in black pen below the picture. Not the same as the brown pen sketch of *Son of Man* (© K&B 1941).

Thorn-crowned Christ

1926; pencil sketch on paper; Covenant Archives. Done in an Edgewater Covenant Church Sunday School class, and given originally to Beatrice Ringquist, a member of the class.

Portrait of the Rev. Gust F. Johnson

1926; charcoal on cardboard; Covenant Archives. Johnson was a well-known pastor of the Covenant Tabernacle in Minneapolis. Given to Covenant Archives in August 1995 by James and Gene Sallman.

Head of Christ

1927; charcoal on brown paper; James and Gene Sallman private collection. A note in Sallman's hand says, "Sketched about 1927–used as a templet for my early chalk talks. Warner '62." Accompanying this is another templet of the same drawing on white paper.

Clown with Flag
     1928; pen sketch; signed "Elias;" location unknown. A clown races across a stage with an American flag in one hand, and a miniature doll of King George in the other. A billboard in front of the stage announces a continuous performance of "America First" pledges: flood control; deep waterways; farm relief; and draft Coolidge. A crow perched atop the billboard is making "caw" noises. A political cartoon printed for April Fools Day in *Lightnin'* 2/6 (April 1928): 1.

Tax Payers Feast and Fast
     1928; two pen sketches; signed "Elias;" location unknown. A simulated eyeglass-look into a Chicago hotel where the rich are feasting, and into a modest city house where the poor are fasting. A political sketch on unjust taxes printed in *Lightnin'* 2/6 (April 1928): 12.

Mary and Joseph with the Baby
     1929; pen sketch; signed "Elias;" Marion Sallman private collection. Used for the Sallman Christmas card in 1929. Below is a verse from 2 Corinthians 4:6.

Gustavus Adolphus efter Van Dyke
     1932; color chalk on paper, mounted on board; Covenant Archives. Drawn for the tercentenary celebration of Gustav Adolphus' death, held at Moody Church, Chicago.

Naming the Salvation Army
     [1933]; pencil sketch on paper on cardboard; Marion Sallman private collection. This piece is one of the drawings created for the Salvation Army Exhibit at Chicago's Century of Progress, 1933-1934.

Kneeling Man in Beam of Light
     1933; charcoal sketch on heavy paper; signed "Elias;" Marion Sallman private collection. A barefoot young man, on one knee, looks up into a beam of light. He appears to be an athlete. He extends both his hands forward and has an open Bible on his knee. Behind him stand large city buildings.

Sunday School Kickoff
     [1934]; pencil sketch on paper; Marion Sallman private collection. The same picture as the cartoon of the same name (1934), which appears on the front cover of *WC* Central 732 (5 January 1935). The sketch is done on a dummy of *The War Cry*.

Head of Christ
[1934] © Messenger Corp. 1935; color pastel on white paper circa 16½ inches by 24½ inches; Renaissance Publishing Company, Auburn, Indiana. The 1924 *Head of Christ* with a halo in the colors of the rainbow. Used for a 1935 Scripture Text Calendar published by the Messenger Corporation. The original hangs in the office of President Jeffry C. Meyer.

The Blessed Mother/Our Lady of the Atonement
[1936]; color pastel on white paper circa 16½ inches by 24½ inches; Renaissance Publishing Co., Auburn, Indiana. Not the same as the later oil, *(Mary the) Mother of Christ* (1948 © K&B 1948). Mary, with hands folded, looks pensively upward. The picture is signed, but without a date. Used for a 1938 Scripture Text Calendar published by the Messenger Corporation. The original hangs in the office of President Jeffry C. Meyer.

Woman, Why Weepeth Thou?
[1936] © The Messenger Corp. 1937; color pastel; Renaissance Publishing Co., Auburn, Indiana. A picture of Mary Magdalene meeting Jesus on Easter morning; similar to *Rabboni* [1952] and *Behold the Lord* (1952 © K&B 1953). Used for calendars and church art published by the Messenger Corporation between 1939 and 1960.

Face of Young Girl
1938; possible charcoal; location unknown. Identity of the girl unknown. Photographic reproduction is in the Marion Sallman private collection.

Old Covered Bridge and Mill Site–Turkey Run, Indiana
1940; watercolor; James and Gene Sallman private collection. Turkey Run is a state park in Indiana.

French Bark on Reefs of Brottö at Föglö, Åland-Finland
1941; watercolor; James and Gene Sallman private collection. Made from an oil done by Sallman's father. Elias Sallman was born in the village of Brattö on the island of Föglö, one of the Åland Islands now part of Finland. A French sailing vessel is seen here caught on the reefs.

Son of Man
© K&B 1941; brown pen sketch, simulated etching; Wilson Galleries, Anderson University. This sketch of the 1924 Christ head is on the left page of an open Bible. On the right page is written at the top: "Jesus said–." A blank space is underneath. Flowers hang over the first letter in Jesus. Signed,

"Sallman," but undated. Made for a series of "Jesus said" plaques to be produced by the Felsenthal Co. of Chicago.

Crown of Thorns

1941 © Warner E. Sallman 1943; © K&B 1956; watercolor and chalk; Wilson Galleries, Anderson University. One of Sallman's finest pictures of the Crucified, also a very fine watercolor. Jesus is pictured here in portrait, with unopened eyes and a crown of thorns on his head. The top of his light purple robe shows at the neck, which Jesus has a hold of with the right hand. On his face and down his hair and neck are drippings of blood. Below in pencil is written, "'yet when he was afflicted he opened not his mouth' Isaiah 53:7." Printed on the front cover of *WC* Central 1164 (17 April 1943). Issued in prints and wallet-size cards; also used as a bulletin cover.

Christ in Gethsemane

[1942] pencil sketch on paper; Marion Sallman private collection. The same picture as like-named oils done for Kriebel and Bates (1941 © K&B 1942) and the Covenant Church in Manchester, Connecticut (1942).

The Exodus

1942; watercolor and chalk; Covenant Archives. A sketch signed "Elias," with a date of 8 January 1942. Two other dates are given at the lower right: 4 March 1943 and 8 August 1943. Given as a gift by Warner and Ruth Sallman to Sally and Karl A. Olsson in June 1966. Scripture at lower right is Exodus 13:18-22. On the frame below are printed verses 18 and 21 of this text.

This very sketchy work depicts a large band of people marching along a rock-lined path towards the Red Sea. At the front, standing at the edge of the sea, is Moses with arms outstretched. The expanse of sea is not large. Above the sea is a pillar of cloud. Beyond is mountainous land under a deep blue sky. In the foreground are two bare-chested men with capes; one has a sack thrown over his shoulder.

Colonial Church

1942; watercolor and chalk? Wilson Galleries, Anderson University. This colonial-type church appears in other Sallman pictures. Here a sectioned steeple narrows to a spire, and a cross is on top. Two people stand in the church doorway. Colored trees flank the center path. Clouds are over the church, but the rest of the sky is blue. Probable church bulletin cover.

Moses Meets God in the Mountain

1942; chalk and watercolor on paper; signed "Elias;" Marion Sallman private collection. Moses is praying here on a large mountain rock. Lightning flashes in the clouds above him, and to the left one sees the wandering Israelites in the desert. The supporting scripture is Exodus 23:1-9. Date on the sketch: 8 January 1942.

The Dial of WMBI

1943; two pen sketches; location unknown. A cartoon and sketched envelope, dated 15 January 1943, which Sallman sent in to WMBI, Chicago, in support of its radio ministry. Printed in *Moody Monthly* 43/7 (March 1943): 448.

The Crusading Christ

[1944]; oil or watercolor; location unknown. Christ is passing hastily through a world newly-ravaged by war. A pie-shaped section at the top shows a bombed-out church. Sections on either side contain the faces of people, who were originally "hosts of Christ-inspired Methodists." In the lower left is more war damage, with women and children looking at the passing Christ. In the lower right men are attending to the ruins of a half-destroyed house. Above is a colorful rainbow.

Sallman did this painting originally for a Methodist Crusade for Christ. It was printed on the front cover of *The Christian Advocate* 119/50 (14 December 1944), where it is called "Christ, the Power of God." An accompanying statement by the Federal Council of Churches concludes, "the cross of Jesus Christ demonstrated the power of God to overcome evil in its very moment of victory." This same figure of Christ is later used on *Christ of the Harvest Fields* (1946).

The Compassionate Christ

1944; pen and charcoal? location unknown. A thorn-crowned Christ looks down upon a globe swirling in space. Below, a hand carries a Christian flag, set over against clouds. This collage appears on the front cover of *The Christian Advocate* for 15 February 1945, and was used the following year on a poster advancing a "Crusade for Christ" sponsored by the Methodist Church. The picture was reprinted in *OYC* for 11 November 1945, and later in *CW* for 30 March 1951.

Boy Christ Sketches

© K&B 1945; nine small pen sketches from *Boy Christ* (1944 © K&B 1945) on cardboard; Wilson Galleries, Anderson University. Done for a booklet by Howard W. Ellis, *Story of Sallman's "Boy Christ"* ([Chicago]: Kriebel and Bates, 1945). Sketches from this artwork are the following: head of *The Boy Christ,* head of the lamb, foreground thorns, thistles and wheat (but slightly rearranged), cluster of grapes, shadow of the cross, background stag, dove above

Easter lilies, mountain village, and mountains and stream–which actually come from *The Lord Is My Shepherd* (1942 © K&B 1943).

Go Ye

1945; black and white sketch on masonite; Covenant Archives. At the upper right it says, "'Go ye...' Matthew 28:19, 20;" at the bottom right, "'Behold, I send you forth...' Matthew 10:16." This sketch makes only minor changes from the oil, *Behold I Send You Forth*, done for Bob Jones College (1944). Here the girl carries only a Bible, and the boy has both a Bible and a suitcase. Sallman is seen doing this sketch in the *Chicago Sunday Tribune* Neighborhood Section Part 3, (6 June 1954,) 1.

Christ of the Harvest Fields

1946; watercolor? Sallman Collection, Valparaiso University. Jesus with robe flapping in the wind passes above a field containing bales of hay. Created originally for Methodists. The figure of Christ is the same as in *The Crusading Christ* [1944]. Date on the artwork: 22 March 1946. The picture was reprinted in support of the 1954 Covenant Quadrennial at Mission Springs in California (*CYT*, 7 February 1954: 1); a Covenant Youth of America Bible study program (*CYT*, 1 August 1954: 5); and the figure of Christ alone in support of Covenant Youth Week (*CYT*, 30 January 1955: 1).

Jesus, the Children's Friend

1946; pencil, watercolor and qouache; Wilson Galleries, Anderson University. Unfinished. Like the K&B oil done the same year, this rendition does not show the sandaled foot of Jesus, as the K&B print does. Minor differences from the oil: color of clothing differs; woman in foreground left has no design on her sleeve; and the girl held by Jesus has her left hand upraised. The woman behind Jesus, who approaches with a child, is only barely sketched. The sky, too, remains unfinished.

Jesus the Children's Friend

1946 © K&B 1947; black and white reproduction with paint; on paper attached to cardboard; Wilson Galleries; Anderson University. This is the same as the K&B copyrighted picture, including the sandaled foot of Jesus.

Head of Christ in Simulated Glass

1946 © K&B 1946; watercolor and pen; location unknown. The familiar *Head of Christ* is done here in simulated stained glass. Background colors are yellow (for the halo) and brown. It appears on the bulletin cover, *Let's Go to Church*

(1947), where it became a window in the church narthex. Compare *Head of Christ against Stained Glass* (n.d.), where the colors are blues, pinks, and yellows.

Let's Go to Church
1947; watercolor on cardboard; Wilson Galleries, Anderson University. This bulletin cover artwork shows nicely-dressed people of various ages entering a church narthex. They pass by a head of Christ in stained glass (*Head of Christ in Simulated Glass*, 1946 © K&B 1946).

Head of Christ
1947; pastel over a sepia print; James and Gene Sallman private collection. A Christmas gift from Sallman to son and wife, Jim and Gene Sallman.

We Would See Jesus
[1947]; watercolor on cardboard; Marion Sallman private collection. The same basic picture as the like-named oil (1947 © K&B 1948), except that figures in the crowd surrounding Jesus are different.

The Nativity (Of Christ)
[1947]; pencil sketch on paper; Marion Sallman private collection. Same as the like-named watercolor or chalk (1947 © K&B 1948), except that the overhead lamp is missing.

The Nativity (of Christ)
1947 © K&B 1948; watercolor or chalk; Wilson Galleries, Anderson University. Similar to the oil, *The Little Lord Jesus* (1956 © K&B 1956). In the present work Sallman's familiar-looking Mary sits in the center of the picture on straw, holding baby Jesus on her lap. In front of her is a rumpled cloth. Next to the cloth sit two pottery vessels. Joseph stands behind Mary, head erect and staff in hand. The stall in which Mary sits has a wall of hewn stone, about waist-high, separating her from a donkey and an ox. The ox is eating straw.
In the background are three shepherds clustered together. They have just come in the door, which stands ajar. The one in the center holds a staff with a crook. The stable ceiling has large exposed wooden beams. From one hangs a Herodian lamp, which lights the stable. The walls are made of large hewn rock. Colors here are bright: Mary wears a red garment with a light green cape; Joseph is dressed in blue; the cloths for the baby are bright yellow. Used on a bulletin cover.

The Carpenter of Nazareth

[1948]; red pencil sketch on paper; Marion Sallman private collection. The head only of the like-named watercolor and chalk (1948 © K&B 1948 & 1951).

The Carpenter of Nazareth

1948 © K&B 1948 & 1951; watercolor and chalk; Wilson Galleries, Anderson University. Alternate title: *Jesus the Carpenter*. This picture shows Jesus as a young adult, perhaps in his early twenties, working in the carpenter shop (cf. Mark 6:3). Here he is making a plow, which rests on a log block. A hammer is in his hand and wood shavings cover the floor. Behind him, on the wall, hangs a yoke. On the carpenter's bench, amidst shavings, lies a plane, and further to the right, a shallow basket with handles.

The carpenter's shop has a wooden beam ceiling. To the right, in an adjoining room, mother Mary has been working at the loom, but now she is looking through the open doorway at Jesus. In the background left, a bearded man stands under an archway. This appears to be Joseph, who was also a carpenter. In the foreground left is a jug with handles, also a robe belonging to Jesus draped over a wooden sawhorse. In the foreground right, two young children—a boy and a girl—look on. They are said to be listening to a story Jesus is telling them about his heavenly Father. Mary too listens. Both the boy and Jesus wear red and white turbans, like those worn by the merchants in a recently-done oil, *We Would See Jesus* (1947 © K&B 1948). Jesus wears a white garment. This picture was reprinted on a 1995 Warner Press calendar.

The Holy Family

1948; large color chalk 7 feet wide and 4½ feet high; James and Gene Sallman private collection. This fine chalk was drawn for the Edgewater Covenant Church 1948 Christmas program. Mary lies in a stable on a bed of straw with the baby Jesus. Joseph at right has folded hands. The face of Joseph looks like the face of the 1924 *Christ head*. A small lamb in the foreground is looking up at the baby. In the foreground right is a wooden bucket filled with water. In the background left can be seen—in the dark—the heads only of an ox and a donkey. Stars fill the sky.

Christ Looking Down

1948; brown chalk with white on paper; Marion Sallman private collection. This is the familiar Sallman Christ head, only with a sorrowful downward glance. Done for Neighborhood Nite, 12 February 1948, at the North Park Covenant Church, Chicago.

D. L. Moody Sketches

[1948]; Twenty-seven sketches in charcoal and quoache; Moody Bible Institute. Done in collaboration with Reinhold Palenske, an artist for Brown & Bigelow, Ruthrauff & Ryan, and various Chicago newspapers.[1] Seven sketches by Palenske were published in *Moody Monthly* 48/6 (February 1948): 403-405. An inventory of the twenty-seven charcoals, nineteen of which are extant, contains the following:

1) Moody's first Sunday School effort in Chicago leads eighteen ragamuffins into the Wells Street Mission. Printed in *MM* 48/6 (February 1948): 404.

2) Moody recruits on his "missionary pony." Not extant.

3) Getting North Market Street Hall ready for Sunday School. Not extant.

4) Reading Bible stories by candlelight to a black boy in an abandoned saloon.

5) Farwell is nominated for Sunday School superintendent, before chairs were provided in Sunday School. Collage.

6) Moody subdues blasphemers by prayer; praying with a young boy. Printed in *MM* 48/6 (February 1948): 405.

7) Moody captures an elusive little girl for Sunday School. Collage. Printed in *MM* 48/6 (February 1948): 404.

8) Last resort treatment for an incorrigible boy.

9) The leader of a gang of young "gutter-snipes," dressed in shreds of clothing with newspapers around his feet, is secured finally for Sunday School, and is ushered courteously by Moody into class.

10) President-elect Abraham Lincoln visits North Market Street Sunday School and makes brief address. Not extant.

11) Moody is trapped by angry man whose whiskey Moody had emptied in the street. Collage. Moody's prayer wins the people over and gets children for Sunday School.

12) Moody preaches on the steps of the old Chicago Court House.

13) Moody finally secures admission to a camp of Confederate prisoners to hold an evangelistic service. Not extant. Printed in *MM* 48/6 (February 1948): 405.

14) Moody is angrily rebuffed by a man because of his inquiry as to the man's salvation. Collage. Happy sequel. Printed in *MM* 48/6 (February 1948): 404.

15) Moody and church deacons make two hundred New Year's Day calls on parishioners. Collage. Printed in *MM* 48/6 (February 1948): 405.

16) Moody organizes a coffee house in Chicago while a preacher merely talks about the need to a large audience.[2] Collage.

17) Farewell meeting in Glasgow in 1874. Crowd overflows Kibble Palace in Botanical Gardens. Not extant.

18) Moody preaches in Agricultural Hall, London (1875). Collage. Being greeted by Gladstone (in insert).

19) Moody preaches in Royal Opera House, Haymarket, London. Printed in *MM* 48/6 (February 1948): 403.

20) Moody preaches in the Hippodrome, New York City, 29-30 March 1876.

21) Moody quits morning study to drive heavily-laden student to railroad station. Collage.

22) Moody preaches on the Mount of Olives. Not extant.

23) Moody leads prayer service on sinking Steamer Spree. Later they are towed to safety in South Hampton. Not extant.

24) Moody shines shoes of English guest after a student refuses (1893). Places them afterwards at the door in early morning.

25) Congress Street, Chicago, jammed with overflow from an auditorium meeting in 1897. Collage. Moody in insert.

26) Moody preaches in Chicago's largest opera house in 1897. Not extant.

27) Moody is greeted by Mt. Hermon students on return from his experience on the Spree.

He Leadeth Me

1949 © K&B 1951; watercolor/colored chalk, 30 inches by 24 inches; Wilson Galleries, Anderson University. This picture is similar to *The Lord Is My Shepherd* (1942 © K&B 1943), only Jesus is leading his sheep in the other direction. The sheep are seen from behind. Jesus and the sheep are on a grassy mountain plateau. In the background are steep, Colorado-type mountains, like the ones in *The Lord Is My Shepherd*. Used on a bulletin cover. Printed on a 1995 Warner Press calendar.

Indian Trail Tree

1949; color chalk; originally at Edgewater Covenant Church; now at Covenant Archives. This drawing, done at Edgewater Covenant, is dated 9 October 1949. The tree was said to be located in Evanston on Chicago's North Shore. According to tradition, it had been bent by Indians while still a sapling for the purpose of marking a trail. The trunk is thus bent 90 degrees to the right, with two of the lower branches now growing upwards. The remaining trunk has been cut. The branch on the left goes straight up; the one on the right leans left, touching the other to make a triangle. Background trees are in brilliant fall colors of yellow and red. A watercolor of this same artwork was done later for Dr. Robert and Adrian Swanson (1957).

Mary the Mother of Christ

1950; large colored chalk on paper attached to board; Covenant Archives. Done at Nyvall Hall, North Park Theological Seminary, for a Seminary Wives Meeting, 8 May 1950. This side view of Mary looking left is the same as in the oil, *(Mary the) Mother of Christ* (1948 © K&B 1948).

Head of Christ

1950; chalk with paint touch-up on masonite; Immanuel Covenant Church, Chicago. Done at Edgewater Sunday School Rally and Parents Night, 20 October 1950. At the lower left is printed,

Edgewater Mission Covenant Church

Leslie Ostberg, Minister

Malcom V. Bowman, Superintendent of the Sunday School

Sallman later gave this very fine head of Christ to the Immanuel Covenant Church to replace a chalk done for the congregation some years earlier. At Immanuel the present artwork hung for about thirty years (until 1992) in the church chancel.

Feed My Sheep

1950; medium and location unknown. Jesus stands at left with one hand outstretched toward a crowd of people behind him; the other hand beckons the viewer. Storm clouds symbolizing sin and evil in the world overshadow the multitude, but a beam of light shines down upon Jesus, who wears a crimson-purple robe draped over the left shoulder. Published on the front cover of the *Upper Room* 16/2 (May-June 1950).

Christ Our Pilot

[1950]; pencil sketch; James and Gene Sallman private collection. Same picture as the like-named oil (1950 © K&B 1950). Four churches—apparently where the picture was drawn—are listed at the bottom: Austin Methodist Church [Chicago], First Covenant Church, Jamestown [New York], Bethesda Covenant Church, Rockford, [Illinois], and Polytechnic Methodist Church, Fort Worth, Texas.

Christ Setting a Man Free

1951; black chalk with white paint; James and Gene Sallman private collection. A note in Sallman's hand says that this is a "rough sketch." Jesus is taking shackles and chains from a man who is kneeling before him. A multitude of faces looks on from above. The accompanying text is John 8:36: "So if the Son makes you free, you will be free indeed."

Thine Is the Power

[1951]; pencil and pen sketch on paper; Marion Sallman private collection. Same picture as the like-named oil (1951). The top part is in pen, and the bottom part in pencil.

Teach Me Thy Way

[1951]; pencil sketch on paper; Marion Sallman private collection. Same as the like-named oil (1951 © K&B 1952), except that here a large tree branch is at upper right.

Follow Thou Me

1951; chalk; Polytechnic Methodist Church, Fort Worth, Texas. This picture hangs in the Mizpah Room of the church.

Rabboni

[1952]; colored pencil on cardboard; Marion Sallman private collection. A version of *Behold the Lord* (1952). Below is written, "Rabboni; which is to say MASTER John 20:16." Notations at the bottom—in a hand not Sallman's—give the following critical comments: "Get full figure of Christ;" "Too stiff and unnatural;" "Show nail holes in hands (not too pronounced);" "Show crosses (3) on hill ____;" and "Woman too squatted, not natural pose."

Behold the Lord

1952 © K&B 1953; watercolor; Wilson Galleries, Anderson University. In this richly-colored work, Mary Magdalene is at the door of the open tomb greeting the resurrected Lord (John 20). Both have outstretched arms, although the arms of Jesus reach more upward than towards Mary. Mary Magdelene, as in other Sallman paintings, has curly hair waist-length. Her deep purple robe covers a white garment. There is a rainbow behind Jesus made by a bright light emanating from the upper left. Easter lilies and trumpet daffodils are at the lower left of the picture. To the right is a square tomb entrance—a Sallman signature—and a large round stone rolled to the left of the opening. Done for a bulletin cover.

Compare the painting from Malden, Massachusetts (Gramstorff Bros.), printed in *WC* Central Easter issue 1110 (4 April 1942): 25, which is a similar depiction of Mary Magdelene.

The Son of God

[1952]; pencil sketch on paper; Marion Sallman private collection. Same as the like-named oil (1952 © K&B 1952), except that Mary and the boy Jesus face the other way.

Thine Is the Victory!

1952; watercolor with pen; Wilson Galleries, Anderson University. This sketch for a bulletin cover reworks an ink drawing Sallman did for *FV 359* (30 March 1920): 1. Here the resurrected Christ emerges out of the crucified Christ, the whole of which is framed by an Easter lily. The bulletin caption reads, "Thine is the Victory." This picture also has coloration making a V (V for Victory). The resurrected Christ reaches down to grasp the upward extended arms of the Crucified. At the foot of the cross there appears to be barbed wire. In the background, at the bottom of the picture, is Jerusalem, upon which light has just dawned.

Head of Christ

1952; watercolor; Newell and Gladys Johnson private collection. This exceptionally fine watercolor was a wedding gift to Sallman's niece and her husband. It is inscribed, "To Gladys and Newell on their wedding day, January third, 1953."

He Careth for You

1952; crayon; James and Gene Sallman private collection. A sketch of the oil painting of the same name (1954 © K&B 1954). The one difference is that here in the upper right a nurse is holding a baby. A gift from Sallman to Sylvia Peterson Knudson in 1967, as a memorial to Sylvia's husband, Ray Knudson.

Christ Our Pilot

1952; chalk; Polytechnic Methodist Church, Fort Worth, Texas. Drawn at the church and dated Easter Sunday 13 April 1952. The picture hangs in the foyer of the chapel.

The Annunciation

1953 © K&B 1953; watercolor on cardboard; Wilson Galleries, Anderson University. Here Mary wears a lime green cape. Her right hand touches the cape above the breast. Inspiration derives from Luke 1:28, which is written below.

Behold My Mother

1953; chalk; James and Gene Sallman private collection. Same as the oil, *The Son of God / Behold My Mother / Jesus Was a Little Boy* (1952 © K&B 1952).

The Light That Shineth

[1954]; pencil sketch on paper; Marion Sallman private collection. Same as like-named oil (1954 © K&B 1954), except that here no cross appears on the front of the pulpit.

Ready to Go–Ready to Stay–!
[1954]; pencil sketch on paper; Marion Sallman private collection. Same as like-named oil (1954 © K&B 1954).

Mary and Baby in Manger
1954 © K&B 1954; watercolor and paint; Wilson Galleries, Anderson University. In this watercolor, which is predominantly in light green, Mary and the baby in a manger dominate the foreground. It is the Mary we are accustomed to seeing in *(Mary the) Mother of Christ* (1948 © K&B 1948), *The Son of God* (1952 © K&B 1952), *The Annunciation* (1953 © K&B 1953), and *Madonna and Christ Child* (1955 © K&B 1956). She faces here to the right, the same way as in *Madonna and Christ Child*. But the face is the face of Mary in *The Annunciation*. She holds the cloths at the side of the crib, looking intently at the baby. The baby gazes up at her, with arms outstretched. The baby has a generous amount of golden curly hair. Two sheep in the foreground look on. Overhead are two winged angels in flowing gowns, their hands held together as if praying, but not folded. They are curved so as to make the shape of a heart. A small amount of starry sky in the upper corners completes the picture.
This picture was reprinted on a 1995 Warner Press calendar.

Peace Be Unto You
1956 © K&B 1956; color chalk; Wilson Galleries, Anderson University. This is another frontal head and shoulders picture of Jesus. Jesus has the right hand raised and a rose at his heart. Used on a 1957 bulletin cover, where it was placed in a white circular frame set against a purple background. Easter lilies are at the top and bottom. Above the picture it says, "Peace be unto you" (Luke 24:36). Compare *In Remembrance of Me* (1956 © K&B 1956), completed the same year.

Forward with Christ
[1956]; pencil sketch on paper; Marion Sallman private collection. Same picture as the like-named watercolor (1956 © K&B 1956).

Forward with Christ
1956 © K&B 1956; watercolor; Wilson Galleries, Anderson University. This painting, done for a 1957 bulletin cover, is of young people marching with flags. Prominent are the American flag to the left, a flag with the 1924 Christ head and John 3:16 in the center, and the Christian flag at right. Other flags say, "Forward with Christ," "Onward," "Forward," "Come," "Rally" and "Upward." The girl holding "Upward" has a Bible in hand. Over the top is written, "His Banner Over Us Is Love." Maple leaves in autumn orange and gold are in the upper corners.

In Remembrance of Me

1956 © K&B 1956; charcoal; Wilson Galleries, Anderson University. Jesus here stands behind a church communion table with a plate of bread in his right hand and a chalice in his left. On the communion table lies an open Bible. On the front of the table is inscribed, "In Remembrance of Me." Drapes and a cross complete the background. The face of Jesus looks a bit like *Portrait of Jesus* (1966 © K&B 1966).

The Bible Speaks Today

1956; poster drawing; location unknown. Two hands reach out of the clouds and point at an open Bible in the center of the picture. Above and below the Bible is printed, "The Bible Speaks Today." Published on the front cover of the *Bible Society Record* 101/8 (October 1956) for a Universal Bible Sunday sponsored by the American Bible Society.

Girl at Bedside Praying

1957; watercolor on cardboard; Wilson Galleries, Anderson University. Here a small girl is kneeling at the side of her bed praying. Hands are folded on a dark pink bedspread. Tucked into the covers at lower left is her doll; behind the girl is a small kitten. Above the girl's head, in an oval frame, is Sallman's *Madonna and Christ Child* (1955 © K&B 1956).

The girl resembles the little Canadian girl in one of the stained glass windows of the Children's Chapel at the Methodist Children's Home in Detroit (1952). The view there, however, is more frontal.

Christ at Prayer

1957 © K&B 1958; charcoal on cardboard; Marion Sallman private collection. In the background of this picture is the upward-looking face of Christ from *Christ in Gethsemane* (1941 © K&B 1942), reproduced also in *Our Redeemer* (1941 © K&B 1942). Folded hands, unconnected to the praying Christ, are in the foreground.

Christ Looking at the City

[1957]; medium and location unknown. Used for the Best Seller Publicity Campaign. A head and shoulders profile of Christ, wearing a cape and looking at tall city buildings accompanies the scripture: "…whosoever liveth and believeth in Me shall never die" (John 11:26). This picture appears together with a syndicated article in a local Chicago newspaper dated 4 January 1957.

It Is Finished

1958 © K&B 1958; watercolor, chalk, and pen; Wilson Galleries, Anderson University. Here the resurrected Christ, with hands uplifted, rises up behind three men on crosses. The whole is framed by the rent veil of the temple. The rend is wide at the top and narrow at the bottom. The title is from John 19:30. Similar to *Christ Rending the Veil* (1929), which appeared in *FV 779* (26 March 1929): 1.

On the center cross hangs Jesus, with blood dripping from his hands and feet. The man on the cross at the left looks up at a resurrected Christ. The man on the cross at the right has been deliberately eclipsed so his face does not show. Below, in the narrow portion of the rent veil, appears a winged serpent in tones of red. He has horns, a flaming tongue, and the tail of a coiled snake. This picture was used as a bulletin cover. On the back of the cardboard Sallman has written

St. Matthew 27:51....."And behold the veil of the temple was rent in twain..."
St. Mark 15:38.........."from top to bottom"
St. Luke 23:44-46......"veil of the temple was rent..."
St. John 19:30.........."It is finished."

Added in red pen are two additional verses, John 17:4 and John 4:34.

Christ on Easter Hill

1958; watercolor, chalk, and pen sketch; Wilson Galleries, Anderson University. Christ here is out walking on a hill covered with grass and spring flowers. He has just left the tomb, which is seen at the lower right. The tomb has the familiar Sallman look–a door-like entrance with a large round stone rolled to one side. Here the stone is to the right of the entrance. Above the tomb, on a rocky hill, appear three empty crosses and an Easter morning sky of blues, pinks, and yellows. It is dawn, and there is brightness on the horizon.

The Holy Communion

1958 © K&B 1958; watercolor, chalk, and pen sketch; Wilson Galleries, Anderson University. This picture with its square top and oval bottom takes the shape of a parament. The parament is bright red. At the top is a thorn-crowned head of Jesus—also in red—positioned at the intersection of a cross. The thorns on the head are the same as those in *Crown of Thorns* (1941 © Sallman 1943 © K&B 1956), but the face here is different. Below the face is a detailed gold chalice, and below it a gold communion plate with wafers, some of which are broken. The chalice and communion plate are surrounded by white light. The chalice looks very similar to the *Chalice of Antioch*, displayed at the Chicago Century of Progress in 1933-1934.[3] That chalice had a slightly smaller pedestal.

Jesus Our Savior

1959; chalk on board; Trinity Evangelical Covenant Church, Oak Lawn, Illinois. This picture is essentially the same as the like-named oil (1959 © K&B 1959). It was done for the dedication of the new church building.

Up From the Grave He Arose

1959; colored chalk; Wilson Galleries, Anderson University. The title comes from the chorus of an Easter hymn.[4] In this drawing, done for a bulletin cover, the upper body of the resurrected Christ ascends out of the tomb on Easter morning. The square doorway of the tomb is visible. Both hands of Christ are outstretched at shoulder height, palms facing inward, perhaps in a gesture of welcome. A background hill contains three empty crosses. In the foreground grow large Easter lilies, all but one of them open. A bright yellow light floods Christ and the hilltop crosses.

This picture was reprinted on a 1995 Warner Press calendar.

Face of Our Lord in Space

1959; color chalk and watercolor; Wilson Galleries, Anderson University. This face of Christ has the gentle look of *Portrait of Jesus* (1966 © K&B 1966), only it is completely frontal with no tilt of the head. It is set over against a green earth, where portions of North and South America are visible. The earth serves as a frame. Above and to the sides, the blue space envelope planets—one with a ring (Saturn?)—and numberless stars. This artwork was done for a Kriebel and Bates Triumphant Life Calendar. At the bottom, an open scroll bears John 16:33: "Be of Good Cheer; I have overcome the World." A reproduced cut-out of the face only was later used, together with 2 Corinthians 4:6, for a bulletin cover (*Face of Our Lord* 1959 © K&B 1961).

Springs of Grace are Streaming

1959; colored chalk; Wilson Galleries, Anderson University. This beautifully-colored chalk serves as another bulletin cover. In a spring scene of flowering fruit trees, a sheep and lamb bound through grass. A large tree sprouting new leaves dominates the foreground right. On one of the tree's branches sits a robin. A background hill contains three empty crosses. Brightly-colored red and pink blossoms—which first strike the eye in this picture—make a winding path from the foreground to the hill in back. A small portion of blue sky contains random clouds.

Portrait of the Rev. Frederic E. Pamp

1959; charcoal sketch; Christopher and Susan Norborg private collection. Pamp was student pastor of Edgewater Covenant Church, and later pastor of the Covenant Congregational Church of Boston. This appeared as sketch #1 in a display of seven former pastors of Edgewater, presented at the Edgewater Covenant Church.

Portrait of the Rev. C. J. Andrews

1959; charcoal sketch; Norman Andrews Jr. private collection. Andrews was pastor of Edgewater Covenant Church from 1914-1916, and superintendent of Swedish Covenant Hospital from 1921-1932. This appeared as sketch #2 in a display of seven former pastors of Edgewater, exhibited at the Edgewater Covenant Church.

Portrait of the Rev. C. V. Bowman

1959; charcoal sketch; Keith and Alpha Olson private collection. Bowman was pastor of Edgewater Covenant Church (1917-1920), and later president of the Mission Covenant Church. This appeared as sketch #3 in a display of seven former pastors of Edgewater, exhibited at the Edgewater Covenant Church.

Portrait of the Rev. F. O. Kling II

1959; charcoal on cardboard; Covenant Archives. Not the pen drawing (1922). Kling served as pastor of Edgewater Covenant Church from 1922-1927. This appeared as sketch #4 in a display of seven former pastors of Edgewater, exhibited at the Edgewater Covenant Church. Given to Covenant Archives in August 1995 by James and Gene Sallman.

Portrait of the Rev. K. K. Jacobson

[1959]; charcoal on cardboard; location unknown. Jacobson was pastor of Edgewater Covenant Church from 1927-1936. This appeared as sketch #5 in a display of seven former pastors of Edgewater, exhibited at the Edgewater Covenant Church.

Portrait of the Rev. Paul F. Erickson

[1959]; charcoal on cardboard; location unknown. Erickson was pastor of Edgewater Covenant Church from 1938-1941. This appeared as sketch #6 in a display of seven former pastors of Edgewater, exhibited at the Edgewater Covenant Church.

Portrait of the Rev. Arthur N. Johnson

[1959]; charcoal on cardboard; originally Everett Sallman private collection; given to Covenant Archives in July 1997. Johnson was pastor of Edgewater Covenant Church from 1943-1947. This appeared as sketch #7 in a display of seven former pastors of Edgewater, exhibited at the Edgewater Covenant Church.

His Presence

[1960]; red pencil sketch on paper with overlay; Marion Sallman private collection. The same picture as the like-named oil (1946 © K&B 1947). Overlay has the outline of a doorway in the background, but it is not exactly the same as the doorway in the oil, *His Presence*, done for the Covenant Church of Escanaba, Michigan (1960).

God Is Love

1960; color chalk 4 feet by 5 feet; Covenant Archives. From an Edgewater Covenant Church Christmas program. The work contains a cross, the baby Jesus (lower left), a crown (upper right), and palm branches (below). Accompanying scriptures: Luke 2:14 and 1 Corinthians 15:57.

The Emmaus Road

1961; watercolor and chalk; Wilson Galleries, Anderson University. Similar to *The Road to Emmaus* in oil (1961 © K&B 1961), but with less detail. There is no light on the three travelers, no tree with blue blossoms in center foreground, no tree to the left of the travelers, no bird flying, and no clouds over Jerusalem.

The Resurrected Lord

1961; colored chalk; Wilson Galleries, Anderson University. Christ stands at the center of this drawing, looking straight ahead with hands outstretched. Compare Sallman's church painting, *The Triumphant Christ* (1965). The hands show the marks of nail prints. Christ says, "Look, my hands" (John 20:19-20). In *The Triumphant Christ* the complete figure of Christ is visible; here the robe fades out at three-quarter length. The head of Christ is very similar to *Face of Our Lord in Space* (1959), also a colored chalk. At the right is the square door of the tomb and a large round stone, only here the stone is partially rolled to the right of the entrance. Three empty crosses stand on a hill at the left of the picture. Christ is flooded in resurrection light. Used on a bulletin cover.

Christ at Prayer on Globe

1961; watercolor and chalk; Wilson Galleries, Anderson University. This picture is similar to *Christ in Gethsemane* (1941 © K&B 1942), only a globe has replaced the table rock on which Jesus is praying. The upward gaze is the same as *Christ in Gethsemane*. The arms, however, are more visible; in the earlier work they were covered by Jesus' robe. The background also is different. On the globe, at a number of points, appear to be nuclear explosions. But a ray of light descends upon Jesus. In its beam is a shadowed cross.

Not My Will But Thine
1961; watercolor and chalk; Wilson Galleries, Anderson University. Another passion portrayal similar to *Christ in Gethsemane* (1941 © K&B 1942), except that the foreground foliage appears in the left instead of the right. Also the background lacks a large rock. But the trees, the sleeping disciples, and distant Jerusalem are all there. Only the upper portion of Jesus' body is visible. Light shines down from above. The title derives from Jesus' prayer in Gethsemane (Luke 22:42 and parallels).

Road to Emmaus Sketches
[1961]; four pencil sketches preceding the *Road to Emmaus Sketches* in pen (1961 © K&B 1961). Marion Sallman private collection. The set, supposed to number eight, is incomplete. The four completed sketches consist of the following:
   #1 Two travelers on the road
   #6 Jesus prays with the disciples as they break bread
   #7 Jesus appears to the group
   #8 The Ascension at Bethany

Road to Emmaus Sketches
1961 © K&B 1961; eight pen sketches; location of seven unknown; *The Ascension at Bethany* (#8) on cardboard resides in the Wilson Galleries, Anderson University. The eight sketches consist of the following:
   #1 Two travelers on the road
   #2 Two women come to tell the disciples about the empty tomb; disciples stand in the doorway of a village house
   #3 Peter and another disciple arrive at the tomb
   #4 The disciples talk on the Emmaus Road
   #5 Jesus approaches the two disciples from behind
   #6 Jesus prays with the disciples as they break bread
   #7 Jesus appears to the group
   #8 The Ascension at Bethany
   These sketches were done for a booklet by F. M. Bates, *Road to Emmaus* (Indianapolis: Kriebel and Bates, 1961).

Mary and Martha with Jesus
1961 © K&B 1962; watercolor; Wilson Galleries, Anderson University. Very similar to the large oil of the same name done for the Bethany Methodist Home, Chicago (1954). Jesus sits in a Palestinian house talking with Mary, who sits in the center of the picture. An open scroll rests on his lap. Behind Mary, Martha carries in a tray of food and drink. Unlike the oil, there is much detail in

this picture. Through an open window one sees a vine trellis, and a man walking by.

This picture appeared in the *Idaho Free Press* (1 December 1962): 12, and it was reprinted on a 1995 Warner Press calendar. Compare another picture of Jesus with Mary and Martha printed in *CHo* 3/38 (17 September 1950): 3.

Lord and Master

1962 © K&B 1962; brown pen sketch; Wilson Galleries, Anderson University. The same Christ portrait as the like-named watercolor, and the later oil, *The Just One* (1964 © K&B 1964). Compare illustration #1 in *Story of Gethsemane Sketches* [1964], where a similar-looking Jesus appears to be second from the last leaving the Upper Room. At the lower right of the present sketch is printed,

Lord and Master

Savior.......Sovereign

This sketch appeared on the front of *Survival Power*, an inspirational booklet on the Lord's Prayer by F. Martin Bates (Indianapolis: Kriebel and Bates, 1962). It was also used on a poster and on other marketed items by Kriebel and Bates (© 1964). Printed at the top of the poster is "When You are Tired and Afraid...I Give You My Peace," and at the bottom: "Be Still." This picture was reprinted on a 1995 Warner Press calendar.

Lord and Master

1962 © K&B 1962; watercolor in full color with transparency; Wilson Galleries, Anderson University. The same portrait as the brown pen sketch of this title, also the oil entitled, *The Just One* (1964 © K&B 1964). The title, *Lord and Master*, derives from John 13:14 (KJV). On the transparency are advisory comments: "Top of hair and head looks feminine," "Darker under (right) eye," "Smooth down hair, too wavy," "Eye (left) not in line with others," and "Too much white in eyes also." Used on the front cover of a later edition of *Survival Power*, by F. Martin Bates.

The Blind Beggar Healed

1962; sketch composition; James and Gene Sallman private collection. Preliminary sketch for the oil, *Christ Healing the Blind Beggar*, done the same year for the Belmont Methodist Church, Belmont, Massachusetts.

Follow Thou Me

1962; charcoal and colored chalk on brown pressed board; First United Methodist Church, Mason City, Iowa. Presented to youth of the church on 14 October 1962. Hangs in the lower East Lounge (formerly the Youth Room).

We Ought to Pray

1963 © K&B 1963; crayon and paint; Wilson Galleries, Anderson University. This artwork contains three sets of hands: in the foreground right hands are folded; at the upper left hands are unfolded, but together; and in the background center hands are open and uplifted. The hands and shading in the upper left are done in reddish-brown.

Abraham Lincoln and Son

1963; watercolor; Everett Sallman private collection. Dated 21 September 1963. This work depicts Lincoln reading his Bible with his son standing along-side. A quotation at the top and bottom reads,

Good boys who to their books apply

will all be great men by and by.

A. Lincoln

Portrait of Harry Denman

1963; rough charcoal sketch; James and Gene Sallman private collection. Dated 8 January 1963. This is the same portrait as the oil of Denman (1963) in the Upper Room Chapel and Museum in Nashville, Tennessee.

Power and Glory

1963; large brown and white chalk on paper; Northern Baptist Theological Seminary, Lombard, Illinois. This 3 feet by 5 feet chalk in brown and white reproduces the oil, *Power and Glory* (1957 © K&B 1958), which depicts Jesus standing on the world with his right hand lifted up, and a small lamb in his left arm. Though well done, the drawing lacks the rich color and refracted light of the oil. The drawing has circular rings around the person of Jesus, just as the oil does. The head of Jesus, however, looks smaller than the head in the oil; the same is true with the feet. Accompanying scripture is 1 Corinthians 2:9.

The drawing was done before a Fall meeting of the Seminary Women's Auxiliary. The date: 28 October 1963. Mrs. Irma Grosser of the Auxiliary arranged for Sallman's visit. Not long after completion, seminary students objected to the work and it had to be taken down. For some years it remained "hidden" in storage. Now it hangs once again in the Student Commons.

Head of Christ

© K&B 1964; black and white photocopy? of the Christ head that is similar, but not the same, as the 1940 painting; on paper in a cardboard frame with a circular cut-out; Wilson Galleries, Anderson University. Written below in Sallman's hand is "suggestion for medallion." Around the circumference of the picture is written, "'In him was life; and the life was the light of men' John 1:4."

Head of Christ
    1964; 24 inches by 30 inches charcoal on brown paper; James and Gene Sallman private collection. Sketch for a painting of the same size.

Jesus in Gethsemane
    [1964]; pencil sketch on paper; Marion Sallman private collection. This is a sketch of Jesus as he appears in the oil, *The Story of Gethsemane* (1964 © K&B 1964).

Story of Gethsemane Sketches
    [1964]; five sketches in pen on white paper; Wilson Galleries, Anderson University. Unfinished and incomplete. For a K&B *Story of Gethsemane* booklet. The five sketches:
    # 1 Jesus and his disciples leave the Upper Room. Jesus, at the back, looks as he does in the brown pen sketch, *Lord and Master* (1962 © K&B 1962). A disciple in front carries a lantern; two others carry torches. The door and overhang on the background house are similar to what appears in *Christ at Heart's Door* (1942 © K&B 1942), only here the door hinges are on the left.
    # 2 "What, could ye not watch with me one hour." Disciples sleep in the Garden. Jesus, at right, walks towards them. An olive tree is in the background.
    # 4 Judas greets Jesus in the Garden of Gethsemane. Olive trees stand behind Jesus. Roman soldiers with spears and torches are behind Judas. Some in the crowd look to be Jews–turbans are on their heads and they have no swords and no armor.
    # 6 Jesus heals the ear of the high priest's slave (Luke 22:50-51). Roman soldier with spear looks on at left. At right is a disciple. Below the disciple is an "S" for the signature.
    # 7 The bound Jesus is led away by Roman soldiers. Crowd in the background is a mix of Romans and Jews.

Glory to God in the Highest
    1964 ©K&B 1964; watercolor; Wilson Galleries, Anderson University. This Bethlehem scene of Mary, Joseph, and the baby Jesus being visited by shepherds was cropped for use as a bulletin cover. In its bulletin frame is a star in the upper right, shining as a cross. Other stars trail in a circle over the manger scene. On an open scroll is written, "'Glory to God in the highest...' Luke 2:14." At the lower right, in pencil, are two additional texts added by Sallman: Isaiah 34:4 and Revelation 6:14.
    The stable in this picture looks like the inside of a Palestinian house. It has a doorway, a window, walls, and a slightly pitched roof. A donkey is visible in the background behind Joseph. Joseph, staff in hand, stands behind Mary and

looks at the baby Jesus, who lies in a comfortable blanketed manger. Mary and the baby are brightly painted, although no beam of light is present. Two lambs are on the floor at the lower right. Mary, Joseph, and the baby all have the familiar Sallman look. The baby has a crop of curly hair, and both arms are outstretched. The three shepherds are on their knees before the baby. The shepherd in the right foreground has a staff with a crook resting on his shoulder; both hands are together–though not folded–in prayerful adoration. The shepherd at lower left is seen from the back; next to him, on the ground, is a flask with straps.

Face of Christ above Mary and Christchild

[1964]; two charcoal sketches on brown paper. James and Gene Sallman private collection. A preliminary sketch of *Thorn-crowned Christ above Mary and Christchild* (1964), except that here is no crown of thorns.

Thorn-crowned Christ above Mary and Christchild

1964; two color chalks on paper; James and Gene Sallman private collection. Face of Christ looks like *Portrait of Jesus* (1966 © K&B 1966). Mary lies with the baby Jesus on straw; accompanying scripture is 2 Corinthians 4:6.

Christ Our Pilot

1964; watercolor and chalk? with quoache; Rich Port (formerly West Suburban) YMCA, La Grange, Illinois. This large watercolor, about 3½ feet in width and 5 feet in height, is essentially the same picture as the like-named K&B oil (1950 © K&B 1950). It is done in three colors: brown, black and white. The background of the oil has been eliminated: There are no waves outside the boat, and no clouds in the sky. Only the inside of the boat shows, and below the wheel is inscribed "Christ Our Pilot." The face of Christ is also different from the K&B version, which has the familiar 1924 and 1940 face. Here more space above the head allows for a configuration at the upper left of three YMCA symbols: the Y; the triangle, symbolizing fullness of life through equal development of spirit, mind and body; and the circle, symbolizing the eternal union of all YMCA members through Christian fellowship.

The picture hangs in the board room. It was done when the YMCA facility was undergoing expansion, and the plan then was that the picture would serve as an inspiration for a Christ Our Pilot statue to be erected in an outside park area. That statue, however, was never built.

The Triumphant Christ

[1965]; pencil sketch; Marion Sallman private collection. Preliminary drawing for the like-named oil done the same year for the South Jacksonville Presbyterian Church, Jacksonville, Florida.

Safe in the Arms of Jesus

[1965]; photographed sketch? James and Gene Sallman private collection. This picture was done in oil for the Grace Methodist Church of South Bend, Indiana (1965).

Jesus in the Garden

1966; colored chalk; Wilson Galleries, Anderson University. In this chalk, done for another Easter bulletin, Jesus stands in a garden of Easter lilies. Only his upper body shows. Jesus lifts up his right hand to face height, with the palm facing the viewer. Over Jesus' head a rainbow shines against a dark sky. The bulletin frame contains an open Bible below, on which is printed John 20:15, 16–the text reporting a resurrection appearance to Mary Magdalene.

Shepherds Outside Stable

1966; watercolor and pen sketch; Wilson Galleries, Anderson University. This sketch, done for a bulletin cover, is another Bethlehem scene of shepherds—here five in number—who are grouped together outside the stable. They peer in through an open archway. One of the shepherds is a young boy. This stable with its thatched roof looks much like an African hut. Mary and the Christchild can be seen through the doorway. Two lambs are lying on the floor. Behind Mary and the child are the heads of a donkey and an ox. Joseph is not visible. It is night, and the dark blue sky is filled with shining stars. A heavenly beam lights up the entrance to the stable, partially lighting the shepherds who are otherwise in darkness. Below the picture, for the bulletin cover, is a Bible over Christmas holly open to Luke 2:15-16.

Bright Stars in the Darkness

1966; watercolor or chalk; Wilson Galleries, Anderson University. A nocturnal landscape in blue, with a farm house flanked by trees–a large one to the right, and a smaller one to the left. A river or perhaps a pond is in the foreground. Clouds cover most of the sky, but at the top and upper left are bright stars. On the back is written, in Sallman's hand,

> The beauty of the stars
> would be lost, if it
> were not for the
> darkness
> F. M. Bates

Underneath Sallman has also written,

> High above the darkening
> clouds, the stars
> are shining bright.

Passion-Easter Sketches

1966; black pen; Wilson Galleries, Anderson University. Series of incomplete and unfinished passion sketches for a K&B booklet. A description of four of the sketches:

#2 At top, Pilate washes his hands in a bowl held by a servant. Jesus with bound hands is behind him. He wears a crown of thorns and has a robe over his bare chest. A Roman pillar is seen in the background. In the middle are empty lines for a text. At the bottom men look on, all but one of whom are wearing turbans.

#3 At top appear two verses of a poem (by Fred Bates?) with accompanying Bible verses. At bottom: Jesus wears a crown of thorns and carries his cross. Roman and Jewish onlookers are close to him. The city wall of Jerusalem is seen in the background, with the arch of a gate partially visible. At the top right is a hill with two crosses already erected.

#4 At top: three men on crosses–Jesus at the center. Onlookers include three women and a man (John the disciple?) near the foot of the cross. Roman soldiers and others are further distant. Jerusalem appears in the background. One woman with long curly waist-length hair (Mary Magdalene) looks on near the cross; a woman in a cape turns away crying. The third woman shields herself with her cloak and is comforted by the man. At bottom appear two more verses of a poem with accompanying Bible verses (one Bible verse missing).

#5 At top, empty framed boxes for more poetry and biblical texts. At bottom, Jesus greets Mary Magdalene in the Garden (John 20). Mary has long curly hair as in Sketch #4. She kneels before him with both arms outstretched. Jesus has the right hand lifted with a finger pointing upward. The left hand extends to keep Mary at a distance. Trees, rocks, and flora are at each side. Behind is an open tomb with a square, hewn doorway. A round stone to the left of the opening has been rolled back.

Portrait of Jesus

1967; charcoal sketch on brown paper; James and Gene Sallman private collection. Dated 22 February 1967. Templet for an illustrated talk.

Portrait of Jesus

[1967]; colored pen sketch on paper; Wilson Galleries, Anderson University. Very similar to *Portrait of Jesus* (1966 © K&B 1966), only the head is not tilted. Used as a cover for a Kriebel & Bates 1968 catalogue.

Head of Christ

1967; colored crayon; James and Gene Sallman private collection. Originally a gift from Sallman to Sylvia Peterson.

Christ Blessing Young People

1967; blue pen sketch on paper; Marion Sallman private collection. Jesus, dressed in a clerical robe, is pictured here above a boy and a girl with his hands over their heads. Each holds a Bible with a cross on the cover. Palm branches and flowers fill out the bottom, and a Gothic church window frames the whole scene. At the bottom is written "GRACE." The sketch is long and narrow, therefore less likely to be a bulletin cover. It could have been done for a baptism, confirmation, wedding, or, because of the palms, for Palm Sunday.

Madonna and Christ Child

1967; colored chalk in a circular frame; Evelyne Gustafson private collection. Done for Sallman's last Christmas concert at the Edgewater Covenant Church, 10 December 1967, Sallman gave the piece to Gunnar and Evelyne Gustafson following the concert. Evelyne had been the concert organist. Similar, but not the same as the 1955 © K&B 1956 *Madonna and Christ Child.*

A Tree

1968; black pen sketch with whiting; translucent overlay of green chalk or qouache; Wilson Galleries, Anderson University. This sketch surrounds a poem written by F. M. Bates entitled, "A Tree." At the right of the sketch grows a tall tree filled with leaves. In front lies a smaller tree that has been felled. An ax remains in the stump. To the right is a building in classical style, with large front pillars. This represents the campus. To the left is a log cabin with its half-door swung open. Out of the chimney comes a trail of smoke. At the bottom is noted 1 Peter 2:24. The date 1968 on this sketch indicates that it was one of Sallman's last before his death.

Works of Unknown Date

Self Portrait

Watercolor; Marion Sallman private collection. Side view of Sallman as a young man.

Self Portrait

Pen sketch; Everett Sallman private collection. Side view of the young Sallman.

Head of Patriot Soldier

Pencil sketch on paper; Marion Sallman private collection. The hat and uniform coat look like those worn by American patriots during the Revolutionary War.

Military Salutes the Christchild

Pencil sketch on paper; Marion Sallman private collection. In the foreground is Mary and Joseph with the Christchild. Behind are saluting men and women from various branches of the American Armed Forces.

Christ Extending Hand to Soldier

Pencil sketch on paper; Marion Sallman private collection. Christ at the left is extending a hand to a soldier on the battlefield. The soldier is on one knee. Flowers (Easter lilies?) below symbolize Easter and the Resurrection. Another soldier can be seen in the background.

Management and Labor Shaking Hands

Pencil sketch on paper; Marion Sallman private collection. A worker at left, in bib overalls and wearing a hat marked "Labor," shakes hands with a man at right, dressed in a suit. Both have smiles on their faces.

Man and Woman Seated on Couch

Pencil sketch on paper; Marion Sallman private collection. A well-dressed man and woman sit on a small couch. A grandfather clock stands in the background.

David Nyvall Portraits

Two sketches in black paint on paper; Marion Sallman private collection. David Nyvall was a Covenant leader and the first president of North Park College.

Crown of Thorns

Small black and white reproduction of pen sketch on cardboard; with © W. Sallman 1941; Wilson Galleries, Anderson University. The artwork is in a wallet-sized frame, together with a similarly-framed "'God is Love' 1 John 4:16." Paint is added. Date in lower left corner is 27 March 1941.

Christ in Gethsemane

Charcoal sketch on brown paper; James and Gene Sallman private collection. This is the same picture as the oils done for K&B (1941 © K&B 1942) and the Covenant Church in Manchester, Connecticut (1942).

Christ Our Pilot

Charcoal sketch on brown paper; James and Gene Sallman private collection. Same picture as the like-named oil (1950 © K&B 1950).

Boy at Bedside Praying

Brown chalk and collage; Wilson Galleries, Anderson University. Sketch of a boy praying at bedside. A cut-out of *Christ our Pilot* (1950 © K&B 1950), in an oval frame, is above the boy's head. A model ship is in the window at right.

Teach Me Thy Way

Charcoal sketch on brown paper; James and Gene Sallman private collection. Same picture, basically, as the like-named oil (1951 © K&B 1952).

Mary Holding Baby Jesus

Pencil sketch on paper; Marion Sallman private collection. Mary is sitting with the baby Jesus in her lap, facing right.

Christ in the Clouds

Pencil sketch on paper; Marion Sallman private collection. A full figure of Christ similar to *His Presence* (1946 © K&B 1947), except that the left foot is slightly forward.

Jesus Walking with Boy and Girl

Pencil sketch on paper; Marion Sallman private collection. Jesus in the center is walking with a young girl on his left and a young boy on his right, holding their hands. The girl carries a Bible.

Missionary Doctor and Nurse

Pencil sketch on paper; Marion Sallman private collection. A doctor and nurse attend to patients in what appears to be an African mission hospital. The doctor examines a patient on the table. The nurse attends to a small boy in the foreground. She holds a bottle. Other medicine bottles are on a table at the right.

Young People with Flags

Pen sketch; Wilson Galleries, Anderson University. Young people are standing on a church platform holding an array of flags. The boy before the pulpit holds the Christian flag. Behind him, in a semi-circle, are other young people in the dress of different countries. They carry flags from America, the Scandinavian countries (four flags with crosses), Turkey (with a crescent and star), Japan (with the rising sun), Germany (with three stripes) and other countries. At the right is printed Matthew 19:14: "Jesus said, Suffer little children, and forbid them not, to come unto me; for of such is the Kingdom of Heaven."

People Approaching Colonial Church

Watercolor with transparency; Wilson Galleries, Anderson University. This bright watercolor is at the left of a blank 8½ inches by 11 inches portion of cardboard, with a border. People walk to a colonial-style church with a steeple and a cross on top. Painted against the sky, another cross frames the tower and the church cross. At the back of the procession two young people frolic. Notations on the transparency indicate that other things were planned for the blank area.

And the Books Were Opened

Unfinished sketch in brown. Wilson Galleries, Anderson University. For a bulletin cover. At the top, a finger points to Revelation 21:27 in an open Bible. This verse, together with the words of the hymn, "Is My Name Written There?" appear below and to the right. Clouds are at the top; the bottom remains unfinished. To the right, behind the open Bible, are other books.

O Lord Our God

Colored pen sketch circa 20 inches by 20 inches on cardboard; Wilson Galleries, Anderson University. At the left is written a verse from 1 Chronicles 29:16; to the right are folded hands.

Pilate Offering Jesus to Mob

Pen sketch; Wilson Galleries, Anderson University. Two sketches at top and bottom frame a center poem entitled, "The Crucifixion of Jesus." The poem has accompanying Bible verses. In the top sketch, Pilate gestures with his right hand toward Jesus, who stands at his right. Jesus, partially robed and bound at the hands, wears a crown of thorns. Behind Pilate, but only partially seen, is a wreath above which appear the letters SPQR.[5] The bottom sketch shows seven angry men calling for Jesus' death. All but one gesture wildly, and all but one wear turbans or similar headgear; none are Roman soldiers.

Wise Men and Shepherds Approaching Heavenly Angel

Watercolor and pen sketch; has a blank cut-out for a collage; Wilson Galleries, Anderson University. In the foreground of this bright watercolor with pen outlining, simulating stained glass, two wise men arrive in Bethlehem. The head of one camel is visible. To the left are shepherds with three sheep. The large wing of an angel is at the top of the picture. Another angel, out of the picture at right, appears to be the source of the light.

Head of Christ against Stained Glass

Watercolor; location unknown. A stained glass background for the familiar Sallman Christ head. Similar to *Head of Christ in Simulated Glass* (1946 © K&B

1946), appearing on the bulletin cover, *Let's Go to Church* (1947), except that the colors here are blues, pinks, and yellows. In the Everett Sallman private collection is a framed print.

Map of Palestine with Christmas Sketches
    Chalk and perhaps paint—all brown; Wilson Galleries, Anderson University. These Christmas sketches portray Mary and Joseph going to Bethlehem, shepherds in the field, and wise men coming from the East. To be used as background for a centerpiece text that is missing. Possibly for a bulletin cover.

Bible Class Outline
    Color sketch on brown paper; James and Gene Sallman private collection. Outline for a study in the book of Revelation.

He Is Risen
    Watercolor with transparency; Wilson Galleries, Anderson University. This work without a signature appears to be an unfinished drawing for a bulletin cover. There is an open square at the top for a text. Easter lilies are in front of a cross. The drawing is cone-shaped, perhaps to simulate the rent veil of the temple.

Pine Forest and Mountains
    Chalk on plywood 22 inches by 17 inches; Marion Sallman private collection. A mountain scene with a foreground road passing through a grove of pines. Background mountains have a trace of snow. Two leafy trees stand at the far right.

The Flight into Egypt
    Large chalk circa 5 feet by 8 feet, very similar to the 1941 oil © The Salvation Army. Everett Sallman private collection. Mary and Joseph with the baby Jesus are traveling by night to Egypt (Matthew 2:14). Done originally for a Christmas program at the Edgewater Covenant Church. The main difference between this drawing and the oil is that Joseph in this picture is glancing to the side, not looking straight ahead. There are also two pyramids and two trees in the distance.

Mary and the Baby
    Circular chalk circa 4 feet in diameter on paper on board; Everett Sallman private collection. Done originally for a Christmas program at the Edgewater Covenant Church. Mary has a blue garment and a yellow cape. A bed of straw is to the right. Not exactly like any other picture of Mary holding the baby Jesus, but one can see similarities to *Madonna and Christ Child* (1955 © K&B 1956).

Mary with Baby in Cloak

Circular color chalk; James and Gene Sallman private collection. Another chalk done originally for a Christmas program at the Edgewater Covenant Church. Mary, in a full-length cloak of dark blue and purple, lies with the baby Jesus in the Bethlehem stable. Only the legs, lower body, and one arm of the baby are visible; the face is hidden. The baby is a bit large. Light emanates from the baby inside Mary's cloak.

Jesus and the Children of the World

A watercolor preceding a later oil to be done for a Methodist Crusade for Christ Campaign. This piece is the cover for a leader's manual.

[1] The name of this artist is listed in records at Moody Bible Institute as Joseph Palenski, but an obituary to which these records refer in the *Chicago Tribune* gives the artist's name as Reinhold Palenske. See *The Chicago Tribune*, (31 December 1954), 7.

[2] The setting is in dispute. Another description card says the workingmen's coffee house has been organized in Glasgow.

[3] See chapter IX, note 2.

[4] Robert Lowry, "Low in the Grave He Lay," *Covenant Hymnal* 1996, #245.

[5] Senatus Populusque Romanus (=the Senate and People of Rome).

Inventory of Sallman Art

The following inventory of Sallman artwork, though comprehensive, is not complete. Some works have been lost and will never be recovered. Others were given to friends and are now in unrecorded private collections. The inventory does, however, include all the well-known oils copyrighted by Kriebel and Bates; other K&B oils, watercolors, and sketches; known paintings in churches, hospitals, schools, reformatories, and homes for the children and the elderly; Sallman artwork known to exist in private collections; and a miscellaneous collection of sketches, drawings, and cartoons published in church papers and elsewhere. No attempt has been made to include the many Christ heads in chalk, despite the fact that they too are originals and represent an important part of the Sallman output. There are simply too many of these scattered across the country, and no inventory of them has ever been made. Titles not in italics are works having no title, or else works that at one time were titled, but whose title is not now known. If a work has gone by more than one title, the one better-known is given first. Dates in square brackets are assumed or approximate dates.

1902
Bob-o-Link on a Reed [1902]; oil; not extant.
Home Scene [1902]; oil; not extant.

1904
Horse and Man Drinking Water [1904]; small oil; Elsie Norman private
    collection.

1906-08
Binder of pencil sketches [1906–]; James and Gene Sallman private collection.

1909
Abraham Lincoln [1909]; oil; location unknown.
Mother 1909; pen sketch; James and Gene Sallman private collection.
LeRoy Sallman 1909; pen sketch; location unknown.

1910
Brass Bowl 1910; watercolor; James and Gene Sallman private collection.

Christmas Light in Children's Eyes [circa 1910]; watercolor; location unknown. Printed in *WC*.

Country Scene 1910; small oil on canvas; Everett Sallman private collection.

1913

Mother Knitting [1913]; oil; location unknown. Printed in Art Institute of Chicago catalogue.

Bouquet of Lilacs 1913; oil on canvas; Everett Sallman private collection.

Nudes [1913]; 10 pencil drawings on white paper; James and Gene Sallman private collection.

Santa Claus 1913; oil on canvas on board; Marion Sallman private collection.

1914

Face of Christ 3 April 1914; black and white sketch; Everett Sallman private collection.

1916

Mother 1916; color chalk; Marion Sallman private collection.

Red Swedish Church 1916; oil on canvas; Everett Sallman private collection.

Our Colossus 1916; poster drawing; location unknown.

1918

Edgebrook Forest Preserve I [1918]; small oil; James and Gene Sallman private collection.

Edgebrook Forest Preserve II 1918; small oil; James and Gene Sallman private collection.

Frid på jorden. 1918; pen sketch; location unknown. Printed in *FV* and in Christmas 1918 issue of *Edgewater Missionsblad.*

Mänskorna ett gott behag. 1918; pen sketch; location unknown. Printed in *FV*.

Hope for the New Year [1918]; pen sketch; location unknown. Printed in *FV*.

Three Men on Parade 1918; pen sketch; Marion Sallman private collection.

1919

Winter in Sweden 1919; pen sketch; James and Gene Sallman private collection. Printed in *FV*.

Angels Blowing Trumpets 1919; two pen sketches; location unknown. Printed in *FV*.

Christmas Tree with Snow-covered House [1919]; pen sketch; location unknown. Printed in *FV*.

Tell Me the Old, Old Story 1919; large sketch; location unknown. Printed in *FV* and in *The Family Altar.*

1920

Resurrected Christ Rising from the Crucified Christ © W. E. Sallman 1920; pen sketch; location unknown. Printed in *FV.*

Tacksägelse 1920; charcoal with whiting; Covenant Archives. Printed in *FV.*

Here Am I, Lord, Send Me 1920; pen sketch; location unknown. Printed in *FV.*

Apostate Religionists 1920; collage; simulated etching in pen; location unknown. Printed in *The Evangelistic Note,* and later in the *WC.*

American Indian and the US Capitol 1920; black paint sketch on cardboard; Marion Sallman private collection.

Cable Midget Upright 1920; pen sketch; location unknown. Printed advertisement.

Pianos in Walnut [1920]; pen sketch; location unknown. Printed advertisement.

1921

Christian Family Life 1921; pen sketch; location unknown. Printed in *The Family Altar.*

Eskimo Child [1921]; pen sketch; location unknown. Printed in *FV.*

Self-Denial, Self-Indulgence 1921; collage; pen sketch; Marion Sallman private collection. Printed in *FV.*

Memories of Julotta 1921; charcoal on cardboard; Marion Sallman private collection. Printed in *FV.*

1922

Mother Reading the Easter Story 1922; pen sketch; location unknown. Printed in *FV.*

Mother Reading the Easter Story [1922]; charcoal sketch; location unknown; photocopy in Marion Sallman private collection.

Hallelujah Scroll 1922; pen sketch; location unknown. Printed in *FV.*

Don't Forget 1922; pen sketch; location unknown. Printed in *The Christian Home Magazine.*

Portrait of the Rev. F. O. Kling I [1922]; pencil sketch; James and Gene Sallman private collection.

Portrait of the Rev. F. O. Kling I 1922; pen drawing; Covenant Archives.

Chicago at the Michigan Avenue Bridge 1922; watercolor or oil; location unknown. Printed on the cover of *Chicago Plan, by the Board of Local Improvements, City of Chicago.*

1923

Christ Holding an Easter Lily 1923; charcoal on cardboard; Marion Sallman private collection. Printed in *FV.*

A Thank Offering? [1923]; cartoon sketch; location unknown. Printed in *FV.*

Family Altar of the American Home 1923; sketch; location unknown. Printed in *CC* Old Series.

Snow-Covered Pines 1923; watercolor? location unknown. Printed in *FV*.

Snow-Covered Tree and Bush 1923; sketch in brown and white; location unknown. Printed in *CC* Old Series.

Only Mother 1923; probable charcoal; location unknown, Printed in *Sunday School Friend.*

1924

Son of Man 1924 © 1941 Covenant Book Concern; charcoal; Sallman private collection. Printed first in *CC* Old Series.

Son of Man 1924; two small black and white reproductions of pen sketches on cardboard; Wilson Galleries, Anderson University.

Up from the Grave 1924; watercolor? location unknown. Printed in *CC* Old Series.

Saved for Service 1924; pen sketch; location unknown. Printed in *CC* Old Series.

Harvest Time 1924; watercolor? location unknown. Printed in *CC* Old Series.

Christmas 1924 [1924]; pen sketch; location unknown. Printed in *FV*.

Green Forest with Lake I 1924; small oil on masonite; Everett Sallman private collection.

1925

Jesus Leaving Gethsemane 1925; pen sketch? location unknown. Printed in *FV*.

Snow-Covered Pines and Bells [1925]; pen sketch; location unknown. Printed in *FV*.

1926

Thorn-crowned Christ 1926; pencil sketch on paper; Covenant Archives.

The Ascension © 1926; large oil painting; Evangelical Covenant Church, South Bend, Indiana.

Behold the Man 1926; mixed media; Sallman Collection at Valparaiso University.

Portrait of a Man 1926; charcoal with paint touch-up; Marion Sallman private collection.

Portrait of the Rev. Gust F. Johnson 1926; charcoal on cardboard; Covenant Archives.

1927

Head of Christ 1927; charcoal on brown paper; James and Gene Sallman private collection.

1928

Clown with Flag 1928; pen sketch; signed "Elias;" location unknown. Printed in *Lightnin'*.

Tax Payers Feast and Fast 1928; two pen sketches; signed "Elias;" location unknown. Printed in *Lightnin'*.

Prayer of an Aged Minister 1928; pen sketch; location unknown. Printed in *CC* Old Series.

Woman with Corsage 1928; charcoal sketch on cardboard; Marion Sallman private collection.

1929

Young Man Kneeling on Jesus [1929]; pen sketch; signed "Elias;" location unknown. Printed in *FV*.

The Lamp of My Life 1929; pen sketch; signed "Elias;" location unknown. Printed in *FV*.

Christ Rending the Veil 1929; pen sketch; signed "Elias;" location unknown. Printed in *FV*.

Waldenström on the Radio 1929; cartoon; signed "Elias;" location unknown. Printed in *FV*.

Look and Live 1929; pen sketch; signed "Elias;" location unknown. Printed in *FV*.

The Benediction of Christian Education [1929]; pen sketch; location unknown. Printed in *CC* Old Series.

Turn the Radio On 1929; collage; pen sketch signed "Elias;" location unknown. Printed in *FV*.

Radio Audiences [1929]; collage; pen sketch unsigned; location unknown. Printed in *FV*.

Pilgrims on Their Way to Church 1929; watercolor or charcoal; signed "Elias;" location unknown. Printed in *FV*.

A Mirror for the Soul [1929]; pen sketch; location unknown. Printed in *CC* Old Series.

Japanese Woman Carrying Baby 1929; charcoal or watercolor; location unknown. Printed in *OYC* and *OJ*.

Mary and Joseph with the Baby 1929; pen sketch; signed "Elias;" Marion Sallman private collection.

1930

Riding the Pony Express 1930; pen sketch; signed "Elias;" location unknown. Printed in *OYC* and *OJ*.

Chinese Boy Working on Model Airplane 1930; pen sketch; signed "Elias;" location unknown. Printed in *OYC* and *OJ*.

Behold, I Am Alive 1930; pen sketch; signed "Elias;" Marion Sallman private collection. Printed in *OCLF*.

1932

Gypsie Girl 1932; charcoal; signed "Elias;" Helen Larson private collection. Printed in *OYC* and *OJ*.

A Birthday Party 1932; charcoal; signed "Elias;" location unknown. Printed in *OYC* and *OJ*.

Gustavus Adolphus efter Van Dyke 1932; color chalk on paper, mounted on board; Covenant Archives.

The Abyss of Ruin 1932; charcoal; signed "Elias;" location unknown. Printed for National Christian-Family Defense League, Washington, DC by the National Poster Service.

Framåt i Jesu Namn 1932; pen sketch?; signed "Elias;" location unknown.

1933

American Bible Society Exhibit (frieze of six paintings) at A Century of Progress, 1933-1934. Not extant.

Salvation Army Exhibit (frieze of 30 drawings in three-colored sepia crayon) at A Century of Progress, 1933-1934. Not extant.

Naming the Salvation Army [1933]; pencil sketch on paper on cardboard; Marion Sallman private collection.

Kneeling Man in Beam of Light 1933; charcoal sketch on heavy paper; signed "Elias;" Marion Sallman private collection.

1934

Frieze and stage artwork in Cherokee Hall, Salvation Army's Camp Shagbark, Camp Lake, Wisconsin 1934. Not extant, except for isolated pieces.

Head of Christ [1934] © Messenger Corp. 1935; color pastel; Renaissance Publishing Co., Auburn, Indiana.

Portrait of Dr. T. W. Anderson 1934; oil on canvas; Covenant Archives.

Palm Sunday 1934; charcoal; signed "Elias;" location unknown. Printed in *OYC* and *OJ*.

The Ascension 1934; large oil on masonite; Evangelical Covenant Church, Braham, Minnesota.

Sunday School Kickoff [1934]; pencil sketch on paper; Marion Sallman private collection.

Sunday School Kickoff 1934; two cartoons; location unknown. Printed in *WC*.

Portrait of Signe Lund 1934; oil on canvas; Mildred Lund private collection.

1935

Four Covenant Presidents 1935; cartoon sketch; location unknown. Printed in *CW*.

Talking about Sunday School 1935; charcoal? location unknown. Printed in *OCY*.

Head of Christ 1935; large oil; location unknown.

Portrait of the Rev. C. A. Björk 1935; oil on canvas; Covenant Archives.

Portrait of C. J. Wilson 1935; oil on canvas; Wilson Hall, North Park University.

On to 50,000 Campaign [1935]; pen and watercolor cartoon; location unknown. Printed in *WC*.

World for God Campaign [1935]; pen (and watercolor?) drawing; location unknown. Printed in *WC*.

Christmas Morning 1935; two watercolors; location unknown. Printed in *WC*.

1936

Roman Soldiers and Barabbas 1936; watercolor; location unknown. Printed in *WC*.

Horse Riders at Bethlehem 1936; two illustrations in unknown media; location unknown. Printed in *WC*.

The Blessed Mother / Our Lady of the Atonement [1936]; color pastel; Renaissance Publishing Co., Auburn, Indiana.

Woman, Why Weepeth Thou? [1936] © The Messenger Corp. 1937; color pastel; Renaissance Publishing Co., Auburn, Indiana.

1937

Head of Christ 1937; oil on masonite; Evangelical Covenant Church, Nelson, BC.

Woman with a Dog [1937]; pen sketch; location unknown. Printed in *OYC* and *OJ*.

Girl Praying 1937; two crayons or charcoals; location unknown. Printed in *WC*.

Come unto Me 1937; color sketch; location unknown. Printed on 1938 calendar for Chicago Christian Business Men's Committee.

1938

Best Seller Publicity Ads (in Chicago streetcars, buses and elsewhere); 1938–.

Miracle and Menial Tasks 1938; five charcoal sketches; location unknown. Printed in *WC*.

The Centurion of Faith 1938; two watercolors; location unknown. Printed in *WC*.

The Innkeeper 1938; watercolor; location unknown. Printed in *WC*.

Face of Young Girl 1938; possible charcoal; location unknown.

1939

The Ascension 1939; large oil on canvas; Swedish Mission Church, Iron Mountain, Michigan. Not extant.

Portrait of the Rev. F. M. Johnson 1939; oil on masonite; Covenant Archives.

Portrait of the Rev. Otto Högfeldt 1939; oil on masonite; Don and Kay Olson private collection.

1940

He Loved the Sheep [1940]; pen sketch; signed "Elias;" location unknown. Printed in CW.

Women at the Village Well [1940]; medium and location unknown. Printed in *WC.*

Service Men and Women Salute Prince of Peace 1940; charcoal; location unknown. Printed on Mission Covenant Church Christmas card to the military.

Head of Christ 1940 © K&B 1941; oil on canvas; Wilson Galleries, Anderson University.

Head of Christ 1940; oil over a print on masonite; Covenant Archives.

Christ in Gethsemane 1940; large oil on canvas; Lund Mission Covenant Church, Lund, Wisconsin. An adaptation of Hofmann.

Christ in Gethsemane 1940; large oil on canvas; originally South Chicago Evangelical Covenant Church; presently in the possession of the Central Conference of the Evangelical Covenant Church. An adaptation of Hofmann.

Christ in Gethsemane 1940; large oil on canvas; First Covenant Church, Red Wing, Minnesota. An adaptation of Hofmann.

Green Forest with Lake II 1940; oil; James and Gene Sallman private collection.

Old Covered Bridge and Mill Site–Turkey Run, Indiana 1940; watercolor; James and Gene Sallman private collection.

1941

French Bark on Reefs of Brottö at Föglö, Åland-Finland 1941; watercolor; James and Gene Sallman private collection.

Son of Man © K&B 1941; unfinished brown pen sketch on cardboard; Wilson Galleries, Anderson University.

Illustrations (circa 500) for *Thorndike Century Senior Dictionary* (Chicago: Scott Foresman, 1941).

The Ascension 1941; large oil painting; Mt. Greenwood Corps of the Salvation Army, Chicago.

Women Talking in a Garden 1941; two watercolors; location unknown. Printed in *WC.*

Puppy in a Basket 1941; watercolor; location unknown. Printed in *WC.*

Salvation Army Woman Selling Flowers 1941; charcoal or crayon; location unknown. Printed in *WC*.

Down the Cellar Passageway 1941; charcoal or crayon; location unknown. Printed in *WC*.

Telling the Easter Story 1941; charcoal or crayon; location unknown. Printed in *WC*.

Christ on the Clouds 1941 © Warner Sallman 1941; charcoal; location unknown. Printed in *WC*.

The Prince of Peace 1941 © The Salvation Army 1941; oil; Salvation Army National Headquarters, Alexandria, Virginia. Printed in *WC*.

A Bethlehem Shepherd 1941; three artworks—the second said to be an oil, the media of the other two unknown; location unknown. Printed in *WC*.

The Boy Jesus 1941 © The Salvation Army 1941; oil; Don Rose private collection. Printed in *WC*.

The Flight into Egypt © The Salvation Army 1941; oil; Salvation Army National Headquarters, Alexandria, Virginia. Printed in *WC*.

Christ in Gethsemane 1941; large oil on canvas; First Covenant Church, Fresno, California. An adaptation of Hofmann.

Christ in Gethsemane 1941; large oil on canvas; Calvary Covenant Church, Stockholm, Wisconsin. An adaptation of Hofmann.

(Christ in) Gethsemane 1941 © K&B 1942; oil on canvas; Wilson Galleries, Anderson University.

Our Redeemer 1941 © K&B 1942; charcoal on paper; Wilson Galleries, Anderson University. Printed in *WC* and on 1995 Warner Press calendar.

Crown of Thorns 1941 © Warner E. Sallman 1943; © K&B 1956; watercolor and chalk on cardboard; Wilson Galleries, Anderson University. Printed in *WC*.

Achieving with Christ 1941; watercolor and pen sketches; location unknown. Printed in *WC*.

1942

The Exodus 1942; watercolor and chalk on paper attached to cardboard; signed "Elias;" Covenant Archives.

Colonial Church 1942; watercolor and chalk? on paper attached to cardboard; Wilson Galleries, Anderson University.

Moses Meets God in the Mountain 1942; chalk and watercolor on paper; signed "Elias;" Marion Sallman private collection.

Wheat Field 1942; pastel 12 inches by 18 inches; Sandy Sallman private collection.

Christ in Gethsemane [1942]; pencil sketch on paper; Marion Sallman private collection.

Christ in the Garden of Gethsemane 1942; oil on canvas; Trinity Covenant Church, Manchester, Connecticut.

Christ at Heart's Door 1942 © K&B 1942; oil on cardboard; Wilson Galleries, Anderson University.

Christ at Heart's Door 1942 © K&B 1942; oil on canvas; Wilson Galleries, Anderson University.

The Lord Is My Shepherd / Good Shepherd 1942 © K&B 1943; oil on canvas; Wilson Galleries, Anderson University.

Head of Christ 1942 © Warner E. Sallman 1942; probable oil; location unknown. Printed in *WC*.

A Mother's Reflections 1942; three watercolors; location unknown. Printed in *WC*.

Consider the Lilies © The Salvation Army 1942; medium and location unknown. Printed in *WC*.

Thorn-crowned Christ on the World 1942; crayon and watercolor? location unknown. Printed in *WC*.

An Army on the March 1942; watercolor; location unknown. Printed in *WC*.

The Christmas Story © The Salvation Army 1942; medium and location unknown. Printed in *WC*.

The Christmas Story [1942]; unfinished oil on canvas; James and Gene Sallman private collection.

Servant of the Bethlehem Inn 1942; three crayons or charcoals; location unknown. Printed in *WC*.

The Wise Men © The Salvation Army 1942; oil; location unknown. Printed in *WC*.

Faithful unto Death © The Salvation Army 1942; medium and location unknown. Printed in *WC*.

Christ Carrying the Cross 1942 © The Salvation Army 1943; pastel; location unknown. Printed in *WC*.

1943

The Christ Triumphant 1943 © The Salvation Army 1943; medium and location unknown. Printed in *WC*.

Pilate and Claudia 1943; two watercolors; location unknown. Printed in *WC*.

The Unseen Easter Guest 1943 © The Salvation Army 1943; medium and location unknown. Printed in *WC*.

Thoughts at Christmastime 1943 © The Salvation Army 1943; medium and location unknown. Printed in *WC*.

Pilate and the Angry Crowd 1943; two watercolors; location unknown. Printed in *WC*.

Woman Journeying to Bethlehem 1943; two watercolors; location unknown. Printed in *WC*.

A Home Away from Home 1943 © The Salvation Army 1943; medium and location unknown. Printed in *WC.*

The Good Shepherd 1943; large oil painting; Bethlehem Covenant Church, Stephenson, Michigan.

The Good Shepherd 1943; large oil painting; Salvation Army Evanston Corps, Evanston, Illinois.

Peter Matson Praying at a Minnesota Haystack 1943; oil; World Missions Office, Covenant Headquarters, Chicago.

Girls' Bible Class 1943; charcoal and pen sketch; location unknown. Printed in *CF.*

The Dial of WMBI 1943; two pen sketches; location unknown. Printed in *Moody Monthly.*

1944

The Crusading Christ [1944]; oil or watercolor; location unknown. Printed in *CA.*

The Compassionate Christ 1944; pen and charcoal? location unknown. Printed in *CA* and *OCY.*

Lest We Forget 1944 © Warner Sallman 1944; oil. location unknown. Printed in *WC.*

Madonna and Child / The Babe of Bethlehem 1944 © Warner Sallman 1944; © The Salvation Army 1944? oil; Salvation Army National Headquarters, Alexandria, Virginia. Printed in *WC.*

(The) Boy Christ / My Father's World 1944 © K&B 1945; oil on canvas; Wilson Galleries, Anderson University.

People Going to Church 1944; oil on canvas; Wilson Galleries, Anderson University.

Behold I Send You Forth 1944; oil on canvas on board; Bob Jones University, Greenville, South Carolina.

First Covenant Church, Chicago, Edifices 1944; pen sketches of three edifices of the First Mission Covenant Church, Chicago, printed in the church's 75th Anniversary booklet.

1945

Christ at Dawn 1945 © K&B 1945; oil on canvas; Wilson Galleries, Anderson University.

Boy Christ Sketches © K&B 1945; nine small pen sketches from *The Boy Christ* (1944 © K&B 1945) on cardboard; Wilson Galleries, Anderson University. Printed in Ellis, *Story of Sallman's "Boy Christ."*

Go Ye 1945; black and white sketch on masonite; Covenant Archives.

Ye Men of Athens 1945; pastel 12 inches by 18 inches; Sandy Sallman private collection.

1946

Tis Easter, Tis Easter [1946]; pen sketch; location unknown. Printed in *OCLF*.

(Christ in) Gethsemane 1946 © K&B 1946; pen sketch on paper attached to cardboard; Wilson Galleries, Anderson University.

(Christ in) Gethsemane 1946 © K&B 1946; photocopy of pen sketch with whiting touch-up; on paper attached to cardboard; Wilson Galleries, Anderson University.

Christ at Heart's Door 1946 © K&B 1946; pen sketch on paper attached to cardboard; Wilson Galleries, Anderson University.

Christ at Heart's Door 1946 © K&B 1946; photocopy of pen sketch with whiting touch-up; on paper attached to cardboard; Wilson Galleries, Anderson University.

The Lord Is My Shepherd / Good Shepherd 1946 © K&B 1946; pen sketch on paper attached to cardboard; Wilson Galleries, Anderson University.

The Lord Is My Shepherd / Good Shepherd 1946 © K&B 1946; photocopy of pen sketch with whiting touch-up; on paper attached to cardboard; Wilson Galleries, Anderson University.

(The) Boy Christ 1946 © K&B 1946; pen sketch on paper attached to cardboard; Wilson Galleries, Anderson University.

(The) Boy Christ 1946 © K&B 1946; photocopy of pen sketch with whiting touch-up; on paper attached to cardboard; Wilson Galleries, Anderson University.

Christ at Dawn 1946 © K&B 1946; pen sketch on paper attached to cardboard; Wilson Galleries, Anderson University.

Christ at Dawn 1946 © K&B 1946; photocopy of pen sketch with whiting touch-up; on paper attached to cardboard; Wilson Galleries, Anderson University.

Christ of the Campus 1946; small oil and watercolor on glass; The Wesley Foundation, The University of Alabama, Tuscaloosa, Alabama.

Christ of the Harvest Fields 1946; watercolor? Sallman Collection at Valparaiso University.

The Children's Friend [1946]; pen sketch; signed "Elias;" location unknown. Printed in *OCLF*.

Jesus, the Children's Friend 1946; unfinished pencil, watercolor, and gouache sketch on cardboard; Wilson Galleries, Anderson University.

Jesus, the Children's Friend 1946 © K&B 1947; oil on canvas; Wilson Galleries, Anderson University. The face was marketed separately as *Portrait of Christ*.

Jesus, the Children's Friend 1946 © K&B 1947; black and white reproduction with paint; on paper attached to cardboard; Wilson Galleries; Anderson University.

His Presence 1946 © K&B 1947;[1] large oil on canvas; Wilson Galleries, Anderson University.

Head of Christ in Simulated Glass 1946 © K&B 1946; watercolor and pen; location unknown.

1947

Let's Go to Church 1947; watercolor on cardboard; Wilson Galleries, Anderson University.

Head of Christ 1947; pastel over a sepia print; James and Gene Sallman private collection.

We Would See Jesus [1947]; watercolor on cardboard; Marion Sallman private collection.

We Would See Jesus 1947 © K&B 1948;[2] oil on canvas; Wilson Galleries, Anderson University.

Christ Knocking at the Door 1947; oil on canvas on board; First Covenant Church, Fort Dodge, Iowa. An adaptation of Zabateri.

The Nativity (of Christ) [1947]; pencil sketch on paper; Marion Sallman private collection.

The Nativity (of Christ) 1947 © K&B 1948; watercolor or chalk on board; Wilson Galleries, Anderson University.

1948

Kenora–Canada 1948; watercolor; James and Gene Sallman private collection.

(Mary the) Mother of Christ 1948 © K&B 1948; oil on canvas; Wilson Galleries, Anderson University.

The Carpenter of Nazareth / Jesus the Carpenter [1948]; red pencil sketch on paper; Marion Sallman private collection.

The Carpenter of Nazareth 1948[3] © K&B 1948 & 1951;[4] watercolor and chalk on cardboard; Wilson Galleries, Anderson University.

The Holy Family 1948; large color chalk on canvas; James and Gene Sallman private collection.

Follow Thou Me 1948 © K&B 1949;[5] oil on canvas; Wilson Galleries, Anderson University.

Christ Looking Down 1948; brown chalk with white on paper; Marion Sallman private collection.

D. L. Moody Sketches [1948]; twenty-seven sketches in charcoal and quoache on cardboard with transparencies; Moody Bible Institute, Chicago.

1949

The Lord's Supper 1949 © K&B 1949; oil on canvas; Wilson Galleries, Anderson University.

He Leadeth Me 1949 © K&B 1951; watercolor and colored chalk; Wilson Galleries, Anderson University.

Indian Trail Tree 1949; color chalk on masonite; Covenant Archives.

Head of Christ 1949; black chalk on burlap; James and Gene Sallman private collection.

1950

Christ Our Pilot [1950]; pencil sketch; James and Gene Sallman private collection.

Christ Our Pilot 1950 © K&B 1950; oil on canvas; Wilson Galleries, Anderson University.

Prince of Peace © K&B 1950; oil; location unknown.

Sacred Heart of Jesus [© K&B 1950]; oil with watercolor; location unknown.

Mary the Mother of Christ 1950; large color chalk on paper attached to board; Covenant Archives.

Head of Christ 1950; chalk with paint touch-up on masonite; Immanuel Covenant Church, Chicago.

Christ at Heart's Door 1950; large oil on canvas; Dawson Covenant Church, Dawson, Minnesota.

Feed My Sheep 1950; medium and location unknown. Printed in *The Upper Room*.

Mother Holding Baby 1950; charcoal; location unknown. Printed in *CHo*.

1951

Christ Our Pilot 1951; color chalk on black paper; James and Gene Sallman private collection.

Christ Setting a Man Free 1951; black chalk with white paint on brown paper; James and Gene Sallman private collection.

He Arose © K&B 1951; oil? location unknown.

Walk in the Light 1951; large oil on canvas; All Faith Chapel, Illinois Youth Center, St. Charles, Illinois.

Thine Is the Power [1951]; pencil and pen sketch on paper; Marion Sallman private collection.

Thine Is the Power 1951; oil; Covenant Archives. Originally entitled *The Christ of Power*.

Teach Me Thy Way [1951]; pencil sketch on paper; Marion Sallman private collection.

Teach Me Thy Way 1951 © K&B 1952; oil on canvas; Wilson Galleries, Anderson University.

Follow Thou Me 1951; chalk; Polytechnic Methodist Church, Fort Worth, Texas.

1952

Rabboni [1952]; colored pencil on cardboard; Marion Sallman private colection.

Behold the Lord 1952 © K&B 1953; watercolor on cardboard; Wilson Galleries, Anderson University.

The Son of God [1952]; pencil sketch on paper; Marion Sallman private collection.

The Son of God / Jesus Was a Little Boy / Behold My Mother 1952 © K&B 1952; oil on stock; Wilson Galleries, Anderson University.

Thine Is the Victory! 1952; watercolor with pen on paper mounted on cardboard with a border; Wilson Galleries, Anderson University.

The Ascension of Christ © 1952; large oil on canvas; First Covenant Church, Iron Mountain, Michigan.

Head of Christ 1952; watercolor; Newell and Gladys Johnson private collection.

I Have Overcome the World 1952; revised 1959; large oil on canvas; First United Methodist Church, Mason City, Iowa.

The Nativity Scene 1952; three-sectioned stained glass window; Children's Chapel, Methodist Children's Home Society, Detroit, Michigan.

Jesus Blessing the Loaves and Fishes 1952; stained glass window; Children's Chapel, Methodist Children's Home Society, Detroit, Michigan.

Jesus with the Children 1952; stained glass window; Children's Chapel, Methodist Children's Home Society, Detroit, Michigan.

Christ Our Pilot 1952; stained glass window; Children's Chapel, Methodist Children's Home Society, Detroit, Michigan.

The Children of the World 1952; eleven stained glass windows; Children's Chapel, Methodist Children's Home Society, Detroit, Michigan.

He Careth for You 1952; crayon; James and Gene Sallman private collection.

Christ Our Pilot 1952; chalk; Polytechnic Methodist Church, Fort Worth, Texas.

1953

Christ Knocking at Heart's Door 1953; large oil painting; Evangelical Covenant Church, Norway, Michigan.

The Annunciation 1953 © K&B 1953; watercolor on cardboard; Wilson Galleries, Anderson University.

Behold My Mother 1953; chalk; James and Gene Sallman private collection.

Portrait of Otto Schnering 1953; oil; Ann Schnering private collection.

1954

Portrait of King Gustaf VI Adolf 1954; oil; Drottningholm Palace, Stockholm, Sweden.

He Careth for You 1954 © K&B 1954; oil on canvas; Wilson Galleries, Anderson University.

Resurrection Morn 1954 © K&B 1954; oil on masonite; Wilson Galleries, Anderson University.

The Light That Shineth [1954]; pencil sketch on paper; Marion Sallman private collection.

The Light That Shineth 1954 © K&B 1954; oil on masonite; Wilson Galleries, Anderson University.

Ready to Go–Ready to Stay–! [1954]; pencil sketch on paper; Marion Sallman private collection.

Ready to Go–Ready to Stay–! 1954 © K&B 1954; oil on mounted canvas board; Wilson Galleries, Anderson University.

Mary and Baby in Manger 1954 © K&B 1954; watercolor and paint on cardboard; Wilson Galleries, Anderson University.

Mary and Martha with Jesus © 1954; large oil painting; Bethany Methodist Home, Chicago.

1955

Jesus, the Light of the World 1955 © K&B 1956;[7] oil on canvas; Wilson Galleries, Anderson University.

Madonna and Christ Child / The Baby Jesus 1955 © K&B 1956; oil on board; Wilson Galleries, Anderson University.

1956

Head of Christ 1956; large oil on canvas; originally Edgewater Covenant Church, Chicago; presently owned by Central Conference of Evangelical Covenant Church and on loan to the Broadway Covenant Church, Rockford, Illinois.

The Little Lord Jesus 1956 ©K&B 1956; oil on canvas; Wilson Galleries, Anderson University.

Jesus of Nazareth I 1956 © K&B 1956; oil on canvas on masonite; Wilson Galleries, Anderson University.

Peace Be Unto You 1956 © K&B 1956; color chalk on casein/paper; Wilson Galleries, Anderson University.

Forward with Christ [1956]; pencil sketch on paper; Marion Sallman private collection.

Forward with Christ 1956 © K&B 1956; watercolor on cardboard; Wilson Galleries, Anderson University.

In Remembrance of Me 1956 © K&B 1956; charcoal on board; Wilson Galleries, Anderson University.

In Remembrance of Me 1956; colored drawing (reproduction?) on paper attached to cardboard; in a blue frame; Wilson Galleries, Anderson University.

The Bible Speaks Today 1956; poster drawing; location unknown. Printed in *Bible Society Record*.

1957

Jean Sibelius 1957; large oil; Covenant Archives.

Power and Glory / Thine Is the Kingdom (Power) 1957 © K&B 1958; large oil on canvas; Wilson Galleries, Anderson University.

Girl at Bedside Praying 1957; watercolor on cardboard; Wilson Galleries, Anderson University.

Christ at Prayer 1957 © K&B 1958; charcoal on cardboard; Marion Sallman private collection.

Christ Looking at the City [1957]; media and location unknown. Printed for Best Seller Publicity Campaign.

Indian Trail Tree 1957; watercolor; Dr. Robert and Adrian Swanson private collection.

1958

Look unto Me 1958 © K&B 1958; oil on canvas; Wilson Galleries, Anderson University.

It Is Finished 1958 © K&B 1958; watercolor, chalk, and pen on cardboard; Wilson Galleries, Anderson University.

Christ on Easter Hill 1958; watercolor, chalk, and pen sketch on cardboard; Wilson Galleries, Anderson University.

The Holy Communion 1958 © K&B 1958; watercolor, chalk, and pen sketch on cardboard; Wilson Galleries, Anderson University.

Abraham Lincoln 1958 © K&B 1958; oil on canvas; Wilson Galleries, Anderson University.

Cedars of Lebanon 1958; oil; Charles Bates private collection.

The Great Physician © Warner E. Sallman 1958; © Iowa Methodist Hospital 1960; large oil painting; Iowa Methodist Medical Center, Des Moines, Iowa.

1959

Jesus Our Savior 1959 © K&B 1959; oil on canvas; Wilson Galleries, Anderson University.

Jesus Our Savior 1959; chalk on board; Trinity Evangelical Covenant Church, Oak Lawn, Illinois.

His Presence 1959; paint touch-up on a print 1946 © K&B 1947; First United Methodist Church, Mason City, Iowa.

Up From the Grave He Arose 1959; colored chalk on paper with cardboard frame; Wilson Galleries, Anderson University.

Face of Our Lord in Space 1959; color chalk and watercolor on cardboard; Wilson Galleries, Anderson University.

Face of Our Lord 1959 © K&B 1961; cut-out reproduction of face only on blue velvet cardboard; Wilson Galleries, Anderson University.

Springs of Grace Are Streaming 1959; colored chalk on cardboard; Wilson Galleries, Anderson University.

Portrait of the Rev. D. L. Moody 1959; oil; Moody Bible Institute, Chicago.

Portrait of the Rev. Frederic E. Pamp 1959; charcoal sketch; Christopher and Susan Norborg private collection.

Portrait of the Rev. C. J. Andrews 1959; charcoal sketch; Norman Andrews Jr. private collection.

Portrait of the Rev. C. V. Bowman 1959; charcoal sketch; Keith and Alpha Olson private collection.

Portrait of the Rev. F. O. Kling II 1959; charcoal sketch; Covenant Archives.

Portrait of the Rev. K. K. Jacobson [1959]; charcoal sketch; location unknown.

Portrait of the Rev. Paul F. Erickson [1959]; charcoal sketch location unknown.

Portrait of the Rev. Arthur N. Johnson [1959]; charcoal sketch; originally in Everett Sallman private collection; given to Covenant Archives in July 1997.

1960
Study to Show Thyself Approved 1960 © K&B 1960; oil on canvas; Wilson Galleries, Anderson University.

The Youth Christ 1960 © K&B 1960; oil on canvas; Wilson Galleries, Anderson University.

Baptized in Christ 1960; large oil on canvas; North Side Christian Church (Disciples of Christ), Chicago.

The Master Healer 1960 © 1961; large oil on canvas; United Hospital Center, Clarksburg, West Virginia.

His Presence [1960]; red pencil sketch on paper with overlay; Marion Sallman private collection.

His Presence 1960 © K&B 1947; large oil on canvas; originally Evangelical Covenant Church, Escanabas, Michigan; presently at United Evangelical Covenant Church, Gladstone, Michigan.

God Is Love 1960; color chalk; Covenant Archives.

Head of Christ 1960 © K&B 1941; oil–possibly over a print–on masonite. Northbrook Evangelical Covenant Church, Northbrook, Illinois.

For God So Loved the World 1960; mural (in oil?); Woodlawn Baptist Church, 6207 University Avenue, Chicago.

1961

The Resurrected Lord 1961; colored chalk on cardboard; Wilson Galleries, Anderson University.

Christ at Prayer on Globe 1961; watercolor and chalk on paper; Wilson Galleries, Anderson University.

Not My Will But Thine 1961; watercolor and chalk on paper; Wilson Galleries, Anderson University.

The Emmaus Road 1961; watercolor and chalk sketch on light cardboard; Wilson Galleries, Anderson University.

The Road to Emmaus 1961 © K&B 1961; oil on canvas; Wilson Galleries, Anderson University.

The Road to Emmaus 1961; oil; Myrtle Anderson private collection.

The Road to Emmaus [1961]; oil; originally in Sylvia Peterson private collection; location unknown.

Road to Emmaus Sketches [1961]; four pencil sketches on paper; Marion Sallman private collection.

Road to Emmaus Sketches 1961 © K&B 1961; eight pen sketches; location of seven unknown; *The Ascension at Bethany* (#8) on cardboard is in the Wilson Galleries, Anderson University. Printed in Bates, *Road to Emmaus*.

Mary and Martha with Jesus 1961 © K&B 1962; watercolor on board; Wilson Galleries, Anderson University.

1962

Portrait of Bishop William C. Martin 1962; oil; location unknown.

Abraham on the Plains of Mamre 1962; oil on canvas on board; Wilson Galleries, Anderson University.

Pleading Savior 1962; oil on canvas; Wilson Galleries, Anderson University.

Lord and Master 1962 © K&B 1962; brown pen sketch; Wilson Galleries, Anderson University. Printed on Bates, *Survival Power*.

Lord and Master 1962 © K&B 1962; brown sketch (reproduction?) with black pen on cardboard; Wilson Galleries, Anderson University.

Lord and Master 1962 © K&B 1962; watercolor on cardboard with transparency; Wilson Galleries, Anderson University. Printed on Bates, *Survival Power*.

The Blind Beggar Healed 1962; sketch composition; James and Gene Sallman private collection.

Follow Thou Me 1962; charcoal and colored chalk on brown pressed board; First United Methodist Church, Mason City, Iowa.

The Smiling Christ 1962; oil on canvas; Marion Sallman private collection.

1963

We Ought to Pray 1963[8] © K&B 1963; crayon and paint on paper attached to cardboard; Wilson Galleries, Anderson University.

Jesus of Nazareth II 1963 © K&B 1963; oil on canvas; Wilson Galleries, Anderson University.

Christ Healing the Blind Beggar 1963 © Warner Sallman 1963; oil on canvas on masonite; Belmont United Methodist Church, Belmont, Massachusetts.

Abraham Lincoln and Son 1963; watercolor; Everett Sallman private collection. Larger oil was also painted; date and location unknown.

Portrait of Harry Denman 1963; rough charcoal sketch; James and Gene Sallman private collection.

Portrait of Harry Denman 1963; oil on canvas; Upper Room Chapel and Museum, Nashville, Tennessee.

Power and Glory 1963; large brown and white chalk on paper; Northern Baptist Theological Seminary, Lombard, Illinois.

1964

Head of Christ © K&B 1964; black and white photocopy? on paper in a cardboard frame; Wilson Galleries, Anderson University.

Head of Christ 1964 © Messenger Corp. 1935; oil on masonite; Salvation Army Central Territory Headquarters, Des Plaines, Illinois.

Head of Christ 1964; charcoal on brown paper; James and Gene Sallman private collection.

The Just One 1964 © K&B 1964; oil on canvas; Marion Sallman private collection.

Jesus in Gethsemane [1964]; pencil sketch on paper; Marion Sallman private collection.

The Story of Gethsemane 1964 © K&B 1964; oil on canvas; Wilson Galleries, Anderson University.

Story of Gethsemane Sketches [1964]; five unfinished pen sketches on white paper; Wilson Galleries, Anderson University.

Glory to God in the Highest 1964 ©K&B 1964; watercolor on cardboard; Wilson Galleries, Anderson University.

Face of Christ above Mary and Christchild [1964]; two charcoal sketches on brown paper; James and Gene Sallman private collection.

Thorn-crowned Christ above Mary and Christchild 1964; two color chalks on paper; James and Gene Sallman private collection.

Christ Our Pilot 1964; watercolor and chalk? with qouache; Rich Port YMCA, La Grange, Illinois.

Portrait of Dr. John Thompson 1964; oil; First United Methodist Church (Chicago Temple), Chicago.

Portrait of the Rev. Charles Ray Goff 1964; oil; First United Methodist Church (Chicago Temple), Chicago.

1965

The Triumphant Christ [1965]; pencil sketch; Marion Sallman private collection.

The Triumphant Christ 1965; large oil on canvas; South Jacksonville Presbyterian Church, Jacksonville, Florida. Mosaic of this artwork done for St. Luke's Hospital, Jacksonville, Florida; date unknown.

Safe in the Arms of Jesus [1965]; photographed sketch? James and Gene Sallman private collection.

Safe in the Arms of Jesus 1965; small oil; Grace United Methodist Church, South Bend, Indiana.

1966

Portrait of Jesus 1966 © K&B 1966; oil on masonite; Wilson Galleries, Anderson University.

Jesus in the Garden 1966; colored chalk on cardboard; Wilson Galleries, Anderson University.

Shepherds Outside Stable 1966; watercolor and pen sketch on cardboard; Wilson Galleries, Anderson University.

Bright Stars in the Darkness 1966; watercolor or chalk on cardboard; Wilson Galleries, Anderson University.

Passion-Easter Sketches 1966; unfinished sketches in black pen on cardboard; Wilson Galleries, Anderson University.

1967

Portrait of Jesus 1967; charcoal sketch on brown paper; James and Gene Sallman private collection.

Portrait of Jesus [1967]; colored pen sketch on paper; Wilson Galleries, Anderson University.

Portrait of the Rev. Robert Bruce Pierce 1967; oil; First United Methodist Church (Chicago Temple), Chicago.

Head of Christ 1967; colored crayon; James and Gene Sallman private collection.

Head of Christ 1967; oil; Covenant Village, Northbrook, Illinois.

Behold He Cometh 1967; large oil on canvas; First Evangelical Covenant Church, Rockford, Illinois.

Christ Blessing Young People 1967; blue pen sketch on paper; Marion Sallman private collection.

Madonna and Christ Child 1967; colored chalk; Evelyne Gustafson private collection.

1968

A Tree 1968; black pen sketch with whiting on cardboard; translucent overlay of green chalk or qouache; Wilson Galleries, Anderson University.

Portrait of Bishop W. Kenneth Pope 1968; unfinished oil on canvas; Bridwell Library, Perkins School of Theology, Dallas, Texas.

Portrait of Dr. Gaston Foote 1968; unfinished oil on canvas; Fred L. Foote private collection.

Works of Unknown Date

Self Portrait; watercolor; Marion Sallman private collection.

Self Portrait; pen sketch; Everett Sallman private collection.

Going to Julotta; large unmounted oil; Everett Sallman private collection.

Boathouse on a Lake; small oil on canvas; Everett Sallman private collection.

Head of Patriot Soldier; pencil sketch on paper; Marion Sallman private collection.

Military Salutes the Christchild; pencil sketch on paper; Marion Sallman private collection.

Christ Extending Hand to Soldier; pencil sketch on paper; Marion Sallman private collection.

Management and Labor Shaking Hands; pencil sketch on paper; Marion Sallman private collection.

Man and Woman Seated on Couch; pencil sketch on paper; Marion Sallman private collection.

Portrait of Charles Lindberg; sketch in black chalk on paper on cardboard; James and Gene Sallman private collection.

Portrait of Abraham Lincoln; charcoal sketch on brown paper; James and Gene Sallman private collection.

David Nyvall Portraits; two black paint sketches on paper; Marion Sallman private collection.

Portrait of Fred Bates Jr.; oil; Elaine Bates private collection.

Son of Man; pencil sketch on paper in a circular frame; Marion Sallman private collection.

Son of Man; pencil sketch on off-white paper; James and Gene Sallman private collection.

Head of Christ; three pen sketches on white paper; James and Gene Sallman private collection.

Crown of Thorns; small black and white reproduction of pen sketch on cardboard; Wilson Galleries, Anderson University.

Christ in Gethsemane; charcoal sketch on brown paper; James and Gene Sallman private collection.

Christ Our Pilot; charcoal sketch on brown paper; James and Gene Sallman private collection.

Boy at Bedside Praying; collage; brown chalk on paper; Wilson Galleries, Anderson University.

Teach Me Thy Way; charcoal sketch on brown paper; James and Gene Sallman private collection.

Men on Road to Emmaus; unfinished oil on canvas; Patsy Needham private collection.

Mary Holding Baby Jesus; pencil sketch on paper; Marion Sallman private collection.

Christ in the Clouds; pencil sketch on paper; Marion Sallman private collection.

Jesus Walking with Boy and Girl; pencil sketch on paper; Marion Sallman private collection.

Missionary Doctor and Nurse; pencil sketch on paper; Marion Sallman private collection.

Folded Hands; black pencil sketch on paper; Marion Sallman private collection.

Folded Hands; purple pencil sketch on paper; Marion Sallman private collection.

Unidentified Woman; pencil sketch on paper; Marion Sallman private collection.

Young People with Flags; pen sketch on cardboard; Wilson Galleries, Anderson University.

People Approaching Colonial Church; watercolor with transparency on cardboard; Wilson Galleries, Anderson University.

And the Books Were Opened; unfinished pen and crayon sketch on cardboard; Wilson Galleries, Anderson University.

O Lord Our God; colored pen sketch on cardboard; Wilson Galleries, Anderson University.

Pilate Offering Jesus to Mob; pen sketch on white paper attached to canvas panel; Wilson Galleries, Anderson University.

Wise Men and Shepherds Approaching Heavenly Angel; watercolor and pen sketch on cardboard in a paper frame; Wilson Galleries, Anderson University.

Head of Christ against Stained Glass; watercolor; location unknown.

Map of Palestine with Christmas sketches; chalk and perhaps paint–all brown; Wilson Galleries, Anderson University.

Bible Class Outline; color sketch on brown paper; James and Gene Sallman private collection.

He Is Risen; unfinished watercolor on cardboard with transparency; Wilson Galleries, Anderson University.

Pine Forest and Mountains; chalk on plywood; Marion Sallman private collection.

The Flight into Egypt; chalk on pressed board; Everett Sallman private collection.

Mary and the Baby; circular color chalk on paper on board; Everett Sallman private collection.

Mary with Baby in Cloak; circular color chalk on canvas; James and Gene Sallman private collection.

Jesus and the Children of the World; watercolor on paper; Marion Sallman private collection.

Total inventory as of 1 July 1998 consisted of over five hundred individual works, not counting illustrations done for the *Thorndike Dictionary* (1941) and the many chalks–mainly of the Christ head–drawn before live audiences.

[1] Painting says © 1946, but Kriebel and Bates Inventory list dates the © 4 August 1947.

[2] Painting says © 1947, but Kriebel and Bates Inventory list dates the © 8 April 1948.

[3] Earlier signature visible on the picture with the date 1946; at the right is a signature with the date 1948.

[4] The painting contains a copyright date of 1948 by K&B; on the K&B Inventory list the © date is 21 November 1951.

[5] Painting says © 1948, but Kriebel and Bates Inventory list dates the © 10 January 1949.

[6] This title was the one given in Madelon Golden, "*Head of Christ* Artist Finishes New Painting," *Chicago Sun-Times,* (14 June 1952), 10.

[7] Painting says © 1955, but Kriebel and Bates Inventory list dates the © 16 January 1956.

[8] The identification of this work with the K&B © 1963 *We Ought to Pray* is likely, but not certain.

Bibliography

Adler, Jerry. "The Faces of Jesus." *Newsweek* (24 December 1979): 51.

Adolph, R. Edmund. "The World's Famous Modern Pictures." *The Ladies Home Journal* 27/16 (1 December 1910): 10-11.

Alexander, Mrs. Charles M. and J. Kennedy Maclean. *Charles M. Alexander: A Romance of Song and Soul-Winning*, 3rd ed. London: Marshall Brothers, 1920.

Anderson, Margaret. "His Subject Shaped His Life." *The War Cry* Central 2136 (9 December 1961): 7-8, 10.

Anderson, Philip J. and Dag Blank, eds. *Swedish-American Life in Chicago: Cultural and Urban Aspects of an Immigrant People, 1850-1930.* Urbana and Chicago: University of Illinois Press, 1992.

"Art Guild Honors Artist." *North Park College News*, 6 January 1984, 1, 4.

Art Index. New York: H. W. Wilson Co. 1929-.

Baetjer, Katherine. *European Paintings in the Metropolitan Museum of Art.* 3 Volumes. New York: The Metropolitan Museum of Art, 1980.

Bailey, Albert E. "Religion in Art." *Our Covenant Youth* 14/29 (16 July 1933): 1; 14/31 (30 July 1933): 1; 14/34 (20 August 1933): 1; 14/39 (24 September 1933): 1; 14/42 (15 October 1933): 3; 15/9 (4 March 1934): 3; 15/19 (13 May 1934): 3; 15/28 (15 July 1934): 3; 16/40 (6 October 1935): 3; 16/45 (10 November 1935): 1.

Bankson, Ben. "Happy Birthday, Mr. Sallman!" *The Covenant Companion* 56/8 (21 April 1967): 8-9, 26.

Barry, Edward. "Jesus of Nazareth by Louis Jambor." *Chicago Sunday Tribune Grafic Magazine* (10 April 1949): 8, 14.

———. "Christ as Depicted by Modern Artists." *Chicago Sunday Tribune Grafic Magazine* (24 February 1952): 6-7.

Bates, F. M. "Head of Christ." *Time* (20 December 1948): 6, 8.

———. *Story of Sallman's "Follow Thou Me."* [Indianapolis]: Kriebel and Bates, 1949.

———. *Road to Emmaus.* Indianapolis: Kriebel and Bates, 1961.

———. *Survival Power.* Indianapolis: Kriebel and Bates, 1962.

Baylor, Bruce. "A Man's Artist." *Sunday School Promoter* (May 1943): 24-29.

Bergsten, Tennessee. "After 55 Years–Still a Silent Witness." *Power for Living* 50/4 (6 September 1992): 2-3, 6-7.

Bevis, Katherine. "He Painted a Religious Masterpiece." *Sunday School Messenger* (21 March 1965): 4-5.

Bibliographie d'Histoire de l'Art. Nancy Cedex: Vandoeuvre/Santa Monica, CA: J. Paul Getty Trust, 1991-. [Continuation of *Repertoire International de la Litterature de l'Art*].

Bird, William L. "Sallman and His *Head of Christ.*" *The Christian Advocate* 118/10 (11 March 1943): 12-13.

Buechner, Thomas S. *Norman Rockwell: A Sixty Year Retrospective.* New York: Harry N. Abrams, 1972.

"Christ in Modern Art." *The Ladies Home Journal* 24/1 (December 1906): 44-45.

de la Croix, Horst and Richard G. Tansey. *Gardner's Art Through the Ages I-II.* 6th ed. New York: Harcourt Brace Jovanovich, 1975.

Crumm, David. "Debating Jesus' Place: Student Sues to Remove Portrait from Hall." *Detroit Free Press*, 11 January 1993, 1A, 8A.

Daniel, Howard. *Encyclopaedia of Themes and Subjects in Painting.* New York: Harry N. Abrams, [1971].

Doré, Paul Gustave. *The Bible in Pictures.* New York: William H. Wise & Co., 1934.

———. *The Bible Illustrated.* New York: Pilsbury Publishers, 1951.

Duning, Carl H. *Christ in Every Purse.* Richmond, IN: Nicholson Press, 1948.

Eckhardt, Susan. "Covenanters Celebrate the Sallman Legacy." *The Covenant Companion* 73/3 (March 1984): 40-41.

Ellis, Howard W. *Story of Sallman's "Head of Christ."* [Chicago]: Kriebel and Bates, 1944.

———. *Story of Sallman's "Gethsemane."* [Chicago]: Kriebel and Bates, 1944.

———. *Story of Sallman's "Good Shepherd."* [Chicago]: Kriebel and Bates, 1944.

———. *Story of Sallman's "Christ at Door."* [Chicago]: Kriebel and Bates, 1944.

———. *Story of Sallman's "Boy Christ."* [Chicago]: Kriebel and Bates, 1945.

———. "Art with a Message III: How to Paint in Public." *Covenant Youth Today* 3/3 (17 March 1957): part 3, 2-7.

Erickson, Rolf H. "Swedish-American Artists and Their Chicago Exhibitions." In *Swedish-American Life in Chicago.* Eds. Philip J. Anderson and Dag Blank. Urbana and Chicago: University of Illinois Press, 1992, pp. 161-177.

Everett, Glenn D. "Story of a Great Picture." *The Link* 16/4 (April 1958): 12-17, 62-63.

Eversole, Finley, ed. *Christian Faith and the Contemporary Arts.* Nashville and New York: Abingdon Press, 1962.

Fairbanks, Arthur. "The Greatest Pictures of the World." *The Ladies Home Journal* 27/5 (April 1910): 14-15.

Farbman, N. R. and Donald Burke. "Congo Mission: Modern Missionaries Combine Faith with Medicine and Education." *Life* (2 June 1947): 105-113.

Francis, Dale. "Protestant Revolt Sent Religious Art into a Continuous Decline." *The* (San Francisco) *Monitor*, 99/7, 1 June 1956, 1.

Gardner, Jane. "Mental Image Is Model for Christ Sketch." *Chicago Sunday Tribune*, 6 June 1954, Neighborhood Section, part 3, 1-2.

Gest, J. H. "The Greatest Pictures of the World." *The Ladies Home Journal* 27/3 (February 1910): 16-17.

Golden, Madelon. "*Head of Christ* Artist Finishes New Painting." *Chicago Sun-Times*, 14 June 1952, 10.

Hamel, Maurice. *The Salons of 1905*. Translated by Paul Villars. Paris and New York: Goupil & Co. [Manzi, Joyant & Co.], 1905.

Hamilton, Merle J. "Religion at the Fair." *The War Cry* Central 650 (10 June 1933): 9-10.

Harris, Betty. "Warner Sallman's Vision of Christ." *The War Cry* 109/10 (13 May 1989): 3-7.

Haskin, Dorothy C. "The Man Who Painted a Manly Head of Christ: Warner Sallman" in Dorothy C. Haskin, *Christians You Would Like to Know*. Grand Rapids: Zondervan Publishing House, 1954, 65-72.

Hawkinson, James R. "A Genuine Child of God." *The Covenant Companion* 81/7 (July 1992): back cover.

Hedstrand, G. F. "The Twelve in the New Testament, in Tradition, and in Art." *The Covenant Companion* Old Series 12/12 (25 March 1933): 5-7.

———. "Without a Halo." *The Covenant Companion* Old Series 12/13 (1 April 1933): 3.

———. "25th Anniversary of an Inspiration." *Covenant Weekly* 38/4 (28 January 1949): 1, 6.

Henry, Carl F. H. "Sallman Made the Deadline." *Power* (19 September 1943): 4-5, 7.

———. "Sallman Made the Deadline." *The Evangelical Beacon* 13/4 (26 October 1943): 3-4.

———. "Evangelical Piety and Christian Art." *Christianity Today* 11/11 (3 March 1958): 26, 32.

Hieston, Lilian Hayden. "A Painter of the Christ." *Our Covenant Youth* 12/43 (25 October 1931): 1.

"His Likeness." *Newsweek* (7 July 1947): 79.

Ives, Halsey C. "The Greatest Pictures of the World." *The Ladies Home Journal* 27/4 (March 1910): 10-11.

Jeschke, Mrs. William. "Sallman's Paintings of the Master." *The* (General Conference Baptist) *Annual* 2 (1947): 20-21, 46.

Johnson, Gerard. "Friends Fete Artist on Sixtieth Birthday." *Covenant Weekly* 41/20 (16 May 1952): 3.

Johnson, Mae. "Art for the Gospel's Sake." *The Baptist Herald* 20/8 (15 April 1942): 4-5.

Johnson, Paul E. "Young People Present Mural to Their Church." *The Covenant Companion* Old Series 5/6 (June 1926): 23.

[Keeler, Lewis]. "Great Masters and Their Paintings." Article series. *The War Cry* Central 736 (2 February 1935); 737 (9 February 1935); 739 (23 February 1935); 742 (16 March 1935); 744 (6 April 1935); 749 (4 May 1935); 750 (11 May 1935); 753 (1 June 1935); 756 (22 June 1935); 757 (29 June 1935); 760 (20 July 1935).

Knudson, Sylvia Peterson—see Sylvia E. Peterson.

Larson, Sylvia Knudson—see Sylvia E. Peterson.

Lauber, Jane W. "Are We Losing Our Artistic Heritage?" *Christianity Today* 10/23 (2 September 1966): 24.

Lindborg, Olga. "Choosing Pictures That Illustrate Bible Stories I-II." *The Teacher's Companion* 2/4 (September 1923): 5-6; 2/5 (October 1923): 6-7.

———. "Elias." *Our Covenant* 4 (1930): 11-14.

———. "Another Picture of Jesus." *Our Covenant* 17 (1942): 67-73.

Lockerbie, Sarah. "The Ascension–On Sailcloth." *The South Bend Tribune Magazine* (17 April 1960): 8-10.

Lundbom, Jack R. "Warner E. Sallman: A Centenary Tribute to a Covenant Artist." *The Covenant Companion* 81/7 (July 1992): 8-11, 40.

———. "Warner Sallman and His *Head of Christ*." *Swedish-American Historical Quarterly* 47 (1996): 69-83.

Marshall, Paul. "An Evening with Sallman." *The War Cry* Toronto 4249 (30 April 1966): 2.

———. "Warner Sallman Receives 'Well Done,'" *The War Cry* Central 68/26 (29 June 1968): 15.

Marshall, Peter. "Blest Be the Tie that Binds." *Covenant Weekly* 35/4 (25 January 1946): 1.

[Marty, Martin]. "As Ugly As a Rented Bowling Shoe." *Context* (15 February 1990): 4.

Maus, Cynthia Pearl. *Christ and the Fine Arts*. Revised and Enlarged ed. New York: Harper & Bros., 1959.

McCahill, Dolores. "Mulder, Sallman and Ross Cited as 'Laymen of Year.'" *Chicago Sun-Times*, 16 March 1962, 30.

McDermott, William F. "A Visit to a Cathedral." *Chicago Daily News*, 6 February 1943, 7.

———. "Christ...According to Sallman." *Christian Herald* 79/1 (January 1956): 19, 34-36

————. "Paintbrush Miracles." *Power* 14/4 (4 November 1956): part 5, 1-3, 6-7.

————. "Here's How Sallman Painted It." *Together* 1/1 (October 1956): 43-44.

————. "The Miracle Picture." *Christian Life* 24/11 (March 1963): 26-28.

Monro, Isabel Stevenson, and Kate M. Monro. *Index to Reproductions of European Paintings.* New York: H. W. Wilson Co., 1956.

Morgan, David. "Sallman's *Head of Christ*: The History of an Image." *The Christian Century* 109/28 (7 October 1992): 868-870.

————. "Imaging Protestant Piety: The Icons of Warner Sallman." *Religion and American Culture* 3 (1993): 29-47.

————. *Icons of American Protestantism: The Art of Warner Sallman, 1892-1968.* Valparaiso IN: Valparaiso University, 1994.

————, ed. *Icons of American Protestantism: The Art of Warner Sallman.* New Haven and London: Yale University Press, 1996.

————. *Visual Piety: A History and Theory of Popular Religious Images.* Berkeley and London: University of California Press, 1998.

Morris, Harrison S. "The Four Great Paintings in This Number." *The Ladies Home Journal* 33/12 (December 1916): 18-22.

Murphy, Alexandra R. *European Paintings in the Museum of Fine Arts, Boston.* Boston: Museum of Fine Arts, 1985.

Nall, T. Otto. "He Preaches as He Paints." *Our Covenant Youth* 24/49 (5 December 1943): 3-4.

————. "He Preaches as He Paints." *Classmate* 50/50 (12 December 1943): 6-7.

Nelson, Edward O. "Recollections of the Salvation Army's Scandinavian Corps." *Swedish Pioneer Historical Quarterly* (October 1978): 257-276.

————. *Hallelujah! Recollections of Salvation Army Scandinavian Work in the U.S.A.* Chicago: The Salvation Army, 1987.

Norman, Geraldine. *Nineteenth Century Painters and Painting: A Dictionary.* Berkeley: University of California, 1977.

"Not Frail, Not Pale." *Time* (22 November 1948): 70.

Opsal, Bernt C. "The Many-Sided Christ." *The Bible Banner* 39/4 (July-August 1963): 2-3.

Peterson, Sylvia E. *Story of Sallman's "Christ at Dawn."* [Indianapolis]: Kriebel and Bates, 1946.

————. *Story of Sallman's "Jesus, the Children's Friend."* [Indianapolis]: Kriebel and Bates, 1947.

————. "The Ministry of Christian Art." *The Lutheran Companion* 55/14 (2 April 1947): 10-12.

————. "The Ministry of Christian Art." *Sunday School Herald* 11/16 (20 April 1947): 1-2.

————. "The Ministry of Christian Art." *The War Cry* Central 1378 (24 May 1947): 4-5, 8.

————. "The Ministry of Christian Art." *Religious Digest* 141 (June 1947): 54-59.

————. *Story of Sallman's "We Would See Jesus."* [Indianapolis]: Kriebel and Bates, 1948.

————. *Story of Sallman's "His Presence."* [Indianapolis]: Kriebel and Bates, 1948.

————. "The Brush that Ministers." *Our Covenant* 23 (1948): 75-84.

————. "The Brush that Ministers." *Covenant Youth Today* 4/6 Part 1 (3 June 1951): 1-4.

————. "The Brush that Ministers." *The Swedish National Sanitorium Journal* (Englewood CO) 29/2 (September 1951): 1, 4-5.

————. *Story of Sallman's "The Lord's Supper."* [Indianapolis]: Kriebel and Bates, 1950.

————. *Story of Sallman's "Christ Our Pilot."* [Indianapolis]: Kriebel and Bates, 1951.

————. *Story of Sallman's "Teach Me Thy Way."* [Indianapolis]: Kriebel and Bates, 1952.

————. *Story of Sallman's "He Careth for You."* [Indianapolis]: Kriebel and Bates, 1955.

————. *Story of Sallman's "Jesus, The Light of the World."* [Indianapolis]: Kriebel and Bates, 1956.

————. "Sallman's *Head of Christ* Still Blessing." *The Covenant Companion* 63/1 (1 January 1974): 3-5, 29.

————. "Over the Coffee Cup." *The Covenant Companion* [63]/2 (15 January 1974): 15.

————. *Warner Sallman and His Ministry of Christian Art.* Pamphlet printed in connection with the Sallman Exhibit at Covenant Village in Northbrook, IL, January 1984.

Pevsner, Nikolaus. *Academies of Art, Past and Present.* Cambridge: Cambridge University Press, 1940.

Phelps, Arthur Stevens. "*The Last Supper* and Its Great Painter." *The Covenant Companion* Old Series 7/4 (April 1928): 15-17.

Repertoire International de la Litterature de l'Art. New York: J. Paul Getty Trust, 1973-1989. [Succeeded by *Bibliographie d'Histoire de l'Art*].

Roth, Robert Paul. "Christ and the Muses." *Christianity Today* 11/11 (3 March 1958): 8-9.

Rothenstein, William. *Men and Memories.* New York: Coward-McCann Inc., 1931.

Rowland, Ronald. "Christ Comes Alive." *The* (Salvation Army) *Musician* (April 1980): 12.

Sallman, Warner. "My Greatest Spiritual Experience." *Chicago Daily News*, 10 March 1953, 30.

———. "My Greatest Spiritual Experience." *North Park College News*, 25 March 1953, 7.

———. "My Greatest Spiritual Experience." *Covenant Weekly* 42 (4 September 1953): 10.

———. "My Greatest Spiritual Experience." *Covenant Youth Today* (13 May 1956): 6-8].

———. "Head of Christ." *The Upper Room* 23/4 (September-October 1957): 3.

———. "Put Your Hands to Work, Your Heart to God." *The Covenant Companion* 49/3 (15 January 1960): 3.

———. "Two Artists Depict Christ: Warner Sallman and Birger Sponberg...." *The Covenant Companion* 49/16 (15 April 1960): 8.

———. "The Story Behind This Painting." *Guideposts* 16/12 (February 1962): 8-10.

Smith, Cecil D. "The Light of the World." *The Epworth Herald* 40/40 (5 October 1929): 9, 20.

———. "The Light of the World." *Our Covenant Youth* 12/12 (22 March 1931): 1-2.

———. "Behold the Man!" *The Epworth Herald* 40/44 (2 November 1929): 8.

———. "Behold the Man!" *Our Covenant Youth* 17/13 (29 March 1936): 3.

———. "Jesus in Gethsemane." *The Epworth Herald* 41/12 (22 March 1930): 15, 23.

———. "Christ at Emmaus." *The Epworth Herald* 41/15 (12 April 1930): 13.

Sparks, Esther. "A Biographical Dictionary of Painters and Sculptors in Illinois 1808-1945." 2 Volumes. Ph.D. dissertation, Northwestern University, 1971.

Swanson, Mary T. "Chicago and Swedish-American Artists." In *Swedish-American Life in Chicago*. Eds. Philip J. Anderson and Dag Blank. Urbana and Chicago; University of Illinois Press, 1992, pp. 150-160.

"The Face of Christ: A Portfolio of His Image through the Ages." *Fortune* 33/1 (January 1946): 133-144.

"The Life of Christ as Seen by Great Artists." *Life* Special Issue: Christianity (26 December 1955): 18-31.

Thomas, Lillian. "Art Facts: The Man Who Created Jesus." (Chicago) *Reader* 13/14 (6 January 1984): section 1, 7.

Thorndike, E. L. *Thorndike Century Senior Dictionary*. Chicago: Scott, Foresman and Co., 1941.

Troutt, Margaret. "Gospel Artist." *The War Cry* 101/5 (31 January 1981): 5.

Valentiner, William R. "The Greatest Pictures of the World." *The Ladies Home Journal* 27/2 (January 1910): 8-9.

van Dyke, John C. "What Do These Old Pictures Mean?" *The Ladies Home Journal* 24/2 (January 1907): 21.

van Fossen, Lou Ann. "Return to China: Touching the Past Gives Hope for the Future." *inSpirit* 16/1 (1993): 18-21.

Wilson, Colonel, ed. *Picturesque Palestine I*. New York: D. Appelton & Co., 1881.

Wilson, Everett L. "And This Is How It Was." *Covenant Youth Today* 11/3 (18 July 1965): 1-7.

Index of Sallman Artworks

Index of Scripture Texts

Index of Names

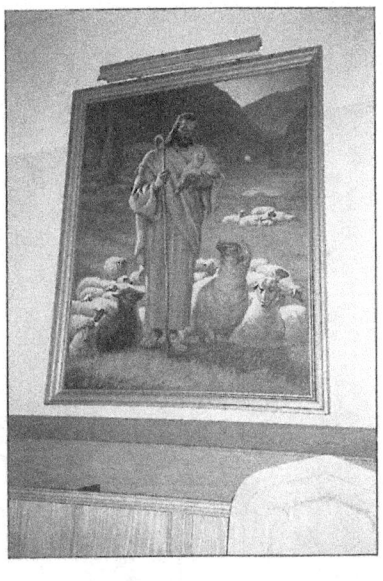

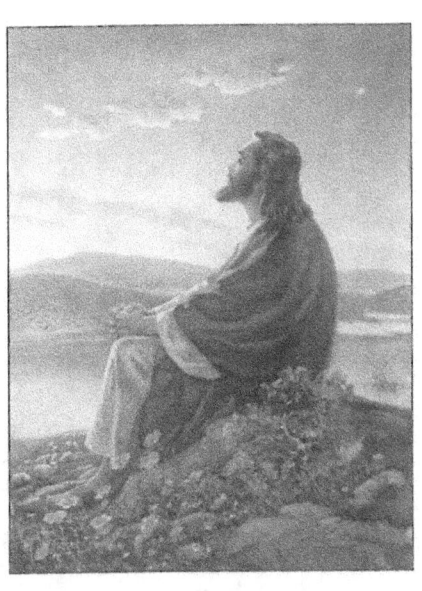

The Good Shepherd (1943) oil.
Bethlehem Covenant Church,
Stephenson, MI.

Christ at Dawn (1945) oil.

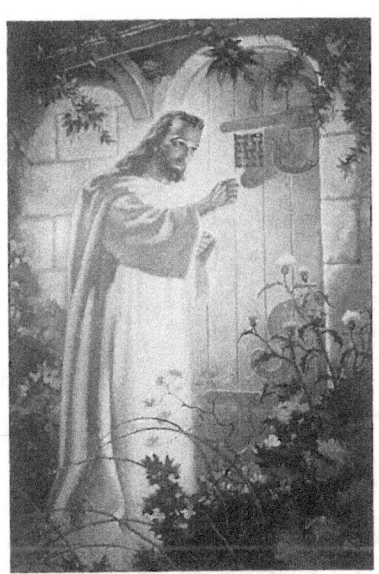

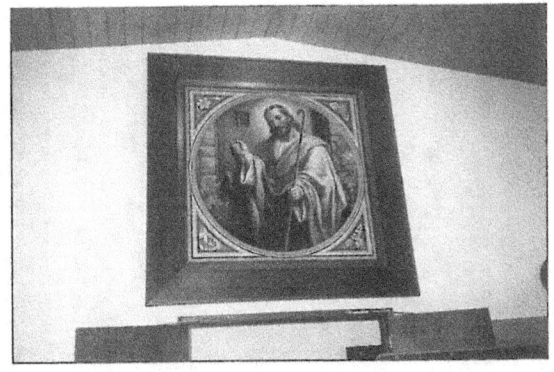

Christ Knocking at the Door (1947) oil. An
adaptation of Zabateri. First Covenant
Church, Fort Dodge, IA.

*Christ Knocking at Heart's
Door* (1953) oil. Evangelical
Covenant Church, Norway,
MI.

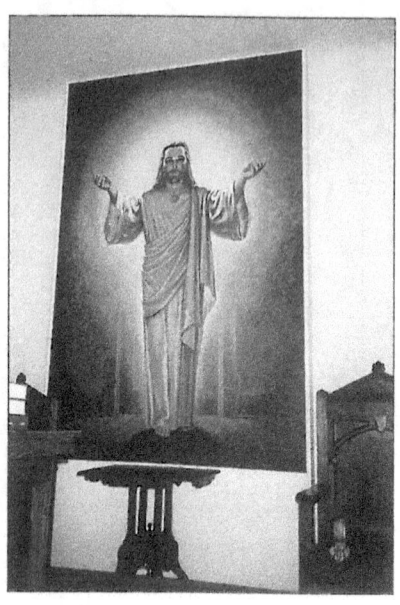

His Presence (1960) oil. United Evangelical Covenant Church, Gladstone, MI.

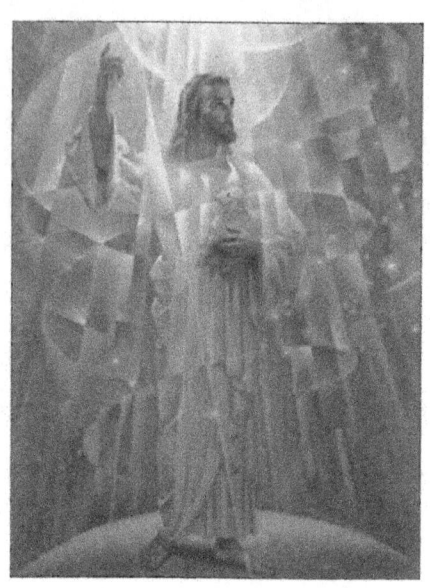

Power and Glory (1957) oil.

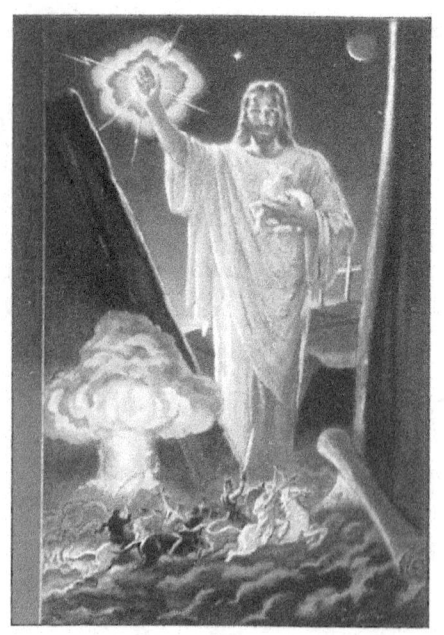

Thine Is the Power (1951) oil.

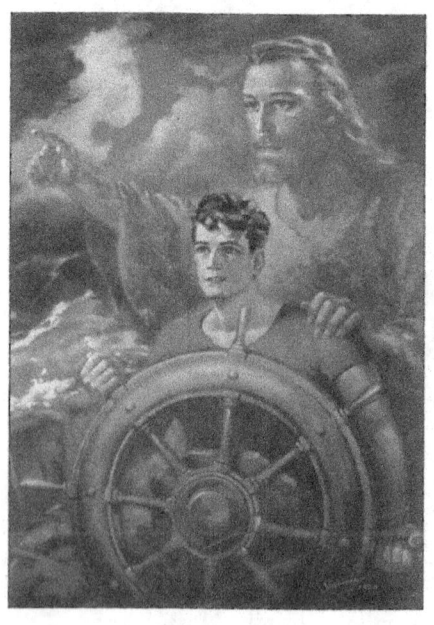

Christ is Our Pilot (1950) oil.

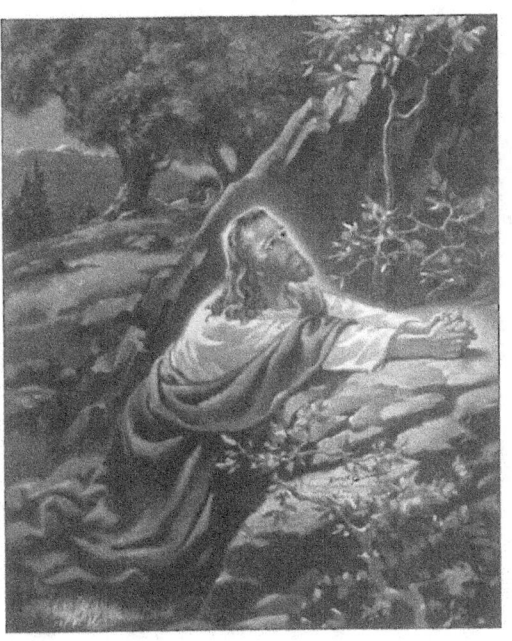

(Christ in) Gethsemane (1941) oil.

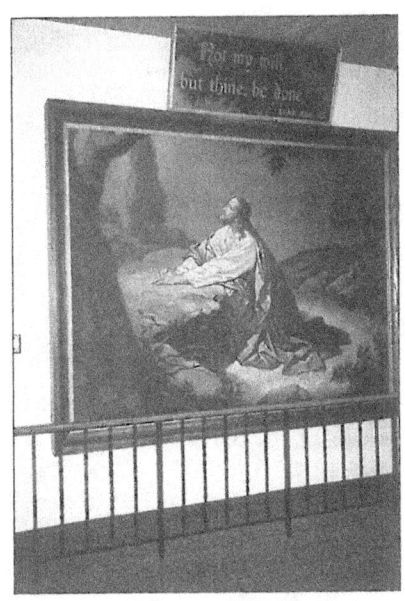

Christ in Gethsemane (1940) oil.
An adaptation of Hoffmann.
First Covenant Church, Red
Wing, MN.

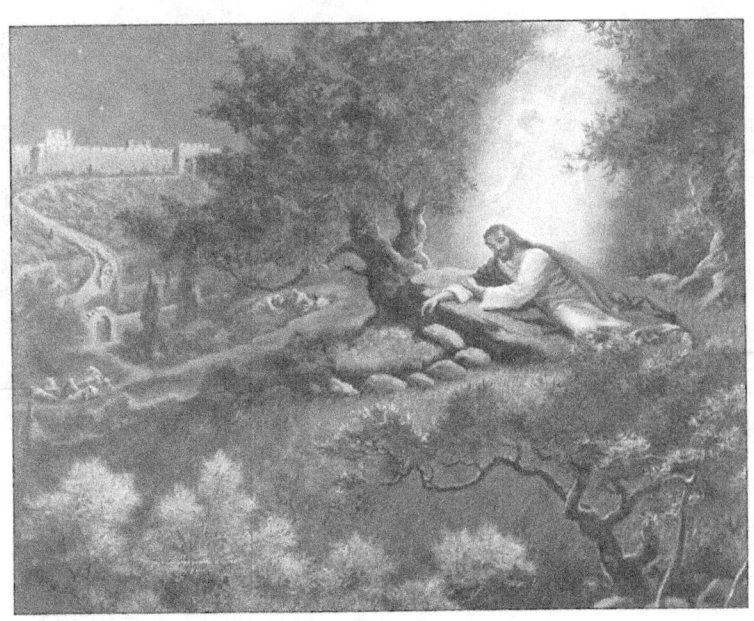

The Story of Gethsemane (1964) oil.

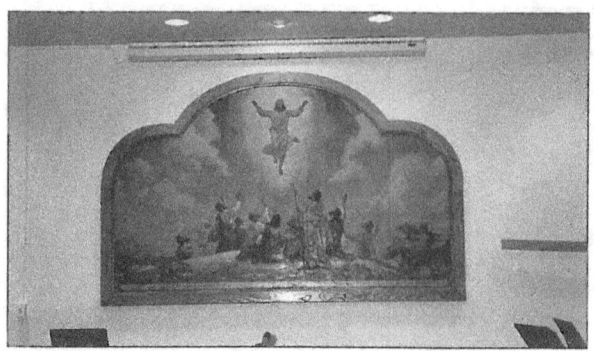

The Ascension (1941) oil. Mount Greenwood Corps of the Salvation Army, Chicago.

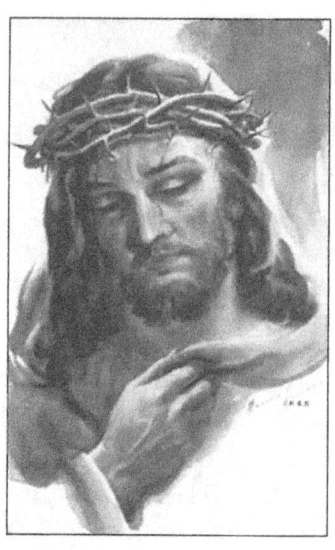

Crown of Thorns (1941) watercolor and chalk.

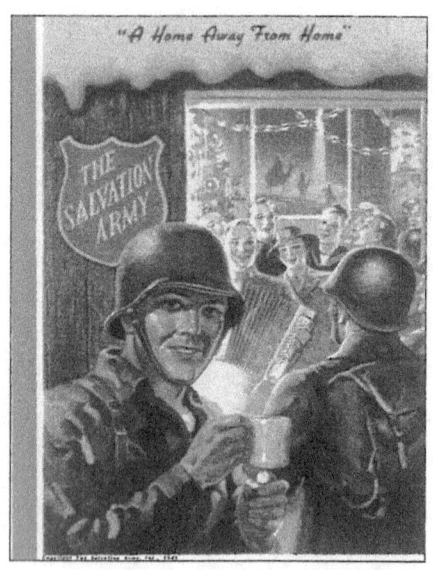

A Home Away from Home (1943) medium unknown. Printed in *The War Cry.*

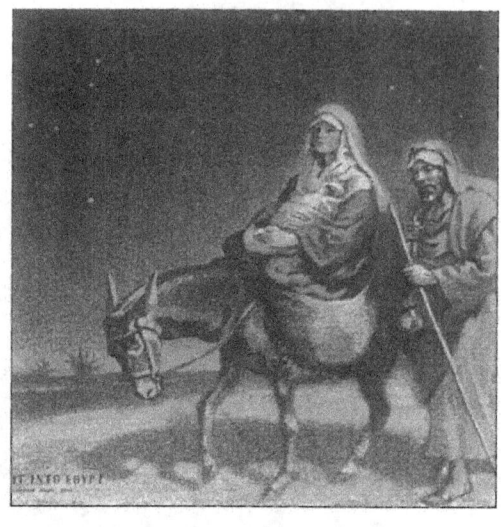

The Flight into Egypt (1941) oil. Salvation Army National Headquarters, Alexandria, VA.

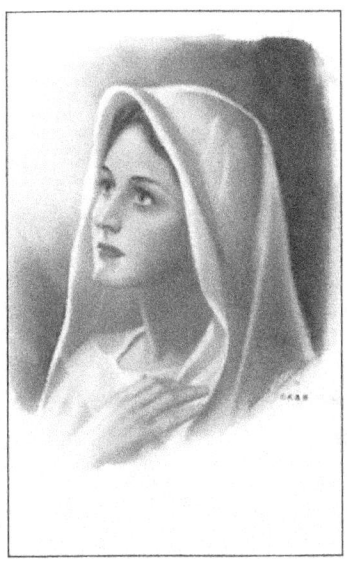

The Anunciation (1953) watercolor.

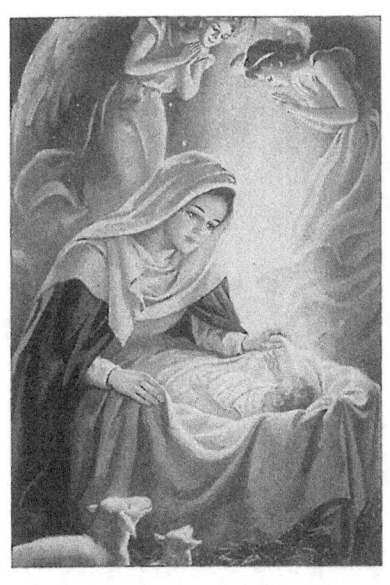

Mary and Baby in Manger (1954) watercolor.

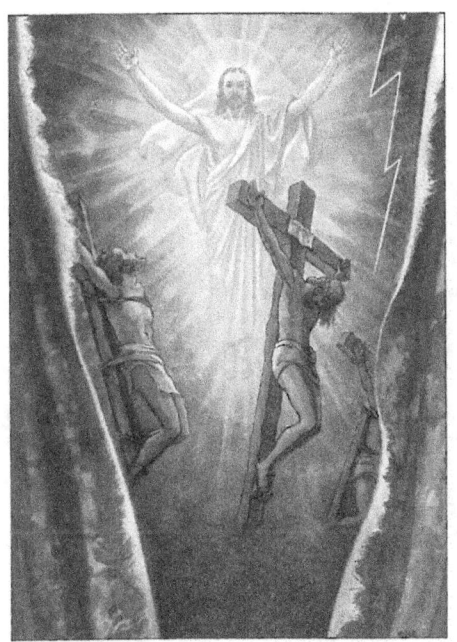

It is Finished (1958) watercolor, chalk and pen.

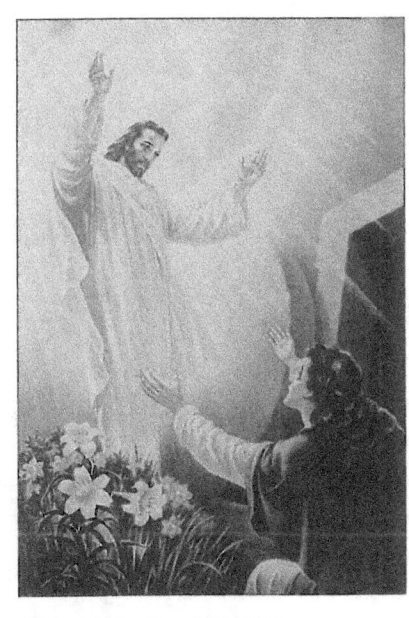

Behold the Lord (1952) watercolor.

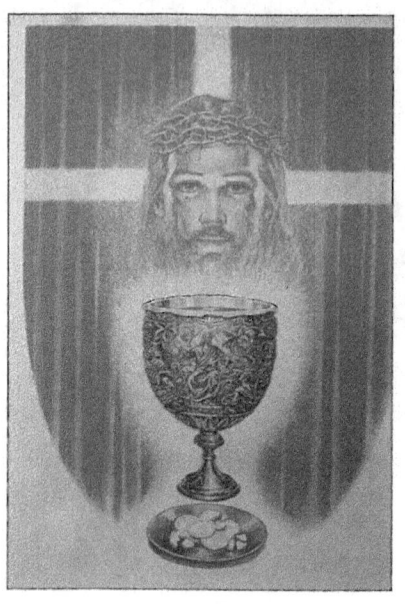

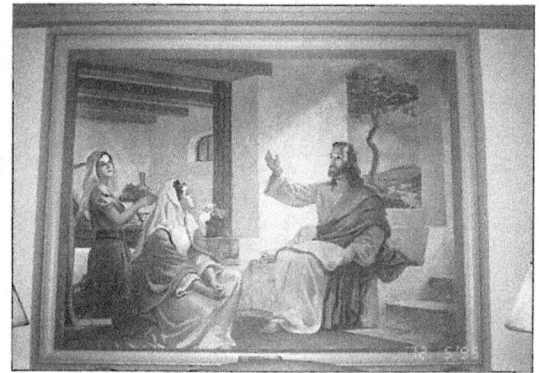

The Holy Communion (1958) watercolor, chalk and pen.

Mary and Martha with Jesus (1954) oil. Bethany Methodist Home, Chicago

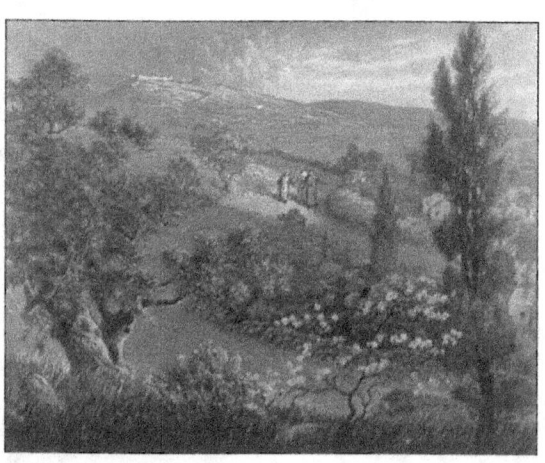

The Road to Emmaus (1961) oil.

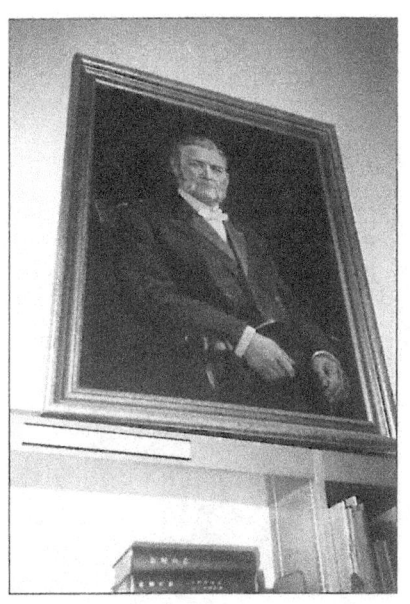

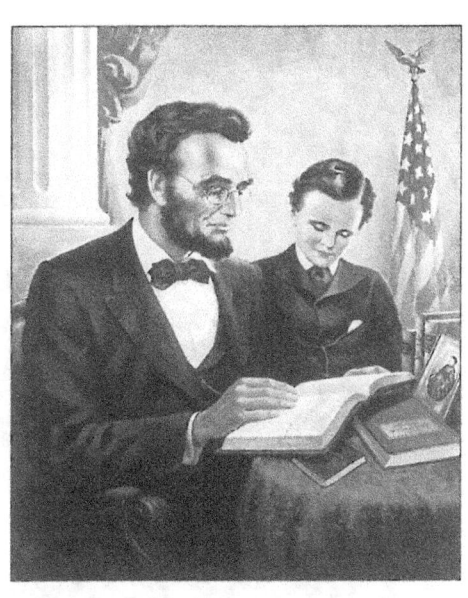

Portrait of the Rev. C. A. Björk
(1935) oil.

Abraham Lincoln and His Son (1963)
watercolor.

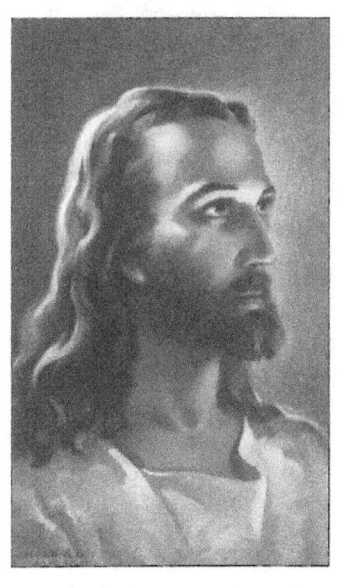

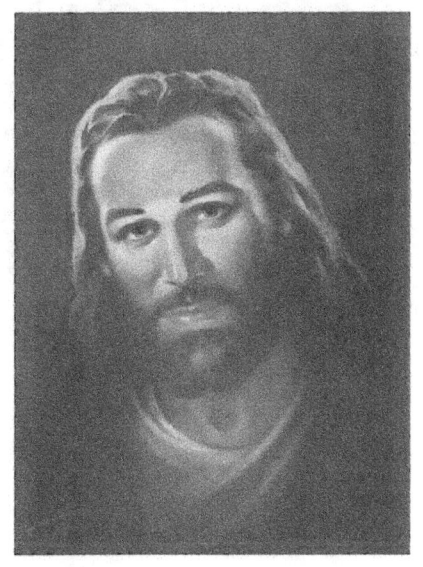

Head of Christ (1940) oil.

Portrait of Jesus (1966) oil.

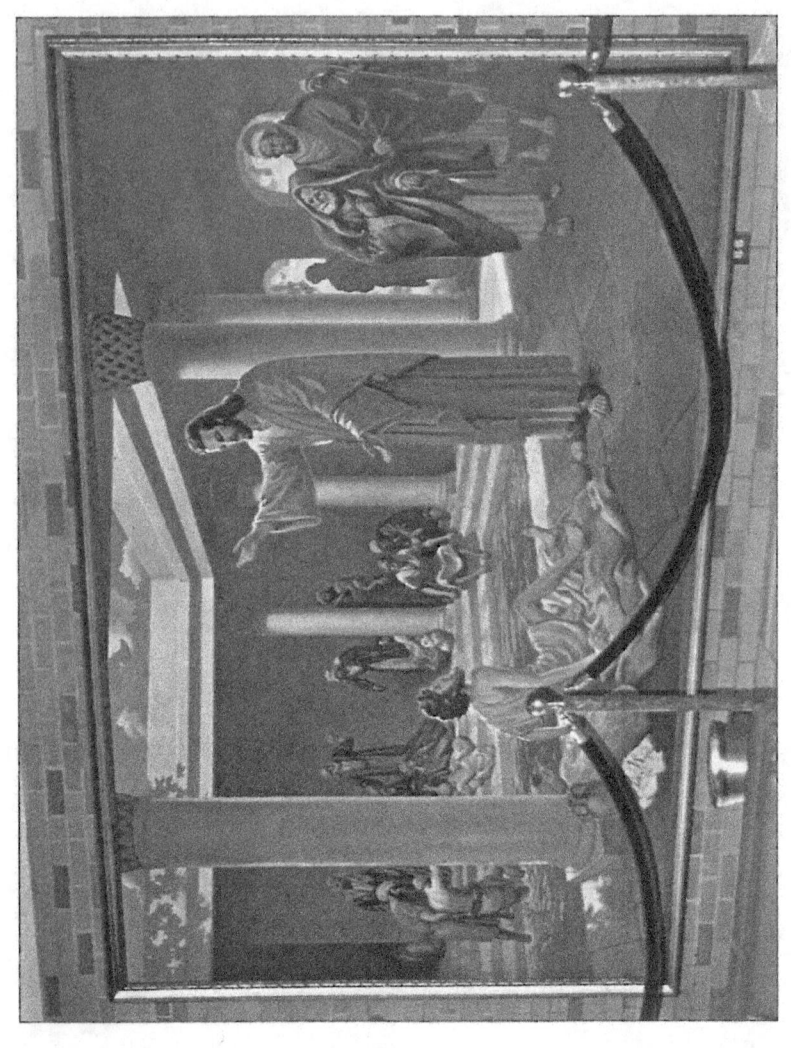

The Master Healer (1960) oil. United Hospital Center, Clarkburg, WV